First Workshop on Gender Bias in Natural Language Processing (GeBNLP 2019)

Florence, Italy
2 August 2019

ISBN: 978-1-5108-9106-7

GeBNLP 2019

Gender Bias in Natural Language Processing

Proceedings of the First Workshop

2 August 2019
Florence, Italy

Google

kaggle

Introduction

Natural Language Processing (NLP) is pervasive in the technologies people use to curate, consume and create information on a daily basis. Moreover, it is increasingly found in decision-support systems in finance and healthcare, where it can have a powerful impact on peoples' lives and society as a whole. Unfortunately, far from the objective and calculating algorithms of popular perception, machine learned models for NLP can include subtle biases drawn from the data used to build them and the builders themselves. Gender-based stereotypes and discrimination are problems that human societies have long struggled with, and it is the community's responsibility to ensure fair and ethical progress. The increasing volume of work in the last few years is a strong signal that researchers and engineers in academia and industry do care about fairer NLP.

This volume contains the proceedings of the First Workshop on Gender Bias in Natural Language Processing held in conjunction with the 57th Annual Meeting of the Association for Computational Linguistics in Florence. The workshop received 19 submissions of technical papers (8 long papers, 11 short papers), of which 13 were accepted (5 long, 8 short), for an acceptance rate of 68%. We have to thank the high-quality selection of research works thanks to the Program Committee members which provided extremely valuable reviews. The accepted papers cover a diverse range of topics related to the analysis, measurement and mitigation of gender bias in NLP. Many of the papers investigate how automatically learned vector space representations of words are affected by gender bias, but the programme also features papers on NLP applications such as machine translation, sentiment analysis and text classification. In addition to the technical papers, the workshop also included a very popular shared task on gender-fair coreference resolution, which attracted submissions from 263 participants. Many of them achieved excellent performance. Of the 11 submitted system description papers, 10 were accepted for publication. We are very grateful to Google for providing a generous prize pool of 25,000 USD for the shared task, and to the Kaggle team for their great help with the organisation of the shared task.

Finally, the workshop counts on two impressive keynote speakers: Melvin Johnson and Pascale Fung, who will provide insides in gender-specific translations in the Google system and the gender roles in the artificial intelligence world, respectively.

We are very excited about the interest that this workshop has generated and we look forward to a lively discussion about how to tackle bias problems in NLP applications when we meet in Florence!

June 2019

Marta R. Costa-jussà
Christian Hardmeier
Will Radford
Kellie Webster

Organizers:

Marta R. Costa-jussà, Universitat Politècnica de Catalunya (Spain)
Christian Hardmeier, Uppsala University (Sweden)
Will Radford, Canva (Australia)
Kellie Webster, Google AI Language (USA)

Program Committee:

Kai-Wei Chang, University of California, Los Angeles (USA)
Ryan Cotterell, University of Cambridge (UK)
Lucie Flekova, Amazon Alexa AI (Germany)
Mercedes García-Martínez, Pangeanic (Spain)
Zhengxian Gong, Soochow University (China)
Ben Hachey, Ergo AI (Australia)
Svetlana Kiritchenko, National Research Council (Canada)
Sharid Loáiciga, University of Gothenburg (Sweden)
Kaiji Lu, Carnegie Mellon University (USA)
Saif Mohammad, National Research Council (Canada)
Marta Recasens, Google (USA)
Rachel Rudinger, Johns Hopkins University (USA)
Bonnie Webber, University of Edinburgh (UK)

Invited Speakers:

Melvin Johnson, Google Translate (USA)
Pascale Fung, Hong Kong University of Science and Technology (China)

Table of Contents

Workshop Program

Friday, August 2, 2019

09:00–09:10   **Opening**

09:10–10:00   **Keynote 1**

Providing Gender-Specific Translations in Google Translate and beyond
Melvin Johnson

10:00–10:30   **Shared Task Overview**

Gendered Ambiguous Pronoun (GAP) Shared Task at the Gender Bias in NLP Workshop 2019
Kellie Webster, Marta R. Costa-jussà, Christian Hardmeier and Will Radford

10:30–11:00   **Refreshments**

11:00–12:30   **Oral presentations 1: Representations**

11:00–11:20   *Proposed Taxonomy for Gender Bias in Text: A Filtering Methodology for the Gender Generalization Subtype*
Yasmeen Hitti, Eunbee Jang, Ines Moreno and Carolyne Pelletier

11:20–11:35   *Relating Word Embedding Gender Biases to Gender Gaps: A Cross-Cultural Analysis*
Scott Friedman, Sonja Schmer-Galunder, Anthony Chen and Jeffrey Rye

11:35–11:50   *Measuring Gender Bias in Word Embeddings across Domains and Discovering New Gender Bias Word Categories*
Kaytlin Chaloner and Alfredo Maldonado

11:50–12:05   *Evaluating the Underlying Gender Bias in Contextualized Word Embeddings*
Christine Basta, Marta R. Costa-jussà and Noe Casas

12:05–12:25   *Conceptor Debiasing of Word Representations Evaluated on WEAT*
Saket Karve, Lyle Ungar and João Sedoc

Fill the GAP: Exploiting BERT for Pronoun Resolution
Kai-Chou Yang, Timothy Niven, Tzu Hsuan Chou and Hung-Yu Kao

On GAP Coreference Resolution Shared Task: Insights from the 3rd Place Solution
Artem Abzaliev

Resolving Gendered Ambiguous Pronouns with BERT
Matei Ionita, Yury Kashnitsky, Ken Krige, Vladimir Larin, Atanas Atanasov and
Dennis Logvinenko

*Anonymized BERT: An Augmentation Approach to the Gendered Pronoun
Resolution Challenge*
Bo Liu

*Gendered Pronoun Resolution using BERT and an Extractive Question Answering
Formulation*
Rakesh Chada

*Gendered Ambiguous Pronouns Shared Task: Boosting Model Confidence by
Evidence Pooling*
Sandeep Attree

15:30–16:00   **Mid-afternoon Snacks (Poster session continues)**

16:00–17:15   **Oral Presentations 2: Applications**

16:00–16:20   *Equalizing Gender Bias in Neural Machine Translation with Word Embeddings
Techniques*
Joel Escudé Font and Marta R. Costa-jussà

16:20–16:40   *Automatic Gender Identification and Reinflection in Arabic*
Nizar Habash, Houda Bouamor and Christine Chung

16:40–16:55   *Quantifying Social Biases in Contextual Word Representations*
Keita Kurita, Nidhi Vyas, Ayush Pareek, Alan W Black and Yulia Tsvetkov

16:55–17:15   *On Measuring Gender Bias in Translation of Gender-neutral Pronouns*
Won Ik Cho, Ji Won Kim, Seok Min Kim and Nam Soo Kim

17:15–17:30   **Closing Remarks**

Gendered Ambiguous Pronouns (GAP)
Shared Task at the Gender Bias in NLP Workshop 2019

Kellie Webster
Google Research
111 8th Avenue
New York, NY, USA
websterk@google.com

Marta R. Costa-jussà
Universitat Politecnica
de Catalunya
Barcelona, Spain
marta.ruiz@upc.edu

Christian Hardmeier
Uppsala Universitet
Sweden
christian.hardmeier@
lingfil.uu.se

Will Radford
Canva
110 Kippax Street
Surry Hills, Australia
will.r@canva.com

Abstract

The 1st ACL workshop on Gender Bias in Natural Language Processing included a shared task on gendered ambiguous pronoun (GAP) resolution. This task was based on the coreference challenge defined in Webster et al. (2018), designed to benchmark the ability of systems to resolve pronouns in real-world contexts in a gender-fair way. 263 teams competed via a Kaggle competition, with the winning system achieving logloss of 0.13667 and near gender parity. We review the approaches of eleven systems with accepted description papers, noting their effective use of BERT (Devlin et al., 2019), both via fine-tuning and for feature extraction, as well as ensembling.

1 Introduction

Gender bias is one of the typologies of social bias (e.g. race, politics) that is alarming the Natural Language Processing (NLP) community. An illustration of the problematic behaviour are the recurrently appearing occupational stereotypes that *homemaker* is to *woman* as *programmer* is to *man* (Bolukbasi et al., 2016). Recent studies have aimed to detect, analyse and mitigate gender bias in different NLP tools and applications including word embeddings (Bolukbasi et al., 2016; Gonen and Goldberg, 2019), coreference resolution (Rudinger et al., 2018; Zhao et al., 2018), sentiment analysis (Park et al., 2018; Bhaskaran and Bhallamudi, 2019) and machine translation (Vanmassenhove et al., 2018; Font and Costa-jussà, 2019). One of the main sources of gender bias is believed to be societal artefacts in the data from which our algorithms learn. To address this, many have created gender-labelled and gender-balanced datasets (Rudinger et al., 2018; Zhao et al., 2018; Vanmassenhove et al., 2018).

We present the results of a shared task evaluation conducted at the 1st Workshop on Gender Bias in Natural Language Processing at the ACL 2019 conference. The shared task is based on the gender-balanced GAP coreference dataset (Webster et al., 2018) and allows us to test the hypothesis that *fair datasets would be enough to solve the gender bias challenge in* NLP.

The strong results of submitted systems tend to support this hypothesis and gives the community a great starting point for mitigating bias in models. Indeed, the enthusiastic participation we saw for this shared task has yielded systems which achieve near-human accuracy while achieving near gender-parity at 0.99, measured by the ratio between F1 scores on feminine and masculine examples. We are excited for future work extending this success to more languages, domains, and tasks. However, we especially note future work in algorithms which achieve fair outcomes given biased data, given the wealth of information from existing unbalanced datasets.

2 Task

The goal of our shared task was to encourage research in gender-fair models for NLP by providing a well-defined task that is known to be sensitive to gender bias and an evaluation procedure addressing this issue. We chose the GAP resolution task (Webster et al., 2018), which measures the ability of systems to resolve gendered pronoun reference from real-world contexts in a gender-fair way. Specifically, GAP asks systems to resolve a target personal pronoun to one of two names, or neither name. For instance, a perfect resolver would resolve that *she* refers to *Fujisawa* and not to *Mari Motohashi* in the Wikipedia excerpt:

(1)   In May, *Fujisawa* joined *Mari Motohashi*'s rink as the team's skip, moving back from Karuizawa to Kitami where **she** had spent her junior days.

The original GAP challenge encourages fairness by balancing its datasets by the gender of the pronoun, as well as using disaggregated evaluation

Proceedings of the 1st Workshop on Gender Bias in Natural Language Processing, pages 1–7
Florence, Italy, August 2, 2019. ©2019 Association for Computational Linguistics

with separate scores for masculine and feminine examples. To simplify evaluation, we did not disaggregate evaluation for this shared task, but instead encouraged fairness by not releasing the balance of masculine to feminine examples in the final evaluation data.[1]

The competition was run on Kaggle[2], a well-known platform for competitive data science and machine learning projects with an active community of participants and support.

2.1 Setting

The original GAP challenge defines four evaluation settings, depending on whether the candidate systems have to identify potential antecedents or are given a fixed choice of antecedent candidates, and whether or not they have access to the entire Wikipedia page from which the example was extracted. Our task was run in *gold-two-mention* with *page-context*. This means that, for our task, systems had access to the two names being evaluated at inference time, so that the systems were not required to do mention detection and full coreference resolution. For each example, the systems had to consider whether the target pronoun was coreferent with the *first*, the *second* or *neither* of the two given antecedent candidates. A valid submission consisted of a probability estimate for each of these three cases. The systems were also given the source URL for the text snippet (a Wikipedia page), enabling unlimited access to context. This minimized the chance that systems could cheat, intentionally or inadvertently, by accessing information outside the task setting.

2.2 Data

To ensure blind evaluation, we sourced 760 new annotated examples for official evaluation[3] using the same techniques from the original GAP work (Webster et al., 2018), with three changes. To ensure the highest quality of annotations for this task, we (i) only accepted examples on which the three raters provided unanimous judgement, (ii) added heuristics to remove cases with errors in entity span labeling, and (iii) did an additional, manual round to remove assorted errors. The final set of

	logloss	F1	Bias
Attree (2019)	0.13667	96.2	0.99
Wang (2019)	0.17289	95.7	0.99
Abzaliev (2019)	0.18397	95.4	0.99

Table 1: Performance of prize-winning submissions on the blind Kaggle evaluation set. logloss was the official task metric, and correlates well with F1 score, which was used in the original GAP work.

760 clean examples was dispersed in a larger set of 11,599 unlabeled examples to produce a set of 12,359 examples that competing systems had to rate. This augmentation was to discourage submissions based on manual labeling.

We note many competing systems used the original GAP evaluation data[4] as training data for this task, given that the two have the same format, base domain (Wikipedia), and task definition.

2.3 Evaluation

The original GAP work defined two official evaluation metrics, F1 score and Bias, the ratio between the F1 scores on feminine and masculine examples. Bias takes a value of 1 at gender parity; a value below 1 indicates that masculine entities are resolved more accurately than feminine ones.

In contrast, the official evaluation metric of the competition was the logloss of the submitted probability estimates:

$$\text{logloss} = -\frac{1}{N} \sum_{i=1}^{N} \sum_{j=1}^{M} y_{ij} \log p_{ij}, \quad (1)$$

where N is the number of samples in the test set, $M = 3$ is the number of classes to be predicted, y_{ij} is 1 if observation i belongs to class j according to the gold-standard annotations and 0 otherwise, and p_{ij} is the probability estimated by the system that observation i belongs to class j.

Table 1 tabulates results based on the original and shared task metrics. Logloss and GAP F1 both place the winners in the same order.

2.4 Prizes

A total prize pool of USD 25,000 was provided by Google. The pool was broken down into prizes of USD 12,000, 8,000, and 5,000 for the top three systems, respectively. This attracted submissions

---

[1] We used 1:1 masculine to feminine examples.

[2] https://www.kaggle.com/c/gendered-pronoun-resolution

[3] Official evaluation ran in Stage 2, following an initial, development stage evaluated on the original GAP data, available at https://github.com/google-research-datasets/gap-coreference

[4] https://github.com/google-research-datasets/gap-coreference

from 263 teams, covering a wide diversity of geographic locations and affiliations, see Section 3.1. Table 1 lists results for the three prize-winning systems: Attree (2019), Wang (2019), and Abzaliev (2019).

3 Submissions

In this section, we describe the diverse set of teams who competed in the shared task, and the systems they designed for the GAP challenge. We note effective use of BERT (Devlin et al., 2019), both via fine-tuning and for feature extraction, and ensembling. Despite very little modeling targeted at debiasing for gender, the submitted systems narrowed the gender gap to near parity at 0.99, while achieving remarkably strong performance.

3.1 Teams

We accepted ten system description papers, from 11 of the 263 teams who competed (Ionita et al. (2019) is a combined submission from the teams placing 5 and 22). Table 2 characterises the teams by their number of members, whether their affiliation is to industry or an academic institution, and the geographic location of their affiliation. Details about participant gender were not collected.

Our first observation is that 7 of the top 10 teams submitted system descriptions, which allows us good insight into what approaches work well for the GAP task (see next, Section 3.2). Also, All these teams publicly release their code, promoting transparency and further development.

We note the geographic diversity of teams: there is at least one team from each of Africa, Asia, Europe, and USA, and one team collaborating across regions (Europe and USA). Five teams had industry affiliations and four academic; the geographically diverse team was diverse here also, comprising both academic and industry researchers.

There is a correlation between team size and affiliation: industry submissions were all from individual contributors, while academic researchers worked in groups. This correlation is somewhat indicative of performance: individual contributors from industry won all three monetary prizes, and only one academic group featured in the top ten submissions. A possible factor in this was the concurrent timing of the competition with other conference deadlines.

3.2 Systems

All system descriptions were from teams who used BERT (Devlin et al., 2019), a method to create context-sensitive word embeddings by pretraining a deep self-attention neural network on a training objective optimizing for cloze word prediction and recognition of adjacent sentences. This is perhaps not surprising, given the recent success of BERT for modeling a wide range of NLP tasks (Tenney et al., 2019; Kwiatkowski et al., 2019) and the small amount of training data available for GAP resolution (which makes LM pretraining particularly attractive). The different models built from BERT are summarized in Table 3.

Eight of the eleven system descriptions used BERT via fine-tuning, the technique recommended in Devlin et al. (2019). To do this, the original GAP data release was used as a tuning set to learn a classifier on top of BERT to predict whether the target pronoun referred to Name A, Name B, or Neither. Abzaliev (2019) also made use of the available datasets for coreference resolution: OntoNotes 5.0 (Pradhan and Xue, 2009), WinoBias (Zhao et al., 2018), WinoGender (Rudinger et al., 2018), and the Definite Pronoun Resolution Dataset (Rahman and Ng, 2012). Given the multiple BERT models available, it was possible to learn multiple such classifiers; teams marked *ensemble* fine-tuned multiple base BERT models and ensembled their predictions, while teams marked *single* produced just one, from a BERT-Large variant.

An alternative way to use BERT in NLP modeling is as a feature extractor. Teams using BERT in this capacity represented mention spans as input vectors to a neural structure (typically a linear structure, e.g. feed-forward network) that learned some sort of mention compatibility, via interaction or feature crossing. To derive mention-span representations from BERT subtoken encodings, Wang (2019) found that pooling using an attention-mediated process was more effective than simple mean-pooling; most teams pooled using AllenAI's SelfAttentionSpanExtractor[5]. An interesting finding was that certain BERT layers were more suitable for feature extraction than others (see Abzaliev (2019); Yang et al. (2019) for an exploration).

The winning solution (Attree, 2019) used a

---

[5]https://github.com/allenai/allennlp/blob/
master/allennlp/modules/span_extractors/self_
attentive_span_extractor.py

	Place	logloss	Members	Affiliation	Region
Attree (2019)	1	0.13667	1	Industry	USA
Wang (2019)	2	0.17289	1	Industry	Asia
Abzaliev (2019)	3	0.18397	1	Industry	Europe
Yang et al. (2019)	4	0.18498	4	Academic	Asia
Ionita et al. (2019)*	5	0.19189	1	Other	Africa
Liu (2019)	7	0.19473	1	Industry	USA
Chada (2019)	9	0.20238	1	Industry	USA
Bao and Qiao (2019)	14	0.20758	2	Academic	Europe
Ionita et al. (2019)*	22	0.22562	4	Mixed	Mixed
Lois et al. (2019)	46	0.30151	3	Academic	Europe
Xu and Yang (2019)	67	0.39479	2	Academic	USA

Table 2: Teams with accepted system description papers. *Note the two teams placing 5 and 22 submitted a combined system description paper.

	Rank	logloss	Fine-tuning	Feature Crossing	Resources
Attree (2019)	1	0.13667	single	–	syntax, coref, URL
Wang (2019)	2	0.17289	single	linear	–
Abzaliev (2019)	3	0.18397	ensemble	linear	synax, URL
Yang et al. (2019)	4	0.18498	ensemble	siamese	–
Ionita et al. (2019)*	5	0.19189	ensemble	linear	syntax, NER, coref
Liu (2019)	7	0.19473	–	linear	–
Chada (2019)	9	0.20238	ensemble	–	–
Bao and Qiao (2019)	14	0.20758	single	SVM & BIDAF	–
Ionita et al. (2019)*	22	0.22562	ensemble	linear	synax, NER, coref
Lois et al. (2019)	46	0.30151	–	–	–
Xu and Yang (2019)	67	0.39479	–	R-GCN	syntax

Table 3: Highlights of systems with accepted description papers. *Note the two teams placing 5 and 22 submitted a combined system description paper.

novel *evidence pooling* technique, which used the output of off-the-shelf coreference resolvers in a way that combines aspects of ensembling and feature crossing. This perhaps explains the system's impressive performance despite its relative simplicity. Two other systems stood out as novel in their approach to the task: Chada (2019) reformulated GAP reference resolution as a question answering task, and Lois et al. (2019) used BERT in a third way, directly applying the masked language modeling task to predicting resolutions.

Despite the scarcity of data for this challenge, there was little use of extra resources. Only two teams made use of the URL given in the example, with Attree (2019) using it only indirectly as part of a coreference heuristic fed into evidence pooling. Two teams augmented the GAP data by using name substitutions (Liu, 2019; Lois et al., 2019) and two automatically created extra examples of the minority label Neither (Attree, 2019; Bao and Qiao, 2019).

4 Discussion

Running the GAP shared task has taught us many valuable things about reference, gender, and BERT models. Based on these, we make recommendations for future work expanding from this shared task into different languages and domains.

GAP Given the incredibly strong performance of the submitted systems, it is tempting to ask whether GAP resolution is solved. We suggest the answer is no. Firstly, the shared task only tested one of the four original GAP settings. A more challenging setting would be *snippet-context*, in which use of Wikipedia is not allowed, which we would extend to LM pre-training. Also, GAP only targets particular types of pronoun usage, and the time is ripe for exploring others. We are particularly excited for future work in languages with different pronoun systems (esp. prodrop languages including Portuguese, Chinese, Japanese), and gender neutral personal pronouns, e.g. English *they*, Spanish *su* or Turkish *o*.

Gender It is encouraging to see submitted systems improve the gender gap so close to parity at 0.99, particularly as no special modeling strategies were required. Indeed, Abzaliev (2019) reported that a handcrafted pronoun gender feature had no impact. Moreover, Bao and Qiao (2019) report that BERT encodings show no significant gender bias on either WEAT (Caliskan et al., 2017) or SEAT (May et al., 2019). We look forward to studies considering potential biases in BERT across more tasks and dimensions of diversity.

BERT The teams competing in the shared task made effective use of BERT in at least three distinct methods: fine-tuning, feature extraction, and masked language modeling. Many system papers noted the incredible power of the model (see, e.g. Attree (2019) for a good analysis), particularly when compared to hand-crafted features (Abzaliev, 2019). We also believe the widespread use of BERT is related to the low rate of external data usage, as it is easier for most teams to reuse an existing model than to clean and integrate new data. As well as the phenomenal modeling power of BERT, one possible reason for this observation is that the public releases of BERT are trained on the same domain as the GAP examples, Wikipedia. Future work could benchmark non-Wikipedia BERT models on the shared task examples, or collect more GAP examples from different domains.

5 Conclusion

This paper describes the insights of shared task on GAP coreference resolution held as part of the 1st ACL workshop on Gender Bias in Natural Language Processing. The task drew a generous prize pool from Google and saw enthusiastic participation across a diverse set of researchers. Winning systems made effective use of BERT and ensembling, achieving near human accuracy and gender parity despite little efforts targeted at mitigating gender bias. We learned where the next research challenges in gender-fair pronoun resolution lie, as well as promising directions for testing the robustness of powerful language model pre-training methods, especially BERT.

Acknowledgements

We would like to extend very many thanks to the Kaggle team (especially Julia Elliot and Will Cukierski) and the Google Data Compute team (especially Daphne Luong and Ashwin Kakarla) who made this shared task possible.

This work is supported in part by the Spanish Ministerio de Economía y Competitividad and the European Regional Development Fund and the Agencia Estatal de Investigación, through the post-doctoral senior grant Ramón y Cajal and by the Swedish Research Council through grant 2017-930.

References

Artem Abzaliev. 2019. On GAP coreference resolution shared task: insights from the 3rd place solution. In *Proceedings of the First Workshop on Gender Bias for Natural Language Processing*, Florence, Italy. Association for Computational Linguistics.

Sandeep Attree. 2019. Gendered Pronoun Resolution Shared Task: Boosting Model Confidence by Evidence Pooling. In *Proceedings of the First Workshop on Gender Bias for Natural Language Processing*, Florence, Italy. Association for Computational Linguistics.

Xingce Bao and Qianqian Qiao. 2019. Transfer Learning from Pre-trained BERT for Pronoun Resolution. In *Proceedings of the First Workshop on Gender Bias for Natural Language Processing*, Florence, Italy. Association for Computational Linguistics.

Jayadev Bhaskaran and Isha Bhallamudi. 2019. Good Secretaries, Bad Truck Drivers? Occupational Gender Stereotypes in Sentiment Analysis. In *Proceedings of the First Workshop on Gender Bias for Natural Language Processing*, Florence, Italy. Association for Computational Linguistics.

Tolga Bolukbasi, Kai-Wei Chang, James Zou, Venkatesh Saligrama, and Adam Kalai. 2016. Man is to computer programmer as woman is to homemaker? debiasing word embeddings. In *Proceedings of the 30th International Conference on Neural Information Processing Systems*, NIPS'16, pages 4356–4364, USA. Curran Associates Inc.

Aylin Caliskan, Joanna J. Bryson, and Arvind Narayanan. 2017. Semantics derived automatically from language corpora contain human-like biases. *Science*, 356(6334):183–186.

Rakesh Chada. 2019. Gendered Pronoun Resolution using BERT and an extractive question answering formulation. In *Proceedings of the First Workshop on Gender Bias for Natural Language Processing*, Florence, Italy. Association for Computational Linguistics.

Jacob Devlin, Ming-Wei Chang, Kenton Lee, and Kristina Toutanova. 2019. BERT: Pre-training of deep bidirectional transformers for language understanding. In *Proceedings of the 2019 Conference of the North American Chapter of the Association for Computational Linguistics: Human Language Technologies, Volume 1 (Long and Short Papers)*, pages 4171–4186, Minneapolis, Minnesota. Association for Computational Linguistics.

Joel Escudé Font and Marta R. Costa-jussà. 2019. Equalizing Gender Biases in Neural Machine Translation with Word Embeddings Techniques. In *Proceedings of the First Workshop on Gender Bias for Natural Language Processing*, Florence, Italy. Association for Computational Linguistics.

Hila Gonen and Yoav Goldberg. 2019. Lipstick on a pig: Debiasing methods cover up systematic gender biases in word embeddings but do not remove them. In *Proceedings of the 2019 Conference of the North American Chapter of the Association for Computational Linguistics: Human Language Technologies, Volume 1 (Long and Short Papers)*, pages 609–614, Minneapolis, Minnesota. Association for Computational Linguistics.

Matei Ionita, Yury Kashnitsky, Ken Krige, Vladimir Larin, and Atanas Atanasov. 2019. Gender-unbiased BERT-based Pronoun Resolution. In *Proceedings of the First Workshop on Gender Bias for Natural Language Processing*, Florence, Italy. Association for Computational Linguistics.

Tom Kwiatkowski, Jennimaria Palomaki, Olivia Redfield, Michael Collins, Ankur Parikh, Chris Alberti, Danielle Epstein, Illia Polosukhin, Matthew Kelcey, Jacob Devlin, Kenton Lee, Kristina N. Toutanova, Llion Jones, Ming-Wei Chang, Andrew Dai, Jakob Uszkoreit, Quoc Le, and Slav Petrov. 2019. Natural Questions: a Benchmark for Question Answering Research. *Transactions of the Association of Computational Linguistics*.

Bo Liu. 2019. Anonymized BERT: An Augmentation Approach to the Gendered Pronoun Resolution Challenge. In *Proceedings of the First Workshop on Gender Bias for Natural Language Processing*, Florence, Italy. Association for Computational Linguistics.

Felipe Alfaro Lois, José A. R. Fonollosa, and Marta R. Costa-jussà. 2019. BERT Masked Language Modeling for Coreference Resolution. In *Proceedings of the First Workshop on Gender Bias for Natural Language Processing*, Florence, Italy. Association for Computational Linguistics.

Chandler May, Alex Wang, Shikha Bordia, Samuel R. Bowman, and Rachel Rudinger. 2019. On measuring social biases in sentence encoders. In *Proceedings of the 2019 Conference of the North American Chapter of the Association for Computational Linguistics: Human Language Technologies, Volume 1 (Long and Short Papers)*, pages 622–628, Minneapolis, Minnesota. Association for Computational Linguistics.

Ji Ho Park, Jamin Shin, and Pascale Fung. 2018. Reducing gender bias in abusive language detection. In *Proceedings of the 2018 Conference on Empirical Methods in Natural Language Processing*, pages 2799–2804, Brussels, Belgium. Association for Computational Linguistics.

Sameer S. Pradhan and Nianwen Xue. 2009. OntoNotes: The 90% solution. In *Proceedings of Human Language Technologies: The 2009 Annual Conference of the North American Chapter of the Association for Computational Linguistics, Companion Volume: Tutorial Abstracts*, pages 11–12, Boulder, Colorado. Association for Computational Linguistics.

Altaf Rahman and Vincent Ng. 2012. Resolving complex cases of definite pronouns: The Winograd schema challenge. In *Proceedings of the 2012 Joint Conference on Empirical Methods in Natural Language Processing and Computational Natural Language Learning*, pages 777–789, Jeju Island, Korea. Association for Computational Linguistics.

Rachel Rudinger, Jason Naradowsky, Brian Leonard, and Benjamin Van Durme. 2018. Gender bias in coreference resolution. In *Proceedings of the 2018 Conference of the North American Chapter of the Association for Computational Linguistics: Human Language Technologies, Volume 2 (Short Papers)*, pages 8–14, New Orleans, Louisiana. Association for Computational Linguistics.

Ian Tenney, Dipanjan Das, and Ellie Pavlick. 2019. BERT Rediscovers the Classical NLP Pipeline.

Eva Vanmassenhove, Christian Hardmeier, and Andy Way. 2018. Getting gender right in neural machine translation. In *Proceedings of the 2018 Conference on Empirical Methods in Natural Language Processing*, pages 3003–3008, Brussels, Belgium. Association for Computational Linguistics.

Zili Wang. 2019. MSnet: A BERT-based Network for Gendered Pronoun Resolution. In *Proceedings of the First Workshop on Gender Bias for Natural Language Processing*, Florence, Italy. Association for Computational Linguistics.

Kellie Webster, Marta Recasens, Vera Axelrod, and Jason Baldridge. 2018. Mind the GAP: A balanced corpus of gendered ambiguous pronouns. *Transactions of the Association for Computational Linguistics*, 6:605–617.

Yinchuan Xu and Junlin Yang. 2019. Look Again at the Syntax: Relational Graph Convolutional Network for Gendered Ambiguous Pronoun Resolution. In *Proceedings of the First Workshop on Gender Bias for Natural Language Processing*, Florence, Italy. Association for Computational Linguistics.

Kai-Chou Yang, Timothy Niven, and Hung-Yu Kao. 2019. Fill the GAP: Exploiting BERT for Pronoun Resolution. In *Proceedings of the First Workshop on Gender Bias for Natural Language Processing*, Florence, Italy. Association for Computational Linguistics.

Jieyu Zhao, Tianlu Wang, Mark Yatskar, Vicente Ordonez, and Kai-Wei Chang. 2018. Gender bias in coreference resolution: Evaluation and debiasing methods. In *Proceedings of the 2018 Conference of the North American Chapter of the Association for Computational Linguistics: Human Language Technologies, Volume 2 (Short Papers)*, pages 15–20, New Orleans, Louisiana. Association for Computational Linguistics.

Proposed Taxonomy for Gender Bias in Text;
A Filtering Methodology for the Gender Generalization Subtype

Yasmeen Hitti* and **Eunbee Jang*** and **Ines Moreno*** and **Carolyne Pelletier***
{hittiyas, jangeunb, morenoin, pelletic}@mila.quebec
Mila, Université de Montréal / 6666 St-Urbain, Montreal, QC H2S 3H1

Abstract

The purpose of this paper is to present an empirical study on gender bias in text. Current research in this field is focused on detecting and correcting for gender bias in existing machine learning models rather than approaching the issue at the dataset level. The underlying motivation is to create a dataset which could enable machines to learn to differentiate bias writing from non-bias writing. A taxonomy is proposed for structural and contextual gender biases which can manifest themselves in text. A methodology is proposed to fetch one type of structural gender bias, Gender Generalization. We explore the IMDB movie review dataset and 9 different corpora from Project Gutenberg. By filtering out irrelevant sentences, the remaining pool of candidate sentences are sent for human validation. A total of 6123 judgments are made on 1627 sentences and after a quality check on randomly selected sentences we obtain an accuracy of 75%. Out of the 1627 sentences, 808 sentence were labeled as Gender Generalizations. The inter-rater reliability amongst labelers was of 61.14%.

1 Introduction

The feminist movement which debuted in the late 1960s was a response to gender discourses that had been problematic and often biased (Messerschmidt et al., 2018). Ever since, more emphasis has been guided towards outlining these issues in societal roles, sports, media, religion, culture, medicine, and education. Haines et al. (2016) have shown, despite time, from the 1980s to 2014, that the perception of gender roles has remained stable for men and women, hence the presence of biased sociocultural expectations to this day. Research concerning gender equality has been focused on quantitative data analysis and has resulted in empirical evidence of inequalities in different sectors.

Examples include school enrollments and job employments, all which have failed to provide the source responsible for these inequalities (Unterhalter, 2015). Although the root of these imbalances remain ambiguous, it is known that social norms have greatly influenced and reinforced inconsistencies while referring to specific genders (Robeyns, 2007).

Language is known to reflect and influence society in its perception of the world. For these reasons there has been constant effort to promote bias-free and non-sexist writing to empower the fairness movement. However, to our knowledge, no quantitative study on gender bias in text at the dataset level has been done. In the era of Machine Learning (ML), gender biases are translated from sourced data to existing algorithms that may reflect and amplify existing cultural prejudices and inequalities (Sweeney, 2013) by replicating human behavior and perpetuating bias. Thus, there is a need to approach this issue in a ML context in the hope that it will help raise awareness and minimize discrimination at the human-level. To do so, rather than removing gender bias in current ML models we want to create a dataset with which to train a model to detect and help correct gender bias in written form. In the long run, our dataset would ideally be extended to encompass all types of bias such as race, religion, sexual orientation, etc.

1.1 Contributions

- Provide a high-level definition of gender bias in text

- Present an approach to find one of the subtypes of gender bias, Gender Generalization

- Provide a small labeled dataset for Gender Generalization bias.

---

*equal contribution

Proceedings of the 1st Workshop on Gender Bias in Natural Language Processing, pages 8–17
Florence, Italy, August 2, 2019. ©2019 Association for Computational Linguistics

2   Related Work

Current ML research has identified gender bias in various models, each with its own evaluation and debiasing methods. In Natural Language Processing (NLP), gender bias has been studied in word embeddings, coreference resolution and recently, in datasets. Previous work on gender bias in writing has been addressed by linguists with the creation of inclusive writing. In the field of gender studies, gender gaps have been explored through social contexts.

2.1   Word Embedding

In NLP, word embeddings have become a powerful means of word representations. Bolukbasi et al. (2016) first experimented with gender in word embeddings and found that the presence of gender stereotypes were highly consistent in popularly used word representation packages such as Glove and word2vec (Bolukbasi et al., 2016). To better understand the gender bias subspace, gender specific words were investigated to compare their distances with respect to other words in the vector space (Bolukbasi et al., 2016). It is claimed that the unequal distances measured are due to the corpora on which an embedding has been trained on and reflect the usage of language which contain cultural stereotypes (Garg et al., 2018).

Hard debiasing was developed following the findings on gender bias in word embeddings. This method introduced by Bolukbasi et al. (2016) has the main objective of debiasing word embeddings while preserving their properties in the embedding space. To achieve the debiasing of an algorithm, the assumption was that a group of words needed to be neutralized to ensure that gender neutral words were not affected in the gender subspace of the embedding. Following this work, Zhao et al. (2018b) have approached the problem differently and have uptaken the task of training on debiased word embeddings from scratch by introducing gendered words as seed words. Furthermore, Gonen and Goldberg (2019) has shown with clustering that debiased word embeddings still contain biases and concluded that the existing bias removal techniques are insufficient, and should not be trusted for providing gender-neutral modeling.

2.2   Coreference Resolution

Coreference resolution is a task aimed at pairing a phrase to its referring entity. In the context of this paper, we are interested in pairing pronouns with their referring entities. Recent studies by Rudinger et al. (2018) suggest, however, that state-of-the-art coreference resolvers are gender biased due in part to the biased data they have been trained on. For example, OntoNotes 5.0, a dataset used in the training of coreference systems, contains gender imbalances (Zhao et al., 2018a). One such example of these imbalances are in the frequency of gendered mentions related to job titles: "Male gendered mentions are more than twice as likely to contain a job title as female mentions". Zhao et al. (2018a) showed that coreference systems are gender biased in this same context of job occupations since they link pronouns to occupations dominated by the gender of the pronoun more accurately than occupations not dominated by the gender of the pronoun.

When coreference resolution decisions are used to process text in automatic systems, any bias present in these decisions will be passed on to downstream applications. This is something that we must keep in mind as we rely on coreference resolution in our filtering system in the later section.

2.3   Datasets

In the past few years, the ML community has created new text datasets with respect to gender discrimination and have focused on hate speech, stereotypes and relatedness to gender ambiguous pronouns. Twitter posts have been the preferred source of investigation when it comes to understanding and capturing human bias although this may only focus on one type of gender bias. The Equity Evaluation Corpus is a dataset of 8,640 English sentences with a race or gendered word and evaluates the sentiment towards these sentences. The measurement of sentiment was achieved by training on the SemEval-2018 Tweets (Kiritchenko and Mohammad, 2018). Abusive language datasets have also been based off of tweets and identify sexist and racist language (Waseem, 2016). GAP is a dataset focused on sentences which have references to entities; this dataset is composed of sentences with proper nouns and ambiguous gendered pronouns (Webster et al., 2018).

2.4 Gender Bias in Writing

2.4.1 Inclusive Writing

Gender-neutral writing was developed to avoid sexism and generic mental images for gender roles (Corbett, 1990). Guidelines for inclusive writing were created following surveys and offer insights on different biases including gender related biases (Schwartz, 1995). A study by Vainapel et al. (2015) demonstrated that male-inflected terms in a survey have affected the responses of women leading to lower task value beliefs. Motivations behind the utilization of gender inclusive writing is to disrupt the current educational system which is tailored for masculinized vocational professions (Ray et al., 2018).

2.4.2 Gender Gap

The gender gap in writing has resurfaced multiple times through history. The meaning of gender was studied by Simone de Beauvoir and was defined as something which is prescribed by society with preferences towards men (Cameron, 2005). This societal role of the toy and media culture has influenced the writing of boys and girls at schools and has related boys to violence and girls to subordinate roles (Newkirk, 2000). The online writing of of women and men on Wikipedia has also been unequal as most editors have been males thus creating a gender gap in their content (Graells-Garrido et al., 2015).

3 Proposed Gender bias Taxonomy

As most work in the ML community related to gender bias has been focused on debiasing existing algorithms, the creation of a dataset will enable to tackle the issue at its root and allow for observation of its impact on different ML models.

The first step to the data creation is to quantify the qualitative definition of gender bias. Thus, a gender bias taxonomy is proposed after consulting language and gender experts. We define gender bias in text as the use of words or syntactic constructs that connote or imply an inclination or prejudice against one gender. Gender bias can manifest itself structurally, contextually or both. Moreover, there can be different intensities of biases which can be subtle or explicit.

3.1 Structural Bias

Under our definition, structural gender bias occurs when bias can be traced down from a specific grammatical construction. This includes looking up of any syntactic patterns or keywords that enforce gender assumptions in a gender neutral setting. This type of bias can be analyzed through popularly used text processing techniques used in NLP.

3.1.1 Gender Generalization

The first subtype of structural bias, that we refer to as Gender Generalization, appears when a gender-neutral term is syntactically referred to by a gender-exclusive pronoun, therefore, making an assumption of gender. Gender-exclusive pronouns include: *he, his, him, himself, she, her, hers and herself.*

- "**A programmer** must always carry **his** laptop with **him**." - gives a fact about an arbitrary programmer and assumes a man to be the programmer by referring to "*he*".

- "**A teacher** should always care about **her** students." - gives a fact about an arbitrary teacher and assumes a woman to be the teacher by referring to "*she*".

Counter example:

- "**A boy** will always want to play with **his** ball." - although representing a stereotype, it is not assuming the gender for a gender neutral word since the word boy (gendered - male) is linked to a male pronoun. Thus, it is not Gender Generalization bias.

3.1.2 Explicit Marking of Sex

A second subtype of structural bias appears with the use of gender-exclusive keywords when referring to an unknown gender-neutral entity or group.

- "**Policemen** work hard to protect our city." - the use of "*policemen*" instead of "*police officers*" directly excludes all women that could also hold that position.

- "The role of **a seamstress** in the workforce is undervalued." - the usage of a gender-marked title for women for a job that can be done by both sexes is biased unless referring only to the female counterpart.

3.2 Contextual Bias

On the other hand, contextual gender bias does not have a rule-based definition. It requires the learning of the association between gender-marked keywords and contextual knowledge. Unlike structural bias, this type of bias cannot be observed through grammatical structure but requires contextual background information and human perception.

3.2.1 Societal Stereotype

Societal stereotypes showcase traditional gender roles that reflects social norms. The assumption of roles predetermines how one gender is perceived in the mentioned context.

- "Senators need their **wives** to **support** them throughout their campaign." - the word *"wife"* is depicted as a supporting figure when we do not know the gender of the senator and the supporting figure can be a male partner, a husband.

- "The event was **kid-friendly** for all the **mothers** working in the company." - assumes women as the principal caretakers of children by using the word *"mothers"* instead of using *"parent"* that would encompass possibly more workers.

3.2.2 Behavioural Stereotype

Behavioural stereotypes contain attributes and traits used to describe a specific person or gender. This bias assumes the behaviour of a person from their gender.

- "**All boys** are **aggressive**." - misrepresentation of all boys as aggressive.

- "**Mary** must **love dolls** because **all girls like playing with them**." - assumes that dolls are only liked by girls.

4 Empirical Pilot Study

Two different surveys were deployed, first to better understand if the proposed definition of gender bias was well accepted and second to decide whether categorical or binary labeling should be used when presenting sentences to human labelers. The definition survey was distributed to individuals from the field of sociolinguistics, linguistics, and gender studies. The second survey on categorical and binary labeling was deployed on Mechanical Turk[1] and to the same gender and language experts for the definition survey.

4.1 Definition Survey

The survey form was designed to be shared with individuals who had some relatedness to the topic in a research context. The motivation was to start a dialogue across disciplines to observe if some sort of consensus could be achieved and to recognize potential factors influencing the bias towards gender. The questions asked were short answers, long answers and multiple choices.

Questions:

1. Do you think gender bias is influenced by demographics (gender, age, geographic location, professional status., etc...)? Please justify your answer.

2. Where is it most likely to find gender bias? (work place, home, legal system, academia, media and other)

3. Do you think there are subtypes of gender bias? (yes/no)

4. If yes, which are the subtypes of gender bias?

5. Our current understanding of gender bias in text is : *Gender bias in text is the use of words/syntactic constructs that connote or imply an inclination or prejudice against one gender. It can be structural (when the construction of sentences show patterns that are closely tied to the presence of gender bias) or contextual (when the tone, the words use or simply the context of a sentence shows gender bias).* Do you agree with this definition?

6. Would you add/remove something to/from the previous definition?

7. Do you have any comments/feedback?

8. Having a well-labeled dataset is key for the success of our project. In the future, would you be willing to help label a subset of sentences as gender biased or non-gender biased?

4.2 Data Presentation Survey

A data presentation survey was sent out to the same group of people and was also launched on a crowdsourcing platform, Mechanical Turk. The survey had two sections of 10 questions; the first section contained categorical labeling with all of

---

[1] https://www.mturk.com/

the potential types of gender bias in text and the second section was binary labeling confirming if a sentence was gender biased or not. At the end of each survey, optional feedback was collected from the participants to ask for their preference and clarity on labeling format. The sentences chosen to be presented to the participants were selected from various journal sources which had been web-scraped previously.

4.3 Deductions

Both surveys provided insightful information for the data collection. The responses from the definition survey included:

- 90% agreed that gender bias is influenced by demographics.

- Respondents had consensus that gender bias can be found in academia, households, media, legal systems, sport coverage, literature and in medical treatments.

- 100% agreed that there are different subtypes of gender bias in writing.

- The top three subtypes identified were stereotypes with 100% agreement, Gender Generalizations with 90% agreement and abusive language with 80% agreement.

A total of 44 participants responded to the data presentation survey and 77.3% preferred binary labeling versus categorical labeling. A good takeaway from this survey was that the presentation of all subtypes of gender bias for categorical labeling may complicate understanding of different definitions we present for future labelers to be able to identify every types of biases. Following both surveys, we decided to focus on extracting one subtype of biases at a time.

5 Methodology

In the previous section, we define different types of biases that can occur which can induce both explicit and implicit biases. In this paper, we focus on one of the structural biases, Gender Generalization, that can be analyzed through observing the syntactic structure of text. Under our definition, Gender Generalization occurs when a gendered pronoun is linked to a gender-neutral term in a gender-free context.

5.1 Corpora Selection

The frequency of Gender Generalizations in texts are unknown and for this reason different types of writing styles were considered for exploration. The biggest challenge in corpus selection was finding sources which talked about human individuals in a general way rather than specific individuals. Our starting point was the IMDB dataset (Maas et al., 2011), followed by multiple corpora from Project Gutenberg [2]. This selection provided a range of writings from the 1800s to modern colloquial English. The texts from Project Gutenberg used for the experiment were: Business Hints for Men and Women, Magna Carta, The Federalists Papers, The Constitution of the United States of America: Analysis and Interpretation, The Common Law, Langstroth on the Hive and the Honey-Bee: A Bee Keeper's Manual, Scouting For Girls: Official Handbook of the Girl Scouts, Boy Scouts Handbook and Practical Mind-Reading. These texts were chosen on the belief that we could capture Gender Generalization sentences; this selection includes guidelines, law and instructions.

5.2 Preprocessing

All texts were preprocessed in order to pass on to the filters and labelers. All texts were split into sentences, no punctuation was stripped and letter cases remained in their original form for integrity purposes. For the IMDB dataset, HTML tags were removed and text was decoded from unicode matching the closest ASCII characters to handle any special symbols present in the text. All text from Project Gutenberg came in a text format in UTF-8 encoding. All document formatting of indentations, blank spaces and quotation marks were removed.

5.3 Design of Filters

The objective behind gathering Gender Generalization sentences is to start constructing a dataset of gender biased sentences with a subtype of bias that is easy to recognize structurally. To gather text data that falls into this category of bias, we have decided to filter sentences based on their syntactic structure. The strategy was to find all the links between expressions that refer to the same entity in text and observe their property with respect to

---

[2]https://www.gutenberg.org/

the gender they are associated with. Following our definition, the main characteristics of Gender Generalization bias is the existence of a link between a gendered pronoun to any human entity that is not tied to any gender.

Identifying gender-free mentions was challenging since they appear in diverse forms and are closely connected with their context in which they appear, making it necessary for human validation. The filters were used as tools to reduce the scope of the labeling pool, which was sent to the labelers for human judgment.

The filters were applied to every sentence and if any sentence did not meet one of the criteria, it was removed from the potential pool of Gender Generalization candidates. The order of filters applied were as such: *coreference resolution, verification of gendered pronoun, human-name removal, gendered-term removal, and pronoun-link.* The coreference resolution was achieved using AllenNLP and the other filters were dependent on the NLTK library.

5.3.1 Coreference Resolution Filter

Coreference resolution was chosen as a filter for fetching Gender Generalizations as it is by definition identifying different mentions referring to the same entity. AllenNLP's[3] pre-trained model was used to gather coreference clusters. This model implements the current state-of-the-art end-to-end neural coreference resolution by Lee et al. (2017) which is trained on a biased word embedding (Bolukbasi et al., 2016). The models utilizes GloVe and Turian embeddings (Pennington et al., 2014) which result in preferred resolution for gendered pronouns. While the accuracy of coreference resolvers given the gender of the pronoun may differ, it did not affect our coreference resolution filter since we were simply interested in using the resolver to indicate the presence of an antecedent linked to a pronoun. As such, the accuracy of the resolver was of diminished concern.

5.3.2 Gendered Pronoun Filter

After acquiring the information of coreference relationships, we filtered out sentences which we know confidently are not human related. Generalization of gender by definition assumes a particular pronoun to be assigned to a person entity with

an unknown gender. Such datapoints were traced down by checking the existence of gendered pronouns in text using simple list manipulations. The gendered pronouns in our list included: *he, him, his, himself, she, her, hers, herself.*

5.3.3 Human Name Filter

While sentences containing human names can be biased, they were not identified as a Gender Generalization. This type of bias requires gender-free context and having a specific person referenced to a gendered pronoun enforces gender in the text as seen in the example below.

- "**Jason** must not abandon the place where **he** was brought up." - The pronoun "*he*" is used because it refers to Jason who is a male.

- "**A politician** must not abandon the place where **he** was brought up." - Exhibiting gender bias because the pronoun "*he*" was used when "*a politician*" is a gender-free term.

To make our system recognize human names, we utilized Named Entity Recognition (NER) from Natural Language Toolkit (NLTK). For every mention in a coreference cluster, we checked if NER classifies the mention as a person-type category when tokenized sentences were fed into the system; identified clusters resulted in the removal of sentences.

5.3.4 Gendered Term Filter

Gendered terms are the words which exhibit specific gender and confirm a person's gender without needing context . For example, the term '*sister*' always refers to female sibling and is always associated with female pronouns whereas '*brother*' refers to male sibling with male pronouns. These types of terms in the coreference relationship were discarded for Gender Generalization bias text mining. Since there is no such system that detected gender assignments of human words, we explored the Lesk algorithm from NLTK which performs Word Sense Disambiguation (WSD) using WordNet. WordNet is a lexical database for the English language and it provides access to dictionary definitions along with related synonyms. The Lesk algorithm utilizes sense-labeled corpus to identify word senses in context using definition overlap.

Our approach was to acquire the adequate word sense of mentions in the coreference cluster given sentences as a context for WSD. The Morphy algorithm in WordNet was then utilized; it uses a

---

combination of inflectional ending rules and exception list to find the base form of the word of interest. When the base forms were attained, we looked up the definitions associated with their synsets (word sense token). If the definitions contained any gendered terms in table 1 , the sentence was removed.

Type	Male Term	Female Term
Base Term	male	female
	man	woman
	boy	girl
Pronoun	he	she
	him	her
	his	hers
	himself	herself
Family Term	husband	wife
	father	mother
	son	daughter
	brother	sister
	grandfather	grandmother
	grandson	granddaughter
	uncle	aunt
	nephew	niece

Table 1: Gendered terms used in the filter.

Below in Table 2 are some example words that have passed through the definitions of human nouns that we have obtained.

Word	Definition	Gendered?
landlord	a landowner who leases to others	No
landlady	a landlord who is a **woman**	Yes
gentleman	a **man** of refinement	Yes
lady	a polite name for any **woman**	Yes
actor	a theatrical performer	No
actress	a **female** actor	Yes

Table 2: Example definitions provided by WordNet.

5.3.5 Pronoun Link Filter

The pronoun link filter detected any coreference clusters that are linked with just pronouns. Our definition of structural Gender Generalization requires at least one gender-neutral human entity in each datapoint. If a cluster contained only pronoun links, the original mention happened in the scope outside of the sentence which was considered. Thus, these sentences were removed from the labeling pool before they were sent to the human labelers.

5.4 Crowdsourcing

The labeling task was designed and implemented on the crowdsourcing platform Figure Eight[4] (previously known as CrowdFlower). The questionnaire form was created based off of a template for categorical labeling of data provided by the crowdsourcing platform. The categories presented to the labelers were *"Gender Generalization"* , *"not a Gender Generalization"* and *"problematic sentence"*. The third option was added as a choice for labelers to indicate when a sentence did not have any mention of a human entity, if the sentence was not grammatical and if the sentence was wrongly picked up by our filters.

Labelers were presented with 10 sentences per page and a limit was set to 100 judgements per labeler. Each page of the task contained a random number of golden sentences to ensure the quality of labelers. The golden set is a set of 20 sentences which were labeled by gender and language experts. The golden sentences were used as a mechanism to filter good labelers from bad labelers. The labelers had to label correctly 80% of the golden sentences presented to them in order for their results to be taken into account. Each sentence needed three trusted judgments at a minimum before obtaining the final label.

To ensure better quality of the data, additional measures were taken to ensure labelers were taking the time to understand the proposed definition of Gender Generalization. Level 2 contributors who were endorsed as experienced, higher accuracy contributors on Figure Eight were chosen to participate in the task. This provides us with a set of labelers that were more experienced. Each time a new page of 10 sentences were presented, the labelers had to spend a minimum of 120 seconds on each page. Equally, the Google translate option on Figure Eight was disabled for labelers while participating in this task in order to preserve the context of the sentences presented to them.

6 Results

Once the 15,000 datapoints from IMDB train set were split into sentences, the dataset contained 180,119 sentences. The 9 Project Gutenberg corpora yielded a total of 55,966 sentences. The

---

search space of IMDB was reduced to 7876 candidate sentences for the labeling pool, representing 4.4% of the original set used. The search space of all Project Gutenberg ebooks was reduced to 1627 sentences, representing 2.7% of the original data. It is important to note that the quality of the pre-trained models used in the filters can impact the sentences retained.

As a preliminary test to validate the quality of sentences filtered from IMDB, randomly chosen 1000 sentences were sent for labeling. It was observed that sentences provided from movie reviews were person specific and they contained information about specific movie characters, actors or directors rather than displaying gender assumptions towards gender-neutral human entities. This introduced too much noise in the data and the quality of the filtration was altered accordingly. Thus, true Gender Generalization sentences were less likely to be found even after going through human validation due to vast noise in the data. This suggests that finding adequate data sources for Gender Generalization is important and confirms our hypothesis that good source for Gender Generalization is dependent on the style of writing.

Corpora from Project Gutenberg on the other hand contained sentences that can be applied to general population, making them more relevant to Gender Generalization bias. We present our result on label quality in the later section. Furthermore, it is observed that the amount of Gender Generalization candidate sentences represented a small fraction of each corpus explored from Project Gutenberg.

As seen in table 3, the search space for Gender Generalization was greatly reduced when the filtering approach was undertaken. This allowed for only the relevant sentences to be validated by human labelers. Reducing the search space helps human labelers to focus on one type of syntactic structure, which can directly impact the quality of final labels. Finally, 808 out of 1627 filtered sentences were accepted as Gender Generalization bias which accounts for 49.7% of filtered data across our corpora and 819 are labeled as not Gender Generalization bias.

6.1 Quality of Judgments

A total of 6123 judgements were made on the potential Gender Generalization candidates (a set of 1627 sentences). Out of the total amount of judge-

Source	S	$\frac{\Sigma C}{\Sigma S}$	$\frac{\Sigma T}{\Sigma C}$
Boy Scouts Handbook	6330	3.6%	61.2%
Business Hints for Men and Women	2162	4.0%	63.6%
The Common Law	6101	5.8%	53.8%
The Constitution of the United States of America	21920	2.2%	44.3%
The Federalists Papers	5981	1.5%	27.0%
the Hive and the Honey-Bee: A Bee Keeper's Manual	4430	4.0%	36.5%
Magna Carta	407	4.4%	55.5%
Official Handbook of the Girl Scouts	7687	1.9%	51.7%
Practical Mind-Reading	948	4.5%	55.8%
All Corpora	55,966	2.9%	49.7%
Mean	-	2.9%	55.4%
Standard deviation	-	1.4%	11.9%

Table 3: Candidate and Gender Generalization sentences by source - {S: total number of sentences in each corpus, C: sentences remaining after filtration, T: sentences identified as true Gender Generalization bias}

ments, 4881 were trusted and accepted as final labels; these judgments represent 79.7% out of the total judgments. Each sentence was validated three times by the labelers who maintained a minimum accuracy of 80% on the golden sentences. 1242 judgements were untrusted, meaning the labelers who did not maintain an accuracy of 80% of the golden sentences were not accounted for in the final labeling; these judgments represent 20.3% of the total judgements.

Full agreement of labels only happened for 637 out of 1627 presented sentences. The remaining 990 sentences had an agreement of 66.7% which means 2 out of 3 labels were in accordance per data point. The inter-rater reliability for the full set of sentences was of 61.14%. Consequently, we decided to investigate a random subset of sentences to evaluate the quality and to better understand the low level of agreement. A total of 108 sentences, 12 sentences from each corpus, were randomly chosen from the final labeled pool to test the quality of labels assigned to each sentence. An f1 score of 73.9% was achieved with 75% accuracy. The percentage of correctly labeled Gender Generalization sentences were 70.4% and correctly labeled not Gender Generalization bias was 79.6% respectively. Sentences falsely classified as true Gender Generalization bias exhibited gender bias that did not fall into the Gender Generalization category. Moreover, sentences which should have been filtered out that remained in the labeling pool also created confusion, suggesting that improving the quality of the filters could impact the quality of the final labels. On the other hand, falsely classified as not Gender Generalization bias sentences tend to be in longer length and contained multiple pronouns linked to different human entities. This suggests that the labeler's judgment is altered when longer attention span is required. Following this, a minimum and maximum time allocation for labeling can be studied in the future as Cooley et al. (2018) observes that predefined social attributions may affect human perception and consequently may affect our labeling.

7 Conclusion and Future Work

In this paper, we propose a gender bias taxonomy as well as a means for capturing Gender Generalization sentences. The purpose of capturing these sentences is to build a dataset so that we can train a ML classifier to identify gender bias writing as well as to see the impact of clean dataset on different ML models. In future work, we hope to propose a method to capture the other types of gender bias in text that we identified in our taxonomy. Capturing qualitative bias is a challenging task and there is a need for designing systems in order to better understand bias. The approach we took was based off the proposed definition that was translated into a fetching mechanism which can aid human validation. With an initial set of 55,966 sentences, the search space was filtered down to 1627 candidates of which 808 were labeled as Gender Generalization. The presence of Gender Generalizations in text was small and represented below 5% of each corpus explored.

Our method suggests that there is a small search space for sentences with Gender Generalizations. Future work to increase the number of fetched sentences an quality of labeling are:

- Explore different state-of-art models for filters

- Upgrade to an automatized filtering and classification mechanism to enhance the quality and quantity of the labeling pool.

- Explore different data presentation for labeling (ie. longer response time, highlighting parts of sentences, etc)

- Create different methodologies to look for different types of gender bias in text.

- Create a full dataset of different gender biases in text.

Acknowledgements

We would like to acknowledge the guidance of our mentors at Mila: Kris Sankaran, Dmitriy Serdyuk, and Francis Grégoire. Also, thank you to Professor Deborah Cameron and Professor Sally McConnell-Ginet for taking the time to speak with us via email and Skype. Lastly, we'd like to acknowledge the aiforsocialgood.ca summer lab, where this project was originally created.

References

Tolga Bolukbasi, Kai-Wei Chang, James Y Zou, Venkatesh Saligrama, and Adam T Kalai. 2016. Man is to computer programmer as woman is to homemaker? debiasing word embeddings. In *Advances in neural information processing systems*, pages 4349–4357.

Deborah Cameron. 2005. Language, gender, and sexuality: Current issues and new directions. *Applied linguistics*, 26(4):482–502.

Erin Cooley, Hannah Winslow, Andrew Vojt, Jonathan Shein, and Jennifer Ho. 2018. Bias at the intersection of identity: Conflicting social stereotypes of gender and race augment the perceived femininity and interpersonal warmth of smiling black women. *Journal of experimental social psychology*, 74:43–49.

Maryann Z Corbett. 1990. Clearing the air: some thoughts on gender-neutral writing. *IEEE Transactions on Professional Communication*, 33(1):2–6.

Nikhil Garg, Londa Schiebinger, Dan Jurafsky, and James Zou. 2018. Word embeddings quantify 100 years of gender and ethnic stereotypes. *Proceedings of the National Academy of Sciences*, 115(16):E3635–E3644.

Hila Gonen and Yoav Goldberg. 2019. Lipstick on a pig: Debiasing methods cover up systematic gender biases in word embeddings but do not remove them. *arXiv preprint arXiv:1903.03862*.

Eduardo Graells-Garrido, Mounia Lalmas, and Filippo Menczer. 2015. First women, second sex: Gender bias in wikipedia. In *Proceedings of the 26th ACM Conference on Hypertext & Social Media*, pages 165–174. ACM.

Elizabeth L Haines, Kay Deaux, and Nicole Lofaro. 2016. The times they are a-changing... or are they not? a comparison of gender stereotypes, 1983–2014. *Psychology of Women Quarterly*, 40(3):353–363.

Svetlana Kiritchenko and Saif M Mohammad. 2018. Examining gender and race bias in two hundred sentiment analysis systems. *arXiv preprint arXiv:1805.04508*.

Kenton Lee, Luheng He, Mike Lewis, and Luke Zettlemoyer. 2017. End-to-end neural coreference resolution. *arXiv preprint arXiv:1707.07045*.

Andrew L Maas, Raymond E Daly, Peter T Pham, Dan Huang, Andrew Y Ng, and Christopher Potts. 2011. Learning word vectors for sentiment analysis. In *Proceedings of the 49th annual meeting of the association for computational linguistics: Human language technologies-volume 1*, pages 142–150. Association for Computational Linguistics.

James W Messerschmidt, Michael A Messner, Raewyn Connell, and Patricia Yancey Martin. 2018. *Gender reckonings: New social theory and research*. NYU Press.

Thomas Newkirk. 2000. Misreading masculinity: Speculations on the great gender gap in writing. *Language Arts*, 77(4):294–300.

Jeffrey Pennington, Richard Socher, and Christopher Manning. 2014. Glove: Global vectors for word representation. In *Proceedings of the 2014 conference on empirical methods in natural language processing (EMNLP)*, pages 1532–1543.

Sarah M Ray, Ovidio Galvan, and Jill Zarestky. 2018. Gender-inclusive educational programs for workforce development. *Adult Learning*, 29(3):94–103.

IAM Robeyns. 2007. When will society be gender just?

Rachel Rudinger, Jason Naradowsky, Brian Leonard, and Benjamin Van Durme. 2018. Gender bias in coreference resolution. *CoRR*, abs/1804.09301.

Marilyn Schwartz. 1995. *Guidelines for Bias-Free Writing*. ERIC.

Latanya Sweeney. 2013. Discrimination in online ad delivery. *arXiv preprint arXiv:1301.6822*.

ES Unterhalter. 2015. Measuring gender inequality and equality in education. In *Proceedings of workshop hosted by UNGEI*. United Nation Girls' Initiative (UNGEI).

Sigal Vainapel, Opher Y Shamir, Yulie Tenenbaum, and Gadi Gilam. 2015. The dark side of gendered language: The masculine-generic form as a cause for self-report bias. *Psychological assessment*, 27(4):1513.

Zeerak Waseem. 2016. Are you a racist or am i seeing things? annotator influence on hate speech detection on twitter. In *Proceedings of the first workshop on NLP and computational social science*, pages 138–142.

Kellie Webster, Marta Recasens, Vera Axelrod, and Jason Baldridge. 2018. Mind the gap: A balanced corpus of gendered ambiguous pronouns. *Transactions of the Association for Computational Linguistics*, 6:605–617.

Jieyu Zhao, Tianlu Wang, Mark Yatskar, Vicente Ordonez, and Kai-Wei Chang. 2018a. Gender bias in coreference resolution: Evaluation and debiasing methods. *arXiv preprint arXiv:1804.06876*.

Jieyu Zhao, Yichao Zhou, Zeyu Li, Wei Wang, and Kai-Wei Chang. 2018b. Learning gender-neutral word embeddings. *arXiv preprint arXiv:1809.01496*.

Relating Word Embedding Gender Biases to Gender Gaps:
A Cross-Cultural Analysis

Scott Friedman, Sonja Schmer-Galunder, Anthony Chen, and Jeffrey Rye
SIFT, Minneapolis, MN USA
`{friedman, sgalunder, achen, rye}@sift.net`

Abstract

Modern models for common NLP tasks often employ machine learning techniques and train on journalistic, social media, or other culturally-derived text. These have recently been scrutinized for racial and gender biases, rooting from inherent bias in their training text. These biases are often sub-optimal and recent work poses methods to rectify them; however, these biases may shed light on actual racial or gender gaps in the culture(s) that produced the training text, thereby helping us understand cultural context through big data. This paper presents an approach for quantifying gender bias in word embeddings, and then using them to characterize statistical gender gaps in education, politics, economics, and health. We validate these metrics on 2018 Twitter data spanning 51 U.S. regions and 99 countries. We correlate state and country word embedding biases with 18 international and 5 U.S.-based statistical gender gaps, characterizing regularities and predictive strength.

1 Introduction

Machine-learned models are the *de facto* method for NLP tasks. Recently, machine-learned models that utilize *word embeddings* (i.e., vector-based representations of word semantics) have come under scrutiny for biases and stereotypes, e.g., in race and gender, arising primarily from biases in their training data (Bolukbasi et al., 2016). These biases produce systematic mistakes, so recent work has developed *debiasing* language models to improve NLP models' accuracy and and remove stereotypes (Zhao et al., 2018; Zhang et al., 2018).

Concurrently, other research has begun to characterize how biases in language models correspond to disparities in the cultures that produced the training text, e.g., by mapping embeddings to survey data (Kozlowski et al., 2018), casting analogies in the vector space to compute that "man

is to woman as doctor is to nurse" (Bolukbasi et al., 2016), or varying the training text over decades and mapping each decade's model bias against its statistical disparities to capture periods of societal shifts (Garg et al., 2018).

Building on previous work, this paper presents initial work characterizing word embedding biases with statistical *gender gaps* (i.e., discrepancies in opportunities and status across genders). This is an important step in approximating cultural attitudes and relating them to cultural behaviors. We analyze 51 U.S. states and 99 countries, by (1) training separate word embeddings for each of these cultures from Twitter and (2) correlating the biases in these word embeddings with 5 U.S.-based and 18 international gender gap statistics.

Our claims are as follows: (1) some cultural gender biases in language are associated with gender gaps; (2) we can characterize biases based on strength and direction of correlation with gender gaps; and (3) themed word sets, representative of values and social constructs, capture different dimensions of gender bias and gender gaps.

We continue with a brief overview of gender gaps (Sec. 2) and then a description of our training data (Sec. 3) and four experiments (Sec. 4). We close with a discussion of the above claims and future work (Sec. 5).

2 Gender Gaps and Statistics

Within the social sciences, anthropologists often attempt to explain the asymmetrical valuations of the sexes across a range of cultures with respect to patterns of social and cultural experience (Rosaldo, 1974). This work contributes to this research by updating traditional qualitative approaches with computational methods.

The public sphere is often associated with male and agents traits (assertiveness, competitiveness)

18

Proceedings of the 1st Workshop on Gender Bias in Natural Language Processing, pages 18–24
Florence, Italy, August 2, 2019. ©2019 Association for Computational Linguistics

in domains like politics and executive rules at work. Private or domestic domains linked to family and social relationships are traditionally related to women, although social relationships are considered more important by people independent of gender (Friedman and Greenhaus, 2000). Gender gaps arise form these asymmetrical valuations, e.g., where men are typically over-represented and have higher salaries compared to women (Mitra, 2003; Vincent, 2013; Bishu and Alkadry, 2017).

We utilize diverse gender gap statistics in this work. For international data, we use 18 gender gap metrics comprising the Global Gender Gap Index (GGGI) originally compiled for the World Economic Forum's 2018 Gender Gap Report.[1] The GGGI measures clearly-defined dimensions for which reliable data in most countries was available (Hawken and Munck, 2013). For domestic data, we use a 2018 report from the U.S. Center for Disease Control (CDC) on male and female exercise rate (Blackwell and Clarke, 2018), wage gap and workforce data published by the U.S. Census Bureau in 2016, female percentages of math and computer science degrees from Society of Women Engineers,[2] and female percentages of each state's legislators from Represent Women's 2018 Gender Parity Report.[3]

3 Training Data

Our training data include public tweets from U.S. and international Twitter users over 100 days throughout 2018, including the first ten days of each of the first ten months. We use tweet's location property to categorize by location, and we include only English tweets in our dataset.

We filtered out all tweets with fewer than three words, and following other Twitter-based embedding strategies (e.g. Li et al., 2017), we replaced URLs, user names, hashtags, images, and emojis with other tokens. We divided the processed tweets into two separate datasets: (1) U.S. states and (2) countries. This helps us validate our approach with multiple granularities and datasets.

The international dataset contains 99 countries with varying number of tweets, ranging from 98K tweets (Mauritius) to 122M tweets (U.K). The U.S. states dataset contains 51 regions (50 states and Washington, D.C.) ranging from 450K tweets

(Wyoming) to 65M tweets (California). For both datasets, we sampled 10 million tweets for all cultures that exceeded that number. These corpora are orders of magnitude smaller than other approaches for tweet embeddings (e.g., Li et al., 2017).

We use Word2Vec to construct word vectors for our experiments, but we compare Word2Vec with other algorithms in our analyses (Sec. 4.3).

4 Experiments

4.1 International Analysis

Our international and U.S.-based analyses have an identical experimental setup, varying only in the gender gap statistics and the word embeddings.

Our materials included word-sets based in part on survey data (Williams and Best, 1990) and recent work on word embeddings (Garg et al., 2018). These word-sets included (1) *female words* including female pronouns and nouns, (2) *male words*, including male pronouns and nouns, and (3) *neutral words* that were grouped thematically. For instance, we used *appearance* and *intellect* adjectives from (Garg et al., 2018), and we generated other thematic word sets representative of social constructs: *government* (democrat, republican, senate, government, politics, minister, presidency, vote, parliament, ...), *threat* (dangerous, scary, toxic, suspicious, threat, frightening ...), *communal* (community, society, humanity, welfare, ...), *criminal* (criminal, jail, prison, crime, corrupt, ...), *childcare* (child, children, parent, baby, nanny, ...), *excellent* (excellent, fantastic, phenomenal, outstanding, ...) and others.

We use the same male and female word sets for international and U.S. state analyses, and we compute per-gender vectors $\overrightarrow{female}$ and $\overrightarrow{male}$ by averaging the vectors of each constituent word, following (Garg et al., 2018). For any country or state's word embedding, we compute the *average axis projection* of a neutral word set W onto the male-female axis as:

$$avg_{w \in W}\left(\vec{w} \cdot \frac{\overrightarrow{female} - \overrightarrow{male}}{||\overrightarrow{female} - \overrightarrow{male}||_2}\right) \quad (1)$$

This average axis projection is our primary measure of gender bias in word embeddings.

For any neutral word list (e.g., government terms), we compute the average axis projection for all countries (or states) and compute its correlation to international (or U.S.) gender gaps. Fig. 2

---

[1] http://reports.weforum.org

[2] http://societyofwomenengineers.swe.org/

[3] http://www.representwomen.org

	govt	intellect	workplace	excellent	childcare	illness	communal	victim	*"pretty"*	r-1	r-2	r-3	r-4
Index: Overall Gender Gap	**.30**	.11	.17	.12	-.01	-.07	-.20	-.06	-.19	-.01	.02	.03	.02
Sex ratio at birth	.00	.01	.03	.00	-.02	-.01	.00	-.02	.00	.00	.03	-.04	.00
Index: Educational Attainment	.03	.05	.10	.03	-.18	-.12	-.19	**-.23**	-.07	-.04	.02	.00	.00
Literacy rate	.07	.08	.05	.07	-.18	-.13	-.21	**-.23**	-.08	-.03	.02	-.05	-.07
Enrollment tertiary education	.06	.10	.07	.02	**-.24**	-.20	-.12	-.11	-.06	-.01	-.01	-.08	-.03
Enrollment secondary education	.02	.01	.03	.00	-.08	-.01	**-.21**	-.13	-.02	.00	.04	-.02	-.01
Enrollment primary education	.01	.01	.05	.01	-.05	-.06	**-.15**	-.12	-.06	-.01	.04	.01	.03
Index: Political Empowerment	**.28**	.02	.10	.01	.04	.01	-.03	.04	-.14	.07	.01	-.04	.00
Women in ministerial positions	**.25**	.03	.17	.09	.00	-.02	-.02	.00	-.08	.04	.03	-.01	-.07
Women in parliament	**.16**	.04	.07	.02	.01	.03	-.02	.05	-.06	.02	.06	-.09	.00
% 50 years female head of state	.05	-.04	.01	-.07	.02	.01	.00	.00	-.06	.01	-.02	-.01	.01
Index: Economic Participation	.10	.04	.13	.10	-.02	-.12	**-.33**	-.09	-.10	-.07	.04	-.05	.04
Professional and technical workers	.20	.23	**.27**	.23	-.15	-.21	-.19	-.12	-.14	-.05	.08	-.08	.06
Legislators, officials, managers	.08	.15	.10	**.18**	-.05	-.14	**-.18**	-.10	-.01	-.05	.04	.00	.03
Labour force participation	.03	.04	.08	.02	-.03	-.09	**-.21**	-.04	-.14	-.09	.02	-.03	.01
Wage equality (survey)	-.02	-.04	-.02	-.02	.03	.04	.00	.00	-.02	.00	-.02	-.03	-.05
Index: Health and Survival	.03	.09	.08	.06	-.12	**-.13**	-.02	-.06	.00	-.02	.09	.01	.00
Healthy life expectancy	.06	.09	.12	.14	-.16	**-.31**	-.07	-.11	-.01	-.02	.07	.01	-.01

Figure 1: Correlation of themed neutral word sets' gender bias (columns) against categories of gender gaps from worldbank.org (rows). Values are R^2 coefficient of determination, where negation is added to indicate inverse correlation. The rightmost four word sets (*r-1 to r-4*) were randomly sampled from the vocabulary for comparison.

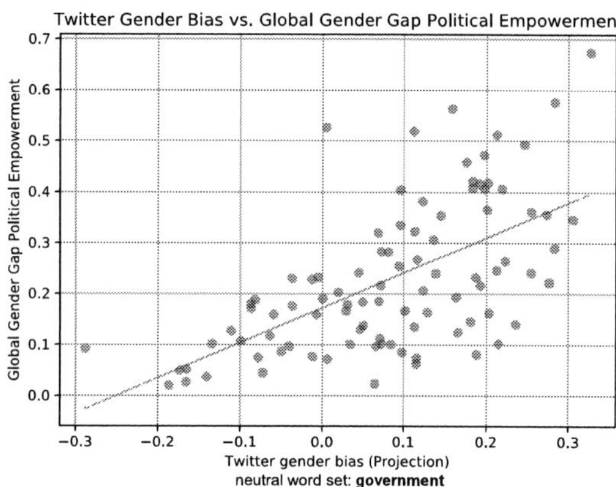

Figure 2: Correlation of country's gender bias of government words (x-axis; female association increases in positive direction) against the World Economic Forum's political empowerment gender gap index (y-axis; gender gap decreases in positive direction).

plots each country's government/political word bias against the World Economic Forum's Political Empowerment Gender Gap sub-index (from 0 to 1, where greater score indicates less gap). The value 0.0 on the x-axis indicates no gender bias, and female bias increases along the x-axis.

Consequently, Fig. 2 is consistent with the hypothesis that— globally, over our set of 99 countries— women's political influence and power increase (relative to men) as political language shows a more female bias.

We present results of each thematic word set regressed against all available international statistics. For each pair of themed word set and gender gap statistic, the algorithm (1) performs feature selection on 20% of the countries to optionally down-select from the set of words in the themed word set, (2) uses the down-selected word set to compute the R^2 determination against the full set of countries, and then (3) repeats a total of five times and averages the answers. Feature selection monotonically increases the R^2, and using 20% of countries helps prevent over-fitting.

Fig. 1 includes our results over this analysis, grouping gender gap sub-indices (bold) with their related statistics. This illustrates that different word sets vary in their correlation direction and strength across different statistic groups: the *political* set is positively correlated with the political empowerment subgroup and marginal on some economic statistics, but weak over health and education; intellectual and workplace terms positively correlate with economic statistics but are weak predictors otherwise; *illness* terms indirectly correlated with health and survival statistics, but are weak correlates elsewhere; and so-forth. The word *"pretty,"* shown in Fig. 1, was the single word with the strongest determination against the overall gender gap and other sub-indices. Fig. 1 also includes four randomly-generated word sets, which do not exceed $R^2 = 0.09$ for any gender gap.

The selective correlation of these thematic word sets with related gender gap statistics supports our claim that gender biases in word embeddings can help characterize and predict statistical gender gaps across cultures. Since we trained our embeddings on tweets alone— with as few as 98K tweets

	threat	unintelligent	criminal	persistent	excellent	stem-alum	childcare	victim	appearance	r-1	r-2	r-3	r-4
CDC Activity Proportion	.09	.05	-.03	.41	.07	-.04	-.02	.03	-.03	-.01	.07	.00	.00
Female State Legislators	-.16	-.22	-.42	.11	.11	.03	-.24	-.04	-.12	.00	-.08	-.03	-.06
Math & CS Degrees	-.15	-.27	-.02	-.07	.01	.28	.01	-.09	-.07	-.03	-.01	.00	-.01
Census Wage Gap	-.51	-.15	-.12	.04	.21	.11	-.06	-.17	-.15	.01	-.06	.02	.04
Census Workforce Ratio	-.06	-.30	-.06	-.04	.00	.03	.01	-.03	-.06	.01	-.03	-.03	-.04

Figure 3: Correlation of themed neutral word sets' gender bias (columns) against U.S. gender disparity statistics from CDC, US Census Bureau, and Represent Women's 2018 Gender Parity Report (rows). Values are R^2 coefficient of determination, where negation is added to indicate inverse correlation. The rightmost four word sets (*rand 1-4*) were randomly sampled from the vocabulary for comparison.

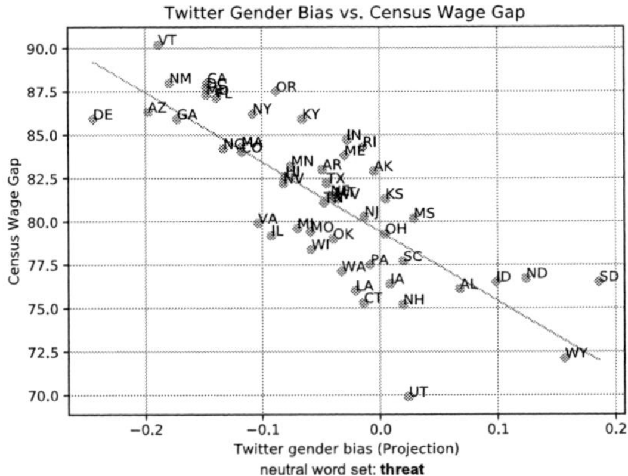

Figure 4: Correlation of states' gender bias of threat words' (x-axis; female association is positive direction) against the pay gap reported by U.S. Census Bureau in 2016 (y-axis; pay gap decreases in positive direction).

for some countries— this also supports our claim that social media is a plausible source to compute a culture's gender bias in language.

None of our themed word sets strongly correlated with: (1) sex ratio at birth, which was 1.0 for the vast majority of countries; (2) percentage of last 50 years with female head of state; and (3) survey-based wage equality. The latter two gender gaps may correlate with other themed word sets, or they may have a more complex or nonlinear relationship to a culture's gender bias in language.

4.2 U.S. State Analysis

Our analysis of 51 U.S. regions (50 U.S. states and Washington, D.C.) is analogous to our Sec. 4.1 international analysis; we only vary the word embeddings and the statistical gender gap data.

Fig. 4 shows an example of indirect correlation ($R^2 = 0.51$) of our *threat* word set (threat, dangerous, toxic, suspicious, scary, frightening, horrifying, ...) against U.S. Census Bureau data reported in 2016 on the gender pay gap. The y-axis indicates cents on the dollar earned by women for the same work as men, ranging from 69.9¢ (UT)

to 91.2¢ (VT). This inverse correlation is consistent with the hypothesis that when masculinity is threatened in some cultures, men react by asserting dominance (Zuo and Tang, 2000; Schmitt and Branscombe, 2001).

Fig. 3 illustrates different word sets' determination on U.S. regions' statistical gender gaps. The word set describing persistence and devotion had strongest direct correlation with reduced gender gap in exercise. The word set for criminal behavior had strongest negative correlation with female proportion of state legislators. Words for STEM disciplines and alumni directly correlated with increased percentages of female math and CS degrees. Threat-based words negatively correlated with pay equality, and words for unintelligent and inept negatively correlated with female percentage of the workforce. Other word sets from the international analysis (e.g., childcare and victimhood) had less determination of gender gaps than in the international setting.

As with our international analysis, this domestic analysis supports our claim that gender biases in cultural language models can predict and characterize statistical gender gaps.

4.3 Algorithm Comparison

We compare four word embedding algorithms and three bias metrics using our gender gap statistics and word sets. We compare four algorithms: (1) GloVe, (2) Word2Vec (skip-gram), (3) CBOW Word2Vec, and (4) FastText (skip-gram). For each algorithm we utilize a window size 10, filter words that occur fewer than 5 times, and produce 200-dimension output vectors.

GloVe (Pennington et al., 2014) uses count-based vectorization to reduce dimensionality by minimizing reconstruction loss. The dot product of two GloVe vectors equals the log of the number of times those two words occur near each other.

Word2Vec (Mikolov et al., 2013) uses a predictive model to learn geometric encodings of words

Gender Gap	Word set	Axis Projection				Rel L2 Diff	Rel L2 Ratio
		w2v	w2v CBOW	GloVe	FastText	w2v	w2v
Census Wage Gap	threat	-0.61	-0.37	-0.30	-0.38	-0.52	-0.49
Female Legislators	criminal	-0.49	-0.33	-0.19	-0.17	-0.39	-0.38
Math & CS Degrees	stem-alum	0.30	0.28	0.30	0.26	0.28	0.29

Figure 5: Comparison of three bias metrics and four word embedding algorithms correlating themed word sets' gender bias with U.S. gender gap statistics. Unlike in Fig. 2, we perform feature selection using all countries.

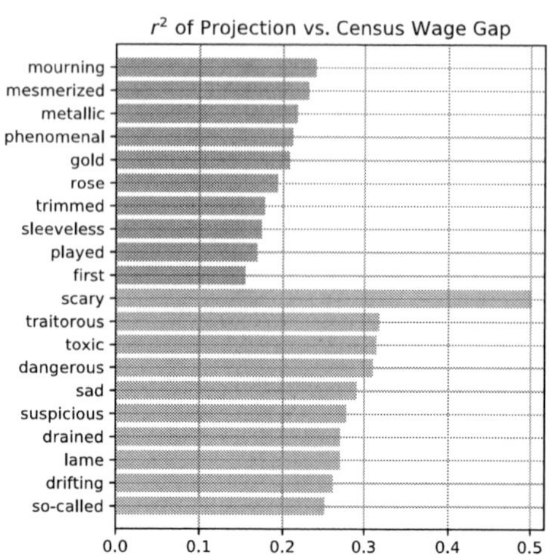

Figure 6: Ten adjectives with highest bias correlations to reduced pay gap (top, blue), and ten with highest correlation to increased pay gap (bottom, red).

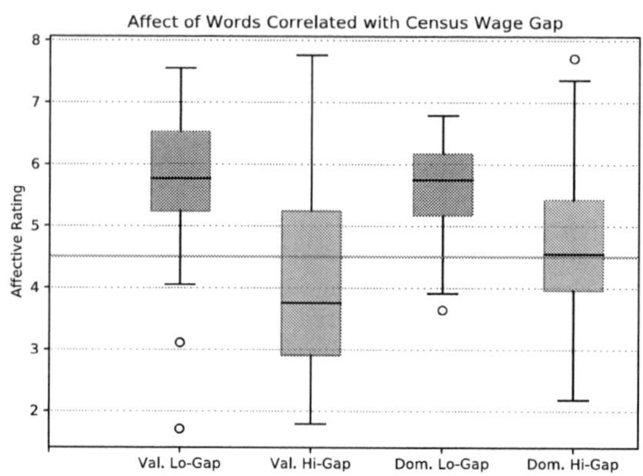

Figure 7: Valence and dominance scores for decreased pay gap words (blue) and increased pay gap words (red). Affect is neutral at 4.5 (plotted in green).

through a feed-forward neural network optimized by stochastic gradient descent. The Word2Vec *continuous bag-of-words* (CBOW) setting predicts the most probable word given a context. The Word2Vec *skip-gram* setting differs slightly by inputting a target word and predicting the context.

FastText (Joulin et al., 2016) characterizes each word as an n-gram of characters rather than an atomic entity. So each word vector is the sum of word vectors of the target word's n-gram (e.g. "app," "ppl," "ple" for "apple"). This is especially useful for rare words that might not exist in the corpus and accounting for misspellings.

Fig. 5 illustrates the above word embedding algorithms used on three different correlated word sets and statistics. In addition to comparing different word embedding algorithms, we also compare three different bias metrics on the Word2Vec algorithm: (1) the *axis projection* metric defined in Sec. 4.1; (2) the *relative L2 norm difference* (Garg et al., 2018); and the (3) *relative L2 norm ratio*. Unlike the axis projection, metrics (2) and (3) both compute the L2 norm from each word in the neutral word set to the $\overrightarrow{male}$ and $\overrightarrow{female}$ vectors, and then subtract or divide the two norms, respectively, returning the average over the word set.

The Fig. 5 results demonstrate that the gender bias is present in the product of all four word embedding algorithms, and is detectable with all three metrics. The Word2Vec approach with axis projection yields the highest coefficient of determination— for both direct and indirect correlation— across all three gender gap and word set pairs. This is the algorithm and bias metric that we use for all other experiments.

4.4 Valence and Dominance Analysis

Our Sec. 4.1 and Sec. 4.2 experiments specified word sets *a priori*, but we can also identify and analyze the individual words whose gender biases directly and indirectly correlate with statistical gender gaps to find trends and commonalities.

We identified all adjectives in the word embeddings using WordNet and then computed each adjective's R^2 score for direct or indirect correlation with each U.S. gender gap statistic. We filtered down the adjectives to those that correlate directly or indirectly with $R^2 > 0.1$. To illustrate, Fig. 6 plots ten highest R^2 words for direct (blue) and indirect (red) correlation against the pay gap, where blue adjectives' female bias correlates with *reduced* pay gap (higher wages) and red adjectives' female bias correlates with *increased* pay gap (lower wages) in U.S. embeddings.

For each statistic, we measured the *valence* and the *dominance* of the directly- and indirectly-correlated adjectives using scores from Warriner et al. (2013). Fig. 7 shows a box plot of the valence and dominance of the reduced-gender-gap adjectives (blue) against increased-gender-gap adjectives (red) for the gender pay gap statistic, where the valence and dominance values for reduced gap (*Lo-Gap*) are significantly higher than the valence and dominance for increased gap (*Hi-Gap*) via t-test, where $p < 1.0e^{-7}$.

The same valence and dominance pattern held for adjectives directly and indirectly correlated with economic and educational gaps (i.e., Census Workforce Ratio, Female State Legislators, and Math & CS Degrees), where the valence and dominance of Lo-Gap words were significantly higher than Hi-Gap words with $p < .005$ throughout. The difference in valence and dominance for CDC Activity gap was not significant.

5 Conclusions

This paper characterized gender biases in Twitter-derived word embeddings from multiple cultures (99 countries and 51 U.S. regions) against statistical gender gaps in those cultures (18 international and 5 U.S.-based statistics).

We demonstrated that thematically-grouped word sets' gender biases correlate with gender gaps intuitively: word sets with a central topic or valence correlate with gender gaps of a similar topic, in a meaningful (positive or negative) direction. This supports our claims (from Sec. 1) that (1) cultural biases in language are correlated with cultural gender gaps and (2) we can characterize biases based on strength and direction of correlation with these gaps. We also demonstrated that these correlations are selective: not all topical word sets' biases correlate with all gender gaps, and random word sets do not correlate. This supports our claim that themed word sets capture different dimensions of gender bias and gender gaps.

Finally, we identified adjectives whose biases were highly correlated with increased and decreased gender gaps in education and economics, and we found that the adjectives correlated with *increased* gender gaps had statistically significantly lower valence and dominance than those correlated with *decreased* gender gaps. This is ev-idence of a cross-cutting attitude towards gender that we can characterize with future work.

The results of our three bias analyses are consistent with the social theory that differences in implicit gender valuation (e.g., linguistic gender bias) manifest in different gender opportunities and status (e.g., gender gaps) (Berger et al., 1972; Rashotte and Webster Jr, 2005). Specifically, when a culture attributes greater competence and social status to a gender, that gender receives higher rewards and evaluations (Dini, 2017).

Limitations and Future Work. Our use of English-only tweets facilitated comparison across embeddings, but it eliminates the native language of many countries and creates cultural blind-spots. Specifically, our use of English tweets does not capture the voices of those that (1) lack access to technology, (2) have poor knowledge of English, and (3) simply do not use Twitter. One might even argue that the gender bias effects may be even more pronounced off-line due to social desirability effects. Expanding to other languages presents additional challenges, e.g., gendered words and many-to-one vector mappings across languages, but recent language transformers facilitate this (Devlin et al., 2018). Incorporating additional languages and cultural texts are important next steps.

Previous Twitter word embedding approaches blend tweets with news or Wikipedia to improve NLP accuracy, using orders of magnitude more text per embedding (Li et al., 2017). Blending tweets with news may improve the embeddings' accuracy for NLP tasks, but it also risks diluting their implicit biases.

Finally, while our analyses illustrate correlations between gender biases and statistical gender gaps, they do not describe causality and they have limited interpretive power. We believe that integrating these methods with additional data and causal models (e.g., Dirichlet mixture models and Bayesian networks) will jointly improve interpretation and accuracy.

Acknowledgments

This research was supported by funding from the Defense Advanced Research Projects Agency (DARPA HR00111890015). The views, opinions and/or findings expressed are those of the authors and should not be interpreted as representing the official views or policies of the Department of Defense or the U.S. Government.

References

Joseph Berger, Bernard P Cohen, and Morris Zelditch Jr. 1972. Status characteristics and social interaction. *American Sociological Review*, pages 241–255.

Sebawit G Bishu and Mohamad G Alkadry. 2017. A systematic review of the gender pay gap and factors that predict it. *Administration & Society*, 49(1):65–104.

Debra L Blackwell and Tainya C Clarke. 2018. State variation in meeting the 2008 federal guidelines for both aerobic and muscle-strengthening activities through leisure-time physical activity among adults aged 18-64: United states, 2010-2015. *National health statistics reports*, (112):1–22.

Tolga Bolukbasi, Kai-Wei Chang, James Y Zou, Venkatesh Saligrama, and Adam T Kalai. 2016. Man is to computer programmer as woman is to homemaker? debiasing word embeddings. In *Advances in neural information processing systems*, pages 4349–4357.

Jacob Devlin, Ming-Wei Chang, Kenton Lee, and Kristina Toutanova. 2018. Bert: Pre-training of deep bidirectional transformers for language understanding. *arXiv preprint arXiv:1810.04805*.

Rachele Dini. 2017. *The second sex*. Macat Library.

Stewart D Friedman and Jeffrey H Greenhaus. 2000. *Work and family–allies or enemies?: what happens when business professionals confront life choices*. Oxford University Press, USA.

Nikhil Garg, Londa Schiebinger, Dan Jurafsky, and James Zou. 2018. Word embeddings quantify 100 years of gender and ethnic stereotypes. *Proceedings of the National Academy of Sciences*, 115(16):E3635–E3644.

Angela Hawken and Gerardo L Munck. 2013. Cross-national indices with gender-differentiated data: what do they measure? how valid are they? *Social indicators research*, 111(3):801–838.

Armand Joulin, Edouard Grave, Piotr Bojanowski, and Tomas Mikolov. 2016. Bag of tricks for efficient text classification. *CoRR*, abs/1607.01759.

Austin C Kozlowski, Matt Taddy, and James A Evans. 2018. The geometry of culture: Analyzing meaning through word embeddings. *arXiv preprint arXiv:1803.09288*.

Quanzhi Li, Sameena Shah, Xiaomo Liu, and Armineh Nourbakhsh. 2017. Data sets: Word embeddings learned from tweets and general data. In *Eleventh International AAAI Conference on Web and Social Media*.

Tomas Mikolov, Ilya Sutskever, Kai Chen, Greg S Corrado, and Jeff Dean. 2013. Distributed representations of words and phrases and their compositionality. In C. J. C. Burges, L. Bottou, M. Welling, Z. Ghahramani, and K. Q. Weinberger, editors, *Advances in Neural Information Processing Systems 26*, pages 3111–3119. Curran Associates, Inc.

Aparna Mitra. 2003. Establishment size, employment, and the gender wage gap. *The Journal of Socio-Economics*, 32(3):317–330.

Jeffrey Pennington, Richard Socher, and Christopher Manning. 2014. Glove: Global vectors for word representation. In *Proceedings of the 2014 conference on empirical methods in natural language processing (EMNLP)*, pages 1532–1543.

Lisa Slattery Rashotte and Murray Webster Jr. 2005. Gender status beliefs. *Social Science Research*, 34(3):618–633.

Michelle Zimbalist Rosaldo. 1974. Woman, culture, and society: A theoretical overview. *Woman, culture, and society*, 21.

Michael T Schmitt and Nyla R Branscombe. 2001. The good, the bad, and the manly: Threats to one's prototypicality and evaluations of fellow in-group members. *Journal of Experimental Social Psychology*, 37(6):510–517.

Carole Vincent. 2013. Why do women earn less than men. *CRDCN Research Highlight/RCCDR en évidence*, 1(5):1.

Amy Beth Warriner, Victor Kuperman, and Marc Brysbaert. 2013. Norms of valence, arousal, and dominance for 13,915 english lemmas. *Behavior research methods*, 45(4):1191–1207.

John E Williams and Deborah L Best. 1990. *Sex and psyche: Gender and self viewed cross-culturally*. Sage Publications, Inc.

Brian Hu Zhang, Blake Lemoine, and Margaret Mitchell. 2018. Mitigating unwanted biases with adversarial learning. In *Proceedings of the 2018 AAAI/ACM Conference on AI, Ethics, and Society*, pages 335–340. ACM.

Jieyu Zhao, Tianlu Wang, Mark Yatskar, Vicente Ordonez, and Kai-Wei Chang. 2018. Gender bias in coreference resolution: Evaluation and debiasing methods. In *Proceedings of the 2018 Conference of the North American Chapter of the Association for Computational Linguistics: Human Language Technologies*, volume 2.

Jiping Zuo and Shengming Tang. 2000. Breadwinner status and gender ideologies of men and women regarding family roles. *Sociological perspectives*, 43(1):29–43.

Measuring Gender Bias in Word Embeddings across Domains and Discovering New Gender Bias Word Categories

Kaytlin Chaloner
ADAPT Centre, SCSS
Trinity College Dublin
Ireland
chalonek@tcd.ie

Alfredo Maldonado
ADAPT Centre, SCSS
Trinity College Dublin
Ireland
alfredo.maldonado@adaptcentre.ie

Abstract

Prior work has shown that word embeddings capture human stereotypes, including gender bias. However, there is a lack of studies testing the presence of specific gender bias categories in word embeddings across diverse domains. This paper aims to fill this gap by applying the WEAT bias detection method to four sets of word embeddings trained on corpora from four different domains: news, social networking, biomedical and a gender-balanced corpus extracted from Wikipedia (GAP). We find that some domains are definitely more prone to gender bias than others, and that the categories of gender bias present also vary for each set of word embeddings. We detect some gender bias in GAP. We also propose a simple but novel method for discovering new bias categories by clustering word embeddings. We validate this method through WEAT's hypothesis testing mechanism and find it useful for expanding the relatively small set of well-known gender bias word categories commonly used in the literature.

1 Introduction

Artificial intelligence (AI) acquired from machine learning is becoming more prominent in decision-making tasks in areas as diverse as industry, healthcare and education. AI-informed decisions depend on AI systems' input training data which, unfortunately, can contain implicit racial, gender or ideological biases. Such AI-informed decisions can thus lead to unfair treatment of certain groups. For example, in Natural Language Processing (NLP), résumé search engines can produce rankings that disadvantage some candidates, when these ranking algorithms take demographic features into account (directly or indirectly) (Chen et al., 2018), while abusive online language detection systems have been observed to produce false positives on terms associated with minorities and women (Dixon et al., 2018; Park et al., 2018). Another example where bias (specifically gender bias) can be harmful is in personal pronoun coreference resolution, where systems carry the risk of relying on societal stereotypes present in the training data (Webster et al., 2018).

Whilst gender bias in the form of concepts of masculinity and femininity has been found inscribed in implicit ways in AI systems more broadly (Adam, 2006), this paper focuses on gender bias on word embeddings.

Word embeddings are one of the most common techniques for giving semantic meaning to words in text and are used as input in virtually every neural NLP system (Goldberg, 2017). It has been shown that word embeddings capture human biases (such as gender bias) present in these corpora in how they relate words to each other (Bolukbasi et al., 2016; Caliskan et al., 2017; Garg et al., 2018). For the purposes of this paper, gender bias is understood as the inclination towards or prejudice against one gender.

Several methods have been proposed to test for the presence of gender bias in word embeddings; an example being the Word Embedding Association Test (WEAT) (Caliskan et al., 2017). WEAT is a statistical test that detects bias in word embeddings using cosine similarity and averaging methods, paired with hypothesis testing. WEAT's authors applied these tests to the publicly-available GloVe embeddings trained on the English-language "Common Crawl" corpus (Pennington et al., 2014) as well as the Skip-Gram (word2vec) embeddings trained on the Google News corpus (Mikolov et al., 2013). However, there is a diverse range of publicly-available word embeddings trained on corpora of different domains. To address this, we applied the WEAT test on four sets of word embeddings trained on corpora from four domains: social media (Twit-

25

Proceedings of the 1st Workshop on Gender Bias in Natural Language Processing, pages 25–32
Florence, Italy, August 2, 2019. ©2019 Association for Computational Linguistics

ter), a Wikipedia-based gender-balanced corpus (GAP) and a biomedical corpus (PubMed) and news (Google News, in order to reproduce and validate our results against those of Caliskan et al. (2017)) (see Section 3).

Caliskan et al. (2017) confirmed the presence of gender bias using three categories of words well-known to be prone to exhibit gender bias: (B1) **career vs. family** activities, (B2) **Maths vs. Arts** and (B3) **Science vs. Arts**. Garg et al. (2018) expanded on this work and tested additional gender bias word categories: (B4) differences on personal descriptions based on **intelligence vs. appearance** and on (B5) physical or emotional **strength vs. weakness**. In this paper, we use these five categories to test for the presence of gender bias in the aforementioned domain corpora. Notice that one of the tested corpora is the gender-balanced GAP corpus (Webster et al., 2018). We specifically chose this corpus in order to test whether the automatic method used to compile it (based on sampling an equal number of male and female pronouns from Wikipedia) yielded a set that was balanced according to these five well-known gender bias word categories. GAP's authors acknowledge that Wikipedia has been found to contain gender biased content (Reagle and Rhue, 2011).

We confirmed bias in all five categories on the Google News embeddings but far less bias on the rest of the embeddings, with the biomedical PubMed embeddings showing the least bias. We did find some bias on GAP. However, given the small size of this corpus, many test words were not present (see Section 4).

The six word categories studied here are word lists manually curated by Psychology researchers based on their studies (e.g. Greenwald et al., 1998). However, it is difficult to establish whether they are exhaustive as there could be other word categories presenting bias, which may well be domain-dependant. In response, we developed a simple method to automatically discover new categories of gender bias words based on word clustering, and measuring statistical associations of the words in each cluster to known female and male attribute words. Assuming that each cluster roughly represents a topic in the corpus, the set of gender bias words in each cluster/topic in the corpus corresponds to a potentially new category of gender-biased words. As far as we are aware, this is the first time a method to discover new gender bias word categories is proposed. We used WEAT's hypothesis testing mechanism to automatically validate the induced gender bias word categories produced by our system. A visual inspection on a sample of these induced categories is consistent with the authors' intuitions of gender bias. We make these induced categories available to other researchers to study.[1] An advantage of this discovery method is that it allows us to detect bias based on a corpus' own vocabulary, even if it is small, as is the case in the GAP corpus embeddings.

2 Previous Work

In word embeddings, words are represented in a continuous vector space where semantically similar words are mapped to nearby points (Goldberg, 2017, ch. 10). The underlying assumption is that words that appear in similar contexts share similar meaning (Harris, 1954; Miller and Charles, 1991). This context-based similarity is operationalised through cosine similarity, a well-established method for measuring the semantic similarity of words in vector space (Schütze, 1998). Recently, however, researchers noticed that cosine similarity was able to exhibit gender biases captured through training on corpora and started developing methods for mitigating this bias (Bolukbasi et al., 2016). Caliskan et al. (2017) then developed the Word Embedding Association Test (WEAT), which is an adaptation of the Implicit Association Test (IAT) from Psychology (Greenwald et al., 1998) to measure biases in word embeddings. The IAT measures a person's automatic association between mental representations of concepts, based on their reaction times. Instead of relying on reaction times, WEAT relies on cosine similarity. WEAT is based on two statistical measures: (1) the effect size in terms of Cohen's d, which measures the association between suspected gender biased words and two sets of reference words (attribute words in WEAT's terminology) known to be intrinsically male and female, respectively; and (2) a statistical hypothesis test that confirms this association. We borrow these statistical measures in this paper. Garg et al. (2018) measured gender bias synchronically across historical data covering 100 years of English language use.

Most work however has concentrated in meth-

---

ods for mitigating gender bias in word embeddings. One approach is debiasing learnt corpora (Bolukbasi et al., 2016), which is achieved using algorithms that modify word embeddings in such a way that neutralises stereotypical cosine similarities. Another approach is creating gender-balanced corpora, such as the GAP corpus (balanced corpus of Gendered Ambiguous Pronouns) (Webster et al., 2018). Roughly speaking, GAP was developed by sampling sentences from Wikipedia in such a way that an equal number of male and female personal pronouns was obtained. Its main use is in the evaluatiation of systems that resolve the coreference of gendered ambiguous pronouns in English. In a similar vain, Dixon et al. (2018) builds a balanced corpora that seeks to neutralise toxic mentions of identity terms.

To the best of our knowledge there has not been work testing for bias on corpora from different domains. Also, we believe this is the first time an unsupervised method for discovering new gender bias word categories from word embeddings is proposed.

3   Choice of Word Embeddings

English-language word embeddings were selected with the intention of giving an insight into gender bias over a range of domains and with the expectation that some word embeddings would demonstrate much more bias than others. The word embeddings selected were: (a) Skip-Gram embeddings trained on the Google News corpus[2], with a vocabulary of 3M word types (Mikolov et al., 2013); (b) Skip-Gram embeddings trained on 400 million Twitter micro-posts[3], with a vocabulary of slightly more than 3M word types (Godin et al., 2015); (c) Skip-Gram embeddings trained on the PubMed Central Open Access subset (PMC) and PubMed[4], with a vocabulary of about 2.2M word types (Chiu et al., 2016) and trained using two different sliding window sizes: 2 and 30 words; (d) FastText embeddings trained on the GAP corpus (Webster et al., 2018) by us[5], with a vocabulary of 7,400 word types.

---

[2] https://tinyurl.com/mpzqe5o

[3] https://github.com/loretoparisi/word2vec-twitter

[4] https://github.com/cambridgeltl/BioNLP-2016

[5] See footnote 1.

4   WEAT Hypothesis Testing

4.1   Experimental Protocol

We largely follow the WEAT Hypothesis testing protocol introduced by Caliskan et al. (2017). The input is a suspected gender bias word category represented by two lists, X and Y, of **target words**, i.e. words which are suspected to be biased to one or another gender. E.g. $X = \{$programmer, engineer, scientist$\}$, $Y = \{$nurse, teacher, librarian$\}$. We wish to test whether X or Y is more biased to one gender or the other, or whether there is not difference in bias between the two lists. Bias is compared in relation to two reference lists of words that represent unequivocally male and female concepts. E.g. $M = \{$man, male, he$\}$, $F = \{$woman, female, she$\}$. In WEAT's terminology these reference lists are called the **attribute words**. Table 1 shows the target and attribute word sets used in our experiments.

The null hypothesis H_o is that there is no difference between X and Y in terms of their relative (cosine) similarity to M and F. Assuming that there is a word embedding vector $\vec{w}$ (trained on some corpus from some domain) for each word w in X, Y, M and F, we compute the following **test statistic**:

$$s(X, Y, M, F) = \sum_{x \in X} s(x, M, F) - \sum_{y \in Y} s(y, M, F) \tag{1}$$

where $s(w, M, F)$ is the **measure of association** between target word w and the attribute words in M and F:

$$s(w, M, F) = \frac{1}{|M|} \sum_{m \in M} \cos(\vec{w}, \vec{m}) - \frac{1}{|F|} \sum_{f \in F} \cos(\vec{w}, \vec{f}) \tag{2}$$

In Caliskan et al. (2017) H_o is tested through a permutation test, in which $X \cup Y$ is partitioned into alternative target lists $\hat{X}$ and $\hat{Y}$ exhaustively and computing the one-sided p-value $p[s(\hat{X}, \hat{Y}, M, F) > s(X, Y, M, F)]$, i.e. the proportion of partition permutations $\hat{X}, \hat{Y}$ in which the test statistic $s(\hat{X}, \hat{Y}, M, F)$ is greater than the observed test statistic $s(X, Y, M, F)$. This p-value is the probability that H_o is true. In other words, it is the probability that there is no difference between X and Y (in relation to M and F) and therefore that the word category is *not* biased. The

Attribute words		M	male, man, boy, brother, he, him, his, son, father, uncle, grandfather
		F	female, woman, girl, sister, she, her, hers, daughter, mother, aunt, grandmother
	B1: career vs family	X	executive, management, professional, corporation, salary, office, business, career
		Y	home, parents, children, family, cousins, marriage, wedding, relatives
	B2: maths vs arts	X	math, algebra, geometry, calculus, equations, computation, numbers, addition
		Y	poetry, art, Shakespeare, dance, literature, novel, symphony, drama
	B3: science vs arts	X	science, technology, physics, chemistry, Einstein, NASA, experiment, astronomy
		Y	poetry, art, Shakespeare, dance, literature, novel, symphony, drama
Target words	B4: intelligence vs appearance	X	precocious, resourceful, inquisitive, genius, inventive, astute, adaptable, reflective, discerning, intuitive, inquiring, judicious, analytical, apt, venerable, imaginative, shrewd, thoughtful, wise, smart, ingenious, clever, brilliant, logical, intelligent
		Y	alluring, voluptuous, blushing, homely, plump, sensual, gorgeous, slim, bald, athletic, fashionable, stout, ugly, muscular, slender, feeble, handsome, healthy, attractive, fat, weak, thin, pretty, beautiful, strong
	B5: strength vs weakness	X	power, strong, confident, dominant, potent, command, assert, loud, bold, succeed, triumph, leader, shout, dynamic, winner
		Y	weak, surrender, timid, vulnerable, weakness, wispy, withdraw, yield, failure, shy, follow, lose, fragile, afraid, loser

Table 1: Target words used for each gender-bias word category and attribute words used as gender reference

higher this p-value is the less bias there is. Following Caliskan et al. (2017), in this work we consider a word category to have statistically significant gender bias if its p-value is below the 0.05 threshold. Given that a full permutation test can quickly become computationally intractable, in this paper we instead use randomisation tests (Hoeffding, 1952; Noreen, 1989) with a maximum of 100,000 iterations in each test.

4.2 WEAT Results

Before experimentation we expected to find a great deal of gender bias across the Google News and Twitter embedding sets and far less in the PubMed and GAP sets. However, results in Table 2 are somewhat different to our expectations:

Google News We detect statistically significant (p-values in bold) gender bias in all 5 categories (B1-B5) on this corpus. Although one would hope to find little gender bias in a news corpus, given that its authors are professional journalists, bias had already been detected by Caliskan et al. (2017) and Garg et al. (2018) using methods similar to ours. This is not surprising given that women represent only a third (33.3%) of the full-time journalism workforce (Byerly, 2011). In addition, it has been found that news coverage of female personalities more frequently mentions family situations and is more likely to invoke matters of superficial nature, such as personality, appearance and fashion decisions, whereas the focus on men in news coverage tends to be be given to their experience and accomplishments (Armstrong et al., 2006).

Twitter On this social media set, we surprisingly only detected bias on the career vs. family (B1) category, although science vs. maths (B2) is a borderline case with a p-value of just 0.0715, and the rest of the values are not particularly high. We also observe that most effect sizes (Cohen's d) are under 1, indicating relatively weaker associations with the gender-specific attribute words from Table 1. We leave for future work further analysis on this set, however we hypothesise that the idiosyncratic language use common in micro-blogging, such as non-standard spelling and hashtags, divide up the semantic signal of word embeddings, perhaps diluting their association bias. Indeed, the word categories showing most gender bias in the discovery experiments (Section 5) include many hashtags, punctuation marks and words with non-standard spellings such as "alwaaaaays", which will not be tested for bias using standard-spelling target words.

PubMed This biomedical set showed the least gender bias, which was expected given its scientific nature. However, it has been documented that gender bias exists in biomedical studies given that more clinical studies involve males than females, and also based on the differences in which male and female patients report pain and other medical complaints and, in turn, the differences in which male and female health practitioners record and understand these complaints (Fillingim et al., 2009). It is possible that gender bias is still present in these texts but it is manifested differently and perhaps cannot be detected through word embed-

Categories	Google News		Twitter		PubMed w2		PubMed w30		GAP	
	p	d	p	d	p	d	p	d	p	d
B1: career vs family	**0.0012**	1.37	**0.0029**	1.31	0.7947	-0.42	0.0962	0.67	**0.0015**	1.44
B2: maths vs arts	**0.0173**	1.02	0.1035	0.65	0.9996	-1.40	0.9966	-1.20	0.0957	1.04
B3: science vs arts	**0.0044**	1.25	0.0715	0.74	0.9797	-0.98	0.7670	-0.37	0.1434	0.71
B4: intelligence vs appearance	**0.0001**	0.98	0.1003	0.37	0.2653	0.18	0.0848	0.36	0.9988	-0.64
B5: strength vs weakness	**0.0059**	0.89	0.2971	0.20	0.0968	0.48	**0.0237**	0.72	**0.0018**	0.77

Table 2: WEAT hypothesis test results for corpora tested for five well-known gender-biased word categories. p-values in bold indicate statistically significant gender bias ($p < 0.05$).

dings. Also of note is that across all five categories, bias is greater (smaller p-values) on the 30-word window set than on the 2-word window set. It is known that window size affects semantic similarity: larger window sizes tend to capture broader, more topical similarities between words whilst smaller windows capture more linguistic or even syntactic similarities (Goldberg, 2017, Sec. 10.5). We leave for future work further analysis on the bias effects of window sizes.

GAP Whilst GAP was specifically developed with gender balance in mind, we did find some degree of gender bias. In fact, given that it is derived from a gender-biased source text (Wikipedia), we actually expected to measure a higher degree of gender bias. This relatively low bias measurement could be due in part to the fact that GAP's vocabulary lacks many of the attribute and target word lists used in the tests. Table 3 shows the number of out-of-vocabulary words from these lists in PubMed and GAP (Google News and Twitter did not have any out-of-vocabulary words). Notice that the category missing most target words (intelligence vs. appearance category, B4) shows the least bias. However, the second category that misses most words (strength vs weakness, B5) does indeed show bias to a medium-high effect size of 0.77. This difficulty in assessing the reliability of these tests, in the face of a relatively high number of out-of-vocabulary attribute and target words, is one of the reasons that inspired us to develop a method for discovering new categories of biased words from an embedding set's own vocabulary. Section 5 covers this method.

5 Discovering New Gender Bias Word Categories

We propose a method for automatically detecting new categories of gender-biased words from a word embedding set. The simplest method in-

	Attrs.		Target Words									
			B1		B2		B3		B4		B5	
	M	F	X	Y	X	Y	X	Y	X	Y	X	Y
TOTAL	11	11	8	8	8	8	8	8	25	25	15	15
PubMed	0	0	0	0	0	0	0	0	0	1	0	0
GAP	0	1	1	1	6	1	4	1	21	18	7	9

Table 3: Number of out-of-vocabulary target and attribute words in the PubMed and GAP embeddings. Google and Twitter embeddings contain all words.

volves constructing a list of male- and female-biased words from a word embedding vocabulary through eq. (2). However, the resulting list would not have a topical or semantic cohesion as the categories B1-B5 have. We propose instead to first cluster the word vectors in an embedding set and then return a list of male- and female-associated word lists per cluster. We expect these cluster-based biased word lists to be more topically cohesive. By controlling for the number and size of clusters it should be possible to find more or less fine-grained categories.

We cluster embedings using K-Means++ (Arthur and Vassilvitskii, 2007), as implemented by scikit-learn (Pedregosa et al., 2011), using 100 clusters for GAP and 3,000 for Google News, Twitter and PubMed (window size 30 only). This algorithm was chosen as it is fast and produces clusters of comparable sizes. For each cluster we then return the list of n most male- and female-associated words (as per eq. 2): these are the discovered gender bias word categories candidates. Table 4 shows a selection of these candidates.[6]

Upon visual inspection, most of these candidates seem to be somewhat cohesive. We notice that on Google News and GAP many of the clusters relate to people's names (Google News cluster 2369) whilst others mix people's names with

---

[6]All candidates in paper repo. See footnote 1.

<table>
<thead>
<tr><th colspan="5">Gender Biased words</th></tr>
<tr><th></th><th>Clus.</th><th>Male</th><th>Female</th><th>d</th></tr>
</thead>
<tbody>
<tr><td rowspan="4">Google News</td><td>2763</td><td>eating_cheeseburgers, Tuna_Helper, Kielbasa, Turtle_Soup, beef_patty_topped, noodle_stir_fry, fried_broiled, trencherman, magnate_Herman_Cain, knockwurst, cracklins, hearty, juicy_steaks, Philly_Cheesesteak, duck_goose, PBJ, loafs, Eat_MREs, Cheddar_cheeses, pizzas_salads</td><td>Gingersnap, Blueberry_Pie, champagne_truffles, bake_brownies, Bon_Bons, Seasonal_Fruit, bakes_cakes, Sinfully, Lemon_Curd, Tagalong, Godiva_Chocolate, brownie_bites, Adoree, apple_crisps, Elinor_Klivans, Mud_Pie, decorate_cupcakes, granola_cereal, baked_apple_pie, cakes_cupcakes</td><td>1.97</td></tr>
<tr><td>2369</td><td>Luke_Schenscher, Stetson_Hairston, Jake_Odum, Maureece_Rice, Errick_Craven, Marcus_Hatten, Jeremiah_Rivers, JR_Pinnock, Tom_Coverdale, Isacc_Miles, Brian_Wethers, Jeff_Varem, Matt_Pressey, Tyrone_Barley, Tavarus_Alston, Kojo_Mensah, Marcellus_Sommerville, Lathen_Wallace, Jordan_Cornette, Willie_Deane</td><td>Jayne_Appel, Cappie_Pondexter, Betty_Lennox, Kara_Lawson, Janel_McCarville, Lisa_Leslie, Deanna_Nolan, Sancho_Lyttle, Seimone_Augustus, Candice_Wiggins, Gearlds, Jessica_Davenport, Plenette_Pierson, Wisdom_Hylton, Lindsey_Harding, Yolanda_Griffith, Elena_Baranova, Loree_Moore, Taurasi, Noelle_Quinn</td><td>1.97</td></tr>
<tr><td>2995</td><td>vetran, defens, ennis, 3AW_Debate, efore, carrer, redknapp, exellent, shanny, slater, shanahan, afridi, brees, westbrook, Thudd, dirk, feild, righ, duhhh, arsene_wenger</td><td>lolita, shiloh, beverly_hills, middleton, extr, leah, dwts, sophie, aniston, kathryn, liza, kristen_stewart, celine, kristin, tess, elena, alexandra, versace, alison, michelle_obama</td><td>1.97</td></tr>
<tr><td>2424</td><td>brewing_vats, Refrigeration_Segment, Sealy_mattress, anesthesia_workstations, outdoor_Jacuzzis, Otis_elevators_Carrier, panels_moldings, Van, CPVC_pipes, refurbed, dome_coverings, covered_amphitheater_Astroturf, JES_Restaurant, beakers_flasks_wiring_Hazmat, Home_3bdrm_2ba, mold_peeling_paint, Zanussi, hoovers, Brendan_Burford, grills_picnic_tables</td><td>Corningware, Lowenborg_Frick, Aveda_bath, upholstery_carpets, bedside_commodes, Janneke_Verheggen_spokeswoman, hipster_tastemaker_Kelly_Wearstler, vacuuming_robot, dinettes, comforters_sheets, robes_slippers, Wolfgang_Puck_Bistro, neck_massager, breakrooms, china_cutlery, jewelers_florists, linen_towels, Frette_sheets, holding_freshly_diapered, china_flatware</td><td>1.97</td></tr>
<tr><td rowspan="3">Twitter</td><td>7</td><td>#HEG_NUMBER_, #zimdecides, #goingconcern, #twobirdswithonestone, #BudSelig, #LeedsUnitedAFC, #Buyout, #Batting, #rickyhatton, #baddeal, #ChaudhryAslam, #radio_NUMBER_today, DETROYT, #findtim, #houndsleadthepack, #Warcriminal, #spil, #kenyakwanza, #commonpurpose, #patriotway</td><td>#Charade, #Icchat, #charlizetheron, #horoscopo, #DiamondJubilee, #paternity, #tombola, #singlepeople, #Fabian, #Flipper, #toilettraining, #eca_NUMBER_, #financialadvisers, #tn_NUMBER_, Swift-boated, #dailytips, #Aramex, #MBCAware, #Glaciers, #RiverValley</td><td>1.97</td></tr>
<tr><td>991</td><td>hewy, Suchecki, furgie, Huebert, bseball, jump-pass, gaudreau, #Thakur, lookalikey, lavalle, _NUMBER_verse, Timonen's, #Kipper, Kouleas, Mannjng, #wetpanda, oriels, Drowney, Brucato, sczesney</td><td>perrrrlease, VoteVictorious, olone, Chick-fi-la, InVasion, #DinahTo_NUMBER_K, Chika's, relaxxxxxxxxxzzzxxzxxzxzxzxzzzzxxsssseee eeeezzzxxx, Heliodore, Kandia, Shakeita, flowers/plants, dress/heels, sexy-times, #sobersunday, Teonia, shrinkies, Kokiri's, solutely, gayke</td><td>1.97</td></tr>
<tr><td>2998</td><td>Swishhhhhh, Johnsonnn, #dadadadadada, Coyh, #HappyBdaySpezz, #RawRivals, #Fastandthefurious, #HedoIsTheBestOnTwitter, LeJames, #spursheat, #sidelined, #BackInYourBox, #fuckmanutd, #FellainiFacts, #LosBravos, #GreatestPlayerIHaveEverSeen, TouchDwn, #celticsvsknicks, Irte, #MSQuotes</td><td>#tiffanymynx, #solvetheriddle, #mandybright, #getthehelloutofhere, #RedSoles, #that'lldopig, #MeetVirginia, #freenudes, #KeepitClassy, #lushlive, #PeaceMessageIn_NUMBER_FromCarolishFamily, #GotOne, #itsnotfine, #thursdayhurryup, #gentletweets, #InDesperateNeed, #PackInMore, masterpieceee, somebodytellmewhy, #biggestflaw</td><td>1.97</td></tr>
<tr><td rowspan="3">PubMed</td><td>2993</td><td>JSK, 1938-1952, Johann-Wolfgang-Goethe, Winstein, Argenteuil, Alfried, Critica, NUST, traumatologie, Saarow, Urologische, carDiac, Neustadt/Saale, Massy, Umgebung, 1925-1927, Eli-Lilly, Commented, Senden, Maisons</td><td>gynecology-important, non-CEE, Breast-, Oketani, RiSk, MIREC, NASPAG, Cervitula, PDCU, cervical-ripening, Step-2, Kimia, Skin-to-Skin, Eeva, AdHOC, NMDSP, lipid-management, CEPAM, NCT00397150, Mass-screening</td><td>1.97</td></tr>
<tr><td>1092</td><td>3beta, 19-NA, Leyding, u-PAI, nonpinealectomized, DHA-s, hydrocortisone-supplemented, misulban, Burd, CHH/KS, NEP28, adrenostasis, JNF, dihydrotestosterone-, appetite-stimulatory, P-hGH, d-Leu6, GIP-treated, alpha-methyl-DHT, pineal-gland, DESPP</td><td>embryo/foetus, hormonally-dependent, gland-stroma, 16α-OHE1, conceptus-produced, Lactogenesis, nERalpha, mid-reproductive, relaxin-deficient, 64.0-kDa, pre-synchronized, 17alpha, 20alpha-dihydroxypregn-4-en-3-one, pseudogestation, foetectomy, E2-dominated, Pinopodes, midpseudopregnancy, estrous-cycle, LH-only, blood-mammary</td><td>1.97</td></tr>
<tr><td>559</td><td>examiniations, cholangiocarcinoma., phlebolithiasis, Celiacography, 79-year-old-woman, 6 cases, spermatocystitis, microbladder, otorhino-laryngological, FACD, neurogen, Cryodestruction, bladder-, Diverticuli, pseudo-angina, epididymo-testicular, Rendu-Weber-Osler, Dystopic, Lazorthes, AISO</td><td>Conisation, TV-US, sonohysterogram, peri, tracheloscopy, Salpingo-oophorectomy, hysteroscopic-guided, endosalpingitis, perifimbrial, previa-percreta, hystero-salpingography, pudendum, auto-amputated, hysterometry, Peritubal, isthmocervical, ovserved, hemosalpinx, Hysterosalpingo, necrosis/dehiscence</td><td>1.97</td></tr>
<tr><td rowspan="4">GAP</td><td>84</td><td>critical, artistic, commercial, vocal, era, pop, article, project, comic, projects, commercials, science, artists, editions, critic, popular, sports, introduction, articles, vocals</td><td>roles, films, television, two, drama, producer, worker, musicians, producers, magazine, produce, programmes, version, products, credits, music, opera, portrayal, features, direct</td><td>1.74</td></tr>
<tr><td>93</td><td>captures, tribe, struck, brain, Asgard, capacity, coin, reinforcements, favour, corpse, assault, license, referee, system, aide, proceedings, strigoi, loyalty, Yu, energy</td><td>Owen, green, parole, rapper, telephone, together, personally, shoe, heroine, chosen, between, storyline, clothes, ghost, daily, Pink, spell, neighborhood, adult, Ramona</td><td>1.95</td></tr>
<tr><td>73</td><td>resulted, responded, considered, constructed, used, respected, accused, committed, ordered, recognized, participated, charged, recommended, focused, devoted, instructed, captured, regarded, demonstrated, controlled</td><td>played, disappeared, stayed, named, arranged, betrayed, hatred, displayed, Damaged, danced, shared, Jared, Named, hosted, abandoned, teamed, separated, Voiced, appealed, welcomed</td><td>1.91</td></tr>
<tr><td>18</td><td>treat, inside, demands, capable, proceeds, crash, skills, buy, far, unable, cash, struggle, promises, guilty, threat, fun, engage, bail, boat, toward</td><td>stolen, actually, friend, even, stays, fallen, Tina, sit, sex, doll, alive, sick, night, totally, boy, sheet, step, knew, still, Esme</td><td>1.91</td></tr>
</tbody>
</table>

Table 4: Selection of induced gender bias word categories per cluster.

more obviously biased words (Google News cluster 2995 and most GAP clusters). It is clear that this method detects thematically-cohesive groups of gender-associated words. However, not all words seem to be genuinely gender biased in a harmful way. We leave for future work the development of a filtering or classification step capable of making this distinction.

In order to test whether the candidates' bias is statistically significant, we applied the full WEAT hypothesis testing protocol, using randomised tests of 1,000 iterations per cluster to make the computation tractable. All clusters across all embedding sets returned a p-value < 0.001. The effect size (Cohen's d) was quite high across all clusters, averaging 1.89 for Google News, 1.87 for Twitter, 1.88 for PubMed and 1.67 for GAP. We leave for future work to conduct a human-based experiment involving experts on gender bias on different domains and languages other than English to further validate our outputs. Emphasis will be placed on assessing the usefulness of this tool for domains and languages lacking or seeking to develop lists of gender bias word categories.

6 Conclusions and Future Work

We have shown that there are varying levels of bias for word embeddings trained on corpora of different domains and that within the embeddings, there are different categories of gender bias present. We have also developed a method to discover potential new word categories of gender bias. Whilst our clustering method discovers new gender-associated word categories, the induced topics seem to mix harmless gender-associated words (like people names) with more obviously harmful gender-biased words. So as a future development, we would like to develop a classifier to distinguish between harmless gender-associated words and harmful gender-biased words. We wish to involve judgements by experts on gender bias in this effort, as well as exploiting existing thematic word categories from lexical databases like WordNet (Fellbaum, 1998), ontologies and terminologies. At the same time, we will also seek to measure the negative impact of discovered categories in NLP systems' performance. We also wish to more closely investigate the relationships between different word embedding hyperparameters, such as sliding window size in the PubMed set, and their learned bias.

Acknowledgements

The ADAPT Centre for Digital Content Technology is funded under the SFI Research Centres Programme (Grant 13/RC/2106) and is co-funded under the European Regional Development Fund. We wish to thank our anonymous reviewers for their invaluable feedback.

References

Alison Adam. 2006. *Artificial knowing: Gender and the thinking machine*. Routledge.

Cory L Armstrong, Michelle LM Wood, and Michelle R Nelson. 2006. Female news professionals in local and national broadcast news during the buildup to the Iraq War. *Journal of Broadcasting & Electronic Media*, 50(1):78–94.

David Arthur and Sergei Vassilvitskii. 2007. k-means++: The Advantages of Careful Seeding. In *Proceedings of the 2007 ACM-SIAM Symposium on Discrete Algorithms*, pages 1027–1035, New Orleans, LA.

Tolga Bolukbasi, Kai-Wei Chang, James Y Zou, Venkatesh Saligrama, and Adam T Kalai. 2016. Man is to computer programmer as woman is to homemaker? Debiasing word embeddings. In *Advances in neural information processing systems*, pages 4349–4357.

Carolyn M Byerly. 2011. *Global Report on the Status Women in the News Media*. Washington, DC: International Women's Media Foundation [IWMF].

Aylin Caliskan, Joanna J Bryson, and Arvind Narayanan. 2017. Semantics derived automatically from language corpora contain human-like biases. *Science*, 356(6334):183–186.

Le Chen, Ruijun Ma, Anikó Hannák, and Christo Wilson. 2018. Investigating the impact of gender on rank in resume search engines. In *Proceedings of the 2018 CHI Conference on Human Factors in Computing Systems*, page 651. ACM.

Billy Chiu, Gamal Crichton, Anna Korhonen, and Sampo Pyysalo. 2016. How to train good word embeddings for biomedical NLP. In *Proceedings of the 15th workshop on biomedical natural language processing*, pages 166–174.

Lucas Dixon, John Li, Jeffrey Sorensen, Nithum Thain, and Lucy Vasserman. 2018. Measuring and Mitigating Unintended Bias in Text Classification. In *AAAI/ACM Conference on AI, Ethics, and Society*, pages 67–73, New Orleans, LA.

Christiane Fellbaum. 1998. *WordNet: An Electronic Lexical Database*. MIT Press, Cambridge, MA.

Roger B. Fillingim, Christopher D. King, Margarete C. Ribeiro-Dasilva, Bridgett Rahim-Williams, and Joseph L. Riley. 2009. Sex, Gender, and Pain: A Review of Recent Clinical and Experimental Findings. *Journal of Pain*, 10(5):447–485.

Nikhil Garg, Londa Schiebinger, Dan Jurafsky, and James Zou. 2018. Word embeddings quantify 100 years of gender and ethnic stereotypes. *Proceedings of the National Academy of Sciences*, 115(16):E3635–E3644.

Fréderic Godin, Baptist Vandersmissen, Wesley De Neve, and Rik Van de Walle. 2015. Multimedia Lab @ ACL WNUT NER Shared Task: Named Entity Recognition for Twitter Microposts using Distributed Word Representations. In *Proceedings of the Workshop on Noisy User-generated Text*, pages 146–153.

Yoav Goldberg. 2017. *Neural Network Methods for Natural Language Processing*. Synthesis Lectures on Human Language Technologies. Morgan & Claypool Publishers.

Anthony G Greenwald, Debbie E McGhee, and Jordan LK Schwartz. 1998. Measuring Individual Differences in Implicit Cognition: The Implicit Association Test. *Journal of personality and social psychology*, 74(6):1464.

Zellig S. Harris. 1954. Distributional structure. *Word*, 10(2-3):146–162.

Wassily Hoeffding. 1952. The large sample power of tests based on permutations. *The Annals of Mathematical Statistics*, 23(2):169–192.

Tomas Mikolov, Kai Chen, Greg Corrado, and Jeffrey Dean. 2013. Efficient estimation of word representations in vector space. *arXiv preprint arXiv:1301.3781*.

George A. Miller and Walter G. Charles. 1991. Contextual correlates of semantic similarity. *Language and Cognitive Processes*, 6(1):1–28.

Eric W. Noreen. 1989. *Computer-intensive methods for testing hypotheses : an introduction*. Wiley.

Ji Ho Park, Jamin Shin, and Pascale Fung. 2018. Reducing Gender Bias in Abusive Language Detection. In *Proceedings of the 2018 Conference on Empirical Methods in Natural Language Processing*, pages 2799–2804, Brus.

F. Pedregosa, G. Varoquaux, A. Gramfort, V. Michel, B. Thirion, O. Grisel, M. Blondel, P. Prettenhofer, R. Weiss, V. Dubourg, J. Vanderplas, A. Passos, D. Cournapeau, M. Brucher, M. Perrot, and E. Duchesnay. 2011. Scikit-learn: Machine learning in Python. *Journal of Machine Learning Research*, 12:2825–2830.

Jeffrey Pennington, Richard Socher, and Christopher D Manning. 2014. GloVe: Global Vectors for Word Representation. In *Proceedings of the 2014 Conference on Empirical Methods in Natural Language Processing*, pages 1532–1543, Doha.

Joseph Reagle and Lauren Rhue. 2011. Gender bias in Wikipedia and Britannica. *International Journal of Communication*, 5:21.

Hinrich Schütze. 1998. Automatic word sense discrimination. *Computational linguistics*, 24(1):97–123.

Kellie Webster, Marta Recasens, Vera Axelrod, and Jason Baldridge. 2018. Mind the GAP: A Balanced Corpus of Gendered Ambiguous Pronouns. *Transactions of the Association for Computational Linguistics*, 6:605–617.

Evaluating the Underlying Gender Bias in Contextualized Word Embeddings

Christine Basta **Marta R. Costa-jussà** **Noe Casas**
Universitat Politècnica de Catalunya
{christine.raouf.saad.basta,marta.ruiz,noe.casas}@upc.edu

Abstract

Gender bias is highly impacting natural language processing applications. Word embeddings have clearly been proven both to keep and amplify gender biases that are present in current data sources. Recently, contextualized word embeddings have enhanced previous word embedding techniques by computing word vector representations dependent on the sentence they appear in.

In this paper, we study the impact of this conceptual change in the word embedding computation in relation with gender bias. Our analysis includes different measures previously applied in the literature to standard word embeddings. Our findings suggest that contextualized word embeddings are less biased than standard ones even when the latter are debiased.

1 Introduction

Social biases in machine learning, in general and in natural language processing (NLP) applications in particular, are raising the alarm of the scientific community. Examples of these biases are evidences such that face recognition systems or speech recognition systems work better for white men than for ethnic minorities (Buolamwini and Gebru, 2018). Examples in the area of NLP are the case of machine translation that systems tend to ignore the coreference information in benefit of a stereotype (Font and Costa-jussà, 2019) or sentiment analysis where higher sentiment intensity prediction is biased for a particular gender (Kiritchenko and Mohammad, 2018).

In this work we focus on the particular NLP area of word embeddings (Mikolov et al., 2010), which represent words in a numerical vector space. Word embeddings representation spaces are known to present geometrical phenomena mimicking relations and analogies between words (e.g. *man* is to

woman as *king* is to *queen*). Following this property of finding relations or analogies, one popular example of gender bias is the word association between *man* to *computer programmer* as *woman* to *homemaker* (Bolukbasi et al., 2016). Pre-trained word embeddings are used in many NLP downstream tasks, such as natural language inference (NLI), machine translation (MT) or question answering (QA). Recent progress in word embedding techniques has been achieved with contextualized word embeddings (Peters et al., 2018) which provide different vector representations for the same word in different contexts.

While gender bias has been studied, detected and partially addressed for standard word embeddings techniques (Bolukbasi et al., 2016; Zhao et al., 2018a; Gonen and Goldberg, 2019), it is not the case for the latest techniques of contextualized word embeddings. Only just recently, Zhao et al. (2019) present a first analysis on the topic based on the proposed methods in Bolukbasi et al. (2016). In this paper, we further analyse the presence of gender biases in contextualized word embeddings by means of the proposed methods in Gonen and Goldberg (2019). For this, in section 2 we provide an overview of the relevant work on which we build our analysis; in section 3 we state the specific request questions addressed in this work, while in section 4 we describe the experimental framework proposed to address them and in section 5 we present the obtained and discuss the results; finally, in section 6 we draw the conclusions of our work and propose some further research.

2 Background

In this section we describe the relevant NLP techniques used along the paper, including word embeddings, their debiased version and contextualized word representations.

33

Proceedings of the 1st Workshop on Gender Bias in Natural Language Processing, pages 33–39
Florence, Italy, August 2, 2019. ©2019 Association for Computational Linguistics

2.1 Words Embeddings

Word embeddings are distributed representations in a vector space. These vectors are normally learned from large corpora and are then used in downstream tasks like NLI, MT, etc. Several approaches have been proposed to compute those vector representations, with word2vec (Mikolov et al., 2013) being one of the dominant options. Word2vec proposes two variants: continuous bag of words (CBoW) and skipgram, both consisting of a single hidden layer neural network trained on predicting a target word from its context words for CBoW, and the opposite for the skipgram variant. The outcome of word2vec is an embedding table, where a numeric vector is associated to each of the words included in the vocabulary.

These vector representations, which in the end are computed on co-occurrence statistics, exhibit geometric properties resembling the semantics of the relations between words. This way, subtracting the vector representations of two related words and adding the result to a third word, results in a representation that is close to the application of the semantic relationship between the two first words to the third one. This application of analogical relationships have been used to showcase the bias present in word embeddings, with the prototypical example that when subtracting the vector representation of *man* from that of *computer* and adding it to *woman*, we obtain *homemaker*.

2.2 Debiased Word Embeddings

Human-generated corpora suffer from social biases. Those biases are reflected in the co-occurrence statistics, and therefore learned into word embeddings trained in those corpora, amplifying them (Bolukbasi et al., 2016; Caliskan et al., 2017).

Bolukbasi et al. (2016) studied from a geometrical point of view the presence of gender bias in word embeddings. For this, they compute the subspace where the gender information concentrates by computing the principal components of the difference of vector representations of male and female gender-defining word pairs. With the gender subspace, the authors identify direct and indirect biases in profession words. Finally, they mitigate the bias by nullifying the information in the gender subspace for words that should not be associated to gender, and also equalize their distance to both elements of gender-defining word pairs.

Zhao et al. (2018b) proposed an extension to GloVe embeddings (Pennington et al., 2014) where the loss function used to train the embeddings is enriched with terms that confine the gender information to a specific portion of the embedded vector. The authors refer to these pieces of information as *protected attributes*. Once the embeddings are trained, the gender protected attribute can be simply removed from the vector representation, therefore eliminating any gender bias present in it.

The transformations proposed by both Bolukbasi et al. (2016) and Zhao et al. (2018b) are downstream task-agnostic. This fact is used in the work of Gonen and Goldberg (2019) to showcase that, while apparently the embedding information is removed, there is still gender information remaining in the vector representations.

2.3 Contextualized Word Embeddings

Pretrained Language Models (LM) like ULMfit (Howard and Ruder, 2018), ELMo (Peters et al., 2018), OpenAI GPT (Radford, 2018; Radford et al., 2019) and BERT (Devlin et al., 2018), proposed different neural language model architectures and made their pre-trained weights available to ease the application of transfer learning to downstream tasks, where they have pushed the state-of-the-art for several benchmarks including question answering on SQuAD, NLI, cross-lingual NLI and named identity recognition (NER).

While some of these pre-trained LMs, like BERT, use subword level tokens, ELMo provides word-level representations. Peters et al. (2019) and Liu et al. (2019) confirmed the viability of using ELMo representations directly as features for downstream tasks without re-training the full model on the target task.

Unlike word2vec vector representations, which are constant regardless of their context, ELMo representations depend on the sentence where the word appears, and therefore the full model has to be fed with each whole sentence to get the word representations.

The neural architecture proposed in ELMo (Peters et al., 2018) consists of a character-level convolutional layer processing the characters of each word and creating a word representation that is then fed to a 2-layer bidirectional LSTM (Hochreiter and Schmidhuber, 1997), trained on language modeling task on a large corpus.

3 Research questions

Given the high impact of contextualized word embeddings in the area of NLP and the social consequences of having biases in such embeddings, in this work we analyse the presence of bias in these contextualized word embeddings. In particular, we focus on gender biases, and specifically on the following questions:

- Do contextualized word embeddings exhibit gender bias and how does this bias compare to standard and debiased word embeddings?

- Do different evaluation techniques identify bias similarly and what would be the best measure to use for gender bias detection in contextualized embeddings?

To address these questions, we adapt and contrast with the evaluation measures proposed by Bolukbasi et al. (2016) and Gonen and Goldberg (2019).

4 Experimental Framework

As follows, we define the data and resources that we use for performing our experiments. The approach motivation is applying the experiments on contextualized word embeddings.

We worked with the English-German news corpus from the WMT18[1]. We used the English side with 464,947 lines and 1,004,6125 tokens.

To perform our analysis, we used a set of lists from previous work (Bolukbasi et al., 2016; Gonen and Goldberg, 2019). We refer to the list of definitional pairs [2] as 'Definitonal List' (e.g. *she-he, girl-boy*). We refer to the list of female and male professions [3] as 'Professional List' (e.g. *accountant, surgeon*). The 'Biased List' is the list used in the clustering experiment and it consists of biased male and female words (500 female biased tokens and 500 male biased token). This list is generated by taking the most biased words, where the bias of a word is computed by taking its projection on the gender direction ($\overrightarrow{he}$-$\overrightarrow{she}$) (e.g. *breastfeeding, bridal* and *diet* for female and *hero, cigar* and *teammates* for male). The 'Extended Biased

List' is the list used in classification experiment, which contains 5000 male and female biased tokens, 2500 for each gender, generated in the same way of the Biased List[4]. A note to be considered, is that the lists we used in our experiments (and obtained from Bolukbasi et al. (2016) and Gonen and Goldberg (2019)) may contain words that are missing in our corpus and so we cannot obtain contextualized embeddings for them.

Among different approaches to contextualized word embeddings (mentioned in section 2), we choose ELMo (Peters et al., 2018) as contextualized word embedding approach. The motivation for using ELMo instead of other approaches like BERT (Devlin et al., 2018) is that ELMo provides word-level representations, as opposed to BERT's subwords. This makes it possible to study the word-level semantic traits directly, without resorting to extra steps to compose word-level information from the subwords that could interfere with our analyses.

5 Evaluation measures and results

There is no standard measure for gender bias, and even less for such the recently proposed contextualized word embeddings. In this section, we adapt gender bias measures for word embedding methods from previous work (Bolukbasi et al., 2016) and (Gonen and Goldberg, 2019) to be applicable to contextualized word embeddings.

We start by computing the gender subspace from the ELMo vector representations of gender-defining words, then identify the presence of direct bias in the contextualized representations. We then proceed to identify gender information by means of clustering and classifications techniques. We compare our results to previous results from debiased and non-debiased word embeddings (Bolukbasi et al., 2016) .

Detecting the Gender Space Bolukbasi et al. (2016) propose to identify gender bias in word representations by computing the direction between representations of male and female word pairs from the Definitional List ($\overrightarrow{he}$-$\overrightarrow{she}$, $\overrightarrow{man}$-$\overrightarrow{woman}$) and computing their principal components.

In the case of contextualized embeddings, there is not just a single representation for each word, but its representation depends on the sentence it

---

[4] Both 'Biased List' and 'Extended Biased List' were kindly provided by Hila Gonen to reproduce experiments from her study (Gonen and Goldberg, 2019)

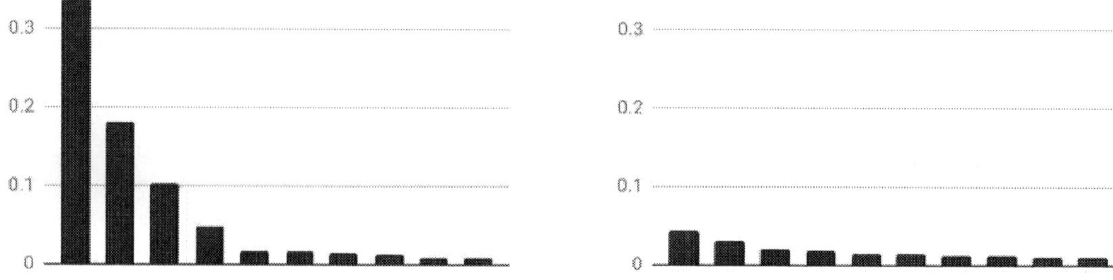

Figure 1: (Left) the percentage of variance explained in the PC of definitional vector differences. (Right) The corresponding percentages for random vectors.

appears in. Hence, in order to compute the gender subspace we take the representation of words by randomly sampling sentences that contain words from the Definitional List and, for each of them, we swap the definitional word with its pair-wise equivalent from the opposite gender. We then obtain the ELMo representation of the definintional word in each sentence pair, computing their difference. On the set of difference vectors, we compute their principal components to verify the presence of bias. In order to have a reference, we computed the principal components of representation of random words.

Similarly to Bolukbasi et al. (2016), figure 1 shows that the first eigenvalue is significantly larger than the rest and that there is also a single direction describing the majority of variance in these vectors, still the difference between the percentage of variances is less in case of contextualized embeddings, which may refer that there is less bias in such embeddings. In the right graph of the figure, we can easily note the difference in the case of random, where the data is not concentrated in a specific direction, as the weight is spread among all components.

A similar conclusion was stated in the recent work (Zhao et al., 2019) where the authors applied the same approach, but for gender swapped variants of sentences with professions. They computed the difference between the vectors of occupation words in corresponding sentences and got a skewed graph where the first component represent the gender information while the second component groups the male and female related words.

Direct Bias Direct Bias is a measure of how close a certain set of words are to the gender vector. To compute it, we extracted from the training data the sentences that contain words in the Professional List. We excluded the sentences that have both a professional token and definitional gender word to avoid the influence of the latter over the presence of bias in the former. We applied the definition of direct bias from Bolukbasi et al. (2016) on the ELMo representations of the professional words in these sentences.

$$\frac{1}{|N|} \sum_{w \epsilon N} |cos(\vec{w}, g)| \tag{1}$$

where N is the amount of gender neutral words, g the gender direction, and $\vec{w}$ the word vector of each profession. We got direct bias of 0.03, compared to 0.08 from standard word2vec embeddings described in Bolukbasi et al. (2016). This reduction on the direct bias confirms that the substantial component along the gender direction that is present in standard word embeddings is less for the contextualized word embeddings. Probably, this reduction comes from the fact that we are using different word embeddings for the same profession depending on the sentence which is a direct consequence and advantage of using contextualized embeddings.

Male and female-biased words clustering. In order to study if biased male and female words cluster together when applying contextualized embeddings, we used k-means to generate 2 clusters of the embeddings of tokens from the Biased list. Note that we cannot use several representations for each word, since it would not make any sense to cluster one word as male and female at the same time. Therefore, in order to make use of the advantages of the contextualized embeddings, we repeated 10 independent experiments, each with a different random sentence of each word from the list of biased male and female words.

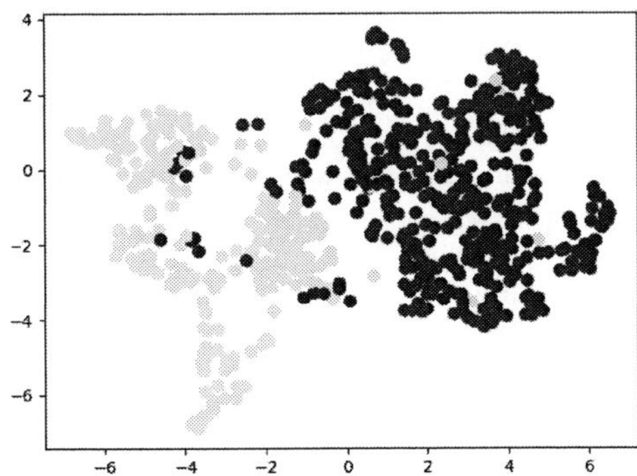

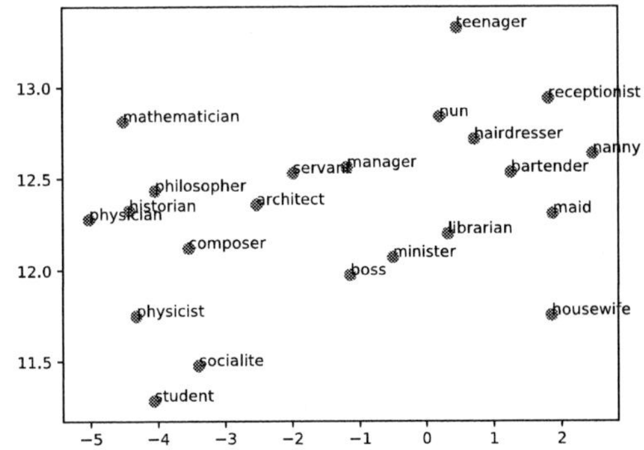

Figure 2: K-means clustering, the yellow color represents the female and the violet represents the male

Figure 3: Visualization of contextualized embeddings of professions.

Among these 10 experiments, we got a minimum accuracy of 69.1% and a maximum of 71.3%, with average accuracy of 70.1%, much lower than in the case of biased and debiased word embeddings which were 99.9 and 92.5, respectively, as stated in Gonen and Goldberg (2019). Based on this criterion, even if there is still bias information to be removed from contextualized embeddings, it is much less than in case of standard word embeddings, even if debiased.

The clusters (for one particular experiment out of the 10 of them) are shown in Figure 2 after applying UMAP (McInnes et al., 2018; McInnes et al., 2018) to the contextualized embeddings.

Classification Approach In order to study if contextualized embeddings learn to generalize bias, we trained a Radial Basis Function-kernel Support Vector Machine classifier on the embeddings of random 1000 biased words from the Extended Biased List. After that, we evaluated the generalization on the other random 4000 biased tokens. Again, we performed 10 independent experiments, to guarantee randomization of word representations. Among these 10 experiments, we got a minimum accuracy of 83.33% and a maximum of 88.43%, with average accuracy of 85.56%. This number shows that the bias is learned in these embeddings with high rate. However, it learns in a lower rate than the normal embeddings, whose classification reached 88.88% and 98.25% for debiased and biased versions, respectively.

K-Nearest Neighbor Approach To understand more about the bias in contextualized embeddings, it is important to analyze the bias in the professions. The question is whether these embeddings

stereotype the professions as the normal embeddings. This can be shown by the nearest neighbors of the female and male stereotyped professions, for example 'receptionist' and 'librarian' for female and 'architect' and 'philosopher' for male. We applied the k nearest neighbors on the Professional List, to get the nearest k neighbor to each profession. We used a random representation for each token of the profession list, after applying the k nearest neighbor algorithm on each profession, we computed the percentage of female and male stereotyped professions among the k nearest neighbor of each profession token. Afterwards, we computed the Pearson correlation of this percentage with the original bias of each profession. Once again, to assure randomization of tokens, we performed 10 experiments, each with different random sentences for each profession, therefore with different word representations. The minimum Pearson correlation is 0.801 and the maximum is 0.961, with average of 0.89. All these correlations are significant with p-values smaller than 1×10^{-40}. This experiment showed the highest influence of bias compared to 0.606 for debiased embeddings and 0.774 for biased. Figure 3 demonstrates this influence of bias by showing that female biased words (e.g. *nanny*) has higher percent of female words than male ones and vice-versa for male biased words (e.g. *philosopher*).

6 Conclusions and further work

While our study cannot draw clear conclusions on whether contextualized word embeddings augment or reduce the gender bias, our results show more insights into which aspects of the final contextualized word vectors get affected by such phenomena, with a tendency more towards reducing the gender bias rather than the contrary.

Contextualized word embeddings mitigate gender bias when measuring in the following aspects:

1. Gender space, which is capturing the gender direction from word vectors, is reduced for gender specific contextualized word vectors compared to standard word vectors.

2. Direct bias, which is measuring how close set of words are to the gender vector, is lower for contextualized word embeddings than for standard ones.

3. Male/female clustering, which is produced between words with strong gender bias, is less strong than in debiased and non-debiased standard word embeddings.

However, contextualized word embeddings preserve and even amplify gender bias when taking into account other aspects:

1. The implicit gender of words can be predicted with accuracies higher than 80% based on contextualized word vectors which is only a slightly lower accuracy than when using vectors from debiased and non-debiased standard word embeddings.

2. The stereotyped words group with implicit-gender words of the same gender more than in the case of debiased and non-debiased standard word embeddings.

While all measures that we present exhibit certain gender bias, when evaluating future debiasing methods for contextualized word embeddings it would be worth putting emphasis on the latter two evaluation measures that show higher bias than the first three.

Hopefully, our analysis will provide a grain of sand towards defining standard evaluation methods for gender bias, proposing effective debiasing methods or even directly designing equitable algorithms which automatically learn to ignore biased data.

As further work, we plan to extend our study to multiple domains and multiple languages to analyze and measure the impact of gender bias present in contextualized embeddings in these different scenarios.

Acknowledgements

We want to thank Hila Gonen for her support during our research.

This work is supported in part by the Catalan Agency for Management of University and Research Grants (AGAUR) through the FI PhD Scholarship and the Industrial PhD Grant. This work is also supported in part by the Spanish Ministerio de Economa y Competitividad, the European Regional Development Fund and the Agencia Estatal de Investigacin, through the postdoctoral senior grant Ramn y Cajal, contract TEC2015-69266-P (MINECO/FEDER,EU) and contract PCIN-2017-079 (AEI/MINECO).

References

Tolga Bolukbasi, Kai-Wei Chang, James Y Zou, Venkatesh Saligrama, and Adam T Kalai. 2016. Man is to computer programmer as woman is to homemaker? debiasing word embeddings. In D. D. Lee, M. Sugiyama, U. V. Luxburg, I. Guyon, and R. Garnett, editors, *Advances in Neural Information Processing Systems 29*, pages 4349–4357. Curran Associates, Inc.

Joy Buolamwini and Timnit Gebru. 2018. Gender shades: Intersectional accuracy disparities in commercial gender classification. In *Conference on Fairness, Accountability and Transparency, FAT 2018, 23-24 February 2018, New York, NY, USA*, pages 77–91.

Aylin Caliskan, Joanna J. Bryson, and Arvind Narayanan. 2017. Semantics derived automatically from language corpora necessarily contain human biases. *Science*, 356:183–186.

Jacob Devlin, Ming-Wei Chang, Kenton Lee, and Kristina Toutanova. 2018. Bert: Pre-training of deep bidirectional transformers for language understanding. *arXiv preprint arXiv:1810.04805*.

Joel Escudé Font and Marta R. Costa-jussà. 2019. Equalizing gender biases in neural machine translation with word embeddings techniques. *CoRR*, abs/1901.03116.

Hila Gonen and Yoav Goldberg. 2019. Lipstick on a pig: Debiasing methods cover up systematic gender biases in word embeddings but do not remove them. *CoRR*, abs/1903.03862.

Sepp Hochreiter and Jürgen Schmidhuber. 1997. Long short-term memory. *Neural Computation*, 9(8):1735–1780.

Jeremy Howard and Sebastian Ruder. 2018. Universal language model fine-tuning for text classification. In *Proceedings of the 56th Annual Meeting of the*

Association for Computational Linguistics (Volume 1: Long Papers), pages 328–339, Melbourne, Australia. Association for Computational Linguistics.

Svetlana Kiritchenko and Saif Mohammad. 2018. Examining gender and race bias in two hundred sentiment analysis systems. In *Proceedings of the Seventh Joint Conference on Lexical and Computational Semantics*, pages 43–53, New Orleans, Louisiana. Association for Computational Linguistics.

Nelson F. Liu, Matt Gardner, Yonatan Belinkov, Matthew E. Peters, and Noah A. Smith. 2019. Linguistic knowledge and transferability of contextual representations. In *Proceedings of the Conference of the North American Chapter of the Association for Computational Linguistics: Human Language Technologies*.

Leland McInnes, John Healy, and James Melville. 2018. UMAP: Uniform Manifold Approximation and Projection for Dimension Reduction. *ArXiv e-prints*.

Leland McInnes, John Healy, Nathaniel Saul, and Lukas Grossberger. 2018. Umap: Uniform manifold approximation and projection. *The Journal of Open Source Software*, 3(29):861.

Tomas Mikolov, Martin Karafit, Luks Burget, Jan Cernock, and Sanjeev Khudanpur. 2010. Recurrent neural network based language model. In *INTERSPEECH*, pages 1045–1048. ISCA.

Tomas Mikolov, Ilya Sutskever, Kai Chen, Greg S Corrado, and Jeff Dean. 2013. Distributed representations of words and phrases and their compositionality. In C. J. C. Burges, L. Bottou, M. Welling, Z. Ghahramani, and K. Q. Weinberger, editors, *Advances in Neural Information Processing Systems 26*, pages 3111–3119. Curran Associates, Inc.

Jeffrey Pennington, Richard Socher, and Christopher Manning. 2014. Glove: Global vectors for word representation. In *Proceedings of the 2014 Conference on Empirical Methods in Natural Language Processing (EMNLP)*, pages 1532–1543, Doha, Qatar. Association for Computational Linguistics.

Matthew Peters, Mark Neumann, Mohit Iyyer, Matt Gardner, Christopher Clark, Kenton Lee, and Luke Zettlemoyer. 2018. Deep contextualized word representations. In *Proceedings of the 2018 Conference of the North American Chapter of the Association for Computational Linguistics: Human Language Technologies, Volume 1 (Long Papers)*, pages 2227–2237, New Orleans, Louisiana. Association for Computational Linguistics.

Matthew Peters, Sebastian Ruder, and Noah A Smith. 2019. To tune or not to tune? adapting pretrained representations to diverse tasks. *arXiv preprint arXiv:1903.05987*.

Alec Radford. 2018. Improving language understanding by generative pre-training.

Alec Radford, Jeff Wu, Rewon Child, David Luan, Dario Amodei, and Ilya Sutskever. 2019. Language models are unsupervised multitask learners.

Jieyu Zhao, Tianlu Wang, Mark Yatskar, Ryan Cotterell, Vicente Ordonez, and Kai-Wei Chang. 2019. Gender bias in contextualized word embeddings. In *Forthcoming in NAACL*.

Jieyu Zhao, Tianlu Wang, Mark Yatskar, Vicente Ordonez, and Kai-Wei Chang. 2018a. Gender bias in coreference resolution: Evaluation and debiasing methods. *arXiv preprint arXiv:1804.06876*.

Jieyu Zhao, Yichao Zhou, Zeyu Li, Wei Wang, and Kai-Wei Chang. 2018b. Learning gender-neutral word embeddings. *arXiv preprint arXiv:1809.01496*.

Conceptor Debiasing of Word Representations Evaluated on WEAT

Saket Karve   **Lyle Ungar**   **João Sedoc**

Department of Computer & Information Science
University of Pennsylvania
Philadelphia, PA 19104
{saketk,ungar,joao} @cis.upenn.edu

Abstract

Bias in word embeddings such as Word2Vec has been widely investigated, and many efforts made to remove such bias. We show how to use *conceptors debiasing* to post-process both traditional and contextualized word embeddings. Our conceptor debiasing can simultaneously remove racial and gender biases and, unlike standard debiasing methods, can make effect use of heterogeneous lists of biased words. We show that conceptor debiasing diminishes racial and gender bias of word representations as measured using the Word Embedding Association Test (WEAT) of Caliskan et al. (2017).

1   Introduction

Word embeddings capture distributional similarities and thus inherit demographic stereotypes (Bolukbasi et al., 2016). Such embedding biases tend to track statistical regularities such as the percentage of people with a given occupation (Nikhil Garg and Zou, 2018) but sometimes deviate from them (Bhatia, 2017). Recent work has shown that gender bias exists in contextualized embeddings (Wang et al., 2019; May et al., 2019).

Here, we provide a quantitative analysis of bias in traditional and contextual word embeddings and introduce a method of mitigating bias (i.e., debiasing) using *the debiasing conceptor*, a clean mathematical representation of subspaces that can be operated on and composed by logic-based manipulations (Jaeger, 2014). Specifically, conceptor negation is a soft damping of the principal components of the target subspace (e.g., the subset of words being debiased) (Liu et al., 2019b) (See Figure 1.)

Key to our method is how it treats word-association lists (sometimes called target lists), which define the bias subspace. These lists include pre-chosen words associated with a target

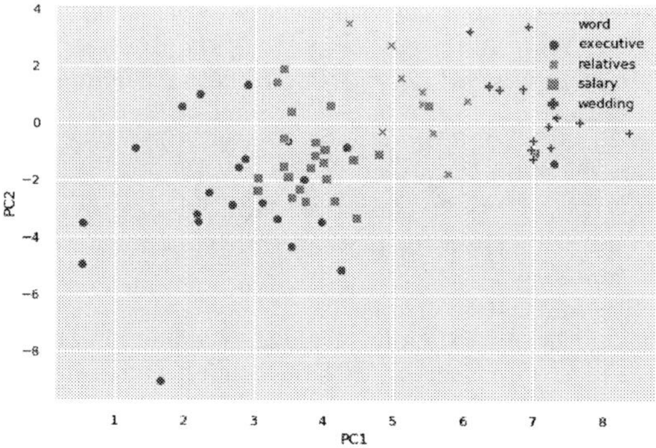

(a) The original space

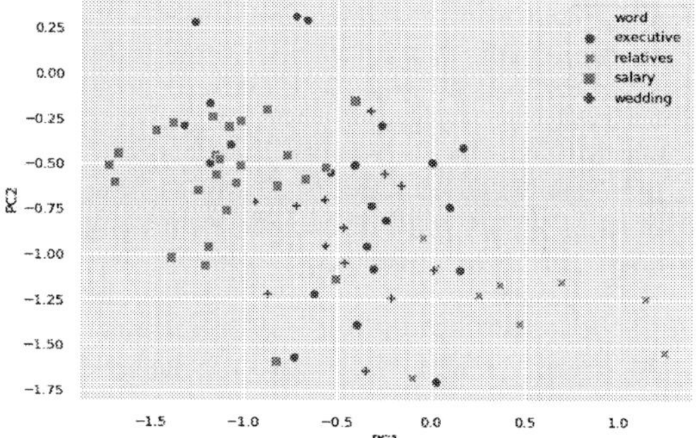

(b) After applying the debiasing conceptor

Figure 1: BERT word representations of the union of the set of contextualized word representations of *relatives, executive, wedding, salary* projected on to the first two principal components of the WEAT gender first names, which capture the primary component of gender. Note how the debiasing conceptor collapses *relatives* and *wedding*, and *executive* and *salary* once the bias is removed.

demographic group (often referred to as a "protected class"). For example, *he / she* or *Mary / John* have been used for gender (Bolukbasi et al., 2016). More generally, conceptors can combine multiple subspaces defined by word lists. Unlike most current methods, conceptor debiasing uses a

Proceedings of the 1st Workshop on Gender Bias in Natural Language Processing, pages 40–48
Florence, Italy, August 2, 2019. ©2019 Association for Computational Linguistics

soft, rather than a hard projection.

We test the debiasing conceptor on a range of traditional and contextualized word embeddings[1] and examine whether they remove stereotypical demographic biases. All tests have been performed on English word embeddings.

This paper contributes the following:

- Introduces *debiasing conceptors* along with a formal definition and mathematical relation to the Word Embedding Association Test.
- Demonstrates the effectiveness of the debiasing conceptor on both traditional and contextualized word embeddings.

2 Related Work

NLP has begun tackling the problems that inhibit the achievement of fair and ethical AI (Hovy and Spruit, 2016; Friedler et al., 2016), in part by developing techniques for mitigating demographic biases in models. In brief, a *demographic bias* is a difference in model output based on gender (either of the data author or of the content itself) or selected demographic dimension ("protected class") such as race. Demographic biases manifest in many ways, ranging from disparities in tagging and classification accuracy depending on author age and gender (Hovy, 2015; Dixon et al., 2018), to over-amplification of demographic differences in language generation (Yatskar et al., 2016; Zhao et al., 2017), to diverging implicit associations between words or concepts within embeddings or language models (Bolukbasi et al., 2016; Rudinger et al., 2018).

Here, we are concerned with the societal bias towards protected classes that manifests in prejudice and stereotypes (Bhatia, 2017). Greenwald and Banaji (1995); implicit attitudes such that "introspectively unidentified (or inaccurately identified) traces of past experience that mediate favorable or unfavorable feeling, thought, or action toward social objects." Bias is often quantified in people using the Implicit Association Test (IAT) (Greenwald et al., 1998). The IAT records subjects response times when asked to pair two concepts. Smaller response times occur in concepts subjects perceive to be similar versus pairs of concepts they perceive to be different. A well known example is where subjects were asked to associate black and white names with "pleasant" and "unpleasant" words. A significant racial bias has been found in many populations. Later, Caliskan et al. (2017) formalized the Word Embedding Association Test (WEAT), which replaces reaction time with word similarity to give a bias measure that does not require use of human subjects. May et al. (2019) extended WEAT to the Sentence Embedding Association Test (SEAT); however, in this paper we instead use token-averaged representations over a corpus.

Debiasing Embeddings. The simplest way to remove bias is to project out a bias direction. For example, Bolukbasi et al. (2016) identify a "gender subspace" using lists of gendered words and then remove the first principal component of this subspace. Wang et al. (2019) used both data augmentation and debiasing of Bolukbasi et al. (2016) to mitigate bias found in ELMo and showed improved performance on coreference resolution. Our work is complementary, as debiasing conceptors can be used in place of hard-debiasing.

Bolukbasi et al. (2016) also examine a soft debiasing method, but find that it does not perform well. In contrast, our debiasing conceptor does a successful soft damping of the relevant principal components. To understand why, we first introduce the conceptor method for capturing the "bias subspaces", next formalize bias, and then show WEAT in matrix notation.

2.1 Conceptors

As in Bolukbasi et al. (2016), our aim is to identify the "bias subspace" using a set of target words, $\mathcal{Z}$ and Z is their corresponding word embeddings. A conceptor matrix, C, is a regularized identity map (in our case, from the original word embeddings to their biased versions) that minimizes

$$\|Z - CZ\|_F^2 + \alpha^{-2}\|C\|_F^2. \tag{1}$$

where α^{-2} is a scalar parameter.[2]

To describe matrix conceptors, we draw heavily on (Jaeger, 2014; He and Jaeger, 2018; Liu et al., 2019b,a). C has a closed form solution:

$$C = \frac{1}{k}ZZ^\top(\frac{1}{k}ZZ^\top + \alpha^{-2}I)^{-1}. \tag{2}$$

Intuitively, C is a soft projection matrix on the linear subspace where the word embeddings Z have

---

[1]Previous work has shown that debiasing methods can have different effects on different word embeddings (Kiritchenko and Mohammad, 2018).

[2]Note that the conceptor and WEAT literature disagree on notation and we follow WEAT. In conceptor notation, the matrix Z would be denoted as X.

the highest variance. Once C has been learned, it can be 'negated' by subtracting it from the identity matrix and then applied to any word embeddings to shrink the bias directions.

Conceptors can represent laws of Boolean logic, such as NOT $\neg$, AND $\wedge$ and OR $\vee$. For two conceptors C and B, we define the following operations:

$$\neg C := \mathbf{I} - C, \tag{3}$$

$$C \wedge B := (C^{-1} + B^{-1} - \mathbf{I})^{-1} \tag{4}$$

$$C \vee B := \neg(\neg C \wedge \neg B) \tag{5}$$

Among these Boolean operations, two are critical for this paper: the NOT operator for debiasing, and the OR operation $\vee$ for multi-list (or multi-category) debiasing. It can be shown that if C and B are of equal sizes, then $C \vee B$ is the conceptor computed from the union of the two sets of sample points from which C and B are computed (Jaeger, 2014); this is not true if they are of different sizes.

Negated Conceptor. Given that the conceptor, C, represents the subspace of maximum bias, we want to apply the negated conceptor, NOT C (see Equation 3) to an embedding space and remove its bias. We call NOT C the *debiasing conceptor*. More generally, if we have K conceptors, C_i derived from K different word lists, we call NOT $(C_1 \vee ... \vee C_K)$ a debiasing conceptor. The negated conceptor matrix has been used in the past on a complete vocabulary to increase the semantic richness of its word embeddings; Liu et al. (2018) showed that the negated conceptor gave better performance on semantic similarity and downstream tasks than the hard debiasing method of Mu and Viswanath (2018).

As shown in Liu et al. (2018), the negated conceptor approach does a soft debiasing by shrinking each principal component of the covariance matrix of the target word embeddings $ZZ^\top$. The shrinkage is a function of the conceptor hyper-parameter α and the singular values σ_i of $ZZ^\top$: $\frac{\alpha^{-2}}{\sigma_i + \alpha^{-2}}$.

3 Formalizing Bias

We follow the formal definition of Lu et al. (2018), where given a class of word sets $\mathcal{D}$ and a scoring function s, the bias of s under the concept(s) tested by $\mathcal{D}$, written $\mathcal{B}_s(\mathcal{D})$, is the expected difference in scores assigned to expected absolute bias across class members,

$$\mathcal{B}_s(\mathcal{D}) \triangleq \mathbb{E}_{D \in \mathcal{D}} |\mathcal{B}_s(D)|.$$

This naturally gives rise to a large set of concepts and scoring functions.

3.1 Word Embedding Association Test

The Word Embeddings Association Test (WEAT), as proposed by Caliskan et al. (2017), is a statistical test analogous to the Implicit Association Test (IAT) (Greenwald et al., 1998) which helps quantify human biases in textual data. WEAT uses the cosine similarity between word embeddings, which is analogous to the reaction time when subjects are asked to pair two concepts they find similar in the IAT. WEAT considers two sets of target words and two sets of attribute words of equal size. The null hypothesis is that there is no difference between the two sets of target words and the sets of attribute words in terms of their relative similarities measured as the cosine similarity between the embeddings. For example, consider the target sets as words representing *Career* and *Family* and let the two sets of attribute words be *Male* and *Female*, in that order. The null hypothesis states that *Career* and *Family* are equally similar (mathematically, in terms of the mean cosine similarity between the word representations) to each of the words in the *Male* and *Female* word lists.

The WEAT test statistic measures the differential association of the two sets of target words with the attribute. The "effect size" is a normalized measure of how separated the two distributions are.

To ground this, we cast WEAT in our formulation where $\mathcal{X}$ and $\mathcal{Y}$ are two sets of target words, (concretely, $\mathcal{X}$ might be *Career* words and $\mathcal{Y}$ *Family* words) and $\mathcal{A}, \mathcal{B}$ are two sets of attribute words ($\mathcal{A}$ might be *female* names and $\mathcal{B}$ *male* names) assumed to associate with the bias concept(s). WEAT is then [3]

$$s(\mathcal{X}, \mathcal{Y}, \mathcal{A}, \mathcal{B})$$

$$= \frac{1}{|\mathcal{X}|} \left[\sum_{x \in \mathcal{X}} \left[\sum_{a \in \mathcal{A}} s(x, a) - \sum_{b \in \mathcal{B}} s(x, b) \right] \right.$$

$$\left. - \sum_{y \in \mathcal{Y}} \left[\sum_{a \in \mathcal{A}} s(y, a) - \sum_{b \in \mathcal{B}} s(y, b) \right] \right],$$

where $s(x, y) = \cos(\text{vec}(x), \text{vec}(y))$ and $\text{vec}(x) \in \mathbb{R}^k$ is the k-dimensional word embedding for word x. Note that for this definition of

---

[3] We assume that there is no overlap between any of the sets $\mathcal{X}, \mathcal{Y}, \mathcal{A},$ and $\mathcal{B}$.

WEAT, the cardinality of the sets must be equal, so $|\mathcal{A}| = |\mathcal{B}|$ and $|\mathcal{X}| = |\mathcal{Y}|$. Our conceptor formulation given below relaxes this assumption.

To motivate our conceptor formulation, we further generalize WEAT to capture the covariance between the target word and the attribute word embeddings. First, let X, Y, A and B be matrices whose columns are word embeddings corresponding to the words in the sets $\mathcal{X}, \mathcal{Y}, \mathcal{A}, \mathcal{B}$, respectively (i.e. the two sets of target words and two sets of attribute words, respectively). To formally define this, without loss of generality choose $\mathcal{X}$, let $X = [x_i]_{i \in I}$ where for i in an index set I with cardinality $|\mathcal{X}|$ and $x_i = \text{vec}(x)$ where the word x is indexed at the ith value of the index set.[4] We can then write WEAT as,

$$\|X^T A - X^T B - (Y^T A - Y^T B)\|_F$$

$$= \|(X - Y)^T (A - B)\|_F,$$

where $\|\cdot\|_F$ is the Frobenius norm. If the embeddings are unit length, then GWEAT is the same as $|\mathcal{X}|$ times WEAT.[5]

Suppose we want to mitigate bias by applying the $k \times k$ bias mitigating matrix, $G = \neg C$, which optimally removes bias from any matrix of word embeddings. We select G to minimize

$$\|(G(X - Y))^T G(A - B)\|_F,$$

$$= \|(X - Y)^T G^T G(A - B)\|_F.$$

Since the conceptor, C, is calculated using the word embeddings of $\mathcal{Z} = \mathcal{X} \cup \mathcal{Y}$, the negated conceptor will mitigate the variance from the target sets, which hopefully identifies the most important bias directions.

4   Embeddings

For context-independent embeddings, we used off-the-shelf Fasttext subword embeddings[6], which were trained with subword information on the Common Crawl (600B tokens), the GloVe embeddings [7] trained on Wikipedia and Gigaword and word2vec[8] trained on roughly 100 billion

words from a Google News dataset. The embeddings used are not centered and normalized to unit length as in Bolukbasi et al. (2016).

For contextualized embeddings, we used ELMo small which was trained on the 1 Billion Word Benchmark, approximately 800M tokens of news crawl data from WMT 2011.[9] We also experimented with the state-of-the-art contextual model "BERT-Large, Uncased" which has 24-layer, 1024-hidden, 16-heads, 340M parameters. BERT is trained on the BooksCorpus (0.8B words) and Wikipedia (2.5B words). We used the last four hidden layers of BERT. We used the Brown Corpus for the word contexts to create instances of the ELMo and BERT embeddings. Embeddings of English words only have been used for all the tests.

5   WEAT Debiasing Experiments

As described in section 3.1, WEAT assumes as its null hypothesis that there is no relative bias between the pair of concepts defined as the target words and attribute words. In our experiments, we measure the effect size (the WEAT score normalized by the standard deviation of differences of attribute words w.r.t target words) (d) and the one-sided p-value of the permutation test. A higher absolute value of effect size indicates larger bias between words in the target set with respect to the words in the attribute set. We would like the absolute value of the effect size to be zero. Since the p-value measures the likelihood that a random permutation of the attribute words would produce at least the observed test statistic, it should be high (at least 0.05) to indicate lack of bias in the positive direction.

Conceptually, the conceptor should be a soft projection matrix on the linear subspace representing the bias direction. For instance, the subspace representing gender must consist of words which are specific to or in some sense related to gender.

A gender word list might be a set of pronouns which are specific to a particular gender such as *he / she* or *himself / herself* and gender specific words representing relationships like *brother / sister* or *uncle / aunt*. We test conceptor debiasing both using the list of such pronouns used by

---

[4]To clarify, in our notation $x_i \in \mathbb{R}^k$ and $x \in \mathcal{X}$.

[5]Our generalization of WEAT is different from Swinger et al. (2018).

[6]https://dl.fbaipublicfiles.com/fasttext/vectors-english/crawl-300d-2M-subword.zip.

[7]https://nlp.stanford.edu/projects/glove/

[8]

[9]https://s3-us-west-2.amazonaws.com/allennlp/models/elmo/2x1024_128_2048cnn_1xhighway/elmo_2x1024_128_2048cnn_1xhighway_weights.hdf5

Embedding	Subspace	Without Debiasing		Mu et al.		Bolukbasi et al.		Conceptor Negation	
		d	p	d	p	d	p	d	p
Glove	Pronouns			1.81	0.00	1.24	0.01	**0.13**	0.40
	Extended List			1.86	0.00	1.24	0.01	0.36	0.26
	Propernouns	1.78	0.00	1.74	0.00	1.24	0.01	0.78	0.07
	All			1.75	0.00	1.20	0.01	0.35	0.27
	OR			NA	NA	NA	NA	-0.51	0.81
word2vec	Pronouns			1.79	0.00	1.55	0.00	1.09	0.02
	Extended List			1.79	0.00	1.59	0.00	1.38	0.00
	Propernouns	1.81	0.00	1.70	0.0	1.59	0.0	1.45	0.00
	All			1.71	0.00	1.56	0.00	1.40	0.00
	OR			NA	NA	NA	NA	**0.84**	0.05
Fasttext	Pronouns			1.70	0.0	1.45	0.00	0.95	0.04
	Extended List			1.70	0.0	1.47	0.00	0.84	0.04
	Propernouns	1.67	0.00	0.86	0.06	1.47	0.00	0.85	0.06
	All			0.82	0.05	1.14	0.01	0.81	0.06
	OR			NA	NA	NA	NA	**0.24**	0.33

Table 1: Gender Debiasing non-contextualized embeddings: (Career, Family) vs (Male, Female)

Embedding	Subspace	Without Debiasing		Mu et. al.		Conceptor Negation	
		d	p	d	p	d	p
ELMo	Pronouns			1.79	0.00	0.70	0.10
	Extended List			1.79	0.00	**0.06**	0.46
	Propernouns	1.79	0.0	1.79	0.00	-0.61	0.89
	All			1.79	0.00	-0.28	0.73
	OR			NA	NA	-0.85	0.96
BERT	Pronouns			1.21	0.01	1.31	0.00
	Extended List			1.27	0.00	1.33	0.01
	Propernouns	1.21	0.01	1.27	0.01	0.92	0.04
	All			1.27	0.01	**0.63**	0.13
	OR			NA	NA	0.97	0.02

Table 2: Gender Debiasing Contextualized embeddings: (Career, Family) vs (Male, Female)

Embedding	Subspace	Without Debiasing		Mu et al.		Bolukbasi et al		Conceptor Negation	
		d	p	d	p	d	p	d	p
Glove	Pronouns			0.89	0.04	-0.53	0.85	1.04	0.01
	Extended List			1.07	0.02	-0.60	0.86	-0.52	0.83
	Propernouns	1.09	0.02	1.04	0.02	-0.56	0.86	0.20	0.33
	All			1.03	0.02	-0.53	0.82	**0.18**	0.35
	OR			NA	NA	NA	NA	-0.48	0.82
Word2vec	Pronouns			0.89	0.03	-1.09	0.99	1.10	0.01
	Extended List			1.00	0.03	-1.14	1.00	-0.49	0.82
	Propernouns	1.00	0.02	0.88	0.04	-1.17	1.00	0.33	0.27
	All			0.90	0.04	-1.07	0.99	**0.25**	0.34
	OR			NA	NA	NA	NA	-0.47	0.81
Fasttext	Pronouns			1.08	0.01	0.18	0.35	-0.36	0.76
	Extended List			0.71	0.08	0.21	0.353	0.73	0.09
	Propernouns	1.19	0.01	0.12	0.43	0.15	0.40	-0.47	0.80
	All			**0.038**	0.47	0.20	0.32	-0.50	0.84
	OR			NA	NA	NA	NA	-0.46	0.78

Table 3: Gender Debiasing non-contextualized embeddings: (Math, Arts) vs (Male, Female)

Embedding	Subspace	Without Debiasing		Mu et. al.		Conceptor Negation	
		d	p	d	p	d	p
ELMo	Pronouns			0.94	0.03	**-0.03**	0.38
	Extended List			0.95	0.02	0.27	0.29
	Propernouns	0.94	0.02	0.94	0.02	0.85	0.05
	All			0.94	0.04	0.87	0.05
	OR			NA	NA	0.53	0.13
BERT	Pronouns			0.23	0.79	0.15	0.15
	Extended List			0.16	0.82	**0.06**	0.53
	Propernouns	0.23	0.777	0.16	0.82	0.75	0.08
	All			0.16	0.85	0.43	0.24
	OR			NA	NA	-0.07	0.59

Table 4: Gender Debiasing contextualized embeddings: (Math, Arts) vs (Male, Female)

Embedding	Subspace	Without Debiasing		Mu et al.		Bolukbasi et al.		Conceptor Negation	
		d	p	d	p	d	p	d	p
Glove	Pronouns			1.23	0.01	-0.46	0.819	**-0.20**	0.66
	Extended List			1.27	0.00	-0.51	0.83	0.93	0.04
	Propernouns	1.34	0.0	1.21	0.011	-0.48	0.839	0.65	0.10
	All			1.21	0.00	-0.45	0.81	0.68	0.10
	OR			NA	NA	NA	NA	0.60	0.12
Word2vec	Pronouns			1.09	0.02	-0.46	0.80	0.45	0.21
	Extended List			1.20	0.01	-0.50	0.80	0.59	0.13
	Propernouns	1.16	0.01	1.08	0.02	-0.55	0.86	0.69	0.10
	All			1.08	0.02	-0.46	0.80	0.66	0.13
	OR			NA	NA	NA	NA	**0.09**	0.45
Fasttext	Pronouns			1.51	0.00	0.88	0.04	0.93	0.03
	Extended List			0.85	0.04	0.85	0.04	1.36	0.00
	Propernouns	1.48	0.00	1.01	0.03	0.85	0.05	**0.75**	0.08
	All			0.98	0.03	0.88	0.03	0.89	0.05
	OR			NA	NA	NA	NA	0.89	0.05

Table 5: Gender Debiasing non-cotextualized embeddings: (Science, Arts) vs (Male, Female)

Embedding	Subspace	Without Debiasing		Mu et. al.		Conceptor Negation	
		d	p	d	p	d	p
ELMo	Pronouns			1.31	0.00	**0.41**	0.22
	Extended List			1.32	0.005	0.52	0.24
	Propernouns	1.32	0.0	1.38	0.00	1.28	0.00
	All			1.34	0.00	0.92	0.03
	OR			NA	NA	0.82	0.05
BERT	Pronouns			-0.91	0.87	-1.23	0.97
	Extended List			-0.90	0.91	-1.10	0.99
	Propernouns	-0.91	0.88	-0.90	0.92	-0.93	0.92
	All			-0.90	0.90	**-0.38**	0.70
	OR			NA	NA	0.97	0.02

Table 6: Gender Debiasing cotextualized embeddings: (Science, Arts) vs (Male, Female)

Caliskan et al. (2017) and using a more comprehensive list of gender-specific words that includes gender specific terms related to occupations, relationships and other commonly used words such as *prince / princess* and *host / hostess*[10]. We further tested conceptor debiasing using male and female

[10] https://github.com/uclanlp/corefBias, https://github.com/uclanlp/gn_glove

names such as *Aaron / Alice* or *Chris / Clary*[11]. We also tested our method with the combination of all lists. The combination of the subspace was done in two ways - either by taking the union of all word lists or by applying the OR operator on the three conceptor matrices computed independently.

The subspace for racial bias was determined using list of European American and African American names.

We tested target pairs of Science vs. Arts, Math vs. Arts, and Career vs. Family word lists with the attribute of the male vs. female names to test gender debiasing. Similarly, we examined European American names vs. African American names as target pairs with the attribute of pleasant vs. unpleasant to test racial debiasing.

Our findings indicate that expanded lists give better debiasing for word embeddings; however, the results are not as clear for contextualized embeddings. The OR operator on two conceptors describing subspaces of pronouns/nouns and names generally outperforms a union of these words. This further motivates the use of the debiasing conceptor.

5.1 Racial Debiasing Results

Embedding	Original		Conceptor Negation	
	d	p	d	p
GloVe	1.35	0.00	0.69	0.01
word2vec	-0.27	**0.27**	-0.55	**0.72**
Fasttext	0.41	0.04	-0.27	**0.57**
ELMo	1.37	0.00	-0.45	**0.20**
BERT	0.92	0.00	0.36	**0.61**

Table 7: Racial Debiasing: (European American Names, African American Names) vs (Pleasant, Unpleasant). d is the effect size, which we want to be close to 0 and p is the p-value, which we want to be larger than 0.05.

Table 7 summarizes the effect size (d) and the one-sided p-value we obtained by running WEAT on each of the word embeddings for racial debiasing. In this experiment we used the same setup as Caliskan et al. (2017) and compare attribute Words of European American / African American names with target words "pleasant" and "unpleasant". In Table 7 we see that racial bias is mitigated

in all cases aside from GloVe. Furthermore, for word2vec the associational bias is not significant. We also found that the conceptor nearly always outperforms the hard debiasing methods of Mu and Viswanath (2018) and Bolukbasi et al. (2016).

5.2 Gender Debiasing Results

Tables 1, 3 and 5 show the results obtained on gender debiasing between attribute words of "Family" and "Career', "Math" and "Arts" and "Science" and "Arts" with the target words "Male" and "Female" respectively for the traditional word embeddings. We show the results for all the word representations; however, the method of Bolukbasi et al. (2016) can only be applied to standard word embeddings.[12] We show the results when embeddings are debiased using conceptors computed using different subspaces. It can be seen in the tables that the bias for the conceptor negated embeddings is significantly less than that of the original embeddings. In the tables, the conceptor debiasing method is compared with the hard-debiasing technique proposed by Mu and Viswanath (2018) where the first principal component of the subspace from the embeddings is completely project off. The debiasing conceptor outperforms the hard debiasing technique in almost all cases. Note that the OR operator can not be used with the hard debiasing technique and thus is not reported.

Similarly, Tables 2, 4 and 6 show a comparison of the effect size and p-value using the hard debiasing technique and conceptor debiasing on conceptualized embeddings. It can be seen that conceptor debiasing generally outperforms other methods in mitigating (has a small absolute value) bias with the ELMo embeddings for all the subspaces. The results are less clear for BERT as observed in Table 6, which we will discuss in the following section. Note that combining all subspaces gives a significant reduction in the effect size.

5.3 Discussion of BERT Results

One of our most surprising findings is that unlike ELMo, the bias in BERT according to WEAT is less consistent than other word representations; WEAT effect sizes in BERT vary largely across different layers. Furthermore, the debiasing conceptor occasionally creates reverse bias in BERT, suggesting that tuning of the hyper-parameter α

---

[11] https://www.cs.cmu.edu/Groups/AI/areas/nlp/corpora/names/

[12] The concurrent work of Wang et al. (2019) was not available in time for us to compare with this method.

may be required. Another possibility is that BERT is capturing multiple concepts, and the presumption that the target lists are adequately capturing gender or racial attributes is incorrect. This suggests that further study into word lists is called for, along with visualization and end-task evaluation. It should also be noted that our results are in line with those from May et al. (2019).

6 Retaining Semantic Similarity

In order to understand if the debiasing conceptor was harming the semantic content of the word embeddings, we examined conceptor debiased embedding for semantic similarity tasks. As done in Liu et al. (2018) we used the seven standard word similarity test set and report Pearson's correlation. The word similarity sets are: the RG65 (Rubenstein and Goodenough, 1965), the WordSim-353 (WS) (Finkelstein et al., 2002), the rare-words (RW) (Luong et al., 2013), the MEN dataset (Bruni et al., 2014), the MTurk (Radinsky et al., 2011), the SimLex-999 (SimLex) (Hill et al., 2015), and the SimVerb-3500 (Gerz et al., 2016). Table 8 shows that conceptors help in preserving and at times increasing the semantic information in the embeddings. It should be noted that these tasks can not be applied to contextualized embeddings such as ELMo and BERT. So, we do not report these results.

	GloVe		word2vec		Fasttext	
	Orig.	CN	Orig.	CN	Orig.	CN
RG65	**76.03**	70.92	74.94	**78.58**	85.87	**85.94**
WS	73.79	**75.17**	69.34	**69.34**	**78.82**	77.44
RW	51.01	**55.25**	55.78	**56.04**	62.17	**62.48**
MEN	**80.13**	80.10	77.07	**77.85**	**83.64**	82.64
MTurk	69.16	**71.17**	**68.31**	67.68	**72.45**	71.34
SimLex	40.76	**45.85**	44.27	**46.05**	50.55	**50.78**
SimVerb	28.42	**34.51**	36.54	**37.33**	**42.75**	42.72

Table 8: Word Similarity comparison with conceptor debiased embeddings using all gender words as conceptor subspace.

7 Conclusion

We have shown that the debiasing conceptor can successfully debias word embeddings, outperforming previous state-of-the art 'hard' debiasing methods. Best results are obtained when lists are broken up into subsets of 'similar' words (pronouns, professions, names, etc.), and separate conceptors are learned for each subset and then OR'd. Conceptors for different protected subclasses such as gender and race can be similarly OR'd to jointly debias.

Contextual embeddings such as ELMo and BERT, which give a different vector for each word token, work particularly well with conceptors, since they produce a large number of embeddings; however, further research on tuning conceptors for BERT needs to be done. Finally, we note that embedding debiasing may leave bias which is undetected by measures such as WEAT Gonen and Goldberg (2019); thus, all debiasing methods should be tested on end-tasks such as emotion classification and co-reference resolution.

References

Sudeep Bhatia. 2017. The semantic representation of prejudice and stereotypes. *Cognition*, 164:46–60.

Tolga Bolukbasi, Kai-Wei Chang, James Y Zou, Venkatesh Saligrama, and Adam T Kalai. 2016. Man is to computer programmer as woman is to homemaker? debiasing word embeddings. In *Advances in neural information processing systems*, pages 4349–4357.

E. Bruni, N. K. Tran, and M. Baroni. 2014. Multimodal distributional semantics. *Journal of Artificial Intelligence Research*, 49(1):1–47.

Aylin Caliskan, Joanna J Bryson, and Arvind Narayanan. 2017. Semantics derived automatically from language corpora contain human-like biases. *Science*, 356(6334):183–186.

Lucas Dixon, John Li, Jeffrey Sorensen, Nithum Thain, and Lucy Vasserman. 2018. Measuring and mitigating unintended bias in text classification. In *Proceedings of the 2018 AAAI/ACM Conference on AI, Ethics, and Society*, pages 67–73. ACM.

L. Finkelstein, E. Gabrilovich, Y. Matias, E. Rivlin, Z. Solan, G. Wolfman, and E. Ruppin. 2002. Placing search in context: the concept revisited. *ACM Transactions on Information Systems*, 20(1):116–131.

Sorelle A Friedler, Carlos Scheidegger, and Suresh Venkatasubramanian. 2016. On the (im) possibility of fairness. *arXiv preprint arXiv:1609.07236*.

D. Gerz, I. Vulic, F. Hill, R. Reichart, and A. Korhonen. 2016. SimVerb-3500: a large-scale evaluation set of verb similarity. In *Proceedings of the EMNLP 2016*, pages 2173–2182.

Hila Gonen and Yoav Goldberg. 2019. Lipstick on a pig: Debiasing methods cover up systematic gender biases in word embeddings but do not remove them. In *North American Chapter of the Association for Computational Linguistics (NAACL)*.

Anthony G Greenwald and Mahzarin R Banaji. 1995. Implicit social cognition: attitudes, self-esteem, and stereotypes. *Psychological review*, 102(1):4.

Anthony G Greenwald, Debbie E McGhee, and Jordan LK Schwartz. 1998. Measuring individual differences in implicit cognition: the implicit association test. *Journal of personality and social psychology*, 74(6):1464.

X. He and H. Jaeger. 2018. Overcoming catastrophic interference using conceptor-aided backpropagation. In *International Conference on Learning Representations*.

F. Hill, R. Reichart, and A. Korhonen. 2015. Simlex-999: Evaluating semantic models with (genuine) similarity estimation. *Computational Linguistics*, 41(4):665–695.

Dirk Hovy. 2015. Demographic factors improve classification performance. In *Proceedings of the 53rd Annual Meeting of the Association for Computational Linguistics and the 7th International Joint Conference on Natural Language Processing (Volume 1: Long Papers)*, volume 1, pages 752–762.

Dirk Hovy and Shannon L Spruit. 2016. The social impact of natural language processing. In *Proceedings of the 54th Annual Meeting of the Association for Computational Linguistics (Volume 2: Short Papers)*, volume 2, pages 591–598.

H. Jaeger. 2014. Controlling recurrent neural networks by conceptors. Technical report, Jacobs University Bremen.

Svetlana Kiritchenko and Saif Mohammad. 2018. Examining gender and race bias in two hundred sentiment analysis systems. In *Proceedings of the Seventh Joint Conference on Lexical and Computational Semantics*, pages 43–53.

T. Liu, J. Sedoc, and L. Ungar. 2018. Correcting the common discourse bias in linear representation of sentences using conceptors. In *Proceedings of ACM-BCB- 2018 Workshop on BioCreative/OHNLP Challenge, Washington, D.C., 2018*.

T. Liu, L. Ungar, and J. Sedoc. 2019a. Continual learning for sentence representations using conceptors. In *Proceedings of the NAACL HLT 2019*.

T. Liu, L. Ungar, and J. Sedoc. 2019b. Unsupervised post-processing of word vectors via conceptor negation. In *Proceedings of the Thirty-Third AAAI Conference on Artificial Intelligence (AAAI-2019), Honolulu*.

Kaiji Lu, Piotr Mardziel, Fangjing Wu, Preetam Amancharla, and Anupam Datta. 2018. Gender bias in neural natural language processing. *arXiv preprint arXiv:1807.11714*.

M. Luong, R. Socher, and C. D. Manning. 2013. Better word representations with recursive neural networks for morphology. In *Proceedings of the CoNLL 2013*.

Chandler May, Alex Wang, Shikha Bordia, Samuel R Bowman, and Rachel Rudinger. 2019. On measuring social biases in sentence encoders. In *North American Chapter of the Association for Computational Linguistics (NAACL)*.

J. Mu and P. Viswanath. 2018. All-but-the-top: Simple and effective postprocessing for word representations. In *International Conference on Learning Representations*.

Dan Jurafsky Nikhil Garg, Londa Schiebinger and James Zou. 2018. Word embeddings quantify 100 years of gender and ethnic stereotypes. *PNAS*.

K Radinsky, E. Agichtein, E. Gabrilovich, and S. Markovitch. 2011. A word at a time: Computing word relatedness using temporal semantic analysis. In *Proceedings of the 20th International World Wide Web Conference*, pages 337–346, Hyderabad, India.

H. Rubenstein and J. B. Goodenough. 1965. Contextual correlates of synonymy. *Communications of the ACM*, 8(10):627–633.

Rachel Rudinger, Jason Naradowsky, Brian Leonard, and Benjamin Van Durme. 2018. Gender bias in coreference resolution. *arXiv preprint arXiv:1804.09301*.

Nathaniel Swinger, Maria De-Arteaga, Neil Thomas Heffernan IV, Mark D. M. Leiserson, and Adam Tauman Kalai. 2018. What are the biases in my word embedding? *CoRR*, abs/1812.08769.

Tianlu Wang, Jieyu Zhao, Mark Yatskar, Ryan Cotterell, Vicente Ordonez, and Kai-Wei Chang. 2019. Gender bias in contextualized word embeddings. In *North American Chapter of the Association for Computational Linguistics (NAACL)*.

Mark Yatskar, Luke Zettlemoyer, and Ali Farhadi. 2016. Situation recognition: Visual semantic role labeling for image understanding. In *Proceedings of the IEEE Conference on Computer Vision and Pattern Recognition*, pages 5534–5542.

Jieyu Zhao, Tianlu Wang, Mark Yatskar, Vicente Ordonez, and Kai-Wei Chang. 2017. Men also like shopping: Reducing gender bias amplification using corpus-level constraints. In *Proceedings of the 2017 Conference on Empirical Methods in Natural Language Processing*, pages 2979–2989.

Filling Gender & Number Gaps in Neural Machine Translation
with Black-box Context Injection

Amit Moryossef[†], Roee Aharoni[†], Yoav Goldberg[†‡]
{first.last}@gmail.com

[†]Bar Ilan University, Ramat Gan, Israel
[‡]Allen Institute for Artificial Intelligence

Abstract

When translating from a language that does not morphologically mark information such as gender and number into a language that does, translation systems must "guess" this missing information, often leading to incorrect translations in the given context. We propose a black-box approach for injecting the missing information to a pre-trained neural machine translation system, allowing to control the morphological variations in the generated translations *without* changing the underlying model or training data. We evaluate our method on an English to Hebrew translation task, and show that it is effective in injecting the gender and number information and that supplying the correct information improves the translation accuracy in up to 2.3 BLEU on a female-speaker test set for a state-of-the-art online black-box system. Finally, we perform a fine-grained syntactic analysis of the generated translations that shows the effectiveness of our method.

1   Introduction

A common way for marking information about gender, number, and case in language is morphology, or the structure of a given word in the language. However, different languages mark such information in different ways – for example, in some languages gender may be marked on the head word of a syntactic dependency relation, while in other languages it is marked on the dependent, on both, or on none of them (Nichols, 1986). This morphological diversity creates a challenge for machine translation, as there are ambiguous cases where more than one correct translation exists for the same source sentence. For example, while the English sentence "I love language" is ambiguous with respect to the gender of the speaker, Hebrew marks verbs

for the gender of their subject and does not allow gender-neutral translation. This allows two possible Hebrew translations – one in a masculine and the other in a feminine form. As a consequence, a sentence-level translator (either human or machine) must commit to the gender of the speaker, adding information that is not present in the source. Without additional context, this choice must be done arbitrarily by relying on language conventions, world knowledge or statistical (stereotypical) knowledge.

Indeed, the English sentence "I work as a doctor" is translated into Hebrew by Google Translate using the masculine verb form *oved*, indicating a male speaker, while "I work as a nurse" is translated with the feminine form *ovedet*, indicating a female speaker (verified on March 2019). While this is still an issue, there have been recent efforts to reduce it for specific language pairs.[1]

We present a simple black-box method to influence the interpretation chosen by an NMT system in these ambiguous cases. More concretely, we construct pre-defined textual hints about the gender and number of the speaker and the audience (the interlocutors), which we concatenate to a given input sentence that we would like to translate accordingly. We then show that a black-box NMT system makes the desired morphological decisions according to the given hint, even when no other evidence is available on the source side. While adding those hints results in additional text on the target side, we show that it is simple to remove, leaving only the desired translation.

Our method is appealing as it only requires simple pre-and-post processing of the inputs and outputs, without considering the system internals, or requiring specific annotated data and training procedure as in previous work (Vanmassenhove et al.,

---

[1]blog.google/products/translate/reducing-gender-bias-google-translate/

Proceedings of the 1st Workshop on Gender Bias in Natural Language Processing, pages 49–54
Florence, Italy, August 2, 2019. ©2019 Association for Computational Linguistics

2018). We show that in spite of its simplicity, it is effective in resolving many of the ambiguities and improves the translation quality in up to 2.3 BLEU when given the correct hints, which may be inferred from text metadata or other sources. Finally, we perform a fine-grained syntactic analysis of the translations generated using our method which shows its effectiveness.

2 Morphological Ambiguity in Translation

Different languages use different morphological features marking different properties on different elements. For example, English marks for number, case, aspect, tense, person, and degree of comparison. However, English does not mark gender on nouns and verbs. Even when a certain property is marked, languages differ in the form and location of the marking (Nichols, 1986). For example, marking can occur on the head of a syntactic dependency construction, on its argument, on both (requiring *agreement*), or on none of them. Translation systems must generate correct target-language morphology as part of the translation process. This requires knowledge of both the source-side and target-side morphology. Current state-of-the-art translation systems do capture many aspects of natural language, including morphology, when a relevant context is available (Dalvi et al., 2017; Bawden et al., 2018), but resort to "guessing" based on the training-data statistics when it is not. Complications arise when different languages convey different kinds of information in their morphological systems. In such cases, a translation system may be required to remove information available in the source sentence, or to add information not available in it, where the latter can be especially tricky.

3 Black-Box Knowledge Injection

Our goal is to supply an NMT system with knowledge regarding the speaker and interlocutor of first-person sentences, in order to produce the desired target-side morphology when the information is not available in the source sentence. The approach we take in the current work is that of *black-box injection*, in which we attempt to inject knowledge to the input in order to influence the output of a trained NMT system, without having access to its internals or its training procedure as proposed by Vanmassenhove et al. (2018).

We are motivated by recent work by Voita et al. (2018) who showed that NMT systems learn to track coreference chains when presented with sufficient discourse context. We conjecture that there are enough sentence-internal pronominal coreference chains appearing in the training data of large-scale NMT systems, such that state-of-the-art NMT systems can and do track sentence-internal coreference. We devise a wrapper method to make use of this coreference tracking ability by introducing artificial antecedents that unambiguously convey the desired gender and number properties of the speaker and audience.

More concretely, a sentence such as "I love you" is ambiguous with respect to the gender of the speaker and the gender and number of the audience. However, sentences such as "I love you, she told him" are unambiguous given the coreference groups {I, she} and {you, him} which determine *I* to be feminine singular and *you* to be masculine singular. We can thus inject the desired information by prefixing a sentence with short generic sentence fragment such as "She told him:" or "She told them that", relying on the NMT system's coreference tracking abilities to trigger the correctly marked translation, and then remove the redundant translated prefix from the generated target sentence. We observed that using a parataxis construction (i.e. "she said to him:") almost exclusively results in target-side parataxis as well (in 99.8% of our examples), making it easy to identify and strip the translated version from the target side. Moreover, because the parataxis construction is grammatically isolated from the rest of the sentence, it can be stripped without requiring additional changes or modification to the rest of the sentence, ensuring grammaticality.

4 Experiments & Results

To demonstrate our method in a black-box setting, we focus our experiments on Google's machine translation system (GMT), accessed through its Cloud API. To test the method on real-world sentences, we consider a monologue from the stand-up comedy show "Sarah Silverman: A Speck of Dust". The monologue consists of 1,244 English sentences, all by a female speaker conveyed to a plural, gender-neutral audience. Our parallel corpora consists of the 1,244 English sentences from the transcript, and their corresponding He-

Speaker	Audience	BLEU
Baseline		18.67
He	–	19.2
He	him	19.25
He	her	19.3
He	them	19.5
I	–	19.84
I	them	20.23
She	–	20.8
She	him	20.82
She	her	20.98
She	them	20.97

Table 1: BLEU results on the Silverman dataset

brew translations based on the Hebrew subtitles.[2] We translate the monologue one sentence at a time through the Google Cloud API. Eyeballing the results suggest that most of the translations use the incorrect, but default, masculine and singular forms for the speaker and the audience, respectively. We expect that by adding the relevant condition of "female speaking to an audience" we will get better translations, affecting both the gender of the speaker and the number of the audience.

To verify this, we experiment with translating the sentences with the following variations: **No Prefix**—The baseline translation as returned by the GMT system. **"He said:"**—Signaling a male speaker. We expect to further skew the system towards masculine forms. **"She said:"**—Signaling a female speaker and unknown audience. As this matches the actual speaker's gender, we expect an improvement in translation of first-person pronouns and verbs with first-person pronouns as subjects. **"I said to them:"**—Signaling an unknown speaker and plural audience. **"He said to them:"**—Masculine speaker and plural audience. **"She said to them:"**—Female speaker and plural audience—the complete, correct condition. We expect the best translation accuracy on this setup. **"He/she said to him/her"**—Here we set an (incorrect) singular gender-marked audience, to investigate our ability to control the audience morphology.

4.1 Quantitative Results

We compare the different conditions by comparing BLEU (Papineni et al., 2002) with respect to the reference Hebrew translations. We use the `multi-bleu.perl` script from the Moses toolkit (Koehn et al., 2007). Table 1 shows BLEU scores for the different prefixes. The numbers match our expectations: Generally, providing an incorrect speaker and/or audience information decreases the BLEU scores, while providing the correct information substantially improves it - we see an increase of up to 2.3 BLEU over the baseline. We note the BLEU score improves in all cases, even when given the wrong gender of either the speaker or the audience. We hypothesise this improvement stems from the addition of the word "said" which hints the model to generate a more "spoken" language which matches the tested scenario. Providing correct information for both speaker and audience usually helps more than providing correct information to either one of them individually. The one outlier is providing "She" for the speaker and "her" for the audience. While this is not the correct scenario, we hypothesise it gives an improvement in BLEU as it further reinforces the female gender in the sentence.

4.2 Qualitative Results

The BLEU score is an indication of how close the automated translation is to the reference translation, but does not tell us what exactly changed concerning the gender and number properties we attempt to control. We perform a finer-grained analysis focusing on the relation between the injected speaker and audience information, and the morphological realizations of the corresponding elements. We parse the translations and the references using a Hebrew dependency parser.[3] In addition to the parse structure, the parser also performs morphological analysis and tagging of the individual tokens. We then perform the following analysis.

Speaker's Gender Effects: We search for first-person singular pronouns with subject case (*ani*, unmarked for gender, corresponding to the English *I*), and consider the gender of its governing verb (or adjectives in copular constructions such as 'I am nice'). The possible genders are 'masculine', 'feminine' and 'both', where the latter indicates a case where the none-diacriticized written form admits both a masculine and a feminine reading. We expect the gender to match the ones

---

[2]The data is obtained from www.opensubtitles.org

[3]https://www.cs.bgu.ac.il/~yoavg/software/hebparsers/hebdepparser/

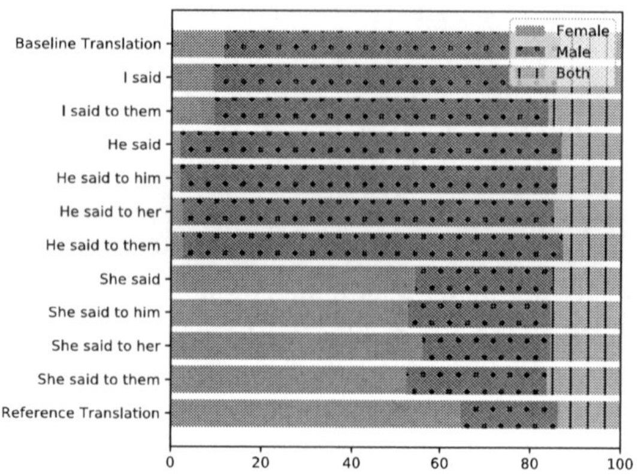

Figure 1: Gender inflection statistics for verbs governed by first-person pronouns.

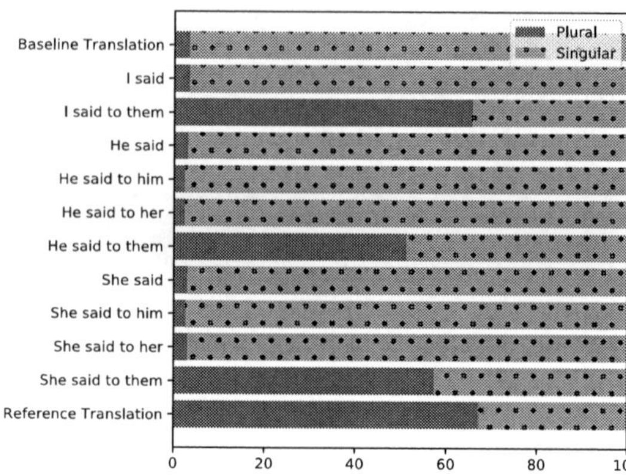

Figure 2: Number inflection statistics for second-person pronouns.

requested in the prefix.

Interlocutors' Gender and Number Effects: We search for second-person pronouns and consider their gender and number. For pronouns in subject position, we also consider the gender and number of their governing verbs (or adjectives in copular constructions). For a singular audience, we expect the gender and number to match the requested ones. For a plural audience, we expect the masculine-plural forms.

Results: Speaker. Figure 1 shows the result for controlling the morphological properties of the speaker (*{he, she, I} said*). It shows the proportion of gender-inflected verbs for the various conditions and the reference. We see that the baseline system severely under-predicts the feminine form of verbs as compared to the reference. The "He said" conditions further decreases the number of feminine verbs, while the "I said" conditions bring it back to the baseline level. Finally, the "She said" prefixes substantially increase the number of feminine-marked verbs, bringing the proportion much closer to that of the reference (though still under-predicting some of the feminine cases).

Results: Audience. The chart in Figure 2 shows the results for controlling the number of the audience (*...to them* vs nothing). It shows the proportion of singular vs. plural second-person pronouns on the various conditions. It shows a similar trend: the baseline system severely under-predicts the plural forms with respect to the reference translation, while adding the "to them" condition brings the proportion much closer to that of the reference.

4.3 Comparison to Vanmassenhove et al. (2018)

Closely related to our work, Vanmassenhove et al. (2018) proposed a method and an English-French test set to evaluate gender-aware translation, based on the Europarl corpus (Koehn, 2005). We evaluate our method (using Google Translate and the given prefixes) on their test set to see whether it is applicable to another language pair and domain. Table 2 shows the results of our approach vs. their published results and the Google Translate baseline. As may be expected, Google Translate outperforms their system as it is trained on a different corpus and may use more complex machine translation models. Using our method improves the BLEU score even further.

	Male	Female
VHW (2018) Baseline	37.58	37.75
VHW (2018) + TAG	38.71	38.97
Google Translate	39.33	39.02
Google Translate + Prefix	39.95	39.95

Table 2: Comparison of our approach (using Google Translate) to Vanmassenhove et al. (2018) on their English-French gender corpus.

4.4 Other Languages

To test our method's outputs on multiple languages, we run our pre-and post-processing steps with Google Translate using examples we sourced from native speakers of different languages. For every example we have an English sentence and two translations in the corresponding language,

	English Text	Masculine	Feminine
Hebrew	I am nice	ani nehmad	ani nehmada
Prefix		ani nehmad	ani nehmada
Spanish	I am delighted	Estoy encantado	Estoy encantada
Prefix		Estoy encantado	Estoy encantada
Portuguese	I was called	Eu fui chamado	Eu fui chamada
Prefix		Eu fui chamado	Eu fui chamado
French	I am patient	je suis patient	je suis patiente
Prefix		je suis patient	je suis patiente
Italian	I am beautiful	Sono bello	Sono bella
Prefix		io sono bello	io sono bella
Russian	I wrote a message	Я написал сообщение	Я написала сообщение
Prefix		Я написал сообщение	Я написал сообщение
Czech	I gave her the flower	já jsem ji dal květinu	já jsem ji dala květinu
Prefix		Dala jsem jí květinu	Dala jsem jí květinu
Romanian	I am patient	Sunt răbdător	Sunt răbdătoare
Prefix		Sunt răbdător	Sunt răbdătoare
Catalan	I am rich	sóc ric	sóc rica
Prefix		sóc ric	sóc ric
Polish	I am nice	Jestem miły	Jestem miła
Prefix		Jestem miły	Jestem miła

Table 3: Examples of languages where the speaker's gender changes morphological markings in different languages, and translations using the prefix "He said:" or "She said:" accordingly

one in masculine and one in feminine form. Not all examples are using the same source English sentence as different languages mark different information. Table 3 shows that for these specific examples our method worked on 6/10 of the languages we had examples for, while for 3/10 languages both translations are masculine, and for 1 language both are feminine.

5 Related Work

Rabinovich et al. (2017) showed that given input with author traits like gender, it is possible to retain those traits in Statistical Machine Translation (SMT) models. Grönroos et al. (2017) showed that incorporating morphological analysis in the decoder improves NMT performance for morphologically rich languages. Burlot and Yvon (2017) presented a new protocol for evaluating the morphological competence of MT systems, indicating that current translation systems only manage to capture some morphological phenomena correctly. Regarding the application of constraints in NMT, Sennrich et al. (2016) presented a method for controlling the politeness level in the generated output. Ficler and Goldberg (2017) showed how to guide a neural text generation system towards

style and content parameters like the level of professionalism, subjective/objective, sentiment and others. Tiedemann and Scherrer (2017) showed that incorporating more context when translating subtitles can improve the coherence of the generated translations. Most closely to our work, Vanmassenhove et al. (2018) also addressed the missing gender information by training proprietary models with a gender-indicating-prefix. We differ from this work by treating the problem in a black-box manner, and by addressing additional information like the number of the speaker and the gender and number of the audience.

6 Conclusions

We highlight the problem of translating between languages with different morphological systems, in which the target translation must contain gender and number information that is not available in the source. We propose a method for injecting such information into a pre-trained NMT model in a black-box setting. We demonstrate the effectiveness of this method by showing an improvement of 2.3 BLEU in an English-to-Hebrew translation setting where the speaker and audience gender can be inferred. We also perform a fine-grained syntactic analysis that shows how our method enables to control the morphological realization of first and second-person pronouns, together with verbs and adjectives related to them. In future work we would like to explore automatic generation of the injected context, or the use of cross-sentence context to infer the injected information.

References

Rachel Bawden, Rico Sennrich, Alexandra Birch, and Barry Haddow. 2018. Evaluating discourse phenomena in neural machine translation. In *Proceedings of the 2018 Conference of the North American Chapter of the Association for Computational Linguistics: Human Language Technologies, Volume 1 (Long Papers)*, volume 1, pages 1304–1313.

Franck Burlot and François Yvon. 2017. Evaluating the morphological competence of Machine Translation Systems. In *2nd Conference on Machine Translation (WMT17)*, volume 1, pages 43–55, Copenhague, Denmark. Association for Computational Linguistics.

Fahim Dalvi, Nadir Durrani, Hassan Sajjad, Yonatan Belinkov, and Stephan Vogel. 2017. Understanding and improving morphological learning in the neural machine translation decoder. In *IJCNLP*.

Jessica Ficler and Yoav Goldberg. 2017. Controlling linguistic style aspects in neural language generation. *CoRR*, abs/1707.02633.

Stig-Arne Grönroos, Sami Virpioja, and Mikko Kurimo. 2017. Extending hybrid word-character neural machine translation with multi-task learning of morphological analysis. In *Proceedings of the Second Conference on Machine Translation*, pages 296–302. Association for Computational Linguistics.

Philipp Koehn. 2005. Europarl: A parallel corpus for statistical machine translation. In *MT summit*, volume 5, pages 79–86.

Philipp Koehn, Hieu Hoang, Alexandra Birch, Chris Callison-Burch, Marcello Federico, Nicola Bertoldi, Brooke Cowan, Wade Shen, Christine Moran, Richard Zens, et al. 2007. Moses: Open source toolkit for statistical machine translation. In *Proceedings of the 45th annual meeting of the ACL on interactive poster and demonstration sessions*, pages 177–180. Association for Computational Linguistics.

Johanna Nichols. 1986. Head-marking and dependent-marking grammar. *Language*, 62(1):56–119.

Kishore Papineni, Salim Roukos, Todd Ward, and Wei-Jing Zhu. 2002. Bleu: a method for automatic evaluation of machine translation. In *Proceedings of the 40th annual meeting on association for computational linguistics*, pages 311–318. Association for Computational Linguistics.

Ella Rabinovich, Raj Nath Patel, Shachar Mirkin, Lucia Specia, and Shuly Wintner. 2017. Personalized machine translation: Preserving original author traits. In *Proceedings of the 15th Conference of the European Chapter of the Association for Computational Linguistics: Volume 1, Long Papers*, pages 1074–1084. Association for Computational Linguistics.

Rico Sennrich, Barry Haddow, and Alexandra Birch. 2016. Controlling politeness in neural machine translation via side constraints. In *Proceedings of the 2016 Conference of the North American Chapter of the Association for Computational Linguistics: Human Language Technologies*, pages 35–40. Association for Computational Linguistics.

Jörg Tiedemann and Yves Scherrer. 2017. Neural machine translation with extended context. In *Proceedings of the Third Workshop on Discourse in Machine Translation*, pages 82–92. Association for Computational Linguistics.

Eva Vanmassenhove, Christian Hardmeier, and Andy Way. 2018. Getting gender right in neural mt. In *Proceedings of the 2018 Conference on Empirical Methods in Natural Language Processing*, pages 3003–3008, Brussels, Belgium. Association for Computational Linguistics.

Elena Voita, Pavel Serdyukov, Rico Sennrich, and Ivan Titov. 2018. Context-aware neural machine translation learns anaphora resolution. In *Proceedings of the 56th Annual Meeting of the Association for Computational Linguistics (Volume 1: Long Papers)*, pages 1264–1274, Melbourne, Australia. Association for Computational Linguistics.

The Role of Protected Class Word Lists in Bias Identification of Contextualized Word Representations

João Sedoc and Lyle Ungar
Computer and Information Science
University of Pennsylvania
Philadelphia, PA 19104
`joao@cis.upenn.edu, ungar@cis.upenn.edu`

Abstract

Systemic bias in word embeddings has been widely reported and studied, and efforts made to debias them; however, new contextualized embeddings such as ELMo and BERT are only now being similarly studied. Standard debiasing methods require large, heterogeneous lists of target words to identify the "bias subspace". We show that using new contextualized word embeddings in conceptor debiasing allows us to more accurately debias word embeddings by breaking target word lists into more homogeneous subsets and then combining ("Or'ing") the debiasing conceptors of the different subsets.

1 Introduction

Contextualized word representations are replacing word vectors in many natural language processing (NLP) tasks such as sentiment analysis, coreference resolution, question answering, textual entailment, and named entity recognition (Peters et al., 2018; Devlin et al., 2018). However, ELMo and BERT have bias similar (Wang et al., 2019; May et al., 2019; Kurita et al., 2019) to the well documented bias in traditional word embedding methods (Bolukbasi et al., 2016; Bhatia, 2017; Caliskan et al., 2017; Nikhil Garg and Zou, 2018; Kiritchenko and Mohammad, 2018; Rudinger et al., 2018; Zhang et al., 2018), and this could cause bias in NLP pipelines used for high stakes downstream tasks such as resume selection or bail setting algorithms (Hansen et al., 2015; Bolukbasi et al., 2016; Ayres, 2002). Traditional word embeddings, such as word2vec (Mikolov et al., 2013), GloVe (Pennington et al., 2014), and Fasttext (Bojanowski et al., 2017) require large sets of target words, since debiasing is generally done in the space of the PCA of the word embeddings. (If one only uses a two words, like

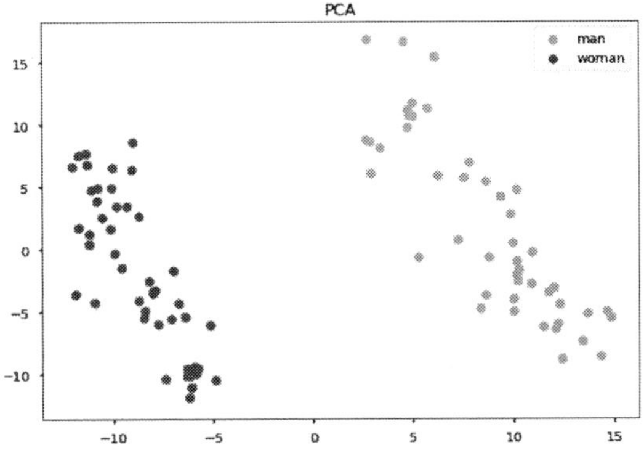

Figure 1: ELMo word representations of tokens of *man* and *woman* projected onto their first and second principal components.

"man" and "woman", the PCA space is just a single vector pointing in the difference between those two vectors.) Context-sensitive embedding such as ELMo and BERT give an embedding for every token (based on its context), giving large numbers of embedding for each word (such as "man"), so that principal components can be calculated even for word lists of size two as shown in Figure 1.

Use of contextualized word embedding allows better debiasing by allowing one (as will be described below) to break up target word lists into smaller homogeneous subsets; it also gives better insight into where the bias may be coming from.

Word embeddings capture distributional similarities; just as humans come to associate certain professions (homemaker or computer programmer) with certain genders (woman or man), word embeddings capture very similar associations (Bolukbasi et al., 2016). Such embedding biases tend to track statistical regularities such as percentage of people with a given occupation (Nikhil Garg and Zou, 2018) but sometimes deviate from them (Bhatia, 2017).

55

Proceedings of the 1st Workshop on Gender Bias in Natural Language Processing, pages 55–61
Florence, Italy, August 2, 2019. ©2019 Association for Computational Linguistics

A number of debiasing methods have been proposed. Most of them use hard debiasing – zeroing out one or more directions in the embedding space, generally selected using principal components (Bolukbasi et al., 2016; Wang et al., 2019). In this paper, we use a soft debiasing method, *conceptor debiasing*, which also works in the principal component space, but does a softer shrinkage of the bias and close-by directions (Liu et al., 2018).

Many debiasing algorithms rely entirely on so called "target lists" of protected classes in order to identify and mitigate the "bias subspace"; however, to our knowledge no work examines the role of these target lists in defining this space. This in part due to the fact that in standard word embeddings there is only one embedding for a token. In contrast, new contextualized word representations such as BERT and ELMo have a different embedding for each word token in a context. This allows us an opportunity to more closely examine what information target word lists are capturing.

This paper:

- Examines bias in ELMo and BERT, taking advantage of their context-sensitivity to give better visualizations.
- Shows how heterogeneity in content and size of the "target list" of gendered or racially marked terms interferes with debiasing, and how conceptors on contextual embeddings can be used to address such target list heterogeneity.

2   Related Work

NLP has begun tackling the problems that are limiting the achievement of fair and ethical AI (Hovy and Spruit, 2016; Friedler et al., 2016), including techniques for mitigating demographic biases in models. In brief, a demographic bias is taken to mean a difference in model output based on gender (either of the data author or within the content itself) or selected demographic dimension ("protected class") such as race. Demographic biases manifest in many ways, from disparities in tagging and classification accuracy depending on author age and gender (Hovy, 2015; Dixon et al., 2018), to over-amplification of demographic differences in language generation (Yatskar et al., 2016; Zhao et al., 2017), to diverging implicit associations between words or concepts within embeddings or language models (Bolukbasi et al., 2016; Rudinger

et al., 2018).

Recent work of Wang et al. (2019) shows bias in ELMo and presents several examples of successful debiasing. However, May et al. (2019) found that bias in BERT may be more difficult to identify, but Kurita et al. (2019) did indeed find bias in BERT. However, prior work has not focused on identifying word lists as a potential area of research.

3   Target Word Lists

To debias word embeddings, an appropriate word list representing the bias in question needs to be used to define the subspace. [1] For example, a gender word list might be a set of pronouns which are specific to a particular gender such as *he / she* or *himself / herself* and gender specific words representing relationships like *brother / sister* or *uncle / aunt*. We test conceptor debiasing both using the list of such pronouns[2] used by Caliskan et al. (2017) and using a more comprehensive list of gender-specific words that also includes gender-specific terms related to occupations, relationships and other commonly used words such as *prince / princess* and *host / hostess*[3]. We further tested conceptor (Jaeger, 2014; Liu et al., 2018) (soft) debiasing using male and female names such as *Aaron / Alice* or *Chris / Clary*.[4]

Previous researchers used a variety of different word lists, but did not study the effect of word list selection; we show below that the word list matters. However, we leave systematic study for future work.

3.1   Word Lists and Principal Components

Recall most debiasing methods rely on principal components of the matrix of embeddings of the target words. Hard debiasing methods remove the first or first several principal components (Bolukbasi et al., 2016; Mu and Viswanath, 2018). Conceptors, as explained below, do soft debiasing in the same principal component space.

Paired nouns and pronouns should provide better support for debiasing than names if we assume that the linguistic markers are unambiguous

---

[1] Some methods also require a list of unbiased words as well, but we will not address those since conceptor debiasing does not require them.
[2] https://github.com/jsedoc/ConceptorDebias/tree/master/lists
[3] https://github.com/uclanlp/corefBias, https://github.com/uclanlp/gn_glove
[4] https://www.cs.cmu.edu/Groups/AI/areas/nlp/corpora/names/

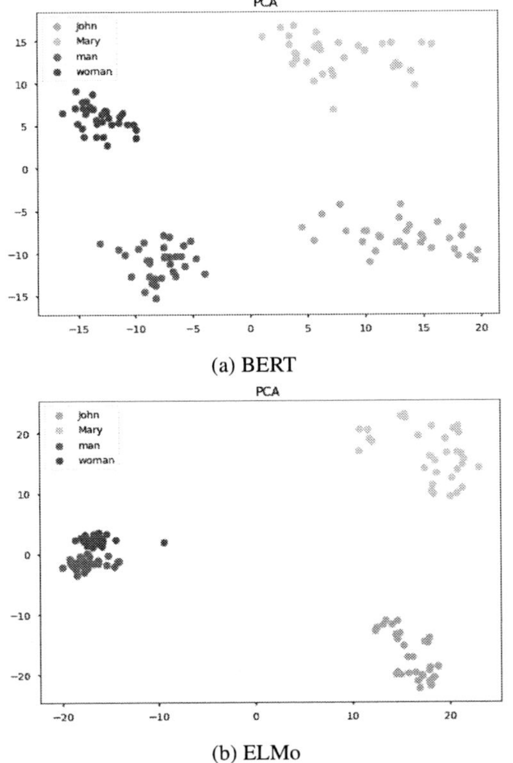

(a) BERT

(b) ELMo

Figure 2: BERT and ELMo word representations of the union of the set of contextualized word representations of the pairs *man / woman* and *Mary / John* projected onto their first and second principal components.

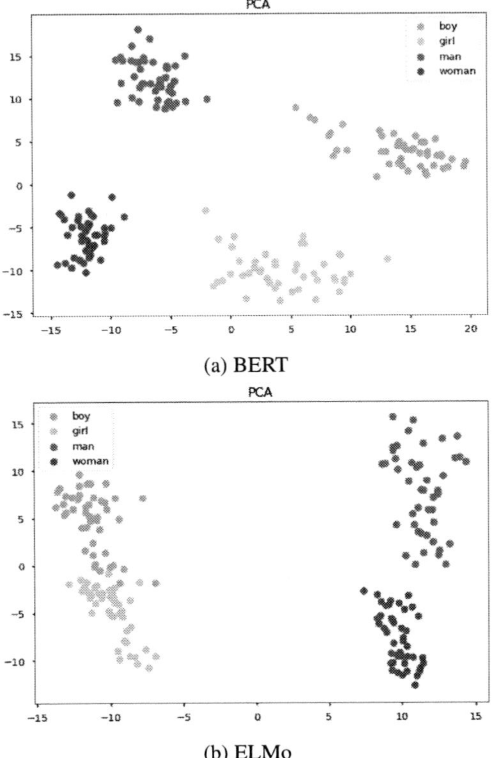

(a) BERT

(b) ELMo

words, say *Mary / John* to the pair *man / woman*, as shown in Figure 2. The first principal component is now capturing pronoun vs proper noun difference, which we do not desire to remove after debiasing.

Figure 3: BERT and ELMo word representations of the union of the set of contextualized word representations of the pairs *man / woman* and *boy / girl* projected onto their first and second principal components.

(a counterexample is "guys"), and there is no polysemy. Names of people can also be ambiguous (e.g. "Pat"). A possible solution for this which we leave for future work is to regress the first few principal components of a word pair with the binary attribute to verify that the pair is properly captures the attribute of interest on out-of-sample lists. In fact, for racial names Gaddis (2017)'s method (using linear regression) can be used to both filter and pair names. While this is difficult to achieve using word embeddings which are at the type level (i.e. one vector per word as in Fasttext and word2vec), for contextualized word representations, which are token level (i.e. one vector per word and context), this is completely feasible.

Figure 1 shows how the pair *man / woman* cleanly separates across the first principal component of the space of their contextualized representations. However, even though one word pair give good results, combining it with a second word pair can have unfortunate effects; debiasing becomes more complicated if we add another pair of

It is also critical to note that contextualized word embeddings are very rich, so while one might think the union of the contextualized word representations of *man / woman* and *boy / girl* would yield a good gender direction, in fact we find that the first principal component of these four words is along the direction of adults vs. children (see Figure 3). There is some separation between "husband" and "wife" in this dimension, but none between "boy" and "girl". Similarly when names such as *Mary / John* are projected onto this subspace, little separation occurs. Since most debiasing methods remove or shrink these principal component directions, this combined word list does poorly for debiasing.

Furthermore, some apparently sensible target word lists are not useful for debiasing contextu-

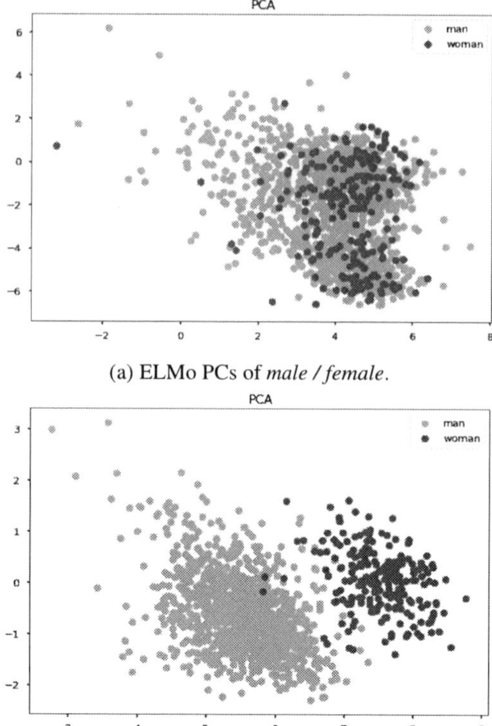

(a) ELMo PCs of *male / female*.

(b) ELMo PC of *John / Mary*

Figure 4: ELMo word representations of *man / woman* projected onto the first and second principal components defined by the pair (a) *male / female* and (b) *John / Mary*.

alized representations. Figure 4 shows that the ELMO vectors of *man* and */woman* separate nicely when projected on to the first two principal components of the *Mary / John* but fail to separate when projected on to the first two principal components of *male / female*. The word *male / female* word pair form a poor target list since they are, in fact, rarely used to refer to people; They are instead applied to animals (*the male parrot*) or to distinguish a break of the social bias (*the male model*).

Note that none of the above figures could have been generated using traditional word embeddings; one cannot get two PCA dimensions for a target word list of only two words.

3.2 Conceptors

Conceptors provide and effective, computationally cheap and mathematically elegant a way of doing soft debiasing of word embeddings. As with many debiasing methods, the input is matrix Z of word embeddings corresponding to a set of target

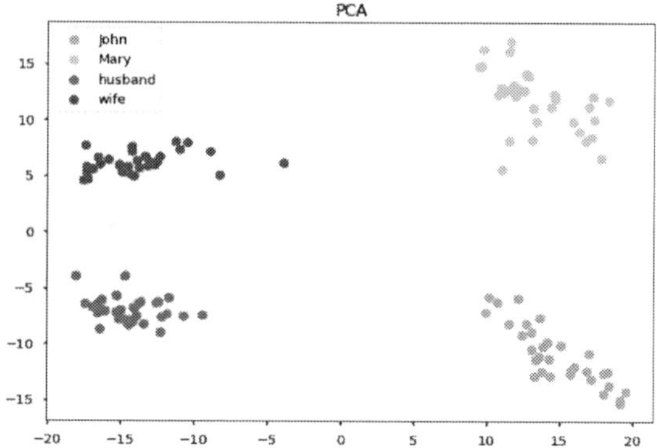

Figure 5: BERT word representations of the union of the set of contextualized word representations of the pairs *husband / wife* and *Mary / John* projected onto the first and second principal components.

words, $\mathcal{Z}$. (These can either be one embedding per word type, for conventional embeddings, or one vector per word token, as we use here for context-sensitive embeddings; for best results, $\mathcal{Z}$ should be mean-centered.) A conceptor matrix, C, is a regularized identity map (in our case, from the original word embeddings to their biased versions) that minimizes

$$\|Z - CZ\|_F^2 + \alpha^{-2}\|C\|_F^2. \qquad (1)$$

where α^{-2} is a scalar parameter. As described in the orignal work on matrix conceptors (Jaeger, 2014; He and Jaeger, 2018; Liu et al., 2019b,a) C has a closed form solution:

$$C = \frac{1}{k}ZZ^\top(\frac{1}{k}ZZ^\top + \alpha^{-2}I)^{-1}. \qquad (2)$$

Intuitively, C is a soft projection matrix on the linear subspace that gives the largest shrinkage where the word embeddings Z have the highest variance. Once C has been learned, it can be 'negated' by subtracting it from the identity matrix and then applied to any word embeddings to shrink their bias directions.

Conceptors can represent laws of Boolean logic, such as NOT ¬, AND ∧, and OR ∨. For two conceptors C and B, we define the following operations:

$$\neg C := \mathbf{I} - C, \qquad (3)$$
$$C \wedge B := (C^{-1} + B^{-1} - \mathbf{I})^{-1} \qquad (4)$$
$$C \vee B := \neg(\neg C \wedge \neg B) \qquad (5)$$

Thus, to minimize bias, we apply the negated conceptor, NOT C (see Equation 3) to an embedding space and reduce its bias. We call NOT C the

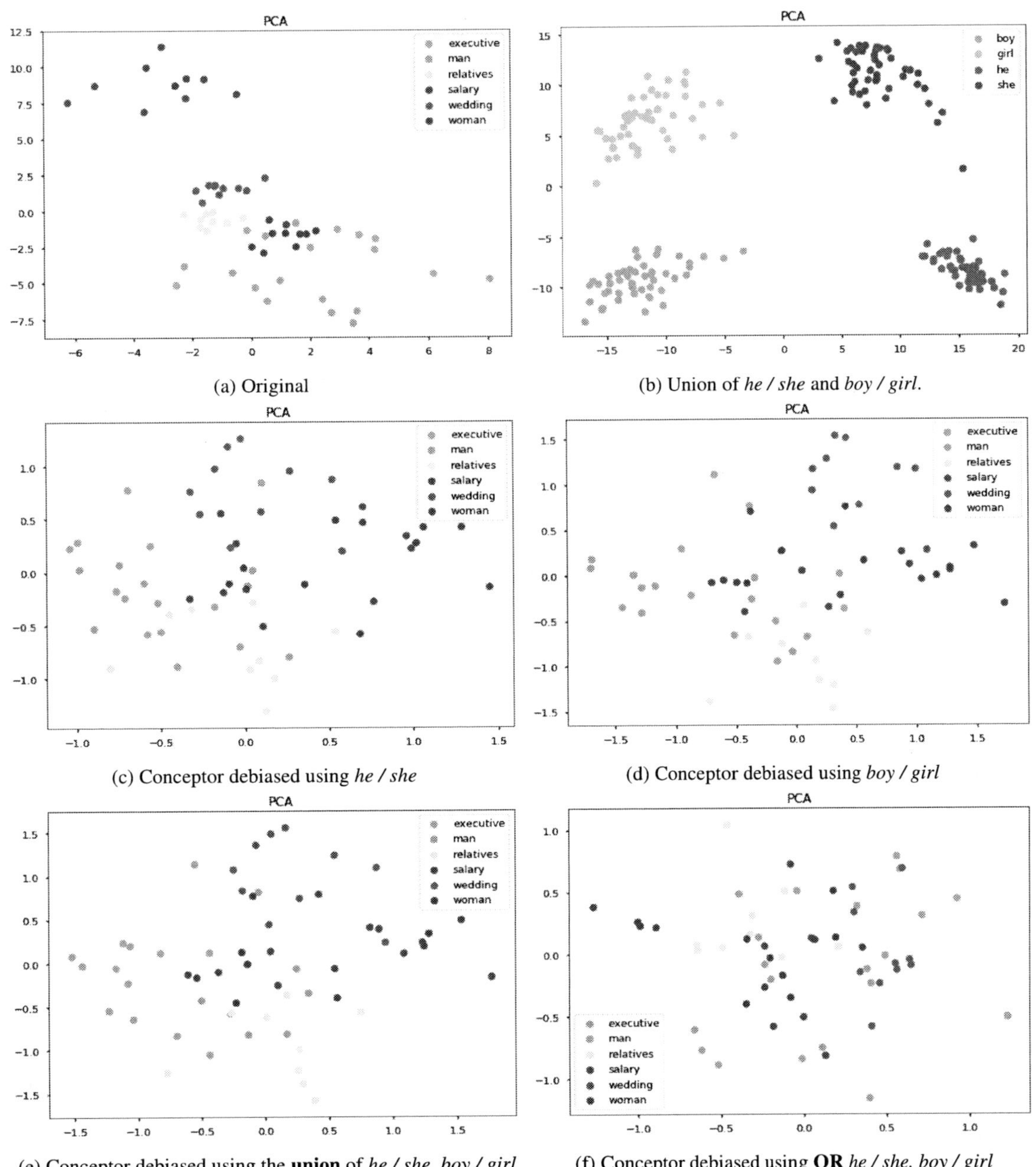

(a) Original

(b) Union of *he / she* and *boy / girl*.

(c) Conceptor debiased using *he / she*

(d) Conceptor debiased using *boy / girl*

(e) Conceptor debiased using the **union** of *he / she, boy / girl*

(f) Conceptor debiased using **OR** *he / she, boy / girl*

Figure 6: Effect of target word lists on debiasing BERT word representations. The union of the set of contextualized word representations of *career, business, family, children, man, woman* projected on to the first two principal components of *he / she*.

debiasing conceptor. More generally, if we have K conceptors, C_i derived from K different word lists, we call NOT $(C_1 \vee ... \vee C_K)$ a debiasing conceptor.

Negated conceptors do soft debiasing, shrinking each principal component of the covariance matrix of the target word embeddings $ZZ^\top$ based on the conceptor hyper-parameter α and the eigenvalues σ_i of $ZZ^\top$: $\frac{\alpha^{-2}}{\sigma_i + \alpha^{-2}}$. (Liu et al., 2018).

4 Conceptor Debiasing

Above we showed that visualizations of gender and racial subspaces gives insight for how word lists for embedding can fail to produce good results. We now show how conceptor negation, applied across homogeneous subsets of the word list can improve performance.

Figure 6a shows that there is a gender bias using career versus family words projected onto the gender space. Figure 6 shows that after debiasing using conceptor negation (Liu et al., 2018) (as defined above) there is substantially less bias.

Nonetheless, one should note that gender bias need not be in the first two dimensions. In fact recent work by Gonen and Goldberg (2019) has pointed out that most "debiasing" methods are simply mitigating bias and thus end task methods will potentially be able to undo this mitigation. As a result, we recommend that a method like Gaddis (2017) be used to identify proper word lists.

5 Conclusion

We showed that one should take care when debiasing word embeddings; well-chosen word lists generally yield better subspaces than poorly-chosen ones. Combining heterogeneous words into a single word list presents a host of problems; a couple of 'bad' words like "male/female" can significantly shift the dominant principal components of the bias space. Conversely, since PCA effectively weights words by their frequency of occurrence, combining small word lists (pronouns) with large word lists (names) means that the longer word lists carry more weight in the principal components (unless the rare words 'stick out' a long way in a different direction).

Conceptor debiasing provides a simple way of addressing the problem of combining word lists of different types and sizes, improving performance over state-of-the art 'hard' debiasing methods. Conceptor debiasing has the further benefit that conceptor negation methods allow one to learn separate conceptors for each word subset and then to OR them. The best results are obtained when lists are broken up into subsets of 'similar' words (pronouns, professions, names, etc). Similarly, conceptors for different protected subclasses such as gender and race can be OR'd to simultaneously debias for both classes. OR'ing has the advantage that word lists of different size are still treated as equally important–a key factor when lists such as pronouns, male and female names and black and white names may be of vastly different sizes.

Contextual embeddings such as ELMo and BERT, which give a different vector for each word token, work particularly well with specialized word lists, since they produce a large number of embeddings, allow principal components to be computed and used for debiasing even for lists of two words.

Finally, the main takeaway from this paper is that word lists matter, especially for debiasing contextualized word embeddings. Remember Figures 3 and 4b where intuition fails entirely!

References

Ian Ayres. 2002. Outcome tests of racial disparities in police practices. *Justice research and Policy*, 4(1-2):131–142.

Sudeep Bhatia. 2017. The semantic representation of prejudice and stereotypes. *Cognition*, 164:46–60.

P. Bojanowski, E. Grave, A. Joulin, and T. Mikolov. 2017. Enriching word vectors with subword information. *Transactions of the Association for Computational Linguistics*, 5:135–146.

Tolga Bolukbasi, Kai-Wei Chang, James Y Zou, Venkatesh Saligrama, and Adam T Kalai. 2016. Man is to computer programmer as woman is to homemaker? debiasing word embeddings. In *Advances in neural information processing systems*, pages 4349–4357.

Aylin Caliskan, Joanna J Bryson, and Arvind Narayanan. 2017. Semantics derived automatically from language corpora contain human-like biases. *Science*, 356(6334):183–186.

Jacob Devlin, Ming-Wei Chang, Kenton Lee, and Kristina Toutanova. 2018. Bert: Pre-training of deep bidirectional transformers for language understanding. *arXiv preprint arXiv:1810.04805*.

Lucas Dixon, John Li, Jeffrey Sorensen, Nithum Thain, and Lucy Vasserman. 2018. Measuring and mitigating unintended bias in text classification. In *Proceedings of the 2018 AAAI/ACM Conference on AI, Ethics, and Society*, pages 67–73. ACM.

Sorelle A Friedler, Carlos Scheidegger, and Suresh Venkatasubramanian. 2016. On the (im) possibility of fairness. *arXiv preprint arXiv:1609.07236*.

S Michael Gaddis. 2017. How black are lakisha and jamal? racial perceptions from names used in correspondence audit studies. *Sociological Science*, 4:469–489.

Hila Gonen and Yoav Goldberg. 2019. Lipstick on a pig: Debiasing methods cover up systematic gender biases in word embeddings but do not remove them. In *North American Chapter of the Association for Computational Linguistics (NAACL)*.

C Hansen, M Tosik, G Goossen, C Li, L Bayeva, F Berbain, and M Rotaru. 2015. How to get the best word vectors for resume parsing. In *SNN Adaptive Intelligence/Symposium: Machine Learning*.

X. He and H. Jaeger. 2018. Overcoming catastrophic interference using conceptor-aided backpropagation. In *International Conference on Learning Representations*.

Dirk Hovy. 2015. Demographic factors improve classification performance. In *Proceedings of the 53rd Annual Meeting of the Association for Computational Linguistics and the 7th International Joint Conference on Natural Language Processing (Volume 1: Long Papers)*, volume 1, pages 752–762.

Dirk Hovy and Shannon L Spruit. 2016. The social impact of natural language processing. In *Proceedings of the 54th Annual Meeting of the Association for Computational Linguistics (Volume 2: Short Papers)*, volume 2, pages 591–598.

H. Jaeger. 2014. Controlling recurrent neural networks by conceptors. Technical report, Jacobs University Bremen.

Svetlana Kiritchenko and Saif Mohammad. 2018. Examining gender and race bias in two hundred sentiment analysis systems. In *Proceedings of the Seventh Joint Conference on Lexical and Computational Semantics*, pages 43–53. Association for Computational Linguistics.

Keita Kurita, Nidhi Vyas, Ayush Pareek, Alan W. Black, and Yulia Tsvetkov. 2019. Measuring bias in contextualized word representations.

T. Liu, J. Sedoc, and L. Ungar. 2018. Correcting the common discourse bias in linear representation of sentences using conceptors. In *Proceedings of ACM-BCB- 2018 Workshop on BioCreative/OHNLP Challenge, Washington, D.C., 2018*.

T. Liu, L. Ungar, and J. Sedoc. 2019a. Continual learning for sentence representations using conceptors. In *Proceedings of the NAACL HLT 2019*.

T. Liu, L. Ungar, and J. Sedoc. 2019b. Unsupervised post-processing of word vectors via conceptor negation. In *Proceedings of the Thirty-Third AAAI Conference on Artificial Intelligence (AAAI-2019), Honolulu*.

Chandler May, Alex Wang, Shikha Bordia, Samuel R Bowman, and Rachel Rudinger. 2019. On measuring social biases in sentence encoders. In *North American Chapter of the Association for Computational Linguistics (NAACL)*.

T. Mikolov, I. Sutskever, K. Chen, G. S. Corrado, and J. Dean. 2013. Distributed representations of words and phrases and their compositionality. In C. J. C. Burges, L. Bottou, M. Welling, Z. Ghahramani, and K. Q. Weinberger, editors, *Advances in Neural Information Processing Systems 26*, pages 3111–3119. Curran Associates, Inc.

J. Mu and P. Viswanath. 2018. All-but-the-top: Simple and effective postprocessing for word representations. In *International Conference on Learning Representations*.

Dan Jurafsky Nikhil Garg, Londa Schiebinger and James Zou. 2018. Word embeddings quantify 100 years of gender and ethnic stereotypes. *PNAS*.

J. Pennington, R. Socher, and C. D. Manning. 2014. Glove: Global vectors for word representation. In *Proceedings of EMNLP*, pages 1532–1543.

Matthew E. Peters, Mark Neumann, Mohit Iyyer, Matt Gardner, Christopher Clark, Kenton Lee, and Luke Zettlemoyer. 2018. Deep contextualized word representations. In *Proc. of NAACL*.

Rachel Rudinger, Jason Naradowsky, Brian Leonard, and Benjamin Van Durme. 2018. Gender bias in coreference resolution. *arXiv preprint arXiv:1804.09301*.

Tianlu Wang, Jieyu Zhao, Mark Yatskar, Ryan Cotterell, Vicente Ordonez, and Kai-Wei Chang. 2019. Gender bias in contextualized word embeddings. In *North American Chapter of the Association for Computational Linguistics (NAACL)*.

Mark Yatskar, Luke Zettlemoyer, and Ali Farhadi. 2016. Situation recognition: Visual semantic role labeling for image understanding. In *Proceedings of the IEEE Conference on Computer Vision and Pattern Recognition*, pages 5534–5542.

Brian Hu Zhang, Blake Lemoine, and Margaret Mitchell. 2018. Mitigating unwanted biases with adversarial learning. In *Proceedings of the 2018 AAAI/ACM Conference on AI, Ethics, and Society, AIES '18*, pages 335–340, New York, NY, USA. ACM.

Jieyu Zhao, Tianlu Wang, Mark Yatskar, Vicente Ordonez, and Kai-Wei Chang. 2017. Men also like shopping: Reducing gender bias amplification using corpus-level constraints. In *Proceedings of the 2017 Conference on Empirical Methods in Natural Language Processing*, pages 2979–2989.

Good Secretaries, Bad Truck Drivers?
Occupational Gender Stereotypes in Sentiment Analysis

Jayadev Bhaskaran
ICME, Stanford University, USA
jayadevbhaskaran@gmail.com

Isha Bhallamudi
Dept. of Sociology, UC Irvine, USA
isha.b@uci.edu

Abstract

In this work, we investigate the presence of occupational gender stereotypes in sentiment analysis models. Such a task has implications for reducing implicit biases in these models, which are being applied to an increasingly wide variety of downstream tasks. We release a new gender-balanced dataset[1] of 800 sentences pertaining to specific professions and propose a methodology for using it as a test bench to evaluate sentiment analysis models. We evaluate the presence of occupational gender stereotypes in 3 different models using our approach, and explore their relationship with societal perceptions of occupations.

1 Motivation

Social Role Theory (Eagly and Steffen, 1984) shows that our ideas about gender are shaped by observing, over time, the roles that men and women occupy in their daily lives. These ideas can crystallize into rigid stereotypes about how men and women ought to behave, and what work they can and cannot do. Gendered stereotypes are powerful precisely for this reason: they define desirable and expected traits, roles and behaviors in people, and go beyond description to prescription. Such biases from the social world, when they map onto machine learning models, serve to reinforce and propagate stereotypes further.

In this paper, we look specifically at occupational gender stereotypes in the context of sentiment analysis. Sentiment analysis is increasingly being applied for recruitment, employee retention and job satisfaction in the corporate world (Costa and Veloso, 2015). Given the prevalence of occupational gender stereotypes, our study primarily deals with the question of whether sentiment analysis models display and propagate these stereotypes. To contextualize and ground our study, we

---

[1]Link to dataset: https://bit.ly/2HLSKnf

first provide a summary of the relevant sociological literature on occupational gender stereotypes.

1.1 Background

Sociological studies as early as 1975 (Shinar, 1975) investigate gender stereotypes of occupations, and rank occupations in terms of how "masculine", "feminine" or neutral they are perceived to be. Cejka and Eagly (1999) successfully predicted the gender distribution of occupations based on beliefs about how specific *gender-stereotypical* attributes (such as "masculine physical") contribute to occupational success. Such beliefs - that success in a *male* dominated profession, for example, requires *male-specific* traits - directly contribute to sex segregation in occupations. The study also found that high occupational prestige and wages are *strongly correlated* with masculine images. Together, this goes to show that occupational structure is deeply shaped by gender. More recently, Haines et al. (2016) investigate how and whether gender stereotypes have changed between 1983 and 2014, and find conclusive evidence that occupational gender stereotypes have *persisted strongly* through the ages and remain stable. There is ample sociological evidence to show that occupational gender stereotypes have *not* undergone substantial modification since the entry of women into the workplace, and that they remain pervasive and widely held by both men *and* women (Glick et al., 1995; Haines et al., 2016).

Since occupational gender stereotypes are shaped by subjective factors and *not* objective reality, they remain resistant to contrary evidence. Theories such as the backlash hypothesis (Rudman and Phelan, 2008) further explain their persistence: this theory shows how women in the workplace must disconfirm female stereotypes in order to be perceived as competent leaders, yet traits of ambition and capability in women evoke negative

Proceedings of the 1st Workshop on Gender Bias in Natural Language Processing, pages 62–68
Florence, Italy, August 2, 2019. ©2019 Association for Computational Linguistics

reactions which present a barrier to every level of occupational success.

The implications of occupational gender stereotypes are profound. Children and adolescents are particularly sensitive to gendered language used to describe occupations and form rigid occupational gender stereotypes based on this (Vervecken et al., 2013). In adults, occupational gender stereotypes directly contribute to the existence of unequal compensation and discriminatory hiring. They also lead to self-fulling prophecies: for instance, individuals may not apply to certain jobs in the first place because they think they don't fit the gender stereotype for occupational success in that field (Kay et al., 2015).

In the following section, we discuss relevant prior work on gender bias from the NLP literature. In Section 3 we describe our methodology, dataset, and experiments in greater detail. In Section 4, we present and analyze our results, and finally, Section 5 describes possible directions of future work and concludes[2].

2   Prior Work

Word embeddings have been the bedrock of neural NLP models ever since the arrival of `word2vec` (Mikolov et al., 2013), and a variety of topics related to biases with word embeddings have been studied in prior literature. Garg et al. (2018) show the presence of stereotypes in word embeddings through the ages, while Bolukbasi et al. (2016) demonstrate explicit examples of social biases that are introduced into word embeddings trained on a large text corpus. Prior work has also dealt with occupational gender stereotypes in different areas of NLP. Caliskan et al. (2017) formulate a method to test biases (including gender stereotypes) in word embeddings, while Rudinger et al. (2018) investigate such stereotypes in the context of coreference resolution. There have also been efforts to *debias* word embeddings (Bolukbasi et al., 2016) and come up with *gender neutral* word embeddings (Zhao et al., 2018). These efforts, however, have attracted criticism suggesting that they do not actually *debias* embeddings but instead *redistribute* the bias across the embedding landscape (Gonen and Goldberg, 2019).

Recent trends have been towards replacing fixed word embeddings with large pretrained *contextual*

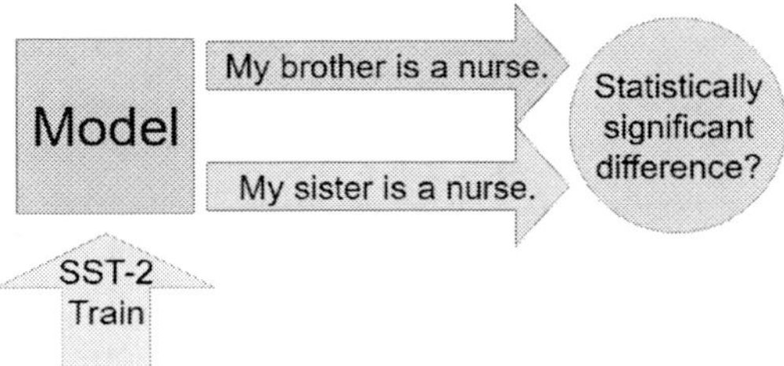

Figure 1: Simple diagram of our task definition.

representations as building blocks for NLP tasks. The rise of this paradigm is characterized by the use of language models for pretraining, exemplified by models such as ELMo (Peters et al., 2018), ULMFit (Howard and Ruder, 2018), GPT (Radford, 2018), and BERT (Devlin et al., 2018).

These models have shown marked improvements over word vector based approaches for a variety of tasks. However, their complexity leads to a tradeoff in terms of interpretability. Recent works have investigated gender biases in such deep contextual representations (May et al., 2019; Basta et al., 2019) as well as their applications to coreference resolution (Zhao et al., 2019; Webster et al., 2018); however, no prior work has dealt with such models in the context of occupational gender stereotypes in sentiment analysis.

Kiritchenko and Mohammad (2018) introduce the Equity Evaluation Corpus, a dataset used for measuring racial and gender biases in sentiment analysis-like systems. It was initially used to evaluate systems that predicted emotion and valence of Tweets (Mohammad et al., 2018). We use a similar approach to create a new dataset for measuring gender differences with a specific focus on occupational gender stereotypes. Our approach is *model-independent* and can be used for *any* sentiment analysis system, irrespective of model complexity.

3   Methodology

We create a dataset of 800 sentences, each with the following structure: **noun is a/an `profession`**. Here, `noun` corresponds to a *male* or *female* noun phrase, such as "This boy"/"This girl", and `profession` is one of 20 different professions. Each sentence is an assertion of fact, and by itself does not seek to exhibit either positive or negative sentiment. Our dataset is balanced across genders and has 20 noun phrases for each gender, leading to a total of 400 sentences per gender.

The rationale behind our selection of the 20 professions is to include a variety of gender distribution characteristics and occupation types, in correspondence with US Current Population Survey 2018 (CPS) data (Current Population Survey, 2018) and prior literature (Haines et al., 2016). We select 5 professions that are male-dominated (*truck driver, mechanic, pilot, chef, soldier*) and 5 that are female-dominated (*teacher, flight attendant, clerk, secretary, nurse*) - with domination meaning greater than 70% share in the job distribution. Next, we add professions that are slightly male-dominated (*scientist, lawyer, doctor*) and slightly female-dominated (*writer, dancer*), with slight domination meaning a $60 - 65\%$ share in the job distribution. We also add *professor*, which does not have a clear definition as per CPS but has been known to have different gender splits at senior and junior levels. Finally, we include two professions that show an approximately neutral divide (*tailor, gym trainer*) and two which have experienced significant changes in their gender distribution over time (*baker, bartender*), with an increasing female representation in recent times (Haines et al., 2016). As mentioned previously, we also select our set of occupations with an eye towards representing a range of occupation types.

We evaluate 3 sentiment analysis models through our experiments. Each model is trained on the Stanford Sentiment Treebank 2 `train` dataset (Socher et al., 2013), which contains phrases from movie reviews along with binary (0/1) sentiment labels. We then evaluate each model on our new corpus and measure the difference in mean predicted positive class probabilities between sentences with male nouns and those with female nouns. We test 3 hypotheses (one for each model), with the *null hypotheses* indicating *no difference* in means between sentences with *male* and *female* nouns. Fig. 1 illustrates our experimental setup.

Our evaluation methodology is very similar to that used in Kiritchenko and Mohammad (2018). For each system, we predict the positive class probability for each sentence. We then apply a *paired* t-test (since each pair contains a *male* and *female* version of the same template sentence) to measure if the mean predicted positive class probabilities are different across genders, using a significance level of 0.01. Since we test *three* hypotheses (one for each system), we apply Bonferroni correction (Bonferroni, 1936) to the p-values

that we obtain. In other words, the null hypothesis is rejected only for calculated p-values less than 0.01/3. We note that we do not perform any correction to account for the fact that the sentences within each gender are *not* iid, and only vary in the `noun` and `profession` words.

The 3 models that we evaluate are as follows:

- **M.1**: Bag-of-words + Logistic Regression (baseline): We build a simple bag-of-words model, apply tf-idf weighting, and use logistic regression (implemented using `scikit-learn` (Pedregosa et al., 2011)) to classify sentiment. This model is a very simple approach that has nevertheless been found to work well in practice for sentiment analysis tasks, and we use it as our baseline model.

- **M.2**: BiLSTM: We use a bidirectional LSTM implemented in `Keras` (Chollet et al., 2015) to predict sentiment. The words in a sentence are represented by 300-dimensional GloVe embeddings (Pennington et al., 2014). This model is more sophisticated than the baseline and captures some contextual information and long-term dependencies (Hochreiter and Schmidhuber, 1997). This model also allows us to investigate gender differences that might be introduced through word embeddings, as described in Bolukbasi et al. (2016).

- **M.3**: BERT (Devlin et al., 2018): We use a pretrained (uncased) BERT-Base model[3] and finetune it the SST-2 dataset. This shows near state-of-the-art performance on a wide variety of NLP tasks, including sentiment analysis (Devlin et al., 2018).

While analysing the results of our experiments, we measure overall predicted mean positive probabilities (across genders) for each of the 20 professions in our newly created dataset, to identify which professions are rated as *high-sentiment* by these models. This helps us investigate relationships between societal perceptions of occupations and corresponding sentiment predictions from the models.

We also examine differences in sentiment among equivalent gender pairs (such as *bachelor* and *spinster*) for the 20 pairs in our dataset, to investigate differences in predicted sentiment between different sets of male/female noun pairs.

---

[3]Model source: `https://bit.ly/2S8w6Jt`

Model	Dev Acc.	F - M
M.1 (BoW+LogReg)	0.827	0.035**
M.2 (BiLSTM)	0.841	0.077**
M.3 (BERT)	0.930	-0.040**

Table 1: Results. Dev Acc. represents accuracy on SST-2 `dev` set. **F - M** represents difference between means of predicted positive class probabilities for sentences with *female* nouns and sentences with *male* nouns. ** denotes statistical significance with $p < 0.01$ (after applying Bonferroni correction).

Model	Top 3 professions
BoW+LogReg	Secretary, Teacher, Writer
BiLSTM	Dancer, Secretary, Scientist
BERT	Scientist, Chef, Dancer
Model	**Bottom 3 professions**
BoW+LogReg	Truck Dr., Fl. Att., (many)
BiLSTM	Truck Dr., Gym Tr., Nurse
BERT	Truck Dr., Clerk, Tailor

Table 2: Top 3 and bottom 3 professions per model, based on predicted positive class probability (agnostic of gender). Note: For BoW+LogReg, (many) denotes all the professions that did not appear in the SST-2 `train` dataset.

Finally, we examine differences between *male* and *female* nouns for each individual occupation, to understand which occupations are susceptible to gender stereotyping.

4 Results/Analysis

The main results of our experiments are shown in Table 1. Our null hypothesis is that the predicted positive probabilities for *female* and *male* sentences have identical means. We notice that **M.1** (Bag-of-words + Logistic Regression) and **M.2** (BiLSTM) show a statistically significant difference between the two genders, with higher predicted positive class probabilities for sentences with *female* nouns. This effectively represents the biases seen in the SST-2 `train` dataset. The dataset has 1182 sentences containing a *male* noun with a mean sentiment of **0.535**, and 601 sentences containing a *female* noun with a mean sentiment of **0.599**. Thus, biases present in training data can get propagated through machine learning models, and our approach can help identify these.

On the contrary, **M.3** (BERT) shows that sentences with *male* nouns have a statistically significant higher predicted positive class probability than sentences with *female* nouns. One possible reason for this might be biases that propagate from the pretraining phase in BERT. This finding indicates a promising direction of future work: investigating the effects of gender biases in the large pretraining corpus versus those in the smaller fine-tuning corpus (in our case, the SST-2 `train` dataset).

4.1 Social Stereotypes of Occupations

We now look at mean distributions of positive class probability (across genders) for each profession, as shown in Table 2. We notice that *secretary* shows up as a high positive sentiment profession in both **M.1** and **M.2**. On further investigation, we notice that this artefact arises because of the 2002 movie *Secretary*, starring Maggie Gyllenhall, that has a number of positive reviews that form a part of the SST-2 `train` dataset. However, **M.3** (BERT) seems to be impervious to this, indicating that extensive pretraining could have the potential to remove certain corpus-specific effects that might have lingered in shallower models.

The profession with the lowest average sentiment score across all 3 models is *truck driver*; other low scoring professions include *clerk*, *gym trainer* and *flight attendant*. We also note that the highest scoring profession (average sentiment 0.99) with **M.3** (BERT) is *scientist* and the lowest (average sentiment 0.34) is *truck driver*, disturbingly reflective of societal stereotypes about white-collar and blue-collar jobs.

To explore this further, we look at data from the Current Population Survey of the US Bureau of Labor Statistics (Current Population Survey, 2018). Fig. 2 shows the relationship between median weekly earnings (for occupations where data is available) and average positive sentiment predicted by BERT. While there are some outliers, the figure shows a positive correlation between earnings and sentiment, indicating that the model may have incorporated societal perceptions around different occupations. We note that this is only a rough analysis, as not all occupations directly correspond to entries from the survey data.

4.2 Gendered Stereotypes

We attempt to analyze differences in gender within occupations by studying the predictions of **M.3** (BERT), which incorporates the largest amount

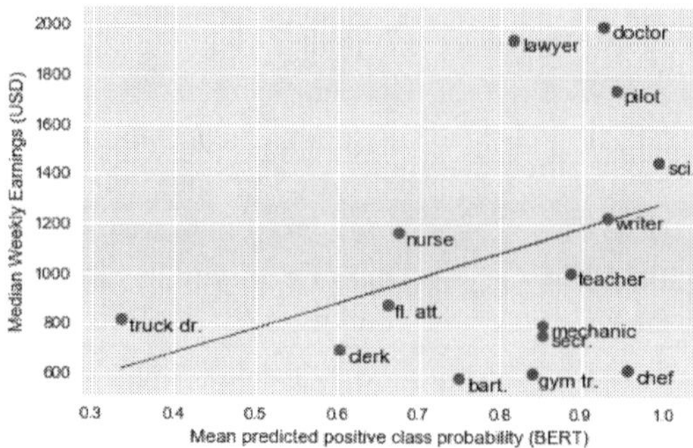

Figure 2: Median weekly earnings (Current Population Survey, 2018) vs. mean predicted positive probability using **M.3** (BERT), per profession.

of external data. First, we analyze differences in mean positive class probability between sentences with male and female nouns for each profession. We notice that *pilot* has the highest *positive* difference between female and male noun sentences (i.e., *female* is *higher*), while *flight attendant* has the *most negative* difference (i.e., *male* is *higher*). This provides an interesting dichotomy: *pilot* is a male-dominated profession, while *flight attendant* is a female-dominated one.

To test whether these are just artefacts of generic gender bias in the model or specific to occupational gendered stereotypes, we replace `profession` with "person" to create 20 sentence pairs such as "This man/this woman is a person.", and predict the sentiment for these 20 pairs. We notice that the difference between *female* and *male* noun sentences for the control experiment is **0.039**, showing that sentences with *female* nouns in the control group exhibit *higher* positive sentiment that those with *male* nouns. The three occupations with the most negative difference (i.e., *female* sentences have lower positive sentiment) are *flight attendant* (−**0.132**), *bartender* (−**0.126**), and *clerk* (−**0.116**). Of these, *flight attendant* (72%) and *clerk* (86%) are female-dominated professions (Current Population Survey, 2018), while *bartender* (55%) is a profession that has been shifting from male to female-dominated in recent times (Haines et al., 2016).

Finally, we study differences between corresponding pairs of female and male nouns, using predictions from **M.3** (BERT). Out of the 20 pairs in our dataset, the pair with the greatest difference in mean positive class probability is *spinster* and *bachelor*, with

spinster − bachelor = −**0.404** ($p < 0.01$). This reflects societal perceptions of *spinster* as someone who is characterized as alone, lonely and resembling an "old maid", versus *bachelor* as someone who might be young, carefree and fun-loving (Nieuwets, 2015). This is an example of *semantic pejoration* seen in society, where the female form of the noun (i.e., *spinster*) gradually acquires a negative connotation. Notably, this pejorative behavior may have also leaked into the model, reflecting societal gender stereotypes.

5 Conclusion/Future Work

In this paper, we introduce a new dataset that can be used to test the presence of occupational gender stereotypes in *any* sentiment analysis model. We then train 3 sentiment analysis models and evaluate them using our dataset. Following that, we analyze our results, exploring social stereotypes of occupations as well as gendered stereotypes. We find that all 3 models that we study exhibit differences in mean predicted positive class probability between genders, though the directions vary. We also see that simpler models may be more susceptible to biases seen in the training dataset, while deep contextual models may exhibit biases potentially introduced during pretraining.

One promising avenue for future work is to explore occupational stereotypes in deep contextual models by analyzing their training corpora. This could also help identify techniques to mitigate biases in such models, since they could be relatively impervious to biases introduced by fine-tuning (especially on smaller datasets).

From a sociological perspective, we plan to investigate occupational gender stereotypes in downstream applications such as automated resume screening. Such a task assumes greater importance with the increased use of these systems in today's world. There is prior work on ethnic bias in such tools (Derous and Ryan, 2018), and we believe that there is significant value in exploring and characterizing gender biases in these systems.

Acknowledgements

We thank Johan Ugander for helping motivate the initial phases of this work. We also thank the anonymous reviewers for their thoughtful feedback and suggestions.

References

Christine Basta, Marta R. Costa-jussà, and Noe Casas. 2019. Evaluating the Underlying Gender Bias in Contextualized Word Embeddings. *arXiv e-prints*.

Tolga Bolukbasi, Kai-Wei Chang, James Zou, Venkatesh Saligrama, and Adam Kalai. 2016. Man is to Computer Programmer As Woman is to Homemaker? Debiasing Word Embeddings. In *Proceedings of the 30th International Conference on Neural Information Processing Systems*, NIPS'16, pages 4356–4364, USA. Curran Associates Inc.

Carlo Bonferroni. 1936. Teoria statistica delle classi e calcolo delle probabilita. *Pubblicazioni del R Istituto Superiore di Scienze Economiche e Commericiali di Firenze*, 8:3–62.

Aylin Caliskan, Joanna J. Bryson, and Arvind Narayanan. 2017. Semantics derived automatically from language corpora contain human-like biases. *Science*, 356(6334):183–186.

Mary Ann Cejka and Alice H. Eagly. 1999. Gender-Stereotypic Images of Occupations Correspond to the Sex Segregation of Employment. *Personality and Social Psychology Bulletin*, 25(4):413–423.

François Chollet et al. 2015. Keras. https://keras.io.

Andre Costa and Adriano Veloso. 2015. Employee analytics through sentiment analysis. In *Brazilian Symposium on Databases*.

Current Population Survey. 2018. 39. Median weekly earnings of full-time wage and salary workers by detailed occupation and sex. Bureau of Labor Statistics, United States Department of Labor.

Eva Derous and Ann Marie Ryan. 2018. When your resume is (not) turning you down: Modelling ethnic bias in resume screening. *Human Resource Management Journal*, 29(2):113–130.

Jacob Devlin, Ming-Wei Chang, Kenton Lee, and Kristina Toutanova. 2018. BERT: Pre-training of Deep Bidirectional Transformers for Language understanding. *CoRR*, abs/1810.04805.

Alice H Eagly and Valerie J Steffen. 1984. Gender stereotypes stem from the distribution of women and men into social roles. *Journal of personality and social psychology*, 46(4):735.

Nikhil Garg, Londa Schiebinger, Dan Jurafsky, and James Zou. 2018. Word embeddings quantify 100 years of gender and ethnic stereotypes. *Proceedings of the National Academy of Sciences*, 115(16):E3635–E3644.

Peter Glick, Korin Wilk, and Michele Perreault. 1995. Images of occupations: Components of gender and status in occupational stereotypes. *Sex Roles*, 32(9):565–582.

Hila Gonen and Yoav Goldberg. 2019. Lipstick on a Pig: Debiasing Methods Cover up Systematic Gender Biases in Word Embeddings But do not Remove Them. *arXiv e-prints*.

Elizabeth L. Haines, Kay Deaux, and Nicole Lofaro. 2016. The Times They Are a-Changing... or Are They Not? A Comparison of Gender Stereotypes, 1983-2014. *Psychology of Women Quarterly*, 40(3):353–363.

Sepp Hochreiter and Jürgen Schmidhuber. 1997. Long Short-Term Memory. *Neural Comput.*, 9(8):1735–1780.

Jeremy Howard and Sebastian Ruder. 2018. Fine-tuned Language Models for Text Classification. *CoRR*, abs/1801.06146.

Matthew Kay, Cynthia Matuszek, and Sean A. Munson. 2015. Unequal representation and gender stereotypes in image search results for occupations. In *Proceedings of the 33rd Annual ACM Conference on Human Factors in Computing Systems*, CHI '15, pages 3819–3828, New York, NY, USA. ACM.

Svetlana Kiritchenko and Saif M. Mohammad. 2018. Examining gender and race bias in two hundred sentiment analysis systems. *CoRR*, abs/1805.04508.

Chandler May, Alex Wang, Shikha Bordia, Samuel R. Bowman, and Rachel Rudinger. 2019. On measuring social biases in sentence encoders.

Tomas Mikolov, Ilya Sutskever, Kai Chen, Greg S Corrado, and Jeff Dean. 2013. Distributed Representations of Words and Phrases and their Compositionality. In C. J. C. Burges, L. Bottou, M. Welling, Z. Ghahramani, and K. Q. Weinberger, editors, *Advances in Neural Information Processing Systems 26*, pages 3111–3119. Curran Associates, Inc.

Saif M. Mohammad, Felipe Bravo-Marquez, Mohammad Salameh, and Svetlana Kiritchenko. 2018. Semeval-2018 Task 1: Affect in Tweets. In *Proceedings of International Workshop on Semantic Evaluation (SemEval-2018)*, New Orleans, LA, USA.

Astrid Nieuwets. 2015. *Fallen Females: On the Semantic Pejoration of Mistress and Spinster*. Bachelor's thesis, Utrecht University.

F. Pedregosa, G. Varoquaux, A. Gramfort, V. Michel, B. Thirion, O. Grisel, M. Blondel, P. Prettenhofer, R. Weiss, V. Dubourg, J. Vanderplas, A. Passos, D. Cournapeau, M. Brucher, M. Perrot, and E. Duchesnay. 2011. Scikit-learn: Machine learning in Python. *Journal of Machine Learning Research*, 12:2825–2830.

Jeffrey Pennington, Richard Socher, and Christopher D. Manning. 2014. Glove: Global Vectors for Word Representation. In *Empirical Methods in Natural Language Processing (EMNLP)*, pages 1532–1543.

Matthew E. Peters, Mark Neumann, Mohit Iyyer, Matt Gardner, Christopher Clark, Kenton Lee, and Luke Zettlemoyer. 2018. Deep contextualized word representations. *CoRR*, abs/1802.05365.

Alec Radford. 2018. Improving Language Understanding by Generative Pre-Training.

Rachel Rudinger, Jason Naradowsky, Brian Leonard, and Benjamin Van Durme. 2018. Gender bias in coreference resolution. *Proceedings of the 2018 Conference of the North American Chapter of the Association for Computational Linguistics: Human Language Technologies, Volume 2 (Short Papers)*.

Laurie A. Rudman and Julie E. Phelan. 2008. Backlash effects for disconfirming gender stereotypes in organizations. *Research in Organizational Behavior*, 28:61 – 79.

Eva H Shinar. 1975. Sexual stereotypes of occupations. *Journal of Vocational Behavior*, 7(1):99 – 111.

Richard Socher, Alex Perelygin, Jean Wu, Jason Chuang, Christopher Manning, Andrew Ng, and Christopher Potts. 2013. Recursive Deep Models for Semantic Compositionality Over a Sentiment Treebank. In *Proceedings of the 2013 Conference on Empirical Methods in Natural Language Processing (EMNLP)*, pages 1631–1642.

Dries Vervecken, Bettina Hannover, and Ilka Wolter. 2013. Changing (S)expectations: How gender fair job descriptions impact children's perceptions and interest regarding traditionally male occupations. *Journal of Vocational Behavior*, 82(3):208 – 220.

Kellie Webster, Marta Recasens, Vera Axelrod, and Jason Baldridge. 2018. Mind the GAP: A Balanced Corpus of Gendered Ambiguous Pronouns. *Transactions of the Association for Computational Linguistics*, 6:605617.

Jieyu Zhao, Tianlu Wang, Mark Yatskar, Ryan Cotterell, Vicente Ordonez, and Kai-Wei Chang. 2019. Gender Bias in Contextualized Word Embeddings. *CoRR*, abs/1904.03310.

Jieyu Zhao, Yichao Zhou, Zeyu Li, Wei Wang, and Kai-Wei Chang. 2018. Learning Gender-Neutral Word Embeddings. *CoRR*, abs/1809.01496.

Debiasing Embeddings for Reduced Gender Bias in Text Classification

Flavien Prost[*]
fprost@google.com

Nithum Thain[*]
nthain@google.com

Tolga Bolukbasi
tolgab@google.com

Abstract

(Bolukbasi et al., 2016) demonstrated that pre-trained word embeddings can inherit gender bias from the data they were trained on. We investigate how this bias affects downstream classification tasks, using the case study of occupation classification (De-Arteaga et al., 2019). We show that traditional techniques for debiasing embeddings can actually worsen the bias of the downstream classifier by providing a less noisy channel for communicating gender information. With a relatively minor adjustment, however, we show how these same techniques can be used to simultaneously reduce bias and maintain high classification accuracy.

1 Introduction

A trend in the construction of deep learning models for natural language processing tasks is the use of pre-trained embeddings at the input layer (Mikolov et al., 2013; Pennington et al., 2014; Bojanowski et al., 2017). These embeddings are usually learned by solving a language modeling task on a large unsupervised corpus, allowing downstream models to leverage the semantic and syntactic relationships learned from this corpus. One issue with using such embeddings, however, is that the model might inherit unintended biases from this corpus. In (Bolukbasi et al., 2016), the authors highlight some gender bias at the embedding layer through analogy and occupational stereotyping tasks, but do not investigate how these biases affect modeling on downstream tasks. It has been argued (Gonen and Goldberg, 2019) that such debiasing approaches only mask the bias in embeddings and that bias remains in a form that downstream algorithms can still pick up.

This paper investigate the impact of gender bias in these pre-trained word embeddings on down-stream modeling tasks. We build deep neural network classifiers to perform occupation classification on the recently released "Bias in Bios" dataset (De-Arteaga et al., 2019) using a variety of different debiasing techniques for these embeddings introduced in (Bolukbasi et al., 2016) and comparing them to the scrubbing of gender indicators. The main contributions of this paper are:

- Comparing the efficacy of embedding based debiasing techniques to manual word scrubbing techniques on both overall model performance and fairness.

- Demonstrating that standard debiasing approaches like those introduced in (Bolukbasi et al., 2016) actually worsen the bias of downstream tasks by providing a denoised channel for communicating demographic information.

- Highlight that a simple modification of this debiasing technique which aims to completely remove gender information can simultaneously improve fairness criteria and maintain a high level of task accuracy.

2 Classification Task

This work utilizes the BiosBias dataset introduced in (De-Arteaga et al., 2019). This dataset consists of biographies identified within the Common Crawl. 397,340 biographies were extracted from sixteen crawls from 2014 to 2018. Biography lengths ranged from eighteen to 194 tokens and were labelled with one of twenty-eight different occupations and a binary gender (see Table 1 for a more detailed breakdown of statistics). The goal of the task is to correctly classify the subject's occupation from their biography. Each comment is assigned to our train, dev, and test split with probability 0.7, 0.15, and 0.15 respectively.

---

[*]Equal contribution.

Proceedings of the 1st Workshop on Gender Bias in Natural Language Processing, pages 69–75
Florence, Italy, August 2, 2019. ©2019 Association for Computational Linguistics

Occupation	Female Bios	Male Bios
accountant	3579	2085
architect	7747	2409
attorney	20182	12531
chiropractor	1973	705
comedian	2223	594
composer	4700	921
dentist	9573	5240
dietitian	289	3696
dj	1279	211
filmmaker	4712	2314
interior designer	282	1185
journalist	10110	9896
model	1295	6244
nurse	1738	17263
painter	4210	3550
paralegal	268	1503
pastor	1926	609
personal trainer	782	656
photographer	15669	8713
physician	20805	20298
poet	3587	3448
professor	65049	53438
psychologist	7001	11476
rapper	1274	136
software engineer	5837	1096
surgeon	11637	2023
teacher	6460	9813
yoga teacher	259	1408

Table 1: Dataset Statistics

In (De-Arteaga et al., 2019), this task is used to explore the level of bias present in three different types of models: a bag of words logistic regression, a word embedding logistic regression, and a bi-directional recurrent neural network with attention. The models are trained with two different tokenization strategies, i.e. with and without scrubbing gender indicators like pronouns. We will use the two variants of the deep neural network model as a baseline in this work.

3 Debiasing Methodology

3.1 Debiasing Word Embeddings

Our DNN models use 100 dimensional normalized GloVe embeddings (Pennington et al., 2014) at the input layer. (Bolukbasi et al., 2016) showed through analogy and occupational stereotyping tasks that such embeddings contain instances of

direct and indirect bias. They also provide a technique that can be used to remove this bias as measured by this task. In this section, we review the specifics of this technique.

The first step to produce debiased word embeddings from our input GloVe embeddings $\{\vec{w} \in \mathbb{R}^d\}$ is to define a collection of word-pairs $D_1, ..., D_n$ which can be used to identify the gender subspace. For this work, we use the same input word pairs as (Bolukbasi et al., 2016). The k-dimensional gender subspace B is then defined to be the first k rows of the singular value decomposition of

$$\frac{1}{2} \sum_{i=1}^{n} \sum_{\vec{w} \in D_i} (\vec{w} - \mu_i)^T (\vec{w} - \mu_i)$$

where $\mu_i := \sum_{\vec{w} \in D_i} \vec{w}/2$. For our experiments, we set $k = 1$.

The next step is to modify the embedding of a set of "neutral" (i.e. non-gendered) words N by projecting them orthogonally to the gender subspace. If we let $\vec{w}_B$ denote the projection of a word embedding $\vec{w}$ orthogonally to the gender subspace B then this would be equivalent to, for all neutral word vectors $\vec{w} \in N$, changing their embedding to:

$$\vec{w} := \vec{w}_B / \|\vec{w}_B\| .$$

The final step in the algorithm is to define a collection of equality sets $E_1, ..., E_m$ of words which we believe should differ only in the gender component. For our purposes we use all the word pairs used in (Bolukbasi et al., 2016) as well as the sets of words that are scrubbed in (De-Arteaga et al., 2019). For each E_i we equalize by taking the mean $\mu = \sum_{\vec{w} \in E_i} \vec{w}/|E_i|$ and projecting that orthogonally to the gender subspace to obtain μ_B. The new embeddings for each word in the equalize set $\vec{w} \in E_i$ can then be set to

$$\mu_B + \sqrt{1 - \|\mu_B\|^2} \frac{\vec{w_B}}{\|\vec{w_B}\|} .$$

To compute these debiased embeddings, we build on the github library[1] provided by the authors of (Bolukbasi et al., 2016).

3.2 Strong Debiasing

In the original work, (Bolukbasi et al., 2016) differentiate between neutral words in the set N and

[1] https://github.com/tolga-b/debiaswe

gender specific words, removing the gender subspace component of the former while preserving it for the latter. While this appears to be a good strategy for maintaining the maximum semantic information in the embeddings while removing as much biased gender information as possible, we show in Sections 5 and 6 that, by providing a clear channel to communicate gender information, this technique can make the gender bias worse in downstream modeling tasks.

To mitigate this effect, we study *strongly debiased embeddings*, a variant of the algorithm in the previous section where we simply set N to be all of the words in our vocabulary. In this case, all words including those typically associated with gender (e.g. he, she, mr., mrs.) are projected orthogonally to the gender subspace. This seeks to remove entirely the gender information from the corpus while still maintaining the remaining semantic information about these words. It should be noted that for words in our equalize sets, i.e. those that differ only by gender, this results in all the words within one set being embedded to the same vector. As we will see in Section 5, this results in an improved performance over techniques like scrubbing which remove this semantic information entirely and disrupt the language model of the input sentence. In Section 6.3, we also perform ablation studies to show how important each of the steps in the algorithm is to achieving high accuracy with low bias.

4 Evaluation Metrics

We will evaluate our models on the dimensions of overall performance and fairness. For the overall performance of these models, we will use the standard accuracy metric of multi-class classification. There are a number of metrics and criteria that offer different interpretations of model fairness (Dixon et al., 2018; Narayanan, 2018; Friedler et al., 2019; Beutel et al., 2019). In this work, we use the method introduced by (Hardt et al., 2016) as Equality of Opportunity.

If your data has binary labels Y and some demographic variable A, in our case whether the biography is about a female, then Equality of Opportunity is defined as

$$\Pr\{\hat{Y} = 1 | Y = 1, A = 1\} = \Pr\{\hat{Y} = 1 | Y = 1, A = 0\}.$$

i.e. the true positive rate of the model should be independent of the demographic variable conditioned on the true label.

In order to measure deviation from this ideal criteria we follow a number of other authors (Garg et al., 2019) and define the True Positive Rate Gap (TPR_{gap}) to be:

$$|\Pr\{\hat{Y} = 1 | Y = 1, A = 1\} - \Pr\{\hat{Y} = 1 | Y = 1, A = 0\}|.$$

Since in our context, we are dealing with a multi-class classifier, we will measure the TPR_{gap} for each class as a separate binary decision and will aggregate by averaging over all occupations.

We can analogously define the TNR_{gap} with the True Negative Rates taking the place of True Positive Rates in the above discussion. We will also report the average TNR_{gap} across occupations.

5 Experiments

To understand how the embedding layer affects our deep learning classifiers, we will train classifiers with a variety of embeddings. As baselines, we will use the GloVe embeddings with and without the gender indicator scrubbing described in (De-Arteaga et al., 2019). Additionally, we train a classifier on GloVe embeddings debiased using both techniques discussed in Section 3. These embeddings are fixed (rather than trainable) parameters of our network. For each of these models, we evaluate their classification performance (accuracy) alongside their overall fairness (TPR_{gap}).

5.1 Model architecture

Our architecture follows the DNN approach used in (De-Arteaga et al., 2019). After tokenization and embedding, we encode the input sentence with a bidirectional Recurrent Neural Network with GRU cells and extract the sentence representation by applying an attention layer over the bi-RNN outputs. After a dense layer with Relu activation, we compute a logit for each class via a linear layer. We use the softmax cross-entropy to compute the loss.

All hyper parameters were tuned for the standard GloVe model and the optimal values were used for the subsequent runs.

5.2 Scrubbing explicit gender indicators

As a baseline with which to compare embedding based debiasing, we implement the scrubbing technique described in (De-Arteaga et al., 2019),

Embedding	Acc.	TPR_{gap}	TNR_{gap}
GloVe	0.818	0.091	0.0031
Scrubbed	0.804	0.070	0.0024
Debiased	0.807	0.119	0.0037
Strongly debiased	0.817	0.069	0.0023

Table 2: Model metrics

Embedding	Accuracy
GloVe	0.86
Scrubbed	0.68
Debiased	0.88
Strong Debiased	0.66

Table 3: Gender classifier accuracy

which consists of preprocessing the text by removing explicit gender indicators. To provide a fair comparison, we scrub explicit gender indicators that combine all the equalizing pairs used in (Bolukbasi et al., 2016) as well as the sets of words that are scrubbed in (De-Arteaga et al.,2019).

5.3 Results

Our results are displayed in Table 2 which records the values of accuracy, TPR_{gap} and TNR_{gap} for each model. We focus on the TPR_{gap} as our primary fairness metric but the results still hold if the TNR_{gap} is used instead.

As we can see, the strongly debiased model performs best overall. It reduces the bias (-.022 TPR_{gap}) slightly more than the scrubbed technique (-.021 TPR_{gap}). However, it has a much smaller cost to classification accuracy than scrubbing (-0.1% vs -1.4%) as the embeddings still retain most of the semantic and syntactic information about the words in the comment.

Our results also indicate that using debiased embeddings has a counter-productive effect on bias as they significantly increase the TPR_{gap}. We explore this further in the next section.

6 Analysis

In this section, we provide some analysis to explain our experimental results. First, we look at the sentence representation of each model and measure how much gender information it contains. We confirm empirically that both strongly debiasing and scrubbing techniques reduce the gender information that is used by the model. Secondly, we explain why using debiased embeddings does not reduce the amount of bias in the classification task and highlight how the algorithm for strongly debiasing addresses this issue. Finally, we explore the relative importance of the two components of the debiasing algorithm: projection and equalization.

6.1 Connecting bias to gender information

The debiasing techniques studied in this paper all modify the way the gender information is fed to the model. The scrubbed technique masks the explicit gender indicators, the debiased algorithm reduces the indirect gender bias in the embeddings and the strongly debiased approach aims at removing the gender component in them entirely.

We investigate how each of these embeddings affect the amount of gender information available to the model for occupation classification. To that end, after each model is trained on occupation labels, we train a separate logistic classifier that takes as input the sentence representation of the previous model (i.e. the last layer before the logits) and predicts the gender of the subject of the biography. We keep the remaining model layers frozen so that we do not change the representation of the sentence. The accuracy of these gender classifiers (reported in Table 3) provide a measure of the amount of gender information contained in each of our models.

We see that the representation of the baseline GloVe model keeps a significant amount of gender information, allowing for a gender classification accuracy of 0.86. With strongly debiased embeddings, the model representation contains much less gender information than the GloVe model and slightly less than scrubbing out the gender indicators. This suggests that both scrubbing and strong debiasing are effective at reducing the amount of gender information the overall model is able to capture, which explains the fairer occupational classifications. Debiased embeddings, on the other hand, slightly increase the gender information that the model can learn. In the next section, we investigate this phenomenon further.

6.2 Impact of debiasing on the gender component

The above experiments show that debiased embeddings cause models to act "less fairly" than

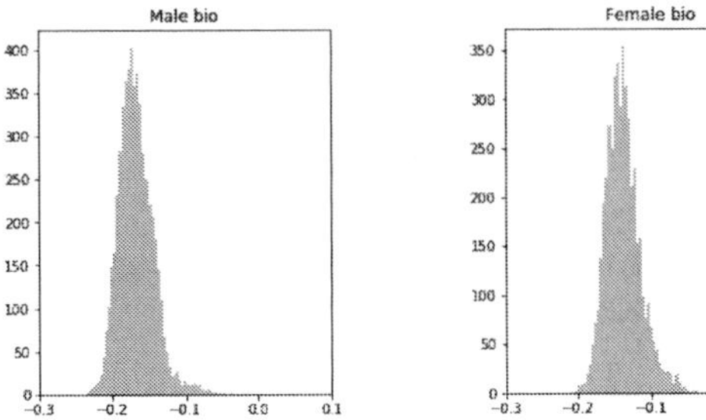

Figure 1: Gender component of a biography

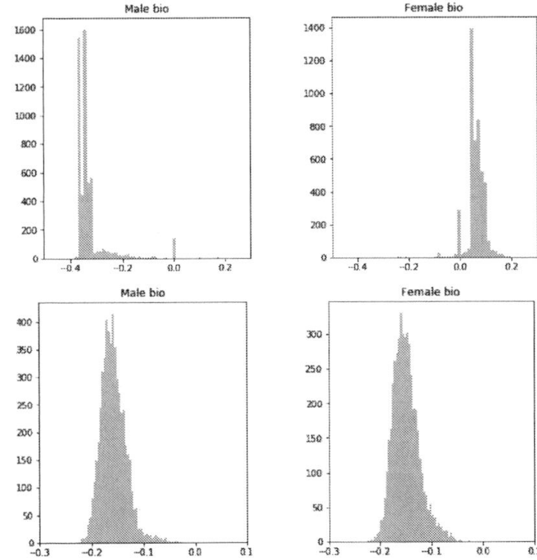

Figure 2: Gender component of a biography based on gender specific words (top) and based on neutral words (bottom)

standard Glove embeddings (20% higher TPR_{gap}) by allowing them to better represent the gender of the subject of the biography. We hypothesize that this is due to an undesirable side-effect of the debiasing algorithm introduced in Section 3.1: it clarifies information coming from gender specific words by removing the noise from coming neutral words and therefore makes it easier for the model to communicate gender features.

To validate this hypothesis, we run the following analysis. Beginning with the standard GloVe embeddings, we define the gender component of a word as its projection on the gender direction and the gender component of a biography to be the average gender component of all the words it contains.

Figure 1 is a histogram of the gender component of the biographies in our data. A negative value means that the gender component of the biography is more male than female. We observe that, surprisingly, all biographies have a negative gender component [2].

As expected, male biographies have a slightly more negative gender component on average than female biographies (-.166 vs -.138), which indicates that they include words that are more associated with male concepts. However, both distributions have a high variance and they are therefore not clearly separable. This plot indicates that, with standard GloVe embeddings, the gender component of a biography is only a weak signal for its gender.

Figure 2 is a histogram of the gender components of biographies which distinguishes the gender-specific words (top) and the neutral words (bottom). We see that the gender component based on gender specific words gives a clear separa-

tion between male and female biographies, with a threshold at 0, whereas the distribution for neutral words (bottom) has more noise and does not clearly indicate the gender of the biography. Interestingly, for neutral words, the average gender component for male biographies is lower than for female ones (-.159 vs -.148), which indicates some indirect bias.

As about 95% of the words of a biography are neutral, its gender component is mostly driven by this set of words and not by the gender-specific ones. This explains why the plot in Figure 1 has a noisy distribution without any clear gender separation. In other words, when using regular Glove embeddings, the neutral words are actually masking the clearer signal coming from gender specific words.

This analysis provides some explanation for the counter-intuitive impact of debiased embeddings. By construction, they remove the gender component of neutral words and leave unchanged that of gender specific words. While this is desirable for analogy tasks, using these embeddings in a text classifier actually allows the model to easily identify the gender of a biography and potentially learn a direct relationship between gender and occupation. On the opposite end, strongly debiased embeddings remove the entire signal and make it harder for the classifier to learn any such relationship.

---

[2] By comparing to other large datasets, we've established that this is an idiosyncrasy of the BiosBias dataset, which overall contains words with a more male gender component.

Embeddings	Acc.	TPR_{gap}	TNR_{gap}
GloVe	0.818	0.091	0.0031
Strongly debias	0.817	0.069	0.0023
Project only	0.815	0.103	0.0032
Equalize only	0.817	0.080	0.0029

Table 4: Ablation study: Metrics for projection and equalization step

6.3 Ablation analysis of debiasing

As mentioned in Section 3.1, the algorithm for strongly debiasing includes two successive steps. First, we project all words orthogonally to the gender subspace. Then we equalize the non-gender part of a predefined list of pairs. We conducted an ablation study to analyze the impact of each step separately. More precisely, we train one model *project only* where we project all the words orthogonally to the gender direction and another one *equalize only* where we equalize all pairs - which is equivalent to replacing each element of a pair by the mean vector.

Results are displayed in Table 4. We observe that the equalization step has the strongest impact in bias reduction, while the projection is inefficient when used separately. We hypothesize that the projection is not able to correctly handle the explicit gender indicator words and therefore leaves too much direct bias. However both combined as in the strong debias technique provide the best results.

7 Conclusion

In this paper, we investigate how debiased embeddings affect both performance and fairness metrics. Our experiments reveal that debiased embeddings can actually worsen a text classifier's fairness, whereas strongly debiased embeddings can reduce gender information and improve fairness while maintaining good classification performance. As these embeddings provide a simple tool that can be injected as is within model architectures, they do not result in much additional burden for ML practitioners (e.g. model tweaks, labelled data). In the future, we would like to confirm that this approach generalizes to a variety of datasets and to other identity groups.

References

Alex Beutel, Jilin Chen, Tulsee Doshi, Hai Qian, Allison Woodruff, Christine Luu, Pierre Kreitmann, Jonathan Bischof, and Ed H Chi. 2019. Putting fairness principles into practice: Challenges, metrics, and improvements. *arXiv preprint arXiv:1901.04562*.

Piotr Bojanowski, Edouard Grave, Armand Joulin, and Tomas Mikolov. 2017. Enriching word vectors with subword information. *Transactions of the Association for Computational Linguistics*, 5:135–146.

Tolga Bolukbasi, Kai-Wei Chang, James Y Zou, Venkatesh Saligrama, and Adam T Kalai. 2016. Man is to computer programmer as woman is to homemaker? debiasing word embeddings. In *Advances in neural information processing systems*, pages 4349–4357.

Maria De-Arteaga, Alexey Romanov, Hanna Wallach, Jennifer Chayes, Christian Borgs, Alexandra Chouldechova, Sahin Geyik, Krishnaram Kenthapadi, and Adam Tauman Kalai. 2019. Bias in bios: A case study of semantic representation bias in a high-stakes setting. In *Proceedings of the Conference on Fairness, Accountability, and Transparency*, pages 120–128. ACM.

Lucas Dixon, John Li, Jeffrey Sorensen, Nithum Thain, and Lucy Vasserman. 2018. Measuring and mitigating unintended bias in text classification. In *Proceedings of the 2018 AAAI/ACM Conference on AI, Ethics, and Society*, pages 67–73. ACM.

Sorelle A Friedler, Carlos Scheidegger, Suresh Venkatasubramanian, Sonam Choudhary, Evan P Hamilton, and Derek Roth. 2019. A comparative study of fairness-enhancing interventions in machine learning. In *Proceedings of the Conference on Fairness, Accountability, and Transparency*, pages 329–338. ACM.

Sahaj Garg, Vincent Perot, Nicole Limtiaco, Ankur Taly, H Chi, and Alex Beutel. 2019. Counterfactual fairness in text classification through robustness. In *Proceedings of the 2019 AAAI/ACM Conference on AI, Ethics, and Society*. ACM.

Hila Gonen and Yoav Goldberg. 2019. Lipstick on a pig: Debiasing methods cover up systematic gender biases in word embeddings but do not remove them. *arXiv preprint arXiv:1903.03862*.

Moritz Hardt, Eric Price, Nati Srebro, et al. 2016. Equality of opportunity in supervised learning. In *Advances in neural information processing systems*, pages 3315–3323.

Tomas Mikolov, Kai Chen, Greg Corrado, and Jeffrey Dean. 2013. Efficient estimation of word representations in vector space. *arXiv preprint arXiv:1301.3781*.

Arvind Narayanan. 2018. Translation tutorial: 21 fairness definitions and their politics. In *Proc. Conf. Fairness Accountability Transp., New York, USA*.

Jeffrey Pennington, Richard Socher, and Christopher Manning. 2014. Glove: Global vectors for word representation. In *Proceedings of the 2014 conference on empirical methods in natural language processing (EMNLP)*, pages 1532–1543.

BERT Masked Language Modeling for Co-reference Resolution

Felipe Alfaro Lois　　**José A. R. Fonollosa**　　**Marta R. Costa-jussà**
TALP Research Center
Universitat Politècnica de Catalunya, Barcelona
`felipe.alfaro@est.fib.upc.edu`
`jose.fonollosa,marta.ruiz}@upc.edu`

Abstract

This paper explains the TALP-UPC participation for the Gendered Pronoun Resolution
shared-task of the 1st ACL Workshop on Gender Bias for Natural Language Processing. We
have implemented two models for mask language modeling using pre-trained BERT ad-
justed to work for a classification problem.
The proposed solutions are based on the word
probabilities of the original BERT model, but
using common English names to replace the
original test names.

1 Introduction

The Gendered Pronoun Resolution task is a natural language processing task whose objective is
to build pronoun resolution systems that identify
the correct name a pronoun refers to. It's called
a co-reference resolution task. Co-reference resolution tackles the problem of different elements
of a text that refer to the same thing. Like for example a pronoun and a noun, or multiple nouns
that describe the same entity. There are multiple
deep learning approaches to this problem. NeuralCoref [1] presents one based on giving every pair
of mentions (pronoun + noun) a score to represent
whether or not they refer to the same entity. In our
current task, this approach is not possible, because
we don't have the true information of every pair of
mentions, only the two names per entry.

The current task also has to deal with the problem of gender. As the GAP researchers point
out (Webster et al., 2018), the biggest and most
common datasets for co-reference resolution have
a bias towards male entities. For example the
OntoNotes dataset, which is used for some of the
most popular models, only has a 25% female representation (Pradhan and Xue, 2009). This creates

a problem, because any machine learning model
is only as good as its training set. Biased training
sets will create biased models, and this will have
repercussions on any uses the model may have.

This task provides an interesting challenge specially by the fact that it is proposed over a gender
neutral dataset. In this sense, the challenge is ori-
ented towards proposing methods that are gender-
neutral and to not provide bias given that the data
set does not have it.

To face this task, we propose to make use of the
recent popular BERT tool (Devlin et al., 2018).
BERT is a model trained for masked language
modeling (LM) word prediction and sentence prediction using the transformer network (Vaswani
et al., 2017). BERT also provides a group of pre-
trained models for different uses, of different languages and sizes. There are implementations for
it in all sorts of tasks, including text classification,
question answering, multiple choice question answering, sentence tagging, among others. BERT
is gaining popularity quickly in language tasks,
but before this shared-task appeared, we had no
awareness of its implementation in co-reference
resolution. For this task, we've used an implementation that takes advantage of the masked LM
which BERT is trained for and uses it for a kind of
task BERT is not specifically designed for.

In this paper, we are detailing our shared-task
participation, which basically includes descriptions on the use we gave to the BERT model and
on our technique of 'Name Replacement' that allowed to reduce the impact of name frequency.

2 Co-reference Resolution System Description

2.1 BERT for Masked LM

This model's main objective is to predict a word
that has been masked in a sentence. For this exer-

---

[1] https://medium.com/huggingface/state-of-the-art-
neural-coreference-resolution-for-chatbots-3302365dcf30

76

cise that word is the pronoun whose referent we're trying to identify. This one pronoun gets replaced by the *[MASKED]* tag, the rest of the sentence is subjected to the different name change rules described in section 2.2.

The text is passed through the pre-trained BERT model. This model keeps all of its weights intact, the only changes made in training are to the network outside of the BERT model. The resulting sequence then passes through what is called the masked language modeling head. This consists of a small neural network that returns, for every word in the sequence, an array the size of the entire vocabulary with the probability for every word. The array for our masked pronoun is extracted and then from that array, we get the probabilities of three different words. These three words are : the first replaced name (name 1), the second replaced name (name 2) and the word *none* for the case of having none.

This third case is the strangest one, because the word *none* would logically not appear in the sentence. Tests were made with the original pronoun as the third option instead. But the results ended up being very similar albeit slightly worse, so the word none was kept instead. These cases where there is no true answer are the hardest ones for both of the models.

We experimented with two models.

Model 1 After the probabilities for each word are extracted, the rest is treated as a classification problem. An array is created with the probabilities of the 2 names and *none* (*[name 1, name 2, none]*), where each one represents the probability of a class in multi-class classification. This array is passed through a softmax function to adjust it to probabilities between 0 and 1 and then the log loss is calculated. A block diagram of this model can be seen in figure 1.

Model 2 This model repeats the steps of model 1 but for two different texts. These texts are mostly the same except the replacement names *name 1* and *name 2* have been switched (as explained in the section 2.2). It calculates the probabilities for each word for each text and then takes an average of both. Then finally applies the softmax and calculates the loss with the average probability of each class across both texts. A block diagram of this model can be seen in figure 2.

2.2   Name Replacement

The task contains names of individuals who are featured in Wikipedia, and some of these names are uncommon in the English language. As part of the pre-processing for both models, these names are replaced. They are replaced with common English names in their respective genders[2]. If the pronoun is female, one of two common English female names are chosen, same thing for the male pronouns. In order to replace them in the text, the following set of rules are followed.

1. The names mentioned on the A and B columns are replaced.

2. Any other instances of the full name as it appears on the A/B columns are replaced.

3. If the name on the A/B column contains a first name and a last name. Instances of the first name are also replaced. Unless both entities share a first name, or the first name of one is contained within the other.

4. Both the name and the text are converted to lowercase

This name replacement has two major benefits. First, the more common male and female names work better with BERT because they appear more in the corpus in which it is trained on. Secondly, when the word piece encoding splits certain words the tokenizer can be configured so that our chosen names are never split. So they are single tokens (and not multiple word pieces), which helps the way the model is implemented.

Both models (1 and 2 presented in the above section) use BERT for Masked LM prediction where the mask always covers a pronoun, and because the pronoun is a single token (not split into word pieces), it's more useful to compare the masked pronoun to both names, which are also both single tokens (not multiple word pieces).

Because the chosen names are very common in the English language, BERT's previous training might contain biases towards one name or the other. This can be detrimental to this model where it has to compare between only 3 options. So the alternative is the approach in model number 2. In model 2 two texts are created. Both texts are basically the same except the names chosen as the

---

[2]https://www.ef.com/wwen/english-resources/english-names/

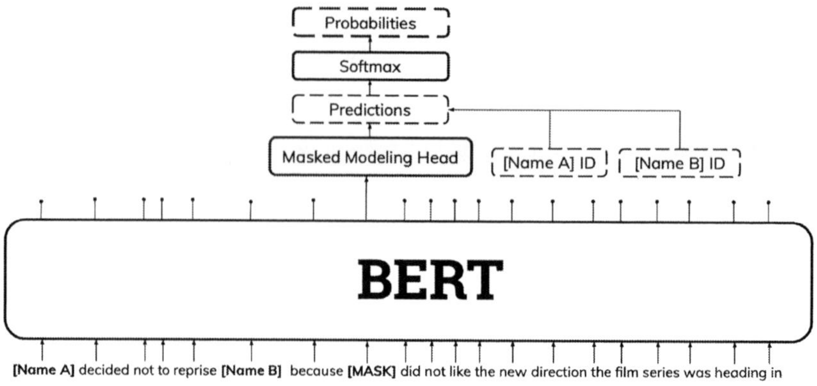

Figure 1: Model 1 representation.

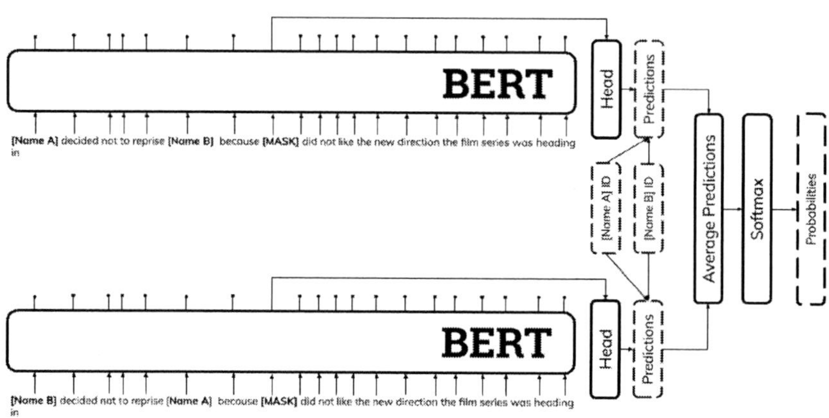

Figure 2: Model 2 representation.

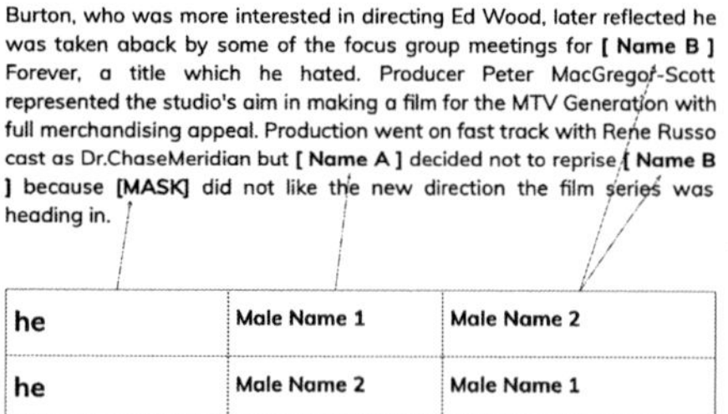

| he | Male Name 1 | Male Name 2 |
| he | Male Name 2 | Male Name 1 |

Figure 3: Example of a text present in the dataset and how the word replacement was done for the model 2.

replacement names 1 and 2 are switched. So, as figure 3 shows, we get one text with each name in each position.

For example lets say we get the text:

"In the late 1980s Jones began working with Duran Duran on their live shows and then in the studio producing a B side single "This Is How A Road Gets Made", before being hired to record the album Liberty with producer Chris Kimsey.",

A is *Jones* and B is *Chris Kimsey*. For the name replacement lets say we choose two common English names like **John** and **Harry**. The new text produced for model 1 (figure 1) would be something like:

*"in the late 1980s **harry** began working with duran duran on their live shows and then in the studio producing a b side single "this is how a road gets made", before being hired to record the album liberty with producer **john**."*

And for model 2 (figure 2) the same text would be used for the top side and for the bottom side it would have the harry and john in the opposite positions.

3 Experimental Framework

3.1 Task details

The objective of the task is that of a classification problem. Where the output for every entry is the probability of the pronoun referencing name A, name B or Neither.

3.2 Data

The GAP dataset (Webster et al., 2018) created by Google AI Language was the dataset used for this task. This dataset consists of 8908 co-reference labeled pairs sampled from Wikipedia, also it's split perfectly between male and female representation. Each entry of the dataset consists of a short text, a pronoun that is present in the text and its offset and two different names (name A and name B) also present in the text. The pronoun refers to one of these two names and in some cases, none of them. The GAP dataset doesn't contain any neutral pronouns such as *it* or *they*.

For the two different stages of the competition different datasets were used.

- For **Stage 1** the data used for the submission is the same as the development set available in the GAP repository. The dataset used for training is the combination of the GAP validation and GAP testing sets from the repository.

- For **Stage 2** the data used for submission was only available through Kaggle[3] and the correct labels have yet to be released, so we can only analyze the final log loss of each of the models. This testing set has a total of 12359 rows, with 6499 male pronouns and 5860 female ones. For training, a combination of the GAP development, testing and validation sets was used. And, as all the GAP data, it is evenly distributed between genders.

The distributions of all the datasets are shown in table 1. It can be seen that in all cases, the *None* option has the least support by a large margin. This, added to the fact that the model naturally is better suited to identifying names rather than the absence of them, had a negative effect on the results.

[3]https://www.kaggle.com/c/gendered-pronoun-resolution/overview

	Stage 1		Stage 2
	Train	Test	Train
Name A	1105	874	1979
Name B	1060	925	1985
None	289	201	490

Table 1: Dataset distribution for the datasets of stages 1 and 2.

3.3 Training details

For the BERT pre-trained weights, several models were tested. BERT base is the one that produced the best results. BERT large had great results in a lot of other implementations, but in this model it produced worse results while consuming much more resources and having a longer training time. During the experiments the model had an overfitting problem, so the learning rate was tuned as well as a warm up percentage was introduced. As table 2 shows, the optimal learning rate was $3e - 5$ while the optimal with a 20% warm up. The length of the sequences is set at 256, where it fits almost every text without issues. For texts too big, the text is truncated depending on the offsets of each of the elements in order to not eliminate any of the names or the pronoun.

Learning Rate	Warmup	Accuracy mean	min	Loss mean	min
0.00003	**0.0**	0.840167	0.8315	0.519565	0.454253
	0.2	0.844444	0.8340	0.502667	0.442313
0.00004	**0.0**	0.822389	0.7970	0.556491	0.473528
	0.2	0.834000	0.7925	0.530862	0.456223
0.00005	**0.1**	0.743500	0.7435	0.666750	0.666750
0.00006	**0.0**	0.756333	0.7040	0.630707	0.544841
	0.2	0.802278	0.7465	0.587041	0.497051

Table 2: Results of the tuning for both models. Minimum and average Loss and Accuracy across all the tuning experiments performed.

The training was performed in a server with an Intel Dual Core processor and Nvidia Titan X GPUs, with approximately 32GB of memory. The run time varies a lot depending on the model. The average run time on the stage 1 dataset for model 1 is from 1 to 2 hours while for model 2 it has a run time of about 4 hours. For the training set for stage 2, the duration was 4 hours 37 minutes for model 1 and 8 hours 42 minutes for model 2. The final list of hyperparameters is in table 3.

Parameter	Value
Optimizer	Adam
Vocabulary Size	28996
Dropout	0.1
Sequence Length	256
Batch Size	32
Learning Rate	$3e-5$
Warm Up	20%
Steps	Stage 1: 81 — Stage 2: 148
Epochs	1
Gradient Accumulation Steps	5

Table 3: Hyperparameters for the model training

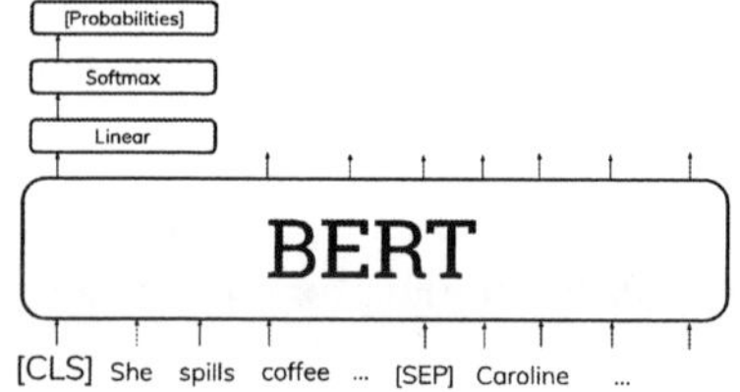

Figure 4: Model: BERT for text classification

4 Results

Tables 4 and 5 report results for models 1 and 2 reported in section 2.1 for stage 1 of the competition. Both models 1 and 2 have similar overall results. Also both models show problems with the None class, model 2 specially. We believe this is because our model is based on guessing the correct name, so the guessing of none is not as well suited to it. Also, the training set contains much less of these examples, therefore making it even harder to train for them.

	Precision	Recall	F1	Support
A	0.83	0.87	0.85	874
B	0.88	0.88	0.88	925
None	0.64	0.52	0.57	201
Avg	**0.83**	**0.84**	**0.84**	**2000**

Table 4: Model 1 results for the testing stage 1.

	Precision	Recall	F1	Support
A	0.81	0.86	0.83	874
B	0.88	0.78	0.82	925
None	0.48	0.62	0.54	201
Avg	**0.81**	**0.80**	**0.80**	**2000**

Table 5: Model 2 results for the testing stage 1.

4.1 Advantages of the Masked LM Model

As well as the Masked LM, other BERT implementations were experimented with for the task. First, a text multi class classification model (figure 4) where the *[CLS]* tag is placed at the beginning of every sentence, the text is passed through a pretrained BERT and then the result from this label is passed through a feed forward neural network.

And a multiple choice question answering model (figure 5), where the same text with the

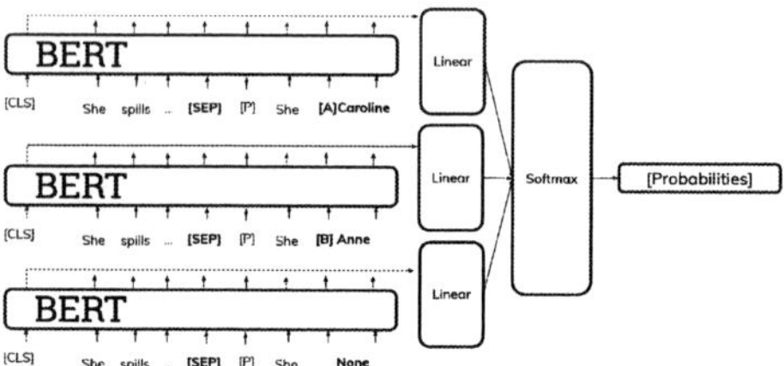

Figure 5: Model: BERT for multiple choice answering

[CLS] label is passed through BERT with different answers and then the result these labels is passed through a feed forward neural network.

These two models, which were specifically designed for other tasks had similar accuracy to the masked LM but suffered greatly with the log loss, which was the competition's metric. This is because in a lot of examples the difference between the probabilities of one class and another was minimal. This made for a model where each choice had low confidence and therefore the loss increased considerably.

	Accuracy	Loss
BERT for Classification	0.8055	0.70488
BERT for Question Answering	0.785	0.6782
BERT for Masked LM	*0.838*	*0.44231*

Table 6: Results for the tests with different BERT implementations.

4.2 Name Replacement Results

As table 2.2 shows, name replacement considerably improved the model's results. This is in part because the names chosen as replacements are more common in BERT's training corpora. Also, a 43% of the names across the whole GAP dataset are made up of multiple words. So replacing these with a single name makes it easier for the model to identify their place in the text.

	Accuracy	Loss
Model 1 Original Names	0.782	0.7021
Model 1 Name Replacement	0.838	0.4423

Table 7: Results for the models with and without name replacement.

4.3 Competition results

In the official competition on Kaggle we placed 46th, with the second model having a loss around 0.301. As the results in table 8 show, the results of stage 2 were better than those of stage 1. And the second model, which had performed worse on the first stage was better in stage 2.

	Model 1	Model 2
Stage 1	0.44231	0.49607
Stage 2	0.31441	0.30151

Table 8: Results for both models across both stages of the competition

5 Conclusions

We have proved that pre-trained BERT is useful for co-reference resolution. Additionally, we have shown that our simple 'Name Replacement' technique was effective to reduce the impact of name frequency or popularity in the final decision.

The main limitation of our technique is that it requires knowing the gender from the names and so it only makes sense for entities which have a defined gender. Our proposed model had great results when predicting the correct name but had trouble with with the *none* option.

As a future improvement it's important to analyze the characteristics of these examples where none of the names are correct and how the model could be trained better to identify them, specially because they are fewer in the dataset. Further improvements could be made in terms of fine-tuning the weights in the actual BERT model.

Acknowledgements

This work is also supported in part by the Spanish Ministerio de Economía y Competitividad, the European Regional Development Fund and the Agencia Estatal de Investigación, through the postdoctoral senior grant Ramón y Cajal, contract TEC2015-69266-P (MINECO/FEDER,EU) and contract PCIN-2017-079 (AEI/MINECO).

References

Jacob Devlin, Ming-Wei Chang, Kenton Lee, and Kristina Toutanova. 2018. Bert: Pre-training of deep bidirectional transformers for language understanding. *arXiv preprint arXiv:1810.04805*.

Sameer S. Pradhan and Nianwen Xue. 2009. OntoNotes: The 90% solution. In *Proceedings of Human Language Technologies: The 2009 Annual Conference of the North American Chapter of the Association for Computational Linguistics, Companion Volume: Tutorial Abstracts*, pages 11–12, Boulder, Colorado. Association for Computational Linguistics.

Ashish Vaswani, Noam Shazeer, Niki Parmar, Jakob Uszkoreit, Llion Jones, Aidan N Gomez, Ł ukasz Kaiser, and Illia Polosukhin. 2017. Attention is all you need. In I. Guyon, U. V. Luxburg, S. Bengio, H. Wallach, R. Fergus, S. Vishwanathan, and R. Garnett, editors, *Advances in Neural Information Processing Systems 30*, pages 5998–6008. Curran Associates, Inc.

Kellie Webster, Marta Recasens, Vera Axelrod, and Jason Baldridge. 2018. Mind the GAP: A balanced corpus of gendered ambiguous pronouns. *Transactions of the Association for Computational Linguistics*, 6:605–617.

Transfer Learning from Pre-trained BERT for Pronoun Resolution

Xingce Bao[*]
School of Engineering, EPFL
Switzerland
xingce.bao@epfl.ch

Qianqian Qiao[*]
School of Engineering, EPFL
Switzerland
qianqian.qiao@epfl.ch

Abstract

The paper describes the submission of the team "We used bert!" to the shared task Gendered Pronoun Resolution (Pair pronouns to their correct entities). Our final submission model based on the fine-tuned BERT (Bidirectional Encoder Representations from Transformers) (Devlin et al., 2018) ranks 14th among 838 teams with a multi-class logarithmic loss of 0.208. In this work, contribution of transfer learning technique to pronoun resolution systems is investigated and the gender bias contained in classification models is evaluated.

1   Introduction

The shared task Gendered Pronoun Resolution aims to classify the pronoun resolution in the sentences, hereby to find the true name referred by a given pronoun, such as **she** in:

*In May, **Fujisawa** joined Mari Motohashi's rink as the team's skip, moving back from Karuizawa to Kitami where **she** had spent her junior days.*

This task for pronoun resolution closely relates to the traditional coreference resolution task in natural language processing. Many works (Wiseman et al., 2016; Clark and Manning, 2016; Lee et al., 2017) related to coreference resolution have been published recently and all of them are evaluated with CoNLL-2012 shared task dataset (Pradhan et al., 2012). However, simply pursuing the best score over the entire dataset may cause the neglect of the model performance gap between the two genders.

To explore the existence of gender bias in such tasks, researchers from Google built and released GAP (Gendered Ambiguous Pronouns) (Webster et al., 2018), a human-labeled corpus of 8908 ambiguous pronoun-name pairs derived

from Wikipedia with balanced gender pronouns. It has been shown that most of the recent representative coreference systems struggled on GAP dataset with a overall mediocre performance and a large performance gap between genders. This may be due to both unbalanced training dataset used by these coreference systems or the design of the systems. Up to now, detecting and eliminating gender bias in such systems still remains a challenge.

In this paper, we explore transfer learning from pre-trained models to improve the performance of tasks with limited data. Various efficient approaches to reuse the knowledge from pre-trained BERT on this shared task are proposed and compared. The final system significantly outperforms the off-the-shelf resolvers, with a balanced prediction performance for two genders. Moreover, gender bias in word and sentence level embeddings is studied with a scientific statistical experiment on Caliskan dataset (Caliskan et al., 2017).

2   Data

This shared task is based on GAP dataset including:

- Test 4,000 pairs: used for official evaluation

- Development 4,000 pairs: used for model development

- Validation 908 pairs: used for parameter tuning

In the first stage, we use part of the released data on Google GAP Github repository, which includes 2000 development pairs, 2000 test pairs, and 454 validation pairs.[1] We refer the test pairs as training

---

[*]Both authors contributed equally in this work.

[1]The testing data from the Kaggle website is the development data in the GAP github repository. So we use the development pairs to evaluate our model, and the test pairs to train in order to conform the Kaggle competition rule.

Proceedings of the 1st Workshop on Gender Bias in Natural Language Processing, pages 82–88
Florence, Italy, August 2, 2019. ©2019 Association for Computational Linguistics

data, the development pairs as testing data and the validation pairs as validation data. Each sample contains a sentence and three mentions, A, B and pronoun. Each pronoun has been labeled as A, B, or NEITHER. Submissions are evaluated using the multi-class logarithmic loss.

Table 1 shows the frequency of the different types of pronouns in the dataset. The number of masculine pronouns and feminine pronouns are strictly equal.

Pronoun type	Training	Test	Validation
he	348	373	93
him	96	98	26
his	556	529	108
her	603	572	140
hers	1	0	0
she	396	428	87
masculine	1000	1000	227
feminine	1000	1000	227

Table 1: Pronoun gender frequency

3 Data Preparation

We introduced the procedure for processing the data before training in detail in this section.

3.1 Data Preprocessing

Data preprocessing can be summarized into the following steps:

BERT embeddings generation: We use pre-trained bert-large-uncased model to obtain contextual embeddings as features. This part is implemented with the bert-as-service library based on Tensorflow (Xiao, 2018).

Dimension reduction: The dimension reduction for the original BERT contextual embeddings is performed to mitigate the overfitting problems. This approach is inspired by the Algorithm 2 (PPA-PCA-PPA) proposed in Raunak (2017).

For large scale vectors with dimension of 1024, instead of directly using PCA (principal component analysis), we train a linear autoencoder to approximate the linear PCA procedure. Namely, we train the autoencoder by minimizing the loss:

$$L(X, W_1, W_2) = ||X - W_2 W_1 X||_2^2, \quad (1)$$

where X is the contextual embedding. W_1 and W_2 are $m \times n$ and $n \times m$ matrices to project vectors to lower dimensional space and recover from

lower dimensional space, respectively ($m < n$). Hence, the PCA part in the original algorithm is performed by computing $W_1 X$, and the PPA part in the original algorithm is performed by computing $X - W_2 W_1 X$.

Here the PPA procedures remove the first 4 principal components. The PCA procedure maps 1024 dimension vectors to 256 dimension vectors.

Processing mention: A mention in the data (A, B or the pronoun) can be a single word or multiple words. Also, since BERT is based on the word piece model (Wu et al., 2016), a word may be cut into multiple word pieces after the BERT tokenization. We define the mention index as the index for the tokenized word piece list which corresponds to the original mention.

The vectors in the BERT contextual embeddings which correspond to the mention index are extracted. Meanwhile, vectors of mentions are the mean value of all the vectors which correspond to the mention. We call this mention vector.

Find names: All names in the sentences except A and B are extracted with the named entity recognition tool. After that, their mention indices are found by the same procedure in the previous step. We call these indices neither mention index. Stanford Named Entity Tagger is used for finding the names in the sentences in this step (Finkel et al., 2005).

An example of tokenization and mention index is shown in table 2.

Sentence: When asked in a 2010 interview with The Mirror what **her** favourite scenes were, **Beverley Callard** replied, "when Jim beat up **Liz**.
Names Except A and B: Jim
Tokens: ['when', 'asked', 'in', 'a', '2010', 'interview', 'with', 'the', 'mirror', 'what', **'her'**, 'favourite', 'scenes', 'were', ',', **'beverley'**, **'call'**, **'##ard'**, 'replied', ',', ' "', ' "', 'when', 'jim', 'beat', 'up', **'liz'**, '.']
Mention A: Beverley Callard   **Mention B: Liz**   **Mention Pronoun: her**   **Mention Neither: Jim**
A Mention Index: 15,16,17   **B Mention Index: 26**   **Pronoun Mention Index: 10**   **Neither Mention Index: 23**

Table 2: An example of tokenization and mention index

3.2 Data Augmentation

We replace the originally referred mention by a different random mention in the sentence, then change the label to neither. This creates 1445 samples labeled neither from training data. Original training data together with augmented neither data make up the augmented training set.

4 Architecture

We mainly explored two sub-categories of models as shown in figure 1. One category is based on fine-tuned BERT with different top layers. For this category, Back-propagation is done to both top layers and the pre-trained BERT model. Another idea is to use BERT as a feature extractor. Different from fine-tuned BERT, models in the second category do not back propagate to BERT weights during training. All of these base models contribute to our final model.[2]

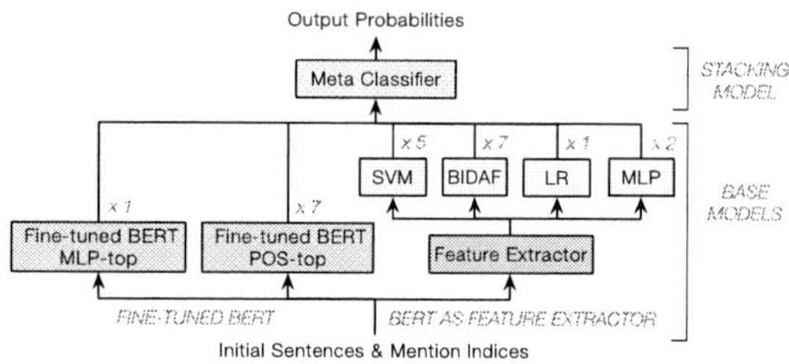

Figure 1: Structure of the final system. It contains 23 base models with different structures, different embedding dimensions and data whether augmented.

4.1 Fine-tuned BERT

We propose two different kinds of top layers to fine-tune BERT model on GAP task and implemented with PyTorch Pretrained BERT library(Hugging-Face, 2018). The first kind of top layer shown in figure 2 is called MLP-top. It extracts and aggregates vectors for all mentions by concatenation, which are then fed into a multiple layer neural network.

The second kind of top layer first map the output of BERT into a scalar by a linear layer whose output size is 1. Then we extract the value corresponding to the mention index and feed it into a softmax layer for a 3-class-probability-output. We call this Positional-top which is illustrated in Figure 3.[3]

---

[2]Due to the space limit, we do not explain all the base models that we use to produce the final ensemble model in detail. The models in the following description are only efficient and representative base models. For a comprehensive list of the base models we use, please check: `https://github.com/bxclib2/kaggle_gender_coref/`

[3]Both figure 2 and figure 3 show the mentions which contain only a single word-piece after tokenization. If one men-

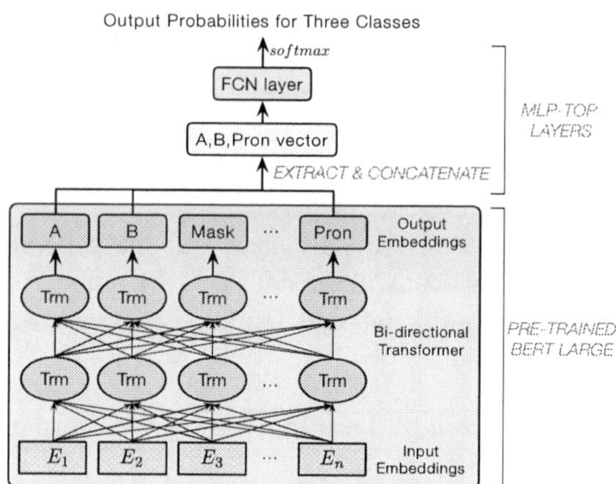

Figure 2: Fine-tuned BERT with MLP-top layer

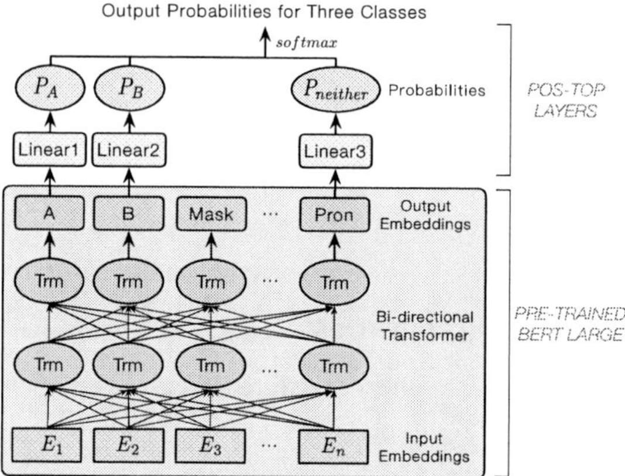

Figure 3: Fine-tuned BERT with Positional-top layer. Linear layers for A,B and Pronoun are with the same parameter.

4.2 BERT as Feature Extractor

When BERT is used as a feature extractor, the contextual embeddings and the mention vectors prepared are passed to the subsequent classifier. Here we use SVM (support vector machine) and BIDAF (bi-directional attention flow layer) (Seo et al., 2017) as classifiers.

SVM: We denote the mention vector of A, B and pronoun as h_A, h_B and h_{pron}. The vector:

$$[h_A, h_B, h_{pron}, h_A \odot h_{pron}, h_B \odot h_{pron}] \quad (2)$$

is fed as the input of the SVM, where the $\odot$ means point-wise product. The multiclass support is handled according to a one-vs-one scheme. The SVM

---

tion contains multiple word-pieces, the mean of the multiple positions in BERT output layer should be computed in order to generate a tensor with desired size to be fed into the top layer.

classifier is implemented with Scikit-Learn library (Pedregosa et al., 2011).

BIDAF: BERT contextual embeddings and the pronoun mention vectors are passed to the bi-directional attention flow layer as the context and the query, respectively. We use the original embedding extracted from BERT large with embedding dimension of 1024 here. Then a two-layer point-wise fully-connected neural network is connected to map the output embedding vectors to scalars. The fully-connected layer has 64 hidden units with ELU as activation function (Djork-Arn Clevert, 2016). Finally, the scalars corresponding to the A, the B and the neither are fed into a softmax layer to generate 3-class probabilities.

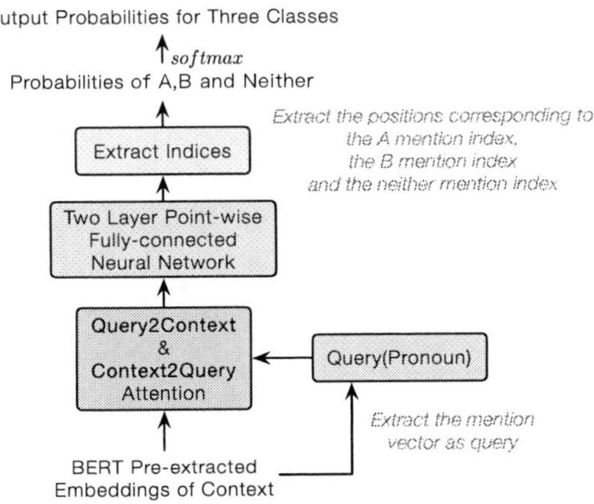

Figure 4: Structure of BIDAF network

The top layer of BIDAF network works similarly to the positional head of the fine-tuned BERT. However, there are two major differences: the positional head of the fine-tuned BERT uses only a linear layer to map the embeddings to scalars, while the BIDAF network uses a two-layer neural network with the ELU activation layer. Also, the output of BIDAF is from the positions corresponding to the A, the B and the neither mention respectively, while the BERT positional head extracts the scalars corresponding to the A, the B and the pronoun mention respectively.

4.3 Model Ensemble

Ensemble learning greatly improves the results compared to single models. Stacking method is used for ensemble. During ensemble, several base classifiers are trained to make preliminary predictions, and a meta classifier is used to make a final prediction based on these predictions.

In order to reduce the data leakage, 5-fold cross validation is performed when building the training data for the meta classifier from the original training data. In other words, we avoid the base classifiers and meta classifier to be trained with the same fold of data (Beaudon, 2016). For each training time 4-fold of data is used to train, and the resulting model predicts the remaining one fold of data to build one fold of training data for the meta classifier, as shown in figure 5. Here we use the logistic regression as the meta classifier.

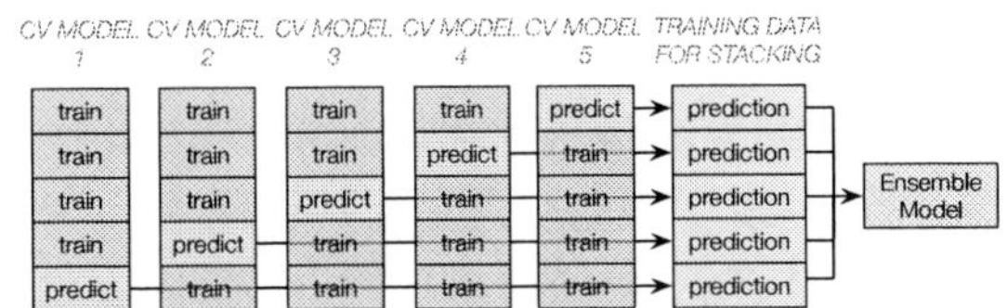

Figure 5: 5-Fold cross validation for stacking

5 Experiment

In this section, we present the result of different classifiers to the shared task.

5.1 Experiment setting

For SVM, C equals to 5.0 and the kernel function is the RBF function. The SVM is trained both with the original 1024 dimension mention vectors and the 256 dimension-reduced mention vectors respectively for comparison.

The BIDAF network is trained for 50 epoches with a batch size of 25. We use the Adam optimizer with a learning rate of 1e-3 for training. For each fully-connected layer in BIDAF, a dropout with probability 0.7 is performed. It is trained both with the original training set and the augmented training set for comparison. This training process takes about 10 minutes with the GTX 1070 GPU.

The fine-tuned BERT models are trained with the Adam optimizer with a learning rate of 2e-5. All the dropout layers in the original BERT model are set to a dropout rate of 0.15. Models are trained for 1 epoch with a batch size of 16. Note that it is not possible to fit 16 training sentences at one time due to the limited GPU memory. Hence, gradient accumulation trick is used. Every time we fit 2 training sentences and we accumulate the gradient for 8 times. This fine-tuning process takes about 10 minutes with the Tesla K80 GPU.

The meta classifier is the logistic regression with l_2 regularization of the regularization constant C which equals to 0.5.

5.2 Evaluation

The results are shown in table 3. The masculine data loss and feminine data loss are shown respectively in order to show the gender bias. We compute the model loss for testing data (stage 1) and the loss caused by the masculine part and the feminine part in stage 1 testing data. We also submit our base model results after the competition finishes in order to get the private testing data (stage 2) loss.

	M	F	T	PT
SVM 256	0.516	0.495	0.506	0.395
SVM 1024	0.619	0.574	0.596	0.475
BIDAF	0.490	0.498	0.494	0.364
BIDAF-aug	0.550	0.579	0.565	0.422
BERT-pos	0.376	0.377	0.377	**0.280**
BERT-mlp	**0.360**	**0.365**	**0.362**	0.351
Ensemble	**0.325**	**0.337**	**0.331**	**0.208**

Table 3: Evaluation results (multi-class logarithmic loss) for models. SVM 256: SVM trained with the mention vector after dimension reduction. SVM 1024: SVM trained with the original 1024 dimension mention vector. BIDAF: BIDAF trained with the original training set. BIDAF-aug: BIDAF trained with the augmented training set. BERT-pos: Fine-tuned BERT with the Positional-top. BERT-mlp: Fine-tuned BERT with the MLP-top. **M**asculine, **F**eminine, **T**esting data and **P**rivate **T**esting data results are shown respectively. Bold indicates the best performance.

We derive the following conclusions:

- The dimension reduction greatly enhances the result of SVM which reduces about 0.1 multi-class logarithmic loss. The SVM 1024 has a loss of 0.184 and 0.597 with respect to training and testing data, while the SVM 256 has a loss of 0.250 and 0.505. Both SVM model overfit a lot, while the dimension reduction of BERT contextual embeddings efficiently mitigate overfitting, which bridges the performance gap between training data and testing data.

- The BIDAF model performs worse when trained with the augmented training set than the original training set, due to the distribution mismatching caused by data augmenta-

tion that, the portion of the neither data is larger in the training set than in the testing set.

- Both two fine-tuned BERT models achieve much more competitive results compared to Bert as Feature Extractor models.[4]

- The ensemble learning with logistic regression greatly enhances the overall classification result.

Although the data augmentation does not improve the BIDAF model directly, it still helps to make more accurate predictions of the neither class in the ensemble model. The BIDAF-aug and the BIDAF reach the loss of 0.982 and 1.095, respectively. In the testing data (stage 1), the respective accuracy of A, B and neither class is 89.8%, 89.5% and 73.1%, indicating that predicting the neither class correctly is much harder than predicting A and B. We can observe that it is easier for the model to choose an answer as A or B than to predict as no reference.

We also evaluate our system F1 score with stage 1 testing dataset to compare to the off-the-shelf resolvers in table 4:

	M	F	B	O
Wiseman et al.	68.4	59.9	0.88	64.2
Lee et al.	67.2	62.2	0.92	64.7
BERT-pos	**86.8**	**86.1**	0.99	**86.5**
BERT-mlp	86.3	85.9	**1.00**	86.1
Our ensemble	**88.1**	**87.9**	**1.00**	**88.0**

Table 4: Comparison to off-the-shelf resolvers, split by **M**asculine and **F**eminine (**B**ias shows F/M), and **O**verall. Bold indicates the best performance.

6 Gender Bias in the Embeddings

To further demonstrate the presence or absence of gender bias in embeddings, we use both the Word Embedding Association Test (WEAT) (Caliskan et al., 2017) and Sentence Embedding Association Test (SEAT) (May et al., 2019) to measure it. As fine-tuned BERT large models with Positional-top contribute a lot to our final ensemble model, we only focus on this category of models in this section.

---

[4]Here the experiment shows that the MLP-top is slightly better than the Positional-top. However, the Positional-top is more stable with different random seeds. Also it is obvious that the MLP-top performs worse than the Positional-top in the private testing data.

6.1 WEAT & SEAT

For both word-level test and sentence level test, let X and Y be two sets of target concept word or sentence embeddings, and let A and B be two sets of attribute word embeddings. The test statistic is the difference between sums of similarities of the respective attributes over target concepts, which can be calculated as:

$$s(X, Y, A, B) = \sum_{x \in X} s(x, A, B) - \sum_{y \in Y} s(y, A, B), \tag{3}$$

where:

$$s(w, A, B) = \text{mean}_{a \in A} \cos(w, a) - \text{mean}_{b \in B} \cos(w, b), \tag{4}$$

the p-values on $s(X, Y, A, B)$ is used to compute the significance between (A, B) and (X, Y),

$$p = \Pr[s(X_i, Y_i, A, B) > s(X, Y, A, B)], \tag{5}$$

where X_i and Y_i are of equal size. Also the effect size d is used to measure the magnitude of associations:

$$d = \frac{\text{mean}_{x \in X} s(x, A, B) - \text{mean}_{y \in Y} s(y, A, B)}{\text{std\_dev}_{w \in X \cup Y} s(w, A, B)} \tag{6}$$

6.2 Experiments and Results

We apply WEAT and SEAT on Caliskan Test of male/female names with career and family, which corresponds to past social psychology studies.

Method	GloVe	ELMo	BERT	F-BERT
WEAT	1.81*	−0.45	0.21	0.38
SEAT	1.74*	−0.38	0.08	0.07

Table 5: Effect sizes for male/female names with career/family task with word and sentence level embeddings. *: significant at 0.01. F-BERT indicates Fine-tuned BERT.

Table 5 shows the result of WEAT and SEAT. Sentence vectors are aggregated by taking the mean value of all word vectors in the sentences for GloVe (Pennington et al., 2014), ELMo (Peters et al., 2018), BERT and Fine-tuned BERT.[5] With p-values lower than 0.01, embeddings by GloVe

on both word level and sentence level show significant gender bias, indicating that women are associated with family while men are associated with career.

However, p-values of all contextual embeddings including ELMo, BERT and Fined-tuned BERT are larger than 0.05, which suggests that there is no evidence suggesting existence of gender bias in these embeddings. One possible explanation is that, by training contextual word embeddings, a single word is usually represented differently in different sentences, resulting in more flexible word representations focusing on single context within a sentence rather than the overall word frequency distribution.

7 Conclusion and Future Work

We propose a transfer-learning-based solution for pronoun resolution. The proposed solution leads to gender balance in both word embeddings and overall predictions. It greatly improves the prediction accuracy of this task by 23.3% F1 against the off-the-shelf solutions proposed by Lee et al. (2017) on the widely studied Google GAP dataset. Meanwhile, among several single models in our ensemble solution, BERT-mlp and BERT-pos model highly outperform others in the experiments. Overall this work shows the efficacy of employing BERT in downstream natural language processing classification tasks.

In the future, we would like to investigate various transfer structures on the top of pre-trained BERT, especially for the sake of enhancing the stability of the fine-tune process. We observe in our experiments that the performance of fine-tune models based on BERT strongly depends on initial random state, thus, further research on building more robust models is indispensable.

Acknowledgments

We thank for Wanhao Zhou, Siyuan Li, Fengyu Cai for useful discussions. We also thank Ruocheng Han, Tian Guo, Xi Fan and Jirou Feng for feedback and writing help.

References

Romain Beaudon. 2016. Cross validation strategy when blending/stacking. https://www.kaggle.com/general/18793.

---

[5] Here we use a different method to aggregate sentence vector for BERT, comparing to the cited paper which uses [CLS] vector as sentence vector for better comparison.

Aylin Caliskan, Joanna Bryson, and Arvind Narayanan. 2017. Semantics derived automatically from language corpora contain human-like biases. *Science*, 356:183–186.

Kevin Clark and Christopher D. Manning. 2016. Improving coreference resolution by learning entity-level distributed representations. In *Proceedings of the 54th Annual Meeting of the Association for Computational Linguistics (Volume 1: Long Papers)*, pages 643–653, Berlin, Germany. Association for Computational Linguistics.

Jacob Devlin, Ming-Wei Chang, Kenton Lee, and Kristina Toutanova. 2018. Bert: Pre-training of deep bidirectional transformers for language understanding. *Computing Research Repository*, arXiv:1810.04805. Version 1.

Sepp Hochreiter Djork-Arn Clevert, Thomas Unterthiner. 2016. Fast and accurate deep network learning by exponential linear units (elus). In *International Conference on Learning Representations*.

Jenny Rose Finkel, Trond Grenager, and Christopher Manning. 2005. Incorporating non-local information into information extraction systems by Gibbs sampling. In *Proceedings of the 43rd Annual Meeting of the Association for Computational Linguistics (ACL'05)*, pages 363–370, Ann Arbor, Michigan. Association for Computational Linguistics.

Hugging-Face. 2018. pytorch-pretrained-bert. `https://github.com/huggingface/pytorch-pretrained-BERT`.

Kenton Lee, Luheng He, Mike Lewis, and Luke Zettlemoyer. 2017. End-to-end neural coreference resolution. In *Proceedings of the 2017 Conference on Empirical Methods in Natural Language Processing*, pages 188–197, Copenhagen, Denmark. Association for Computational Linguistics.

Chandler May, Alex Wang, Shikha Bordia, Samuel R. Bowman, and Rachel Rudinger. 2019. On measuring social biases in sentence encoders. *Computing Research Repository*, arXiv:1903.10561. Version 1.

F. Pedregosa, G. Varoquaux, A. Gramfort, V. Michel, B. Thirion, O. Grisel, M. Blondel, P. Prettenhofer, R. Weiss, V. Dubourg, J. Vanderplas, A. Passos, D. Cournapeau, M. Brucher, M. Perrot, and E. Duchesnay. 2011. Scikit-learn: Machine learning in Python. *Journal of Machine Learning Research*, 12:2825–2830.

Jeffrey Pennington, Richard Socher, and Christopher Manning. 2014. Glove: Global vectors for word representation. In *Proceedings of the 2014 Conference on Empirical Methods in Natural Language Processing (EMNLP)*, pages 1532–1543, Doha, Qatar. Association for Computational Linguistics.

Matthew Peters, Mark Neumann, Mohit Iyyer, Matt Gardner, Christopher Clark, Kenton Lee, and Luke Zettlemoyer. 2018. Deep contextualized word representations. In *Proceedings of the 2018 Conference of the North American Chapter of the Association for Computational Linguistics: Human Language Technologies, Volume 1 (Long Papers)*, pages 2227–2237, New Orleans, Louisiana. Association for Computational Linguistics.

Sameer Pradhan, Alessandro Moschitti, Nianwen Xue, Olga Uryupina, and Yuchen Zhang. 2012. CoNLL-2012 shared task: Modeling multilingual unrestricted coreference in OntoNotes. In *Joint Conference on EMNLP and CoNLL - Shared Task*, pages 1–40, Jeju Island, Korea. Association for Computational Linguistics.

Vikas Raunak. 2017. Simple and effective dimensionality reduction for word embeddings. In *Proceedings of the workshop on the learning with limited labeled data, NIPS'2017*, Long Beach, CA, USA.

Minjoon Seo, Aniruddha Kembhavi, Ali Farhadi, and Hannaneh Hajishirzi. 2017. Bidirectional attention flow for machine comprehension. In *International Conference on Learning Representations*.

Kellie Webster, Marta Recasens, Vera Axelrod, and Jason Baldridge. 2018. Mind the GAP: A balanced corpus of gendered ambiguous pronouns. *Transactions of the Association for Computational Linguistics*, 6:605–617.

Sam Wiseman, Alexander M. Rush, and Stuart M. Shieber. 2016. Learning global features for coreference resolution. In *Proceedings of the 2016 Conference of the North American Chapter of the Association for Computational Linguistics: Human Language Technologies*, pages 994–1004, San Diego, California. Association for Computational Linguistics.

Yonghui Wu, Mike Schuster, Zhifeng Chen, Quoc V. Le, Mohammad Norouzi, Wolfgang Macherey, Maxim Krikun, Yuan Cao, Qin Gao, Klaus Macherey, Jeff Klingner, Apurva Shah, Melvin Johnson, Xiaobing Liu, Lukasz Kaiser, Stephan Gouws, Yoshikiyo Kato, Taku Kudo, Hideto Kazawa, Keith Stevens, George Kurian, Nishant Patil, Wei Wang, Cliff Young, Jason Smith, Jason Riesa, Alex Rudnick, Oriol Vinyals, Greg Corrado, Macduff Hughes, and Jeffrey Dean. 2016. Google's neural machine translation system: Bridging the gap between human and machine translation. *Computing Research Repository*, arXiv:1609.08144. Version 2.

Han Xiao. 2018. bert-as-service. `https://github.com/hanxiao/bert-as-service`.

MSnet: A BERT-based Network for Gendered Pronoun Resolution

Zili Wang
CEIEC
Chengdu, China
`wzlnot@gmail.com`

Abstract

The pre-trained BERT model achieves a remarkable state of the art across a wide range of tasks in natural language processing. For solving the gender bias in gendered pronoun resolution task, I propose a novel neural network model based on the pre-trained BERT. This model is a type of mention score classifier and uses an attention mechanism with no parameters to compute the contextual representation of entity span, and a vector to represent the triple-wise semantic similarity among the pronoun and the entities. In stage 1 of the gendered pronoun resolution task, a variant of this model, trained in the fine-tuning approach, reduced the multi-class logarithmic loss to 0.3033 in the 5-fold cross-validation of training set and 0.2795 in testing set. Besides, this variant won the 2nd place with a score at 0.17289 in stage 2 of the task.

The code in this paper is available at: `https://github.com/ziliwang/MSnet-for-Gendered-Pronoun-Resolution`

1 Introduction

Coreference resolution is an essential field of natural language processing (Sukthanker et al., 2018) and has been widely used in many systems such as dialog system (Niraula et al., 2014; Wessel et al., 2017), relation extraction (Wang et al., 2018) and question answer (Vicedo and Ferrández, 2000). Up to now, various models for coreference resolution have been proposed, and they can be generally categorized as (1) mention-pair classifier model (Webster and Nothman, 2016), (2) entity-centric model (Clark and Manning, 2015), (3) ranking model (Lee et al., 2017, 2018). However, some of these models implicate gender bias (Koolen and van Cranenburgh, 2017; Rudinger et al., 2018). To address this, Webster et al. (2018) presented and

released Gendered Ambiguous Pronouns (GAP) dataset.

Recent work indicated that the pre-trained language representation models benefit to the coreference resolution (Lee et al., 2018). In the past years, the development of deep learning methods of language representation was swift, and the newer methods were shown to have significant effects on improving other natural language processing tasks(Peters et al., 2018; Radford and Salimans, 2018; Devlin et al., 2018). The latest one is Bidirectional Encoder Representations from Transformers (BERT) (Devlin et al., 2018), which is the cornerstone of the state of the art models in many tasks.

In this paper, I present a novel neural network model based on the pre-trained BERT for the gendered pronoun resolution task. The model is a kind of mention score classifier, and it is named as Mention Score Network (MSNet in short) and trained on the public GAP dataset. In particular, the model adopts an attention mechanism to compute the contextual representation of the entity span, and a vector to represent the triple-wise semantic similarity among the pronoun and the entities. Since the MSnet can not be tuned in a general way, I employ a two-step strategy to achieve the tuning-fine, which tunes the MSnet with freezing BERT firstly and then tunes them together. Two variants of MSnet are submitted in the gendered pronoun resolution task, and their logarithmic loss of local 5-fold cross-validation of train dataset is 0.3033 and 0.3042 respectively. Moreover, in stage 2 of the task, they acquired the score at 0.17289 and 0.18361 respectively, by averaging the predictions on the test dataset, and won the 2nd place in the task.

Proceedings of the 1st Workshop on Gender Bias in Natural Language Processing, pages 89–95
Florence, Italy, August 2, 2019. ©2019 Association for Computational Linguistics

2 Model

As the target of the Gendered Pronoun Resolution task is to label the pronoun with whether it refers to entity A, entity B, or NEITHER. I aim to learn the reference probability distribution $P(E_i|D)$ from the input document D:

$$P(E_i|D) = \frac{\exp(s(E_i|D))}{\sum_{j \in E} \exp(s(E_j|D))}$$

where E_i is the candidate reference entity of pronoun, $E = \{A, B, NEITHER\}$ and s is the score function which is implemented by a neural network architecture, which is described in detail in the following subsection.

2.1 The Mention Score Network

The mention score network is build on the pre-trained BERT model (Figure 1). It has three layers, the span representation layer, the similarity layer, and the mention score layer. They are described in detail in the following part.

Span Representation Layer: The contextual representation is crucial to accurately predict the relation between the pronouns and the entities. Inspired by Lee et al. (2017), I adopt the hidden states of transformers of the pre-trained BERT as the contextual representation. As Devlin et al. (2018) showed that the performance of the concatenation of token representations from the top hidden layers of pre-trained Transformer of BERT is close to fine-tuning the entire model, the top hidden states will be given priority to compute the representation of entity spans. Since most entity spans consist of various tokens, the contextual representation of them should be re-computed to maintain the correspondence. I present two methods to re-compute the span representations: 1) **Meanpooling method**:

$$x^*_{(j,l)} = \frac{1}{\hat{N}} \sum_{i \in \text{Span}_j} x_{(i,l)}$$

where $x_{(i,l)}$ denotes the hidden states of i-th token in l-th layer of BERT, and $x^*_{(j,l)}$ denotes the contextual representation of entity span j, and $\hat{N}$ is the token counts of span j. 2) **Attention mechanism:** Instead of weighting each token equality, I adopt the attention mechanism to weight the tokens by:

$$s_{(i,l)} = \frac{1}{\sqrt{d_H}} \text{norm}(x_{(i,l)}) \cdot x_{(p,l)}$$

$$a_{(i,j,l)} = \frac{\exp(s_{(i,l)})}{\sum_{k \in \text{Span}_j} \exp(s_{(k,l)})} \ , i \in \text{Span}_j$$

$$x^*_{(j,l)} = \sum_{i \in \text{Span}_j} a_{(i,j,l)} x_{(i,l)}$$

The weights $a_{(i,j,l)}$ are learned automatically from the contextual similarity $s_{(i,l)}$ between pronoun $x_{(p,l)}$ and the token $x_{(i,l)}$ in the span j. Different from the commonly used attention functions, the above one has no parameters and is more space-efficient in practice. The scaling factor d_H denotes the hidden size of BERT and is designed to counteract the effect of extremely small gradients caused by the large magnitude of dot products (Vaswani et al., 2017).

Similarity Layer: Inspired by the pairwise similarity of Lee et al. (2017), I assume a vector $\hat{s}_l$ to represent the triple-wise semantic similarity among the pronoun and the entities of l-layer in BERT:

$$a_l = x^*_{(a,l)}$$

$$b_l = x^*_{(b,l)}$$

$$p_l = x_{(p,l)}$$

$$\hat{s}_l = \mathbf{W}^T[p_l, a_l, b_l, a_l \circ p_l, b_l \circ p_l] + \mathbf{b}$$

where a_l, b_l and p_l denote the contextual representation of the pronoun, entity A and entity B of the l-th layer in BERT, $\cdot$ denotes the dot product and $\circ$ denotes the element-wise multiplication. The $\hat{s}_l$ can be learned by a single layer feed-forward neural network with the weights $\mathbf{W}$ and the bias $\mathbf{b}$.

Mention Score Layer: Mention score layer is also a feed-forward neural network architecture and computes the mention scores given the distance vector $\mathbf{d}$ between the pronoun and its candidate entities and the concatenated similarity vector $\hat{s}$:

$$d_a = \tanh(w_{\text{dist}}(\text{START(A)} - \text{START(P)}) + b_{\text{dist}})$$

$$d_b = \tanh(w_{\text{dist}}(\text{START(B)} - \text{START(P)}) + b_{\text{dist}})$$

$$\mathbf{d} = [d_a, d_b]$$

$$\hat{s} = [\hat{s}_0, \hat{s}_1, ..., \hat{s}_l, ..., \hat{s}_L]$$

$$s(E_i|D) = \mathbf{W}_{E_i} \cdot [\hat{s}, \mathbf{d}] + b_{E_i}$$

where d_a (or d_b) denotes the distance encoding of entity A (or B), $\hat{s}_l$ denotes the similarity vector computed by the representation of the l-th layer in BERT. L is the total layers for representation, and START denotes the index of the start token of

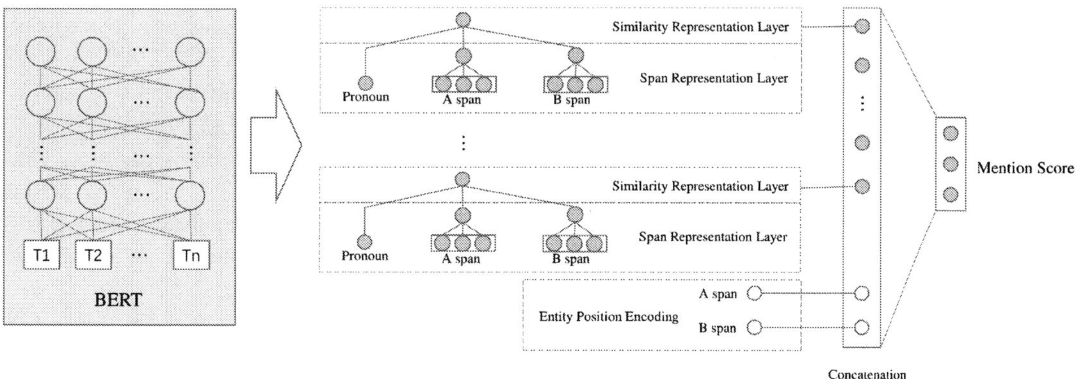

Figure 1: The architecture of MSnet.

the span. w_{dist} is a learnable weight for encoding the distance which corresponds to a learnable bias b_{dist} and $\mathbf{W}_{E_i}$ is the learnable weights for scoring entity E_i which corresponds to a learnable bias b_{E_i}.

3 Experiments

I train the model on the Kaggle platform by using scripts kernel which using the computational environment from the docker-python [1]. I employ pytorch as the deep learning framework, and the `pytorch-pretrained-BERT` package [2] to load and tune the pre-trained BERT model.

3.1 Dataset

The GAP Coreference Dataset [3] (Webster et al., 2018) has 4454 records and officially split into three parts: development set (2000 records), test set (2000 records), and validation set (454 records). Conforming to the stage 1 of Gendered Pronoun Resolution [4] task, the official test set and validation set are combined as the training dataset in the experiments, while the official development set is used as the test set correspondingly.

3.2 Preprocessing

In the experiments, the WordPiece is used to tokenize the documents. To ensure the token counts less than 300 after tokenizing, I remove the head or tail tokens in a few documents. Next, the special tokens `[CLS]` and `[SEP]` are added into the head and end of the tokens sequences.

3.3 Hyper-parameters

Pre-trained BERT model: As increasing model sizes of BERT may lead to significant improvements on very small scale tasks (Devlin et al., 2018), I explore the effect of BERT$_{\text{BASE}}$ and BERT$_{\text{LARGE}}$ in the experiments. I employ the `uncased_L-12_H-768_A-12` [5] as the BERT$_{\text{BASE}}$ and `cased_L-24_H-1024_A-16` [6] as the BERT$_{\text{LARGE}}$, and both of them are transformed into the pytorch-supported format by the script in `pytorch-pretrained-BERT`.

Hidden Layers for Representation: Devlin et al. (2018) showed that using the representation from appropriate hidden layers of BERT can improve the model performance, the hidden layers L (described in Section 2) is therefore utilized as a hyper-parameter tuned in the experiments.

Dimension of Similarity Vector: Since a vector is used to represent the task-specific semantic similarity, its dimension $\hat{s}_{dim}$ may have potential influence the performance. A smaller dimension

---

[1] `https://github.com/Kaggle/docker-python`

[2] `https://github.com/huggingface/pytorch-pretrained-BERT`

[3] `https://github.com/google-research-datasets/gap-coreference`

[4] `https://www.kaggle.com/c/gendered-pronoun-resolution`

[5] `https://storage.googleapis.com/bert_models/2018_10_18/uncased_L-12_H-768_A-12.zip`

[6] `https://storage.googleapis.com/bert_models/2018_10_18/cased_L-24_H-1024_A-16.zip`

will partly lose information, while a bigger one will cause generalization problems.

Span Contextual Representation: As section 2 described, both the meanpooling and attention method can be used to compute the contextual representation of the tokens span of the entity. Therefore, the choice of them is a hyper-parameter in the experiment.

Tunable Layers: I use two different approaches to train the MSnet model. The first one is the feature-based approach which trains MSnet with freezing the BERT part. The second one is the fine-tuning approach, which tunes the parameters of BERT and MSnet simultaneously. Howard and Ruder (2018) showed the discriminative fine-tuning gets a better performance than the ordinary, which possibly means that the pre-trained language model has a hierarchical structure. One possible explanation is that the lower hidden layers extract the word meanings and grammatical structures and the higher layers process them into higher-level semantic information. In this, I freeze the embedding layer and bottom hidden layers of BERT to keep the completeness of word meaning and grammatical structure and tune the top hidden layers L_{tuning}.

3.4 Training Details

For improving the generalization ability of the model, I employ the dropout mechanism (Srivastava et al., 2014) on the input of the feed-forward neural network in the similarity layer and the concatenation in the mention score layer. The rate of dropout is set at 0.6 which is the best setting after tuned on it. I also apply the dropout on the representation of tokens when using the attention mechanism to compute the contextual representation of span, and its dropout rate is set at 0.4. Additionally, I adopt the batch normalization (Ioffe and Szegedy, 2015) before the dropout operation in the mention score layer. As introduced in section 3.3, I use the feature-based approach and the fine-tuning approach separately to train the MSnet, and the training details are described in the following.

Feature-based Approach: In the feature-based approach, I train the model by minimizing the cross-entropy loss with Adam (Kingma and Ba, 2014) optimizer with a batch size of 32. To adapt to the training data in the experiments, I tuned the learning rate and found a learning rate of 3e-4 was the best setting. The maximum epoch set at 30 and early stopping method is used to prevent the over-fitting of MSnet.

Fine-tuning Approach: In the fine-tuning approach, the generic training method was not working. I adopt a two-step tuning strategy to achieve the fine-tuning. In step 1, I train the MSnet in the feature-based approach. And in step 2, MSnet and BERT are tuned simultaneously with a small learning rate.

Since the two steps have the same optimization landscape, in step 2, the model may not escape the local minimum where it entered in step 1. I adopt two strategies of training in step 1 to reduce the probability of those situations: 1) premature. The MSnet is trained to under-fitting by using a small maximum training epoch which is set at 10 in the experiments. 2) mature. In this strategy, MSnet is trained to proper-fitting, and it is applied by adopting a weight decay at 0.01 rate, an early stopping at 4 epoch, and the maximum training epoch at 20 in the experiments. In addition, other training parameters of the two strategies have the same setting as in the feature-based approach.

In step 2, I also trained the model by minimizing the cross-entropy loss but with two different optimizers. For BERT, I used the Adam optimizer with the weight decay fix which implemented by `pytorch-pretrained-BERT`. For MSnet, the generic Adam was used. Both of the two optimizers are set with a learning rate at 5e-6 and a weight decay at 0.01. The maximum training epoch is set at 20, and the early stopping is set at 4 epoch. The batch size was 5 as the GPU memory limitation.

3.5 Evaluation

I report the multi-class logarithmic loss of the 5-fold cross-validation on train and the average of their predictions on the test. Also, the running time of the scripts is reported as a reference of the performance of the MSnet.

4 Results and Discussion

4.1 Feature-based Approach

The results of MSnet variants trained in feature-based approach are shown in Table 1. The comparison between model #1 and model #2 shows that the combination of the top 4 hidden layers for contextual representation is better than the top

Model#	BERT	L	$\hat{s}_{dim}$	Span	5-fold CV on train	test	runtime(s)
1	BASE	1	32	Meanpooling	0.5247±0.0379	0.4891	232.8
2	BASE	4	32	Meanpooling	0.4699±0.0431	0.4270	317.3
3	LARGE	4	32	Meanpooling	0.4041±0.0532	0.3819	358.3
4	LARGE	8	32	Meanpooling	0.3783±0.0468	0.3519	372.2
5	LARGE	12	32	Meanpooling	0.3879±0.0461	0.3546	415.4
6	LARGE	8	8	Meanpooling	0.3758±0.0430	0.3490	436.2
7	LARGE	8	16	Meanpooling	0.3736±0.0465	0.3488	415.0
8	LARGE	8	64	Meanpooling	0.3780±0.0441	0.3518	447.6
9	LARGE	8	16	Attention	0.3582±0.0435	0.3349	828.2

Table 1: Results of Feature-based Aproach.

Model#	Based Model	method	L_{tuning}	5-fold CV on train	test	runtime(s)
10	#9	premature	12	0.3033±0.0367	0.2795	6909.5
11	#9	mature	12	0.3042±0.0352	0.2856	7627.7
12	#9	mature	8	0.3110±0.0352	0.2876	8928.1
13	#9	mature	16	0.3185±0.0465	0.2820	7763.4
14	#9	mature	24	0.3169±0.0440	0.2843	8695.4

Table 2: Results of Fine-tuning Aproach.

layer. The possible reason is that the semantic information about gender may be partly transformed to the higher level semantic information during the hidden layers in BERT. In addition, changing BERT$_{BASE}$ to the BERT$_{LARGE}$ reduces the loss in 5-fold CV on train from 0.4699±0.0431 to 0.4041±0.0532, which demonstrate increasing model size of BERT can lead to remarkable improvement on the small scale task. The exploration of contextual representation layers shows the proper representation layers is proportionate to the number of hidden layers of BERT. In other words, the modeling ability of BERT$_{LARGE}$ is more powerful than BERT$_{BASE}$ by using a more complex function to do the same work.

The comparison among the model #4, model #6, model #7 and model #8 shows the dimension of the similarity vector has a slight affection for the performance of MSnet (Table 1) and the best loss is 0.3736±0.0465 with the dimension set at 16. Changing the method for computing the span contextual representation from meanpooling to attention mechanism reduces the loss in CV on train by ~0.02, which demonstrates that the attention mechanism used in the experiment is effective to compute the contextual representation of the entity span. To the best of my knowledge, it is a novel attention mechanism with no learnable parameters and more space-efficient and more explainable in practice.

4.2 Fine-tuning Approach

The experiments in fine-tuning approach was based on model #9, and the results are shown in table 2. The comparison between model #10 and model #11 shows that their difference on performance is slight. Also, both of them are effective to the fine-tuning of MSnet and reduce loss in the CV of train by ~0.054 compared to the feature-based approach. Furthermore, the tuning on L_{tuning} shows the best setting is tuning top 12 hidden layers in BERT, and more or fewer layers will reduce the performance of MSnet. The possible reason is that tuning fewer layers will limit the ability of the transformation from basic semantic to gender-related semantic while tuning more bottom layers will damage the extraction of the underlying semantics when training on a small data set.

As the apporach transformed from the feature-based to the fine-tuning, the intentions of some hyper-parameters were changed. The obvious one is the hidden layers for contextual representation, which is used to combine the semantic in each hidden layers in the feature-based approach and changed to constrain the contextual representation to include the same semantic in fine-tuning approach. Although, the change on the intentions was not deliberate, the improvement on the performance of the model was observed in the experiments.

4.3 Results in Stage 2

The gendered pronoun resolution was a two-stage task, and I submitted the model #10 and #11 in stage 2 as their best performances in 5-fold cross-validation of the training dataset. The final scores of the models were 0.17289 (model #10) and 0.18361 (model #11). This result featurely demonstrates the premature strategy is better than the mature one and can be explained as former one keeps more explorable optimization landscape in step 2 in the fine-tuning approach.

5 Conclusion

This paper presented a novel pre-trained BERT based network model for the gendered pronoun resolution task. This model is a kind of mention score classifier and uses an attention mechanism to compucate the contextual representation of entity span and a vector to represent the triple-wise semantic similarity among the pronoun and the entities. I trained the model in the feature-based and the two-step fine-tuning approach respectively. On the GAP dateset, the model trained by the fine-tuning approach with premature strategy obtains remarkable multi-class logarithmic loss on the local 5-fold cross-valication at 0.3033, and 0.17289 on the test dataset in stage 2 of the task. I believe the MSnet can serve as a new strong baseline for gendered pronoun resolution task as well as the coreference resolution. The code for training model are available at: `https://github.com/ziliwang/MSnet-for-Gendered-Pronoun-Resolution`

Acknowledgments

I want to thank the kaggle company for its public computing resources.

References

Kevin Clark and Christopher D Manning. 2015. Entity-centric coreference resolution with model stacking. In *Proceedings of the 53rd Annual Meeting of the Association for Computational Linguistics and the 7th International Joint Conference on Natural Language Processing (Volume 1: Long Papers)*, volume 1, pages 1405–1415.

Jacob Devlin, Ming-Wei Chang, Kenton Lee, and Kristina Toutanova. 2018. Bert: Pre-training of deep bidirectional transformers for language understanding. *arXiv preprint arXiv:1810.04805*.

Jeremy Howard and Sebastian Ruder. 2018. Universal language model fine-tuning for text classification. *arXiv preprint arXiv:1801.06146*.

Sergey Ioffe and Christian Szegedy. 2015. Batch normalization: Accelerating deep network training by reducing internal covariate shift. *arXiv preprint arXiv:1502.03167*.

Diederik P Kingma and Jimmy Ba. 2014. Adam: A method for stochastic optimization. *arXiv preprint arXiv:1412.6980*.

Corina Koolen and Andreas van Cranenburgh. 2017. These are not the stereotypes you are looking for: Bias and fairness in authorial gender attribution. In *Proceedings of the First ACL Workshop on Ethics in Natural Language Processing*, pages 12–22.

Kenton Lee, Luheng He, Mike Lewis, and Luke Zettlemoyer. 2017. End-to-end neural coreference resolution. *Proceedings of the 2017 Conference on Empirical Methods in Natural Language Processing*.

Kenton Lee, Luheng He, and Luke Zettlemoyer. 2018. Higher-order coreference resolution with coarse-to-fine inference. *arXiv preprint arXiv:1804.05392*.

Nobal B Niraula, Vasile Rus, Rajendra Banjade, Dan Stefanescu, William Baggett, and Brent Morgan. 2014. The dare corpus: A resource for anaphora resolution in dialogue based intelligent tutoring systems. In *LREC*, pages 3199–3203.

Matthew E. Peters, Mark Neumann, Mohit Iyyer, Matt Gardner, Christopher Clark, Kenton Lee, and Luke Zettlemoyer. 2018. Deep contextualized word representations.

Alec Radford and Tim Salimans. 2018. GPT: Improving Language Understanding by Generative Pre-Training. *arXiv*, pages 1–12.

Rachel Rudinger, Jason Naradowsky, Brian Leonard, and Benjamin Van Durme. 2018. Gender bias in coreference resolution. *arXiv preprint arXiv:1804.09301*.

Nitish Srivastava, Geoffrey Hinton, Alex Krizhevsky, Ilya Sutskever, and Ruslan Salakhutdinov. 2014. Dropout: a simple way to prevent neural networks from overfitting. *The Journal of Machine Learning Research*, 15(1):1929–1958.

Rhea Sukthanker, Soujanya Poria, Erik Cambria, and Ramkumar Thirunavukarasu. 2018. Anaphora and Coreference Resolution: A Review.

Ashish Vaswani, Noam Shazeer, Niki Parmar, Jakob Uszkoreit, Llion Jones, Aidan N. Gomez, Lukasz Kaiser, and Illia Polosukhin. 2017. Attention is all you need. In *NIPS*.

José L Vicedo and Antonio Ferrández. 2000. Importance of pronominal anaphora resolution in question answering systems. In *Proceedings of the 38th Annual Meeting of the Association for Computational Linguistics*.

Yanshan Wang, Liwei Wang, Majid Rastegar-Mojarad, Sungrim Moon, Feichen Shen, Naveed Afzal, Sijia Liu, Yuqun Zeng, Saeed Mehrabi, Sunghwan Sohn, et al. 2018. Clinical information extraction applications: a literature review. *Journal of biomedical informatics*, 77:34–49.

Kellie Webster and Joel Nothman. 2016. Using mention accessibility to improve coreference resolution. In *Proceedings of the 54th Annual Meeting of the Association for Computational Linguistics (Volume 2: Short Papers)*, volume 2, pages 432–437.

Kellie Webster, Marta Recasens, Vera Axelrod, and Jason Baldridge. 2018. Mind the gap: A balanced corpus of gendered ambiguous pronouns. In *Transactions of the ACL*, page to appear.

Michael Wessel, Girish Acharya, James Carpenter, and Min Yin. 2017. An ontology-based dialogue management system for virtual personal assistants. In *Proceedings of the 8th International Workshop On Spoken Dialogue Systems (IWSDS)*.

Look Again at the Syntax: Relational Graph Convolutional Network for Gendered Ambiguous Pronoun Resolution

Yinchuan Xu[*]
University of Pennsylvania
Philadelphia, PA, 19104, USA
yinchuan@seas.upenn.edu

Junlin Yang[*]
Yale University
New Haven, CT, 06511, USA
junlin.yang@yale.edu

Abstract

Gender bias has been found in existing coreference resolvers. In order to eliminate gender bias, a gender-balanced dataset Gendered Ambiguous Pronouns (GAP) has been released and the best baseline model achieves only 66.9% F1. Bidirectional Encoder Representations from Transformers (BERT) has broken several NLP task records and can be used on GAP dataset. However, fine-tune BERT on a specific task is computationally expensive. In this paper, we propose an end-to-end resolver by combining pre-trained BERT with Relational Graph Convolutional Network (R-GCN). R-GCN is used for digesting structural syntactic information and learning better task-specific embeddings. Empirical results demonstrate that, under explicit syntactic supervision and without the need to fine tune BERT, R-GCN's embeddings outperform the original BERT embeddings on the coreference task. Our work significantly improves the snippet-context baseline F1 score on GAP dataset from 66.9% to 80.3%. We participated in the Gender Bias for Natural Language Processing 2019 shared task, and our codes are available online. [1]

1 Introduction

Coreference resolution aims to find the linguistic mentions that refer to the same real-world entity in natural language (Pradhan et al., 2012). Ambiguous gendered pronoun resolution is a subtask of coreference resolution, where we try to resolve gendered ambiguous pronouns in English such as "he" and "she". This is an important task for natural language understanding and a longstanding challenge. According to (Sukthanker et al., 2018), there are two main approaches: heuristics-based

approaches and learning-based approaches, such as mention-pair models, mention-ranking models, and clustering models (McCarthy and Lehnert, 1995; Haghighi and Klein, 2010; Fernandes et al., 2014). Learning-based approaches, especially deep-learning-based methods, have shown significant improvement over heuristics-based approaches.

However, most state-of-art deep-learning-based resolvers utilize one-directional Transformers (Stojanovski and Fraser, 2018), limiting the ability to handle long-range inferences and the use of cataphors. Bidirectional Encoder Representations from Transformers, or BERT (Devlin et al., 2018) learns a bidirectional contextual embedding and has the potential to overcome these problems using both the previous and next context. However, fine-tuning BERT for a specific task is computationally expensive and time-consuming.

Syntax information has always been a strong tool for semantic tasks. Most heuristics-based methods use syntax-based rules (Hobbs, 1978; Lappin and Leass, 1994; Haghighi and Klein, 2009). Many of learning based models also rely on syntactic parsing for mention or entity extraction algorithms and compute hand-crafted features as input (Sukthanker et al., 2018).

Can we learn better word embeddings than BERT on the coreference task with the help of syntactic information and without computationally expensive fine-tuning of BERT? Marcheggiani and Titov et al. (2017) successfully use Graph Convolutional Networks (GCNs) (Duvenaud et al., 2015; Kipf and Welling, 2016) to learn word embeddings for the semantic role labeling task and outperform the original LSTM contextual embeddings.

Inspired by Marcheggiani and Titov (2017), we create a 'Look-again' mechanism which combines BERT with Gated Relational Graph Convolutional

---

[*] Equal contribution.

[1] Our codes and models are available at: https://github.com/ianycxu/RGCN-with-BERT.

Networks (R-GCN) by using BERT embeddings as initial hidden states of vertices in R-GCN. R-GCN's structure is derived from a sentence's syntactic dependencies graph. This architecture allows contextual embeddings to be further learned and encoded into better task-specific embeddings without fine tuning BERT which is computationally expensive.

2   Contributions

Our main contributions are: (1) Our work is the first successful attempt of using R-GCN to boost the performance of BERT contextual embeddings without the need to fine tune BERT. (2) Our work is the first to use R-GCN on the coreference resolution task. (3) Our work improves the snippet-context baseline F1 score on Gendered Ambiguous Pronouns dataset from 66.9% to 80.3%.

3   Methodology

We propose a series connection architecture of pre-trained BERT with Gated Relational Graph Convolutional Network (Gated R-GCN). Gated R-GCN is used for digesting structural syntactic information. This architecture, which we name as 'Look-again' mechanism can help us learn embeddings which have better performance on coreference task than original BERT embeddings.

3.1   Syntactic Structure Prior

As mentioned in the Introduction section, syntactic information is beneficial to semantic tasks. However, how to encode syntactic information directly into deep learning systems is difficult.

Marcheggiani and Titov (2017) introduces a way of incorporating syntactic information into sequential neural networks by using GCN. The syntax prior is transferred into a syntactic dependency graph, and GCN is used to digest this graph information. This kind of architecture is utilized to incorporate syntactic structure prior with BERT embeddings for coreference task in our work.

3.2   GCN

Graph Convolutional Networks (GCNs) (Duvenaud et al., 2015; Kipf and Welling, 2016) take graphs as inputs and conduct convolution on each node over their local graph neighborhoods. The convolution process can also be regarded as a simple differentiable message-passing process. The message here is the hidden state of each node.

Consider a directed graph $\mathcal{G} = (\mathcal{V}, \mathcal{E})$ with nodes $v_i \in \mathcal{V}$ and edges $(v_i, v_j) \in \mathcal{E}$. The original work of GCN (Kipf and Welling, 2016) assumes that every node v contains a self-loop edge, which is $(v_i, v_i) \in \mathcal{E}$. We denote hidden state or features of each node v_i as h_i, and neighbors of each node as $\mathcal{N}(v_i)$, then for each node v_i, the feed-forward processing or message-passing processing then can be written as:

$$h_i^{(l+1)} = ReLU\left(\sum_{u \in \mathcal{N}(v_i)} \frac{1}{c_i} W^{(l)} h_u^{(l)} \right) \quad (1)$$

Note that we ignore the bias term here. l here denotes the layer number, and c_i is a normalization constant. We use $c_i = |\mathcal{N}(v_i)|$, which is the in-degree of the node. Weight $W^{(l)}$ is shared by all edges in layer l.

3.3   R-GCN

Each sentence is parsed into its syntactic dependencies graph and use GCN to digest this structural information. Mentioned in (Schlichtkrull et al., 2018), when we construct the syntactic graph we also allow the information to flow in the opposite direction of syntactic dependency arcs, which is from dependents to heads. Therefore, we have three types of edges: first, from heads to dependents; second, from dependents to heads and third, self-loop (see Fig. 1).

Traditional GCN cannot handle this multi-relation graph. Schlichtkrull (2018) proposed a Relational Graph Convolutional Networks (R-GCNs) structure to solve this multi-relation problem:

$$h_i^{(l+1)} = ReLU\left(\sum_{r \in R} \sum_{u \in \mathcal{N}_r(v_i)} \frac{1}{c_{i,r}} W_r^{(l)} h_u^{(l)} \right) \quad (2)$$

where $\mathcal{N}_r(v_i)$ and $W_r^{(l)}$ denote the set of neighbor of node i and weight under relation $r \in R$ respectively. In our case, we have three relations.

3.4   Gate Mechanism

Because the syntax information is predicted by some NLP packages, which might have some error, we need some mechanism to reduce the effect of erroneous dependency edges.

A gate mechanism is introduced in (Marcheggiani and Titov, 2017; Dauphin et al., 2017; Li

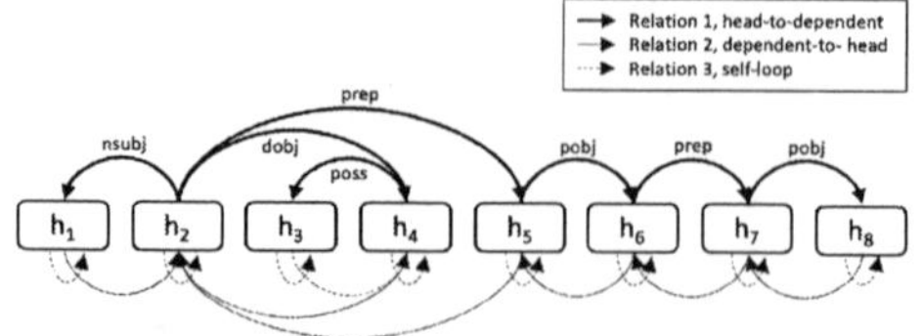

Figure 1: Syntactic dependencies graph with three relations

et al., 2015). The idea is calculating a gate value ranging from 0 to 1, and multiplying it with the incoming message. The gate value is computed by:

$$g_{u,v}^{(l)} = Sigmoid \left(h_u^{(l)} \cdot W_{r,g} \right) \quad (3)$$

The final forward process of Gated R-GCN is:

$$h_i^{(l+1)} = ReLU \left(\sum_{r \in R} \sum_{u \in \mathcal{N}_r(v_i)} g_{u,v_i}^{(l)} \frac{1}{c_{i,r}} W_r^{(l)} h_u^{(l)} \right) \quad (4)$$

3.5 Connect BERT and R-GCN in Series

We use pre-trained BERT embeddings (Devlin et al., 2018) as our initial hidden states of vertices in R-GCN. This series connection between pre-trained BERT and Gated R-GCN forms the 'Look-again' mechanism. After pre-trained BERT encodes tokens' embeddings, Gated R-GCN will 'look again' at the syntactic information which is presented as structural information and further learn semantic task-specific embeddings with the explicit syntactic supervision by syntactic structure.

A fully-connected layer in parallel with Gated R-GCN is utilized to learn a compact representation of BERT embeddings of two mentions (A and B) and the pronoun. This representation is then concatenated with Gated R-GCN's final hidden states of those three tokens. The reason of concatenating R-GCN's hidden states with BERT embeddings' compact representation is that graph convolution of the GCN model is actually a special form of Laplacian smoothing (Li et al., 2018), which might mix the features of vertices and make them less distinguishable. By concatenation, we maintain some original embeddings information. After concatenation, we use a fully-connect layer for the final prediction. The visualization of the final end-to-end model is shown in Fig. 2.

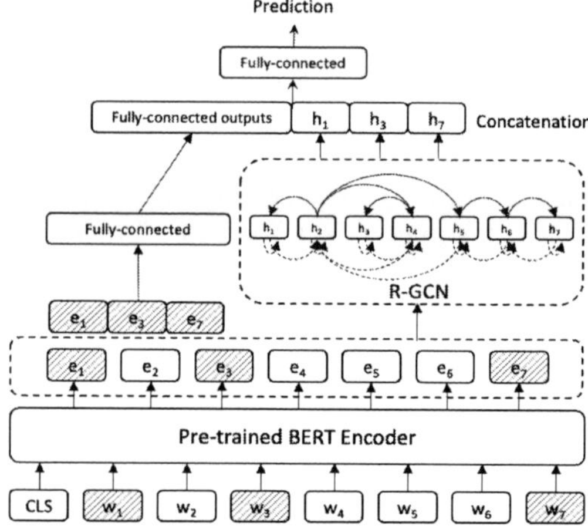

Figure 2: End-to-end coreference resolver

4 Experimental Methodology and Results

In the experiment, it shows that, with the explicit syntactic supervision by syntactic structure, Gated R-GCN structure can learn better embeddings that improve performance on the coreference resolution task. Two sets of experiments were designed and conducted: Stage one experiments and Full GAP experiments.

Stage one experiments used the same setting as stage one of shared-task competition, where we had 4454 data samples in total. 'Gap-validation.tsv' and 'gap-test.tsv' were used as training dataset, while 'gap-development.tsv' was used for testing.[2]

Full GAP experiments used full 8908 samples of Gendered Ambiguous Pronouns (GAP) dataset in order to compare with the baseline result from the GAP paper (Webster et al., 2018).

4.1 Dataset

The dataset provided by the shared task is Google AI Language's Gendered Ambiguous Pronouns (GAP) dataset (Webster et al., 2018), which is a gender-balanced dataset containing 8,908 coreference-labeled pairs of (ambiguous pronoun, antecedent name), sampled from Wikipedia.

In stage one of the shared task, only 2454 samples were used as the training dataset, and 2000 samples were used as the test dataset.

---

[2] https://www.kaggle.com/c/ gendered-pronoun-resolution/data.

4.2 Data Preprocessing

SpaCy was used as our syntactic dependency parser. Deep Graph Library (DGL)[3] was used to transfer each dependency graph into a DGL graph object. Several graphs were grouped together as a larger DGL batch-graph object for batch training setting. R-GCN model was also implemented with DGL.

4.3 Training settings

Adam was used (Kingma and Ba, 2014) as our optimizer. Learning rate decay was applied. $l2$ regularization of both R-GCN's and fully-connected layer's weights was added to the training loss function. Batch-normalization and drop-out were used in all fully-connection layers. We used one layer for R-GCN which captures immediate syntactic neighbors' information. BERT in our model was not fined tuned and was fixed for training. We used 'bert-large-uncased' version of BERT for generating original embeddings.

The five-fold ensemble was used to achieve better generalization performance and more accurate estimation of the model's performance. The training dataset was divided into 5 folds. Each time of training we trained our model on 4 folds and chose the model which had the best validation performance on the left fold. This best model then was used to predict the test dataset. In the end, predicted results from 5 folds were averaged as the final result.

4.4 Stage One Experiments

There are 4 different settings for Stage One experiments for comparisons (see Fig. 3):

1. Only BERT embeddings are fed into an additional MLP for prediction.

2. Connect BERT with Gated R-GCN, but only feed Gated R-GCN's hidden states into MLP for prediction.

3. Connect BERT with R-GCN, and the concatenation is fed into MLP for prediction. The gate mechanism is not applied to R-GCN

4. Connect BERT with Gated R-GCN, and the concatenation is fed into MLP for prediction. The gate mechanism is applied.

4.4.1 Evaluation Metrics

The competition used multi-class log-loss as evaluation metrics.

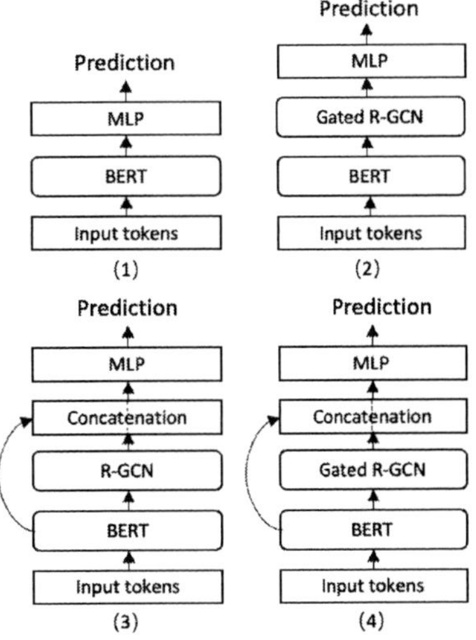

Figure 3: Stage one experiments

$$logloss = -\frac{1}{N} \sum_{i=1}^{N} \sum_{j=1}^{M} y_{ij} \log(p_{ij}),$$

where N is the number of samples in the test set, M is 3, log is the natural logarithm.

4.4.2 Results

Table 1 presents the results of four different settings. it demonstrates that R-GCN structure does learn better embeddings and improve the performance. Setting three and setting four show the effectiveness of the Gate Mechanism.

BERT	R-GCN	Concatenation	Gate	Test Log-loss
Yes	No	No	No	0.5301
Yes	Yes	No	Yes	0.5142
Yes	Yes	Yes	No	0.5045
Yes	Yes	Yes	Yes	**0.4936**

Table 1: Stage one results

By comparing setting two and setting four, we can see that because graph convolution of the R-GCN model brings the potential problem of over-smoothing the information (Li et al., 2018), model without concatenation might lose some performance.

4.5 Full GAP Experiments and Results

We also tested our model on the full GAP dataset which contains 8,908 samples. 4908 samples were used as training data, and 4000 samples were used as test data. We used micro F1 score as our metric.

---

[3]DGL official website: `https://www.dgl.ai/pages/about.html`.

The GAP paper (Webster et al., 2018) introduced several baseline methods: (1) Off-the-shelf resolvers including a rule-based system of Lee et al. (2013) and three neural resolvers from Clark and Manning (2015), Wiseman et al. (2016), and Lee et al. (2017); (2) Baselines based on traditional cues for coreference; (3)Baselines based on structural cues: syntactic distance and Parallelism; (4) Baselines based on Wikipedia cues; (5) Transformer models (Vaswani et al., 2017).

Model	F1 Score
Lee et al. (2017)	64.0%
Parallelism	66.9%
Parallelism+URL	70.6%
BERT only	78.5%
Ours	**80.3%**

Table 2: GAP experiments results

Three best models (Lee et al. (2017), Parallelism, and Parallelism+URL) from above baselines were chosen for comparison. We first used pre-trained BERT embeddings and fully-connected layers for prediction (see Fig. 3 (1)). Not surprising, BERT embeddings outperformed all of the previous work.

We then tested our Gated R-GCN model. The model further improved the F1 score by using explicitly syntactic information and learning coreference-task-specific word representations. The final model largely increased the baseline F1 score from 70.6 % to 80.3 % and the BERT embeddings' result from 78.5 % to 80.3 %.

4.6 Final Submission and Shared-Task Score

For the final submission for stage 2 of the shared task, we averaged our result with a BERT-score-layer (Zhang et al., 2018; Clark and Manning, 2016) result. In stage two, our work reaches log-loss of 0.394 on the private leaderboard showing that our model is quite effective and robust. This result is obtained without any data augmentation prepossessing.

5 Discussion and Conclusion

The Gender Bias for Natural Language Processing (GeBNLP) 2019 shared-task is a competition for building a coreference resolution system on GAP dataset. We participate in this shared-task by using a novel approach which combines Gated R-GCN with BERT. R-GCN is used for digesting syntactic dependency graph and leveraging this syntactic information to help our semantic task. Experiments with four settings were conducted on the shared task's stage one data. We also tested our model on the full GAP dataset where our model improved the best snippet-context baseline F1 score from 66.9 % to 80.3 % (by 20 %). The results showed that, under explicit syntactic supervision and without the need to fine tune BERT, our gated R-GCN model can incorporate syntactic structure prior with BERT embeddings to improve the performance on the coreference task.

References

Kevin Clark and Christopher D Manning. 2015. Entity-centric coreference resolution with model stacking. In *Proceedings of the 53rd Annual Meeting of the Association for Computational Linguistics and the 7th International Joint Conference on Natural Language Processing (Volume 1: Long Papers)*, volume 1, pages 1405–1415.

Kevin Clark and Christopher D Manning. 2016. Deep reinforcement learning for mention-ranking coreference models. In *Proceedings of the 2016 Conference on Empirical Methods in Natural Language Processing*, pages 2256–2262.

Yann N Dauphin, Angela Fan, Michael Auli, and David Grangier. 2017. Language modeling with gated convolutional networks. In *Proceedings of the 34th International Conference on Machine Learning-Volume 70*, pages 933–941. JMLR. org.

Jacob Devlin, Ming-Wei Chang, Kenton Lee, and Kristina Toutanova. 2018. Bert: Pre-training of deep bidirectional transformers for language understanding. *arXiv preprint arXiv:1810.04805*.

David Duvenaud, Dougal Maclaurin, Jorge Aguilera-Iparraguirre, Rafael Gómez-Bombarelli, Timothy Hirzel, Alán Aspuru-Guzik, and Ryan P Adams. 2015. Convolutional networks on graphs for learning molecular fingerprints. In *Proceedings of the 28th International Conference on Neural Information Processing Systems-Volume 2*, pages 2224–2232. MIT Press.

Eraldo Rezende Fernandes, Cícero Nogueira dos Santos, and Ruy Luiz Milidiú. 2014. Latent trees for coreference resolution. *Computational Linguistics*, 40(4):801–835.

Aria Haghighi and Dan Klein. 2009. Simple coreference resolution with rich syntactic and semantic features. In *Proceedings of the 2009 Conference on Empirical Methods in Natural Language Processing: Volume 3-Volume 3*, pages 1152–1161. Association for Computational Linguistics.

Aria Haghighi and Dan Klein. 2010. Coreference resolution in a modular, entity-centered model. In *Human Language Technologies: The 2010 Annual Conference of the North American Chapter of the Association for Computational Linguistics*, pages 385–393. Association for Computational Linguistics.

Jerry R Hobbs. 1978. Resolving pronoun references. *Lingua*, 44(4):311–338.

Diederik P Kingma and Jimmy Ba. 2014. Adam: A method for stochastic optimization. *arXiv preprint arXiv:1412.6980*.

Thomas N Kipf and Max Welling. 2016. Semi-supervised classification with graph convolutional networks. *arXiv preprint arXiv:1609.02907*.

Shalom Lappin and Herbert J Leass. 1994. An algorithm for pronominal anaphora resolution. *Computational linguistics*, 20(4):535–561.

Heeyoung Lee, Angel Chang, Yves Peirsman, Nathanael Chambers, Mihai Surdeanu, and Dan Jurafsky. 2013. Deterministic coreference resolution based on entity-centric, precision-ranked rules. *Computational Linguistics*, 39(4):885–916.

Kenton Lee, Luheng He, Mike Lewis, and Luke Zettlemoyer. 2017. End-to-end neural coreference resolution. In *Proceedings of the 2017 Conference on Empirical Methods in Natural Language Processing*, pages 188–197.

Qimai Li, Zhichao Han, and Xiao-Ming Wu. 2018. Deeper insights into graph convolutional networks for semi-supervised learning. In *Thirty-Second AAAI Conference on Artificial Intelligence*.

Yujia Li, Daniel Tarlow, Marc Brockschmidt, and Richard Zemel. 2015. Gated graph sequence neural networks. *arXiv preprint arXiv:1511.05493*.

Diego Marcheggiani and Ivan Titov. 2017. Encoding sentences with graph convolutional networks for semantic role labeling. In *Proceedings of the 2017 Conference on Empirical Methods in Natural Language Processing*, pages 1506–1515.

Joseph F McCarthy and Wendy G Lehnert. 1995. Using decision trees for coreference resolution. *arXiv preprint cmp-lg/9505043*.

Sameer Pradhan, Alessandro Moschitti, Nianwen Xue, Olga Uryupina, and Yuchen Zhang. 2012. Conll-2012 shared task: Modeling multilingual unrestricted coreference in ontonotes. In *Joint Conference on EMNLP and CoNLL-Shared Task*, pages 1–40. Association for Computational Linguistics.

Michael Schlichtkrull, Thomas N Kipf, Peter Bloem, Rianne Van Den Berg, Ivan Titov, and Max Welling. 2018. Modeling relational data with graph convolutional networks. In *European Semantic Web Conference*, pages 593–607. Springer.

Dario Stojanovski and Alexander Fraser. 2018. Coreference and coherence in neural machine translation: A study using oracle experiments. In *Proceedings of the Third Conference on Machine Translation: Research Papers*, pages 49–60.

Rhea Sukthanker, Soujanya Poria, Erik Cambria, and Ramkumar Thirunavukarasu. 2018. Anaphora and coreference resolution: A review. *arXiv preprint arXiv:1805.11824*.

Ashish Vaswani, Noam Shazeer, Niki Parmar, Jakob Uszkoreit, Llion Jones, Aidan N Gomez, Łukasz Kaiser, and Illia Polosukhin. 2017. Attention is all you need. In *Advances in neural information processing systems*, pages 5998–6008.

Kellie Webster, Marta Recasens, Vera Axelrod, and Jason Baldridge. 2018. Mind the gap: A balanced corpus of gendered ambiguou. In *Transactions of the ACL*, page to appear.

Sam Wiseman, Alexander M Rush, and Stuart M Shieber. 2016. Learning global features for coreference resolution. *arXiv preprint arXiv:1604.03035*.

Rui Zhang, Cicero Nogueira dos Santos, Michihiro Yasunaga, Bing Xiang, and Dragomir Radev. 2018. Neural coreference resolution with deep biaffine attention by joint mention detection and mention clustering. *arXiv preprint arXiv:1805.04893*.

Fill the GAP: Exploiting BERT for Pronoun Resolution

Kai-Chou Yang[1], **Timothy Niven**, **Tzu-Hsuan Chou**, and **Hung-Yu Kao**

Intelligent Knowledge Management Lab
National Cheng Kung University
Tainan, Taiwan
`zake7749@gmail.com`[1]

Abstract

In this paper, we describe our entry in the gendered pronoun resolution competition which achieved fourth place without data augmentation. Our method is an ensemble system of BERTs which resolves co-reference in an interaction space. We report four insights from our work: BERT's representations involve significant redundancy; modeling interaction effects similar to natural language inference models is useful for this task; there is an optimal BERT layer to extract representations for pronoun resolution; and the difference between the attention weights from the pronoun to the candidate entities was highly correlated with the correct label, with interesting implications for future work.

1 Introduction

The Gendered Ambiguous Pronouns (GAP) dataset[1] (Webster et al., 2018) addresses gender bias by providing a dataset balanced over male and female pronouns. The task is made challenging by long paragraph lengths of multiple sentences with a variety of named entities. The text comes from the encyclopedia genre which is more formal and contains numerous technical terms. Furthermore, world knowledge is indispensable to this task. An example is given in Figure 1 where the pronoun is highlighted in green and the entities are highlighted in blue. To know that **She** refers to **Christine** rather than **Elsie Tanne**, a model requires knowing that "never been mentioned again" is a result of having died.

Due to the small size of the dataset (Table 1), our solution was mainly based on transfer learning. Specifically, we used representations of the pronoun and entities from an optimal frozen BERT

Christine sent a telegram to congratulate Elsie and Steve Tanner on their wedding day in 1967. In 1984, Elsie Tanner informed Ken Barlow that Christine had died of liver failure after becoming an alcoholic in the late 1970s. She has never been mentioned again.

Figure 1: An example in GAP dataset. To refer "she" to "Christine", a model has to connect "never been mentioned again" with "had died of liver failure", which requires world knowledge.

layer (Devlin et al., 2018) as inputs to a novel encoder architecture (Figure 2), whose results were then ensembled (Maclin and Opitz, 2011) over various BERT models (base and large, cased and uncased) using shallow neural networks.

Our result achieved fourth place in the Kaggle shared-task competition[2]. The competition is composed of two stages. In the first stage, the the development set of GAP which is used for evaluation and is entirely public to help competitors search for model architectures. In the second stage, a large and unpublished dataset was used to test generalization ability as well as prevent label probing.

Our model makes the following contributions to this task. We propose a multi-head natural language inference (NLI) encoder which resolves co-reference though heuristic interaction and efficiently addresses the redundancy in BERT by applying dropout to inputs directly. With layer-by-layer exploration, we extract the task-specific features from the optimal layer of BERT for coreference resolution where we observe pronouns strongly attend to the corresponding candidate entities.

---

[1] `https://github.com/google-research-datasets/gap-coreference`

[2] `https://www.kaggle.com/c/gendered-pronoun-resolution/over`

Proceedings of the 1st Workshop on Gender Bias in Natural Language Processing, pages 102–106
Florence, Italy, August 2, 2019. ©2019 Association for Computational Linguistics

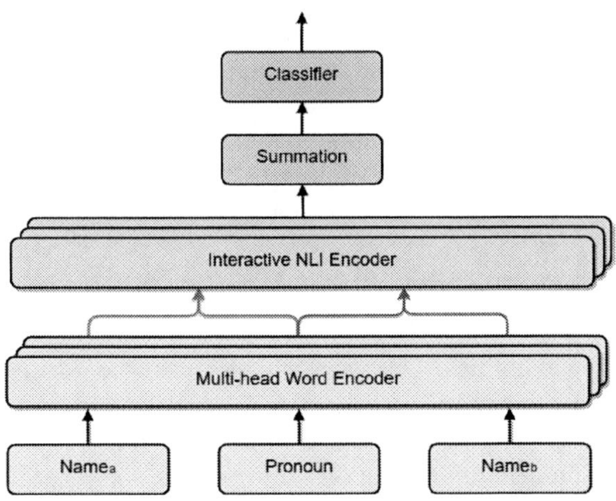

Figure 2: Our multi-head NLI encoder model. The inputs are representations of the pronoun and candidate entities from frozen BERT models.

Dataset	Size	Label Distribution		
		A	B	Neither
Validation	454	0.412	0.452	0.136
Development	2,000	0.437	0.463	0.100
Testing	2,000	0.459	0.428	0.113

Table 1: GAP dataset sizes and label distributions.

2 Methodology

2.1 Overview

We use the GAP dataset to train and evaluate our model. For stage 1, following the evaluation settings of Kaggle, our models were trained with the test set, validation set and evaluated on the development set. For stage 2, the models were trained with the whole GAP dataset. The number of samples and distribution of labels in each dataset is shown in Table 1.

Given a query $(entity_a, entity_b, pronoun)$, we obtain deep contextual representations from the optimal layer of BERT for the pronoun and each entity. Where the entities are composed of multiple word pieces, we take the mean of those vectors.

The relations between query words were modeled by two base neural architectures. The first architecture concatenates the contextual representations and aggregates the features with a shallow MLP, which turns out to be simple yet efficient. The second architecture is based on natural language inference. It projects the contextual representations into several low-dimensional subspaces to extract task-specific features which are

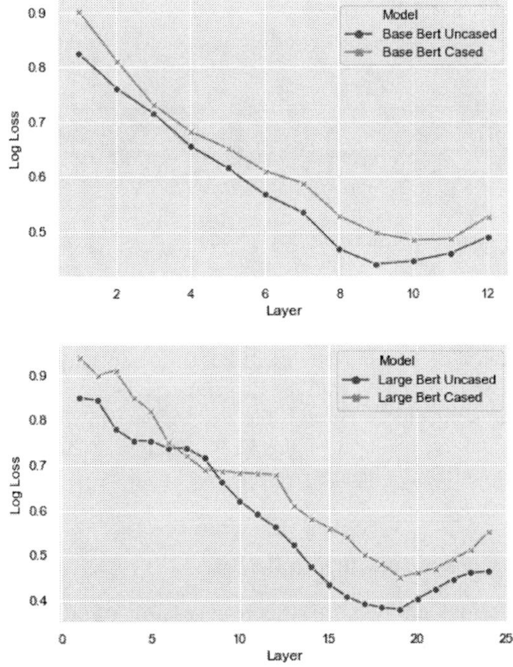

Figure 3: Performance of representations from different BERT layers. Log loss is calculated with the first stage evaluation set.

then passed to an interaction layer and Siamese encoders. We chose the second method as our main model because it is more structural and interpretable. Each base model is trained on frozen BERT Base and Large, and from both cased and uncased versions. The final prediction was an ensemble over all types of base models using a densely connected neural network.

2.2 Optimal BERT Layer

Unlike the common practice of taking the last hidden layer of BERT, we searched for a task-specific layer to obtain the most relevant contextualized representations, which yielded significant improvements. As pointed out by Peters et al. (2018), the hidden layers in language models encode different linguistic knowledge. We therefore conducted a layer by layer analysis to find the best features for this task. As shown in Figure 3, not all BERT layers performed equally well. A similar pattern is observed in both BERT Base and Large, where performance increases until around three quarters of the depth, before becoming worse. The optimal layers turn out to be 8 and 19 for BERT Base and Large, respectively.

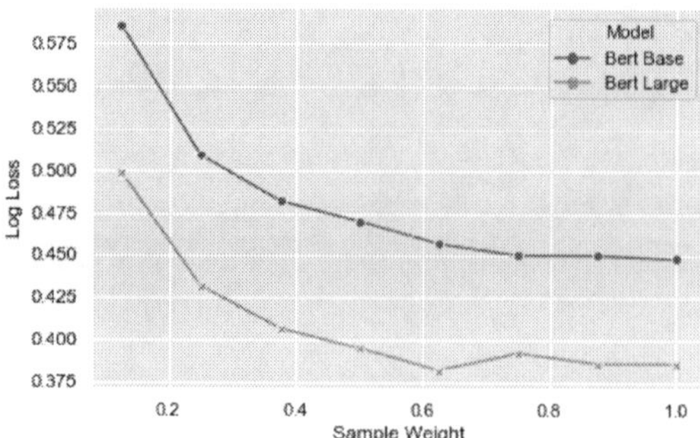

Figure 4: Redundancy in BERT Base and Large. Log loss is calculated with the first stage evaluation set. We can still achieve close to the best log loss in each case by taking a subset of the BERT vectors. This has a regularization benefit overall.

2.3 Redundancy in BERT

Manual analysis of the progression of attention distributions through each layer of BERT indicated the potential for a lot of redundancy in the information attended to, and therefore encoded. We empirically tested this idea by randomly sampling a subset of features in the BERT vectors (held constant through training) and comparing log loss to the sampling rate. Performance degradation halts well before the entire BERT vector is included. This indicates information necessary for this task is present in about 70% to 80% of the BERT vectors (taken from the optimal layer).

Based on this observation, we leverage the redundancy by adding dropout(Srivastava et al., 2014) directly to BERT features, which can be considered a kind of model boosting (Breiman, 1998), similar to training several prototypes with subsets that are randomly sampled from the BERT vector, and letting the neural network figure out the best ensemble architecture through back propagation.

The idea of sampling subsets and then training several models is quite similar to random forests (Breiman, 2001). However, unlike the general situation in random forests where the performance of base models degrade when using less data, our base models can still achieve strong performance because of the redundancy in BERT.

2.4 Word Encoder

Because of the small size of the dataset and the redundancy in the BERT vectors, we chose to project the BERT representations into several lower-dimensional spaces using multiple affine layers with SELU activation (Klambauer et al., 2017), rather than using the whole BERT vector directly. For a k-dimensional word embedding w, the word encoder of the head h encodes it as a n-dimensional vector, which is described as:

$$x_h = \mathrm{SELU}(\mathbf{W_{e_h}} w + b_{e_h}) \tag{1}$$

where $\mathbf{W_{e_h}} \in \mathbb{R}^{n \times k}$ is shared for the pronoun and entities. Our word encoder was also inspired by the multi-head attention (Vaswani et al., 2017), an essential component in BERT, which projects hidden representations into multiple sub-spaces where it can infer the relations between query and key efficiently. We attempted to use more complicated architectures, such as independent transformations for pronouns and entities, or deeper highway transformations (Srivastava et al., 2015), which all resulted in overfitting.

2.5 Modeling Interactions

This task can be considered a sub-task of binary answer selection. We found success modeling interactions between the representations of each entity and the pronoun. We use an established technique from successful natural language inference models (Mou et al., 2015) to model the interaction of encoded results from every head. For the head h, the interaction between encoded entities a_h, b_h and the pronoun p_h is modeled as:

$$i_{ah} = [[a_h; p_h]; a_h - p_h; a_h * p_h] \tag{2}$$
$$i_{bh} = [[b_h; p_h]; b_h - p_h; b_h * p_h] \tag{3}$$

where $i_{ha,hb} \in \mathbb{R}^{4n}$ and $[.;.]$ is the concatenation operator. The interaction vectors are then aggregated to m-dimensional vectors by Siamese encoders which share parameters for (a_h, p_h) and (b_h, p_h), but not shared to different heads:

$$e_{ah} = \mathrm{SELU}(\mathbf{W_{n_h}} i_{ah} + b_{n_h}) \tag{4}$$
$$e_{bh} = \mathrm{SELU}(\mathbf{W_{n_h}} i_{bh} + b_{n_h}) \tag{5}$$

where $W_{n_h} \in \mathbb{R}^{m \times 4n}$. We then sum the results from each Siamese encoder to gather the evidence from all heads:

$$e_a = \sum_h e_{ah} \; ; \; e_b = \sum_h e_{bh} \tag{6}$$

2.6 Handcrafted Features

We also manually create features from parse trees which were generated by spacy,(Honnibal and

Model	Stage 1	Stage 2
Handcrafted features baseline	0.60	-
BERT (B)	0.50	-
BERT (B) + drop.	0.45	0.38
BERT (B) + drop. + inter.	0.43	-
BERT (B) + drop. + inter. + proj.	0.39	0.32
BERT (B) + all*	0.38	0.32
BERT (L) + drop.	0.39	0.31
BERT (L) + drop. + inter. + proj.	0.32	0.24
BERT (L) + all*	0.31	0.24
BERT (B) and BERT (L) ensemble	0.30	0.18

Table 2: The performance gain of each component for both Bert Base and Bert Large, where **all** denotes using input dropout, interaction layers, projection, and handcrafted features at the same time. Performance is log loss from the stage 1 and stage 2 testing data.

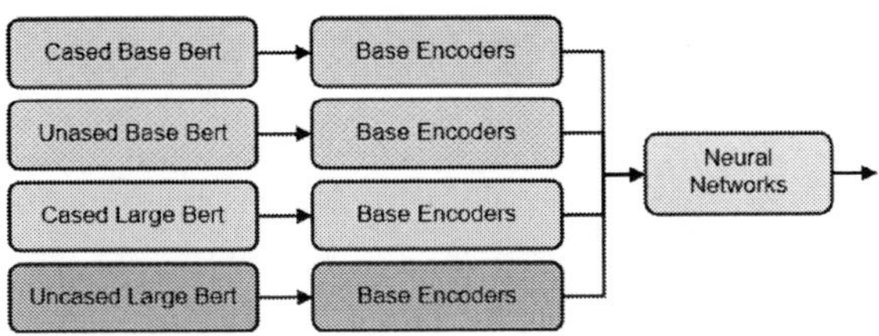

Figure 5: Overview of our ensemble.

Montani, 2017) and from heuristics such as the number of words between the candidate and pronoun. We normalized the hand-crafted features into the range $[0, 1]$ and aggregated them using a feature encoder which consists of an affine layer with SELU activation. To combine the handcrafted features with our encoder architecture, we concatenate the outputs of feature encoder with e_a and e_b.

2.7 Putting it Together

Table 2 shows the performance gains of implementing input dropout, projection, interactions and handcrafted features. In the case **all**, handcrafted features are included. We saw a steady improvement in performance implementing these together that carried over from BERT Base to BERT Large on the both stage 1 and stage 2 evaluation data.

2.8 Ensemble

Figure 5 shows the overview of our ensemble architecture. The ensemble was composed of models whose inputs were from different types of BERTs and handcrafted features. We then aggregated the predictions of the base models with a five-layer densely-connected feedforward network.

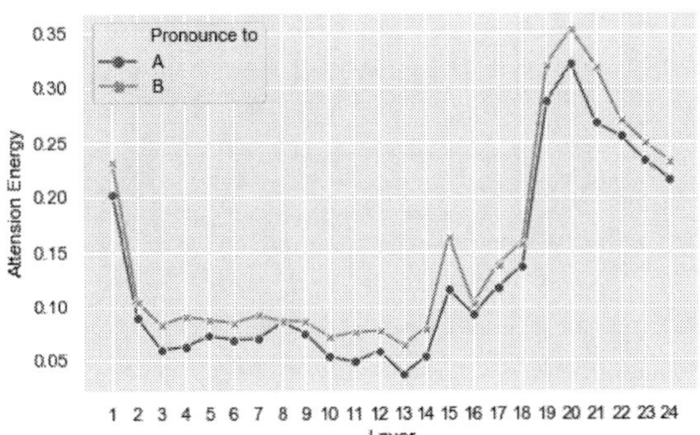

Figure 6: Average attention energy from the pronoun to the entity A and B as a function of layer. Due to imbalance in the dataset, B is more likely to be the correct answer, which explains BERT's preference for B.

2.9 Experiment Setting

Our models were built with Keras. The input dropout rates were 0.6 and 0.7 for BERT Base and Large, respectively. For the concatenation based model, the classifier was composed of a single hidden layer with size 37 following a batch normalization layer and a dropout layer with rate 0.6. For the multi-head NLI encoder, the number of heads was 6 and the dimension of the down-projected vector space was 37. The interactive encoder as composed of a hidden layer with size 37 following SELU activation. To summarize the output from each NLI encoders, we used either a concatenation or summation operation following a dropout layer with rates 0.8, 0.85 respectively. The classifier of the multi-head NLI encoder was exactly the same as the concatenation based encoder.

For training, we validated our models with 7-fold cross-validation and early-stopping on cross-entropy with patience 20. The batch size was 32 and the optimizer was Adam (Kingma and Ba, 2014) with initial learning rate $1e^{-3}$ for all models. We regularized the output layer with 0.1 L2 penalty. The overall training time was about 8 hours for stage 1. For other detailed settings and hyper-parameters please refer to our public code repository.[3]

3 Conclusion

We have demonstrated that BERT has an optimal layer for this task. We also showed that BERT's representations contain redundant infor-

---

[3] https://github.com/zake7749/Fill-the-GAP

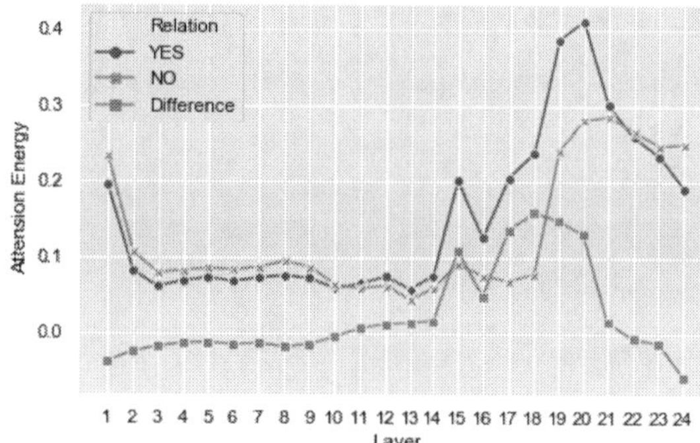

Figure 7: Average attention energy from the pronoun to the correct (YES) and incorrect entity (NO), and the difference between them. These attention distributions provide a signal may be useful for further improvements to our solution.

mation, and that dropout can be used to overcome this problem. Projecting to lower dimensions with multiple heads also allowed us to consider multiple perspectives on this information in more tractable space. Considering interactions between these perspectives also proved beneficial for this task. However, manual error analysis still revealed a large number of world knowledge cases, a major limitation of our solution.

4   Future Work

Post-competition analysis revealed that the difference between attention weights from the target pronoun to the candidate entities in the optimal layer was found to be highly predictive of the correct label. In Figure 6 we can see the overall energy of attention from the pronoun to the candidate entities' peaks. Notice that due to imbalance in the dataset, B is more likely to be the correct answer, which explains BERT's preference for B. Figure 7 shows the average difference in attention energy from the pronoun to the entity that is referred to, or not referred to, and the difference. There are significant gaps between the correct and incorrect candidates in layers 17 to layers 20. The pattern of attention energies is consistent as the observations in section 2.2, which indicates that instead of using the attended vectors, the energies in the attention process can also be efficient and highly-interpretable features for correference resolution.

In future work, we intend to add features from BERT's attention layers to see if we can improve our performance. Furthermore, this discovery could lead to a more general pronoun resolution technique based on BERT that doesn't require candidate entity labeling. We would also like to investigate using this signal for unsupervised and semi-supervised pronoun resolution.

References

Leo Breiman. 1998.   Arcing classifier (with discussion and a rejoinder by the author). *Ann. Statist.*, 26(3):801–849.

Leo Breiman. 2001. Random forests. *Machine Learning*, 45(1):5–32.

Jacob Devlin, Ming-Wei Chang, Kenton Lee, and Kristina Toutanova. 2018.   BERT: pre-training of deep bidirectional transformers for language understanding. *CoRR*, abs/1810.04805.

Matthew Honnibal and Ines Montani. 2017. spacy 2: Natural language understanding with bloom embeddings, convolutional neural networks and incremental parsing. *To appear*.

Diederik P Kingma and Jimmy Ba. 2014.   Adam: A method for stochastic optimization. *arXiv preprint arXiv:1412.6980*.

Günter Klambauer, Thomas Unterthiner, Andreas Mayr, and Sepp Hochreiter. 2017. Self-normalizing neural networks. *CoRR*, abs/1706.02515.

Richard Maclin and David W. Opitz. 2011.   Popular ensemble methods: An empirical study. *CoRR*, abs/1106.0257.

Lili Mou, Rui Men, Ge Li, Yan Xu, Lu Zhang, Rui Yan, and Zhi Jin. 2015.   Recognizing entailment and contradiction by tree-based convolution. *CoRR*, abs/1512.08422.

Matthew E. Peters, Mark Neumann, Mohit Iyyer, Matt Gardner, Christopher Clark, Kenton Lee, and Luke Zettlemoyer. 2018. Deep contextualized word representations. *CoRR*, abs/1802.05365.

Nitish Srivastava, Geoffrey Hinton, Alex Krizhevsky, Ilya Sutskever, and Ruslan Salakhutdinov. 2014. Dropout: A simple way to prevent neural networks from overfitting. *J. Mach. Learn. Res.*, 15(1):1929–1958.

Rupesh Kumar Srivastava, Klaus Greff, and Jürgen Schmidhuber. 2015. Highway networks. *CoRR*, abs/1505.00387.

Ashish Vaswani, Noam Shazeer, Niki Parmar, Jakob Uszkoreit, Llion Jones, Aidan N. Gomez, Lukasz Kaiser, and Illia Polosukhin. 2017. Attention is all you need. *CoRR*, abs/1706.03762.

Kellie Webster, Marta Recasens, Vera Axelrod, and Jason Baldridge. 2018. Mind the gap: A balanced corpus of gendered ambiguous pronouns. In *Transactions of the ACL*, page to appear.

On GAP coreference resolution shared task: insights from the 3rd place solution

Artem Abzaliev

GfK SE

Global Data Science

Bamberger Strasse 6, Nuremberg 90425, Germany

`artem.abzaliev@gfk.com`

Abstract

This paper presents the 3rd-place-winning solution to the GAP coreference resolution shared task. The approach adopted consists of two key components: fine-tuning the BERT language representation model (Devlin et al., 2018) and the usage of external datasets during the training process. The model uses hidden states from the intermediate BERT layers instead of the last layer. The resulting system almost eliminates the difference in log loss per gender during the cross-validation, while providing high performance.

1 Introduction

The GAP coreference resolution shared task promotes gender fair modelling with its GAP dataset (Webster et al., 2018). GAP is a coreference dataset for the resolution of ambiguous pronoun-name pairs in real-world context. GAP has a particular focus on the balance of masculine and feminine pronouns and allows for gender-specific evaluation. The challenge was hosted by Kaggle and consisted of two stages. Stage 1 attracted 838 participants, and stage 2 involved 263 participants.

GAP training examples look the following way:

> Burnett Stone (Peter Fonda) is **Lily's** grandfather and **Lady's** caretaker. He keeps **her** in Muffle Mountain.

where **her** is ambiguous pronoun, **Lily** is candidate mention A, and **Lady** is the candidate mention B. The data was extracted from Wikipedia, so, in addition to the text, the source URL of the article is given. The goal is to predict whether the ambiguous pronoun refers to the mention A, to the mention B or to NEITHER of them. The problem was treated as gold-two-mention task, where the model has the access to the position of the mentions.

2 The data

The GAP dataset is split into training, validation and test set. Training and test set contain 2000 examples each, validation includes 454 examples. During the stage 1 of the competition, the test set was used to evaluate the model performance, while train and validation sets together were used for training with 5 fold cross-validation scheme. This choice initially was made because of the relatively little amount of data and the instability of the predictions (the score on one fold can significantly differ from the other fold). There were several errors in labels of all three GAP dataset, reported by the competition participants[1]. The current solution employs the GAP data with manual corrections.

During the stage 2 of the competition, all three datasets with resulting 4454 observations were used for the training, while the new test set with 12,359 examples was used for the prediction.

2.1 Additional data

There are several coreference datasets available for training and evaluating. Besides GAP data, the presented solution uses four external data sources: Winobias (Zhao et al., 2018), Winogender (Rudinger et al., 2018), The Definite Pronoun Resolution (DPR) Dataset (Rahman and Ng, 2012; Peng et al., 2015) and Ontonotes 5.0 (Pradhan et al., 2012). Each of them was processed to be compatible with the GAP format. After the cleaning this resulted in 39,452 training examples for Ontonotes 5.0, 360 for Winogender, 3162 for Winobias and 1400 for DPR. In this paper, this external data (Ontonotes 5.0, Winobias, Winogdender, DPR) will be called *warm-up data*, because it was used to fine-tune the BERT embeddings, and the weights learned from this data served as 'warm

---

[1] https://www.kaggle.com/c/gendered-pronoun-resolution/discussion/81331

Proceedings of the 1st Workshop on Gender Bias in Natural Language Processing, pages 107–112

Florence, Italy, August 2, 2019. ©2019 Association for Computational Linguistics

up' for the training on the GAP dataset.

There was one more candidate to the additonal datasets pool, namely PreCo (Chen et al., 2018), but despite many efforts this dataset did not provide any score improvement. Presumably, this is mainly due to the different structure of the data, and the high amount of noise. For instance, some training examples contained the same word as both mention and pronoun, which may have worsen the model performance.

There were several attempts to include all the additional datasets to the training procedure. The naive attempt to concatenate GAP data and additional data into one big training set did not work, because the additional data has a different structure and does not have the URL feature. The second attempt was to use a two-step approach:

1. Warm-up step: pretrain the part of the model (namely the head, see section 3 for the explanations) on the external data only. Then, select the weights from the model that performs best on the warm-up validation set.

2. GAP step: continue training on GAP data, using the weight from the best-performing warm-up model instead of randomly initialized weights.

The warm-up data was randomly split into training and validation set with 95%-5% proportions. This strategy slightly improved the model performance, showing that warming-up on external dataset can be a promising direction. One possible explanation is that starting with pretrained weights allowed the model to reach flatter optimum and generalize better. In addition, the external data contained many more training examples for the category NEITHER (see Table 1), resulting in better performance for this group.

During the third attempt, the validation set was not randomly chosen, but replaced by Winobias only. It was done to ensure that gender fair representation will be chosen as initialization weights for the GAP step. This action further provided small improvement in the evaluation metric. However, the negative effect of choosing Winobias as validation data was the complete exclusion of the class NEITHER from the validation data (see Table 1). Surprisingly, this effect was not detrimental to the performance, most likely because the training data contained enough training examples for this class.

	GAP train	Warm-up train	Warm-up val
A	43.71%	31.91%	50%
B	44.65%	31.40%	50%
NEITHER	11.63%	36.68%	0

Table 1: Class distribution for the datasets used. GAP train includes all the gap datasets available (gap development, gap val, gap test). Warm-up train includes Ontonotes, DPR and Winogender. Warm-up val only includes Winobias.

The final version of the model also fine-tunes the particular layers of BERT embeddings, in addition to the warm-up of the head. For a full description, see section 3.

2.2 Evaluation metrics and class distributions

Class distributions Table 1 shows the class distributions for the three final datasets used: GAP train, which includes all GAP data, warm-up train, which includes Ontonotes 5.0, Winogdender, DPR and warm-up validation, which is Winobias. As can be seen, warm-up train has the most balanced distribution of classes, while GAP train has a lower portion of the category NEITHER.

Evaluation metrics Solutions were evaluated using the multi-class logarithmic loss. For each pronoun, the participants had to provide the probabilities of it belonging to A, B, or NEITHER. The formula to evaluate the performance of the model is:

$$logloss = -\frac{1}{N}\sum_{i=1}^{N}\sum_{j=1}^{M} y_{ij} log(p_{ij})$$

where N is the number of samples in the test set, M is number of classes, 3, log is the natural logarithm, y_{ij} is 1 if observation i belongs to class j and 0 otherwise, and p_{ij} is the predicted probability that observation i belongs to class j.

2.3 Features

Besides the direct textual input, the current solution uses some manually constructed features. The majority of them were already mentioned by Webster et al. (2018) as single baseline models. The following features were used:

- **Token Distance**. Distance between mentions and the pronoun, and also between the mentions themselves.

- **Syntactic distance between mentions and pronoun**. The distances were extracted with the StandfordCoreNLP.

- **URL**. Whether the Wikipedia URL contains the mention.

- **Sentence of the mention**. Index of the sentence, where the mention is located, divided by total number of sentences in the snippet.

- **Syntactic distance to the sentence root**. The distance between the mention and its syntactic parent.

- **Character position**. The relative character position of the mention in the text.

- **Pronoun gender**. Gender of the pronoun. It was noticed that in some examples, mentions were of different gender, so the hope was that this feature could help. It did not help, but it did not hurt either. The fact that this feature did not affect the performance can be a good indicator of gender-neutral learning.

The features that provided the biggest improvements were URL (0.07 decrease on log loss) and syntactic distance between mentions and pronoun (0.01). The contribution of other features was very limited.

3 The system

The final solution uses an ensemble of four neural networks. They are: fifth-to-last-layer with cased BERT, fifth-to-last-layer with uncased BERT, sixth-to-last-layer with uncased BERT, sixth-to-last-layer with cased BERT. The explanation is in the next subsection of the paper. Each network consists of two main parts:

- BERT part: contextual representations of the text with fine-tuned BERT embeddings

- Head part: using the embeddings together with manually crafted features to produce softmax probabilities of the three classes

All networks have the same architecture for the head part and the only difference is in the BERT part.

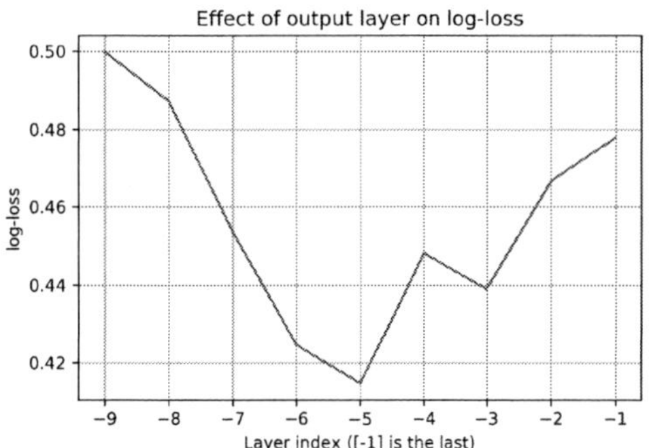

Figure 1: The effect of the output layer choice on the performance of the model. Layer index [-5] means fifth-to-last output layer. Log loss is reported on the stage 1 test dataset, at the beginning of the competition, keeping all the other parameters fixed.

3.1 BERT part

BERT is general purpose language model, pretrained on Wikipedia and BookCorpus. It leverages high amount of unannotated data on the web and produces context-aware word embeddings. The current solution uses pytorch-pretrained-BERT[2]. Besides fine-tuning BERT weights, the set of possible parameters for the pretrained BERT is limited. The possibilities are:

- Amount of layers in the Transformer model: 12-layer (bert-base) or 24-layer (bert-large)

- Cased or uncased model

- Multilingual or single-language model

One additional peculiarity, discovered by several contestants independently, is that using the output of the last layer may be an inferior option compared to the deeper ones. For the architecture presented in this paper, optimal layers were fifth-to-last ([-5]) and sixth-to-last ([-6]). Figure 1 shows the log loss during stage 1 for different ouput layers, keeping all other parameters of the network fixed.

One possible explanation for this phenomenon is that the last output layer specializes on predicting the masked words, while the intermediate layers contain more general information. The U-shaped curve also shows that taking much deeper layers negatively affect the model performance.

Fine-tuning. As mentioned in the section 2.1, initially only the head part was fine-tuned on the

---

[2]https://github.com/huggingface/pytorch-pretrained-BERT

warm-up dataset and the learned weights were used as initialization weights for the GAP training. The logical step would also be to fine-tune the BERT embeddings themselves. It was done in the following way: first, the head was trained for 16 epochs, with the parameters of BERT being frozen. Afterwards, all of the parameters of the head were frozen, and one particular layer (either fifth-to-last or sixth-to-last) of BERT was fine-tuned. The small learning rate was very crucial at this step, because the number of parameters is high (12,596,224). The current solution uses $4e^{-5}$ as learning rate, trained for 16 epochs with batch size of 32. Every 400 steps the network performance was estimated on the evaluation data, and only the best performing model was used after the training was done.

3.2 Head part

The head network always takes BERT contextual embeddings of shape [batch_size, seq_len, 1024] (for BERT-large). These embeddings are processed with the 1d-convolutional layer of size 64 and kernel=1 in order to reduce the dimensionality. Interestingly, increasing kernel size to 2 or 3 deteriorates the performance. This may be due to the fact that the context just around the mentions was not that informative.

Because the positions of mentions and pronoun are known in advance, the embeddings of only those three phrases are extracted. This is done by using SelfAttentiveSpanExtractor from AllenNLP (Gardner et al., 2017). This span extractor will generate 3 vectors of size 64 - for A, B and Pronoun. For single token mentions the span representation is just the original vector itself, while for mentions with more than two tokens, the span extractor will produce weighted representation by using the attention scores. Other span extractors from AllenNLP did not perform as good as the self-attentive span extractor.

The resulting three vectors of size 64 are concatenated and processed with the standard fully-connected block: BatchNorm1d(192) $\rightarrow$ Linear (192, 64) $\rightarrow$ ReLU $\rightarrow$ BatchNorm1d $\rightarrow$ Dropout (0.6). This output is concatenated with all the manual features mentioned in the section 2.3, which results in the vector of length 96. Adding features directly to the last layer is important, otherwise they do not bring any improvement. Finally, Linear (96, 3) layer on top produces the log-

its. The softmax probabilities are computed in the numerically stable way in the loss function.

3.3 Training details

For the GAP training, Adam optimizer with the learning rate $2e^{-3}$ is used. The batch size is 20. For both BERT fine-tuning and GAP training the triangular learning rate schedule is used (Smith, 2017). The loss used is CrossEntropyLoss, which combines numerically stable computation of softmax probabilities with negative log-likelihood loss function.

The predictions for each of the four networks are done in 10 fold cross-validation stratified by the class distribution, i.e. the model is trained on 90% of the data and the other 10% is used for the evaluation. The final predictions is the average across all folds and all models, overall of 40 models. Final predictions were clipped to be in the interval $(1e^{-2}, 1 - 1e^{-2})$, because log loss penalizes the predictions heavily as they drift away from ground truth.

The training runs approximately one day on single NVIDIA Tesla P100. This can be substantially reduced with proper code optimization (for instance, removing BERT computations for all layers after the fifth-to-last). The framework used for the implementation is PyTorch[3]

4 Results

The described solution provides the log loss of 0.1839 on the test stage 2 data, which results in the third place on Kaggle leaderboard. The results of single models are presented in the Table 3. As can be seen, the cased version performs generally better. One reason may be given by the variety of personal names in the GAP, and the cased version is able to recognize them better.

On the *cleaned* stage 1 test data, the best-performing single model (cased BERT, fifth-to-last layer) provided the log loss of 0.23819. Because the true labels are available for the test stage 1 data, the loss for the masculine and the feminine pronouns was estimated separately. For masculine pronouns the log loss was equal to 0.24014, while for feminine it was equal to 0.23623. The difference is $3e^{-3}$, which can be considered insignificant.

The error matrix for the whole stage one dataset (10-fold cross-validated) is presented in the Table

---

[3]https://pytorch.org/

	A pred	B pred	NEITHER pred
A	1849	72	26
B	57	1908	24
NEITHER	58	59	401

Table 2: Confusion matrix on the whole stage 1 data with 10 fold cross validation.

Model name	Log loss
Cased [-5]	0.20592
Cased [-6]	0.20429
Uncased [-5]	0.22834
Uncased [-6]	0.21088
Ensemble	0.18397

Table 3: Performance of the models on the test stage 2 data.

2. As can be seen, the performance for the category NEITHER is worse than for other categories. Most likely this is because of the lower amount of training examples. Even though the warm-up data contained many observations with this category, these examples were quite trivial, and the final model still struggles on the GAP data. This indicates a potential area for the improvement of the model. For the wrong predictions, some additional metrics were also examined, like the length of the text or the number of words in the mentions. These properties are not significantly different from those for the correct predictions. After manual examination, it appears that the model makes mistakes on the examples that are also quite challenging for humans.

5 Discussion

One of the weaknesses of the presented system is the training and prediction time. Because there are four networks, training takes a long time, and the prediction on the test set requires almost 2 hours. The attempt to concatenate several intermediate BERT layers, or to use a linear combination of them did not work, although it was reported to have a positive effect (Tenney et al., 2018). Using the information from the whole Wikipedia page also did not provide any improvements.

During the early stages of the competition, when only GAP data was used, the sources of model mistakes were analyzed. It was found, that despite the best efforts of the authors, there are still some mislabelled examples in the GAP data itself.

dataset	errors female	errors male
gap_development	35	31
gap_val	12	9
gap_test	45	28

Table 4: Number of mislabelled examples in the datasets per gender.

Other participants reported errors as well[4]. Some of these errors are quite simple, but the majority require substantial human efforts and sometimes were impossible to detect without reading the corresponding Wikipedia article.

The number of erroneous labels for different GAP datasets separated by gender is reported in Table 4. This list is based on the mistakes reported on the forum, as well as own single checks, but it is not comprehensive. It can be seen that mislabelled examples represent less than 5% of all cases. They are usually equally distributed between genders, besides gap_test, where mislabelled examples for female cases are 30% higher.

6 Conclusion

This paper presents the solution for the coreference resolution on GAP shared task. The solution utilizes the pretrained contextual embeddings from BERT and fine-tunes them for the coreference problem on additional data. One of the findings is that the output of BERT's intermediate layers gives better representation of the input text for the coreference task. Another contribution is that the gender bias in external data can be mitigated by using gender-fair datasets as validation data during the pretraining phase.

References

Hong Chen, Zhenhua Fan, Hao Lu, Alan L Yuille, and Shu Rong. 2018. Preco: A large-scale dataset in preschool vocabulary for coreference resolution. *arXiv preprint arXiv:1810.09807*.

Jacob Devlin, Ming-Wei Chang, Kenton Lee, and Kristina Toutanova. 2018. Bert: Pre-training of deep bidirectional transformers for language understanding. *arXiv preprint arXiv:1810.04805*.

Matt Gardner, Joel Grus, Mark Neumann, Oyvind Tafjord, Pradeep Dasigi, Nelson F. Liu, Matthew Peters, Michael Schmitz, and Luke S. Zettlemoyer.

---

[4]https://www.kaggle.com/c/gendered-pronoun-resolution/discussion/81331

2017. Allennlp: A deep semantic natural language processing platform.

Haoruo Peng, Daniel Khashabi, and Dan Roth. 2015. Solving hard coreference problems. In *Proceedings of the 2015 Conference of the North American Chapter of the Association for Computational Linguistics: Human Language Technologies*, pages 809–819.

Sameer Pradhan, Alessandro Moschitti, Nianwen Xue, Olga Uryupina, and Yuchen Zhang. 2012. Conll-2012 shared task: Modeling multilingual unrestricted coreference in ontonotes. In *Joint Conference on EMNLP and CoNLL-Shared Task*, pages 1–40. Association for Computational Linguistics.

Altaf Rahman and Vincent Ng. 2012. Resolving complex cases of definite pronouns: the winograd schema challenge. In *Proceedings of the 2012 Joint Conference on Empirical Methods in Natural Language Processing and Computational Natural Language Learning*, pages 777–789. Association for Computational Linguistics.

Rachel Rudinger, Jason Naradowsky, Brian Leonard, and Benjamin Van Durme. 2018. Gender bias in coreference resolution. *arXiv preprint arXiv:1804.09301*.

Leslie N Smith. 2017. Cyclical learning rates for training neural networks. In *2017 IEEE Winter Conference on Applications of Computer Vision (WACV)*, pages 464–472. IEEE.

Ian Tenney, Patrick Xia, Berlin Chen, Alex Wang, Adam Poliak, R Thomas McCoy, Najoung Kim, Benjamin Van Durme, Samuel R Bowman, Dipanjan Das, et al. 2018. What do you learn from context? probing for sentence structure in contextualized word representations.

Kellie Webster, Marta Recasens, Vera Axelrod, and Jason Baldridge. 2018. Mind the gap: A balanced corpus of gendered ambiguous pronouns. *Transactions of the Association for Computational Linguistics*, 6:605–617.

Jieyu Zhao, Tianlu Wang, Mark Yatskar, Vicente Ordonez, and Kai-Wei Chang. 2018. Gender bias in coreference resolution: Evaluation and debiasing methods. *arXiv preprint arXiv:1804.06876*.

Resolving Gendered Ambiguous Pronouns with BERT

Matei Ionita
University of Pennsylvania
matei@sas.upenn.edu

Yury Kashnitsky
Moscow Institute of Physics and Technology
yury.kashnitsky@phystech.edu

Ken Krige
Kitsong
kenkrige@gmail.com

Vladimir Larin
PJSC Sberbank
vlarine@gmail.com

Denis Logvinenko
Jet Infosystems
dennis_l@rambler.ru

Atanas Atanasov
Sofia University
a.atanasov1@ocado.com

Abstract

Pronoun resolution is part of coreference resolution, the task of pairing an expression to its referring entity. This is an important task for natural language understanding and a necessary component of machine translation systems, chat bots and assistants. Neural machine learning systems perform far from ideally in this task, reaching as low as 73% F1 scores on modern benchmark datasets. Moreover, they tend to perform better for masculine pronouns than for feminine ones. Thus, the problem is both challenging and important for NLP researchers and practitioners. In this project, we describe our BERT-based approach to solving the problem of gender-balanced pronoun resolution. We are able to reach 92% F1 score and a much lower gender bias on the benchmark dataset shared by Google AI Language team.

1 Introduction

In this work, we are dealing with gender bias in pronoun resolution. A more general task of coreference resolution is reviewed in Sec. 2. In Sec. 3, we give an overview of a related Kaggle competition. Then, Sec. 4 describes the GAP dataset and Google AI's heuristics to resolve pronomial coreference in a gender-agnostic way, so that pronoun resolution is done equally well in cases of masculine and feminine pronouns. In Sec. 5, we provide the details of our BERT-based solution while in Sec. 6 we analyze pleasantly low gender

bias specific for our system (our code is shared on GitHub[1]). Lastly, in Sec. 7, we draw conclusions and express some ideas for further research.

2 Related work

Among popular approaches to coreference resolution are:[2] rule-based, mention pair, mention ranking, and clustering. As for rule-based approaches, they describe naïve Hobbs algorithm (Hobbs, 1986) which, in spite of being naïve, has shown state-of-the-art performance on the OntoNotes dataset[3] up to 2010.

Recent state-of-the-art approaches (Lee et al., 2018, 2017; Peters et al., 2018a) are pretty complex examples of mention ranking systems. The 2017 version is the first end-to-end coreference resolution model that didn't utilize syntactic parsers or hand-engineered mention detectors. Instead, it used LSTMs and attention mechanism to improve over previous NN-based solutions.

Some more state-of-the-art coreference resolution systems are reviewed in (Webster et al., 2018) as well as popular datasets with ambiguous pronouns: Winograd schemas (Levesque et al., 2012), WikiCoref (Ghaddar and Langlais, 2016), and

---

[1] https://github.com/Yorko/
gender-unbiased_BERT-based_pronoun_
resolution
[2] https://bit.ly/2JbKxv1
[3] https://catalog.ldc.upenn.edu/
LDC2013T19

Proceedings of the 1st Workshop on Gender Bias in Natural Language Processing, pages 113–119
Florence, Italy, August 2, 2019. ©2019 Association for Computational Linguistics

The Definite Pronoun Resolution Dataset (Pradhan et al., 2007). We also refer to the GAP paper for a brief review of gender bias in machine learning.

We further outline that e2e-coref model (Lee et al., 2018), in spite of being state-of-the-art in coreference resolution, didn't show good results in the pronoun resolution task that we tackled, so we only used e2e-coref predictions as an additional feature.

3 Kaggle competition "Gendered Pronoun Resolution"

Following Kaggle competition "Gendered Pronoun Resolution",[4] for each abstract from Wikipedia pages we are given a pronoun, and we try to predict the right coreference for it, i.e. to which named entity (A or B) it refers. Let's take a look at this simple example:

"John entered the room and saw [A] Julia. [Pronoun] She was talking to [B] Mary Hendriks and looked so extremely gorgeous that John was stunned and couldn't say a word."

Here "Julia" is marked as entity A, "Mary Hendriks" – as entity B, and pronoun "She" is marked as Pronoun. In this particular case the task is to correctly identify to which entity the given pronoun refers.

If we feed this sentence into a coreference resolution system (see Fig. 1 and online demo[5]), we see that it correctly identifies that "she" refers to Julia, it also correctly clusters together two mentions of "John" and detects that Mary Hendriks is a two-word span.

For instance, if you take an abstract like this it's pretty hard to resolve coreference.

"Roxanne, a poet who now lives in France. Isabel believes that she is there to help Roxanne during her pregnancy with her toddler infant, but later realizes that her father and step-mother sent her there so that Roxanne would help the shiftless Isabel gain some direction in life. Shortly after she (pronoun) arrives, Roxanne confides in Isabel that her French husband, Claude-Henri has left her."

Google AI and Kaggle (organizers of this competition) provided the GAP dataset (Webster et al., 2018) with 4454 snippets from Wikipedia articles, in each of them named entities A and B are labeled along with a pronoun. The dataset is labeled, i.e. for each sentence a correct coreference is specified, one of three mutually-exclusive classes: either A or B or "Neither". Thus, the prediction task is actually that of multiclass classification type.

Moreover, the dataset is balanced w.r.t. masculine and feminine pronouns. Thus, the competition was supposed to address the problem of building a coreference resolution system which is not susceptible to gender bias, i.e. works equally well for masculine and feminine pronouns.

These are the columns provided in the dataset (Webster et al., 2018):

- ID - Unique identifier for an example (matches to Id in output file format)

- Text - Text containing the ambiguous pronoun and two candidate names (about a paragraph in length)

- Pronoun - target pronoun (text)

- Pronoun-offset - character offset of Pronoun in Text

- A - first name candidate (text)

- A-offset - character offset of name A in Text

- B - second name candidate

- B-offset - character offset of name B in Text

- URL - URL of the source Wikipedia page for the example

Evaluation metric chosen for the competition[6] is multiclass logarithmic loss. Each pronoun has been labeled with whether it refers to A, B, or "Neither". For each pronoun, a set of predicted probabilities (one for each class) is submitted. The formula is then

$$logloss = -\frac{1}{N} \sum_{i=1}^{N} \sum_{j=1}^{M} y_{ij} \log p_{ij},$$

where N is the number of samples in the test set, M is 3, log is the natural logarithm, y_{ij} is 1 if observation i belongs to class j and 0 otherwise, and p_{ij} is the predicted probability that observation i belongs to class j.

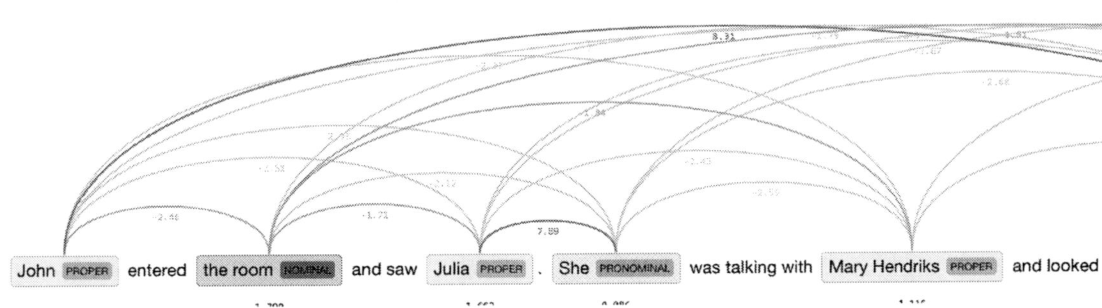

Figure 1: Coreference resolution visualized with HuggingFace demo `https://huggingface.co/coref/`.

Unfortunately, the chosen evaluation metric does not reflect the mentioned above goal of building a gender-unbiased coreference resolution algorithm, i.e. the metric does not account for gender imbalance - logarithmic loss may not reflect the fact that e.g. predicted pronoun coreference is much worse for masculine pronouns than for feminine ones. Therefore, we explore gender bias separately in Sec. 6 and compare our results with those published by the Google AI Language team (reviewed in Sec. 4).

4 Mind the GAP: A Balanced Corpus of Gendered Ambiguous Pronouns

Google AI Language team addresses the problem of gender bias in pronoun resolution (when systems favor masculine entities) and a gender-balanced labeled corpus of 8,908 ambiguous pronoun-name pairs sampled to provide diverse coverage of challenges posed by real-world text (Webster et al., 2018) (further referred to as the GAP dataset). They run 4 state-of-the-art coreference resolution models (Lee et al., 2013; Clark and Manning, 2015; Wiseman et al., 2016; Lee et al., 2017) on the OntoNotes and GAP datasets reporting F1 scores separately for masculine and feminine pronoun-named entity pairs (metrics **M** and **F** in the paper). Also they measure "gender bias" defined as $\mathbf{B} = \mathbf{F} / \mathbf{M}$. In general, they conclude, these models perform better for masculine pronoun-named entity pairs, but still pronoun resolution is challenging - all achieved F1 scores are less than 0.7 for both datasets.

Further, they propose simple heuristics (called surface, structural and Wikipedia *cues*). The best reported cues are "Parallelism" (if the pronoun is a subject or direct object, select the closest candidate with the same grammatical argument) and "URL" (select the syntactically closest candidate which has a token overlap with the page title). They compare the performance of "Parallelism + URL" cue with e2e-coref (Lee et al., 2017) on the GAP dataset and, surprisingly enough, conclude that heuristics work better achieving better F1 scores (0.742 for **M** and 0.716 for **F**) at the same time being less gender-biased (some of heuristics are totally gender-unbiased, for "Parallelism + URL" $\mathbf{B} = \mathbf{F} / \mathbf{M} = 0.96$).

Finally, they explored Transformer architecture (Vaswani et al., 2017) for this task and observed that the coreference signal is localized on specific heads and that these heads are in the deep layers of the network. In Sec. 5 we confirm this observation. Actually, they select the candidate which attends most to the pronoun ("Transformer heuristic" in the paper). Even though they conclude that Transformer models implicitly learn language understanding relevant to coreference resolution, as for F1 scores, they didn't make it work better than e2e-coref or Parallelism cues (F1 scores lower that 0.63). More to that, proposed Transformers heuristics are a bit biased towards masculine pronouns with **B** from 0.95 to 0.98.

Further we report a much stronger gender-unbiased BERT-based (Devlin et al., 2018) pronoun resolution system.

5 System

BERT (Devlin et al., 2018) is a transformer architecture, pre-trained on a large corpus (Wikipedia + BookCorpus), with 12 to 24 transformer layers. Each layer learns a 1024-dimensional representation of the input token, with layer 1 being similar to a standard word embedding, layer 24 specialized for the task of predicting missing words from context. At the same time BERT embeddings are learned for a second auxiliary task of resolving whether two consequent sentences are connected to each other or not.

In general, motivated by (Tenney et al., 2019), we found that BERT provides very good token embeddings for the task in hand.

Our proposed pipeline is built upon solutions by teams "Ken Krige" and "[ods.ai] five zeros" (placed 5 and 22 in the final leaderboard[7] correspondingly). The way these two teams approached the competition task are described in two Kaggle posts.[8][9] The combined pipeline includes several subroutines:

- Extracting BERT-embeddings for named entities A, B, and pronouns

- Fine-tuning BERT classifier

- Hand-crafted features

- Neural network architectures

- Correcting mislabeled instances

5.1 Extracting BERT-embeddings for named entities A, B, and pronouns

We concatenated embeddings for entities A, B, and Pronoun taken from Cased and Uncased large BERT "frozen" (not fine-tuned) models.[10] We noticed that extracting embeddings from intermediate layers (from -4 to -6) worked best for the task. Also we added pointwise products of embeddings for Pronoun and entity A, Pronoun and entity B as well as AB - PP. First of these embedding vectors expresses similarity between pronoun and A, the second one expresses similarity between pronoun and B, the third vector is supposed to represent the extent to which entities A and B are similar to each other but differ from the Pronoun.

5.2 Fine-tuning BERT classifier

Apart from extracting embeddings from original BERT models, we also fine-tuned BERT classifier for the task in hand. We made appropriate changes to the "run_classifier.py" script from Google's repository.[11] Preprocessing input data for the BERT input layer included stripping text to 64 symbols, then into 4 segments, running BERT Wordpiece for each segment, adding start and end tokens (with truncation if needed) and concatenating segments back together. The whole preprocessing is reproduced in a Kaggle Kernel[12] as well as in our final code on GitHub.[13]

5.3 Hand-crafted features

Apart from BERT embeddings, we also added 69 features which can be grouped into several categories:

- Neuralcoref,[14] Stanford CoreNLP (Manning et al., 2014) and e2e-coref (Lee et al., 2017) model predictions. It turned out that these models performed not really well in the task in hand, but their predictions worked well as additional features.

- Predictions of a Multi-Layered Perceptron trained with ELMo (Peters et al., 2018b) embeddings

- Syntactic roles of entities A, B, and Pronoun (subject, direct object, attribute etc.) extracted with SpaCy [15].

- Positional and frequency-based (distances between A, B, Pronoun and derivations, whether they all are in the same sentence or Pronoun is in the following one etc.). Many of these features we motivated by the Hobbs algorithm (Hobbs, 1986) for coreference resolution.

- Named entities predicted for A and B with SpaCy

[7]https://www.kaggle.com/c/
gendered-pronoun-resolution/leaderboard

[8]https://www.kaggle.com/c/
gendered-pronoun-resolution/discussion/
90668

[9]https://www.kaggle.com/c/
gendered-pronoun-resolution/discussion/
90431

[10]https://github.com/google-research/
bert

[11]https://github.com/google-research/
bert

[12]https://www.kaggle.com/kenkrige/
bert-example-prep

[13]https://github.com/Yorko/
gender-unbiased_BERT-based_pronoun_
resolution

[14]https://github.com/huggingface/
neuralcoref

[15]https://spacy.io/

- GAP heuristics outlined in the corresponding paper (Webster et al., 2018) and briefly discussed in Sec. 4

We need to mention that adding all these features had only minor effect on the quality of pronoun resolution (resulted in a 0.01 decrease in logarithmic loss when measured on the Kaggle test dataset) as compared to e.g. fine-tuning BERT classifier.

5.4 Neural network architectures

Final setup includes:

- 6 independently trained fine-tuned BERT classifiers with preprocessing described in Subsec. 5.2. In Tables 1, 2, and 3, we refer to their averaged prediction as to that of a "fine-tuned" model (🔥)

- 5 multi-layered perceptrons trained with different combinations of BERT embeddings for A, B, Pronoun (see Subsec. 5.1) and hand-crafted features (see Subsec. 5.3), all together referred to as "frozen" in Tables 1, 2, and 3 (❄). Using MLPs with pre-trained BERT embeddings is motivated by (Tenney et al., 2019). Two MLPs- separate for Cased and Uncased BERT models - both taking 9216-d input and outputting 112-d vectors. Two Siamese networks were trained on top of distances between Pronoun and A-embeddings, Pronoun and B-embeddings as inputs. One more MLP took only 69-dimensional feature vectors as an input. Finally, a single dense layer mapped outputs from the mentioned 5 models into 3 classes corresponding to named entities A, B or "Neither".

- Blending (🔍) involves taking predicted probabilities for A, B and "Neither" with weight 0.65 for the "fine-tuned" model and summing the result with 0.35 times corresponding probabilities output by the "frozen" model.

In the next Section, we perform the analysis identical to the one done in (Webster et al., 2018) to measure the quality of pronoun resolution and the severity of gender bias in the task in hand.

	GAP test	Kaggle test
🔥 **fine-tuned**	0.29	0.192
❄ **frozen**	0.299	0.226
🔍 **blend**	0.257	0.185

Table 1: Logarithmic loss reported for the GAP test set, and Kaggle test (Stage 2) data for the model with fine-tuned BERT classifier (🔥), MLPs with pre-trained BERT embeddings and hand-crafted features (❄) and a blend of the previous two (🔍). There are 66 corrections done for GAP test labels as described in Subsec. 5.5.

5.5 Correcting mislabeled instances

During the competition, 158 label corrections were proposed for the GAP dataset[16] - when Pronoun is said to mention A but actually mentions B and vice versa. For the GAP test set, this resulted in 66 pronoun coreferences being corrected. It's important to mention that the observed mislabeling is a bit biased against female pronouns (39 mislabeled feminine pronouns versus 27 mislabeled masculine ones), and it turned out that most of the gender bias for F1 score and accuracy comes from these mislabeled examples.

6 Results

In Table 1, we report logarithmic loss that we got on GAP test ("gap-test.tsv"), and Kaggle test (Stage 2) datasets. Kaggle competition results can also be seen on the final competition leaderboard.[17] We report GAP test results as well to further compare with the results reported in the GAP paper: measured are logarithmic loss, F1 score and accuracy for masculine and feminine pronouns (Table 2). Logarithmic loss and accuracy are computed for a 3-class classification problem (A, B, or Neither) while F1 is computed for a 2-class problem (A or B) to compare with results reported by the Google AI Language team in (Webster et al., 2018).

We also incorporated 66 label corrections as described in 5.5 and, interestingly enough, this lead to a conclusion that with corrected labels, models are less susceptible to gender bias. Table 3 reports the same metric in case of corrected labeling, and we see that in this case the proposed models are

---

[16]https://www.kaggle.com/c/gendered-pronoun-resolution/discussion/81331

[17]https://www.kaggle.com/c/gendered-pronoun-resolution/leaderboard

	Logarithmic loss				Accuracy				F1 score			
	M	F	O	B	M	F	O	B	M	F	O	B
fine-tuned	0.294	0.398	0.346	0.738	0.908	0.884	0.896	0.974	0.927	0.9	0.914	0.971
frozen	0.308	0.368	0.338	0.837	0.883	0.866	0.874	0.981	0.904	0.882	0.893	0.976
blend	0.259	0.338	0.299	0.766	0.907	0.883	0.895	0.974	0.923	0.898	0.911	0.973

Table 2: Performance of the proposed two models and their blending on the GAP test set, split by **M**asculine, **F**eminine (**B**ias shows F/M in case of F1 and accuracy, and M/F in case of logarithmic loss), and **Overall**.

almost gender-unbiased.

These results imply that:

- Overall, in terms of F1 score, the proposed solution compares very favorably with the results reported in the GAP paper, achieving as high as 0.911 overall F1 score, compared to 0.729 for "Parallelism + URL" heuristic from (Webster et al., 2018);

- Blending model predictions improves logarithmic loss pretty well but does not impact F1 score and accuracy that much. It can be explained: logarithmic loss is high for confident and at the same time incorrect predictions. Blending averages predicted probabilities so that they end up less extreme (not so close to 0 or 1);

- With original labeling, all models are somewhat susceptible to gender bias, especially in terms of logarithmic loss. However, in terms of F1 score, gender bias is still less than for e2e-coref and "Parallelism + URL" heuristic reported in (Webster et al., 2018);

- Fixing some incorrect labels almost eliminates gender bias, when we talk about F1 score and accuracy of pronoun resolution.

7 Conclusions and further work

We conclude that we managed to propose a BERT-based approach to pronoun resolution which results in considerably better quality (as measured in terms of F1 score and accuracy) than in case of pronoun resolution done with heuristics described in the GAP paper. Moreover, the proposed solution is almost gender-unbiased - pronoun resolution is done almost equally well for masculine and feminine pronouns.

Further we plan to investigate which semantic and syntactic information is carried by different BERT layers and how it refers to coreference resolution. We are also going to benchmark our system on OntoNotes, Winograd, and DPR datasets.

Acknowledgments

Authors would like to thank Open Data Science[18] community for all insightful discussions related to Natural Language Processing and, more generally, to Deep Learning. Authors are also grateful to Kaggle and Google AI Language teams for organizing the Gendered Pronoun Resolution challenge.

References

Kevin Clark and Christopher D. Manning. 2015. Entity-centric coreference resolution with model stacking. In *Proceedings of the 53rd Annual Meeting of the Association for Computational Linguistics and the 7th International Joint Conference on Natural Language Processing (Volume 1: Long Papers)*, pages 1405–1415, Beijing, China. Association for Computational Linguistics.

Jacob Devlin, Ming-Wei Chang, Kenton Lee, and Kristina Toutanova. 2018. Bert: Pre-training of deep bidirectional transformers for language understanding. Cite arxiv:1810.04805Comment: 13 pages.

Abbas Ghaddar and Phillippe Langlais. 2016. Wikicoref: An english coreference-annotated corpus of wikipedia articles. In *Proceedings of the Tenth International Conference on Language Resources and Evaluation (LREC 2016)*, Paris, France. European Language Resources Association (ELRA).

J Hobbs. 1986. Readings in natural language processing. chapter Resolving Pronoun References, pages 339–352. Morgan Kaufmann Publishers Inc., San Francisco, CA, USA.

Heeyoung Lee, Angel Chang, Yves Peirsman, Nathanael Chambers, Mihai Surdeanu, and Dan Jurafsky. 2013. Deterministic coreference resolution based on entity-centric, precision-ranked rules. *Comput. Linguist.*, 39(4):885–916.

Kenton Lee, Luheng He, Mike Lewis, and Luke Zettlemoyer. 2017. End-to-end neural coreference resolution. In *Proceedings of the 2017 Conference on Empirical Methods in Natural Language Processing*, pages 188–197, Copenhagen, Denmark. Association for Computational Linguistics.

---

[18]`https://ods.ai`

	Logarithmic loss				Accuracy				F1 score			
	M	**F**	**O**	**B**	**M**	**F**	**O**	**B**	**M**	**F**	**O**	**B**
🔥 fine-tuned	0.268	0.311	0.29	0.863	0.914	0.905	0.91	0.99	0.932	0.919	0.926	0.987
❄ frozen	0.292	0.306	0.299	0.954	0.886	0.89	0.888	1.005	0.908	0.906	0.907	0.997
🔍 blend	0.241	0.273	0.257	0.882	0.913	0.908	0.91	0.995	0.928	0.921	0.924	0.992

Table 3: Performance of the proposed two models and their blending on the GAP test set with 66 corrected labels, split by **M**asculine, **F**eminine (**B**ias shows F/M in case of F1 and accuracy, and M/F in case of logarithmic loss), and **Overall**.

Kenton Lee, Luheng He, and Luke Zettlemoyer. 2018. Higher-order coreference resolution with coarse-to-fine inference. In *Proceedings of the 2018 Conference of the North American Chapter of the Association for Computational Linguistics: Human Language Technologies, Volume 2 (Short Papers)*, pages 687–692, New Orleans, Louisiana. Association for Computational Linguistics.

Hector J. Levesque, Ernest Davis, and Leora Morgenstern. 2012. The winograd schema challenge. In *Proceedings of the Thirteenth International Conference on Principles of Knowledge Representation and Reasoning*, KR'12, pages 552–561. AAAI Press.

Christopher D. Manning, Mihai Surdeanu, John Bauer, Jenny Finkel, Steven J. Bethard, and David McClosky. 2014. The Stanford CoreNLP natural language processing toolkit. In *Association for Computational Linguistics (ACL) System Demonstrations*, pages 55–60.

Matthew E. Peters, Mark Neumann, Mohit Iyyer, Matt Gardner, Christopher Clark, Kenton Lee, and Luke Zettlemoyer. 2018a. Deep contextualized word representations. Cite arxiv:1802.05365Comment: NAACL 2018. Originally posted to openreview 27 Oct 2017. v2 updated for NAACL camera ready.

Matthew E. Peters, Mark Neumann, Mohit Iyyer, Matt Gardner, Christopher Clark, Kenton Lee, and Luke Zettlemoyer. 2018b. Deep contextualized word representations. *CoRR*, abs/1802.05365.

Sameer Pradhan, Lance Ramshaw, Ralph Weischedel, Jessica Macbride, and Linnea Micciulla. 2007. Unrestricted coreference: Identifying entities and events in ontonotes. *International Conference on Semantic Computing*, 0:446–453.

Ian Tenney, Patrick Xia, Berlin Chen, Alex Wang, Adam Poliak, R. Thomas McCoy, Najoung Kim, Benjamin Van Durme, Samuel R. Bowman, Dipanjan Das, and Ellie Pavlick. 2019. What do you learn from context? probing for sentence structure in contextualized word representations. In *International Conference on Learning Representations*.

Ashish Vaswani, Noam Shazeer, Niki Parmar, Jakob Uszkoreit, Llion Jones, Aidan N Gomez, Ł ukasz Kaiser, and Illia Polosukhin. 2017. Attention is all you need. In I. Guyon, U. V. Luxburg, S. Bengio, H. Wallach, R. Fergus, S. Vishwanathan, and R. Garnett, editors, *Advances in Neural Information Processing Systems 30*, pages 5998–6008. Curran Associates, Inc.

Kellie Webster, Marta Recasens, Vera Axelrod, and Jason Baldridge. 2018. Mind the gap: A balanced corpus of gendered ambiguous pronouns. In *Transactions of the ACL*.

Sam Wiseman, Alexander M. Rush, and Stuart M. Shieber. 2016. Learning global features for coreference resolution. In *Proceedings of the 2016 Conference of the North American Chapter of the Association for Computational Linguistics: Human Language Technologies*, pages 994–1004, San Diego.

Anonymized BERT: An Augmentation Approach to the Gendered Pronoun Resolution Challenge

Bo Liu

S&P Global

New York, NY

`bo.liu@spglobal.com`

Abstract

We present our 7th place solution[1] to the Gendered Pronoun Resolution challenge, which uses BERT without fine-tuning and a novel augmentation strategy designed for contextual embedding token-level tasks. Our method anonymizes the referent by replacing candidate names with a set of common placeholder names. Besides the usual benefits of effectively increasing training data size, this approach diversifies idiosyncratic information embedded in names. Using same set of common first names can also help the model recognize names better, shorten token length, and remove gender and regional biases associated with names. The system scored 0.1947 log loss in stage 2, where the augmentation contributed to an improvements of 0.04. Post-competition analysis shows that, when using different embedding layers, the system scores 0.1799 which would be third place.

1 Introduction

Gender bias has been an important topic in natural language processing in recent years (Bolukbasi et al., 2016; Reddy and Knight, 2016; Chiappa and Gillam, 2018; Madaan et al., 2018). GAP (Gendered Ambiguous Pronouns) dataset is a gender balanced labeled corpus of 8,908 ambiguous pronoun-name pairs sampled from English Wikipedia, built and released by Webster et al. (2018) to challenge the community for gender unbiased pronoun resolution systems.

In the Gendered Pronoun Resolution challenge which is based on GAP dataset, we designed a unique augmentation strategy for token-level contextual embedding models and applied it to feature based BERT (Devlin et al., 2019) approach for a 7th place finish. BERT is a large bidirectional transformer trained with masked language

model, which is fine-tuned to state-of-the-art results on a variety of NLP benchmark tasks. Four version of BERT model weights were released in October 2018, following a family of NLP transfer learning models in the same year, ELMo (Peters et al., 2018), ULMFit (Howard and Ruder, 2018) and OpenAI GPT (Radford et al., 2018).

Although augmentation has been shown to be very effective in deep learning (Xie et al., 2019), most NLP augmentation methods are on document or sentence level, such as synonym replacement (Zhang et al., 2015), data noising (Xie et al., 2017) and back-translation (Yu et al., 2018). For token level tasks like pronoun resolution, only the name and pronoun embeddings are in the model input. Even though altering whole document also affect these embeddings, direct change to the names has much bigger impact to the model.

The main idea of our augmentation is to replace each name in the name-pronoun pair by a set of common placeholder names, in order to (1) diversify the idiosyncratic information embedded in individual names and leave only the contextual information and (2) remove any gender or region related bias in names. In other words, to *anonymize* the names and make BERT extract name-independent features purely about context. With the same set of common first names from the training corpus as the placeholders, the model can recognize candidate names more easily and embed contextual information more compactly into single tokens. This technique could also be used in other token level tasks to anonymize people or entity names.

2 Model

Our system is an ensemble of two neural network models, the "End2end" model and the "Pure Bert" model.

---

[1]The code is available at https://github.com/boliu61/gendered-pronoun-resolution

Proceedings of the 1st Workshop on Gender Bias in Natural Language Processing, pages 120–125
Florence, Italy, August 2, 2019. ©2019 Association for Computational Linguistics

End2end model: This model uses the scoring architecture proposed in Lee et al. (2017), but with BERT embeddings. Since candidate names A and B are already given in this task, the model doesn't have mention scores, only antecedent scores, which is a concatenation of BERT embeddings of the name (A or B); BERT embeddings of the pronoun; their element-wise similarity (between A/B and P); and non-BERT features such as distance between the name and the pronoun, whether the name is in the URL and linguistic features (syntactic distances and parts of sentence etc).

Pure BERT model: The input of this model is only the concatenated BERT embeddings of name A, name B and the pronoun, which are fed into two fully connected hidden layers of dimensions 512 and 32 before the softmax output layer.

2.1 Augmentation

Our augmentation strategy works this way: for each sample, replace all the occurrences of names A and B by 4 sets of placeholder names during both training and inference unless certain conditions are met. In training, it will make the epoch size 5 times as big. In inference, the model will make 5 predictions for each sample which are to be ensembled—this is also known as TTA (test time augmentation).

The 4 sets of placeholder names are

> **F:** Alice, Kate, **M:** John, Michael
>
> **F:** Elizabeth, Mary, **M:** James, Henry
>
> **F:** Kate, Elizabeth, **M:** Michael, James
>
> **F:** Mary, Alice, **M:** Henry, John

The names were chosen from most common names in stage 1 data. For each sample, use the male pair if the pronoun is masculine ("he", "him", or "his") and female pair otherwise.

We have experimented with fewer or more sets of placeholder names, and alternative name choices which are more "modern" (common names in GAP are mostly old fashioned, as many articles are about historical figures), but none worked better than the original set of names we initially chose.

The conditions for *not* applying augmentation are:

1. If the placeholder name already appear in original document. e.g. in the following document, do not apply the augmentation sets that have "Alice" as a placeholder name,

   > **Alice** went to live with Nick's sister Kathy, who desperately tried to ...

2. If A or B is full name (first and last name), but the first name or last name appear alone elsewhere in the document. e.g. If we replace "Candace Parker" (name B) by "Kate" in the following sentence, the model would not known "Kate" and "Parker" are the same person

   > ... the Shock's Plenette Pierson made a hard box-out on **Candace Parker** , causing both players to become entangled and fall over. As **Parker** tried to stand up, ...

3. If the name has more than two words, such as "Elizabeth Frances Zane" or "Jose de Venecia Jr", We don't replace it because it would be difficult to implement rule 2.

4. If one of name A or B is a substring of the other, e.g. name A is "Erin Fray" and name B is "Erin". These are likely tagging errors.

In stage 1 data, for each set of placeholder names there are 8%, 2%, 1% and 1% data that met these conditions respectively and 88% was augmented. Note that the first 8% are different for each set of placeholder names—only the 4% corresponding to conditions 2-4 wasn't augmented at all.

3 Experiments

We used the official GAP dataset to build the system. There are 2000 data in both test and development sets and 454 in validation set. We used all of test and development plus 400 random rows in validation set (4400 in total) to train the system and left 54 as a sanity check to test the inference pipeline. The gender is nearly equally distributed in the training data with 2195 male and 2205 female examples.

There are 12359 samples in stage 2 test data, but only 760 were revealed to have been labeled and used for scoring. Effectively, there are 760 stage 2 test data—all the others were presumably added to prevent cheating. The gender distribution is again almost equal with 383 female and 377 male examples.

The meta information for both End2end and Pure Bert model is shown in Table 1. For each model, we trained two versions, one based on BERT Large Uncased, the other based on BERT Large Cased. For the competition, we used layer -4 (fourth to last hidden layer) embeddings for the End2end model and a concatenation of layers -3 and -4 for the Pure BERT model. As will be shown in the results section, we re-trained the models after the competition with layers -5 and -6 and achieved better results.

Pre-processing: As reported in the competition discussion forum, there are some clear label mistakes in GAP dataset. We identified 159 mislabels (74 development, 68 test, 17 validation) to the best of our ability by going through all the examples with a log loss of 1 or larger. We trained the system using corrected labels but report all results evaluated with original labels.

Post-processing: The problem with using clean labels to train and dirty labels to evaluate is that, loss will be huge for very confident predictions if the label is wrong (i.e. when the predicted probability for the wrong-label class is very small). We solved this problem by clipping predicted probabilities smaller than a threshold 0.005, which was tuned with cross validation. The idea is similar to label smoothing (Szegedy et al., 2016) and confidence penalty (Pereyra et al., 2017)

All the training was done in Google Colab with a single GPU. We used 5-fold cross validation for stage 1 results, and 5-fold average for stage 2 test results. End2end model was trained 5 times using different seeds with each seed taking about 30 minutes; Pure BERT model was trained only once which took about 50 minutes.

Each team is allowed two submissions for this shared task. Above described is our submission A. Submission B is the same except that (1) it was trained on GAP test and validation sets only (2454 training samples instead of 4400), and (2) it didn't use the linguistic features. Submission B has worse results than A in both stage 1 and stage 2 as expected.

4   Results and discussion

4.1   Augmentation results

In Table 2, we show the contribution of augmentation to the End2end model. In both uncased and cased versions and their ensemble, stage 1 log loss improved by about 0.01 when augmentation is added in training but not inference. And another massive 0.05 and 0.04 improvement for the uncased and cased version respectively is achieved when TTA is used. For the ensemble, augmentation improved the score from 0.3470 to 0.3052.

The reason that this augmentation method worked so well can be explained in number of ways.

1. BERT contextual embeddings of a name contain information of both the context and the name itself. Only the contextual information is relevant for coreference resolution—whether the name is Alice or Betty or Claire does not matter at all. By replacing all names by the same set of placeholders, only the useful contextual information remains for the model to learn.

2. By using the same set of names in both training and inference, the noise from individual names are further reduced, i.e., the model will likely know they are names when it sees the same placeholder names during inference. This is even more so for foreign (non Western) names, as there are some articles in GAP about foreign figures. Without augmentation, it's less likely that BERT model trained on English corpus can recognize, for example, a lowered cased (Romanized) Chinese name as a name.

3. For gender-neutral names (including certain foreign names) and males with a typically feminine name or females with a typically masculine name, the model can much easily resolve the gender after augmentation.

4. When a long name or uncommon name is tokenized into multiple word-piece tokens, we use the average embeddings of all these tokens. Since all the placeholder names are common first names thus tokenized into single token, the syntactic information may be embedded better into a single vector than the average of a few.

5. TTA will generate four additional predictions for each sample. Ensemble of them and the unaugmented one gives an extra boost.

Reason #1 is related to training only, #5 related to inference only, #2-4 to both training and inference. An indirect proof of #2-4 is: in TTA, the

Model	End2end	Pure BERT
ensemble weights	0.9	0.1
BERT embeddings	layer -4	concatenation of layer -3 and -4
architecture	Lee et al. (2017)	concatenation of A, B, Pronoun embeddings and FCN
non-BERT features	yes	no
model size	5 MB	36 MB
seed average	average of 5 seeds	only 1 seed
training time per seed	30 min	50 min

Table 1: Meta information of two models.

model	uncased	cased	ensemble
no augmentation	0.3878	0.3771	0.3470
augmentation only in training	0.3796	0.3671	0.3355
augmentation in both training and inference	0.3308	0.3308	0.3052

Table 2: Stage 1 results improvements in End2end model due to augmentation

order of the 4 augmentations' scores varies depending on the model (not reported due to space limit), but they all always outperform the one without augmentation. In other words, given a trained model, the prediction on any of four augmented version is better than prediction on original data.

4.2 Overall results

In Table 3, we report the log loss scores of single models and the ensemble. For stage 1, we use the 5-fold cross validation scores, trained with cleaned labels and evaluated using original labels. We also tuned the ensemble weights based on scores with cleaned labels (not shown).

During the competition, we experimented with BERT embedding layers -1 to -4 by trying different combinations of layers and their sum and concatenation and settled on layer -4 for End2end model and concatenation of -3 and -4 for Pure BERT model. After the competition ended, we realized lower layers work better on this task. So we re-trained the models using layer -5 for End2end model and layer -5 and -6 for Pure BERT model.

The results are significantly better across the board, as shown in Table 4. In fact, the stage 2 score 0.1799 is good enough for third place on the leaderboard. The ensemble weights were tuned on stage 1 data using clean labels as before.

After the competition, we also calculated the gender breakdown for all single and ensemble models based on the gender of the pronoun, reported also in Table 3 and 4. During the competi-

tion, we trained the system and tuned the ensemble weights solely based on overall score. As a result, it exhibits some degree of gender bias in both stages, similar to Webster et al. (2018) and the systems cited therein. The final ensemble's bias is 0.93 in stage 1 and 0.96 in stage 2, with bias represented by the ratio of masculine and feminine scores.

Interestingly, the 4 single models demonstrate different level of bias, ranging from 0.91 to 1.03 in stage 1, and from 0.85 to 1.09 in stage 2. The larger variance is due to the much smaller stage 2 test size. Had the evaluation metrics been different than the overall log loss, we could have addressed it by assigning different weights to each single model. For instance, if systems were judged by the worse of feminine and masculine scores (to penalize heavily biased systems), we would have tuned the weights differently, sacrificing some overall score for a more balanced performance. For example, with ensemble weights [0.18, 0.42, 0.12, 0.28] and clipping threshold of 0.006, the overall score and gender bias of our post-competition system would be 0.2855 and 0.97 in stage 1 instead of the original version with better overall (0.2846) and a larger bias (0.93), as shown in the last row of Table 4. On stage 2 data, the bias became slightly worse to 0.96 from 0.97. But since the stage 1 dataset is about six times as large as stage 2, the latter version is still the more gender unbiased system considering both sets.

During results checking, we noticed a clear

discrepancy between the document styles of two stages. There are many more shorter documents in stage 2, as shown in the top plot of Figure 1. In many of the shorter documents, the pronoun refers to name A, which is the page entity. The average predicted probabilities of the three classes A, B and Neither are 0.61, 0.35 and 0.05, compared with 0.44, 0.46 and 0.10 in stage 1.

However, as revealed by the stage 2 solution, 94% of the stage 2 data are unlabeled, which was probably generated differently (e.g. most unlabeled data have length smaller than 455). The length distribution of the 760 "real" labeled data used for scoring is very close to stage 1, as shown in the bottom plot of Figure 1. So is the predicted probability distribution (0.45, 0.46, 0.09). Then what could explain the 0.1 log loss difference between the two stage 2? We boostrapped 760 samples from stage 1 predictions for 10,000 times, the simulated stage 2 score is smaller than actual stage 2 score for only once (0.01%). So the discrepancy is not solely due to variance from smaller sample size in stage 2.

Our best educated guess is cleaner labels: our stage 1 score evaluated using clean labels is 0.1993, which is much closer to stage 2 score. The organizer likely spent more effort quality-checking the smaller stage 2 labels. Obviously, different pre-processing criteria during data preparation could also have made stage 2 data inherently easier to resolve.

5 Conclusion

We presented a simple yet effective augmentation strategy that helped us finishing 7th place in the Gendered Pronoun Resolution challenge without fine-tuning. We reasoned how this technique helped the model achieving higher scores by anonymizing idiosyncrasy in individual names while also handling gender and other biases to some degree. We demonstrated how the system could be altered slightly to (1) get a better score good for 3rd place by only changing BERT embedding layers or (2) become more gender-unbiased by using different ensemble weights.

Even though our solution only used feature-based approach, we expect this augmentation method to work as well with fine-tune BERT approach, which could potentially further improve the score.

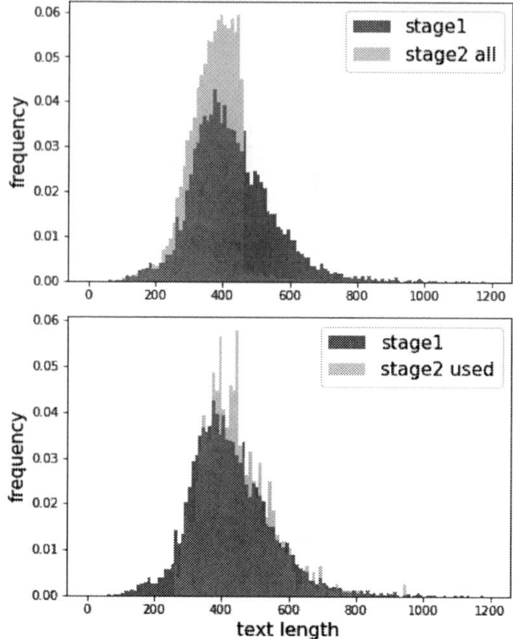

Figure 1: Comparisons of document length distributions of two stages. Top: all 12359 documents in stage 2. Bottom: the 760 "real" documents used for scoring in stage 2.

References

Tolga Bolukbasi, Kai-Wei Chang, James Y Zou, Venkatesh Saligrama, and Adam T Kalai. 2016. Man is to computer programmer as woman is to homemaker? debiasing word embeddings. In *Advances in neural information processing systems*, pages 4349–4357.

Silvia Chiappa and Thomas PS Gillam. 2018. Path-specific counterfactual fairness. *arXiv preprint arXiv:1802.08139*.

Jacob Devlin, Ming-Wei Chang, Kenton Lee, and Kristina Toutanova. 2019. Bert: Pre-training of deep bidirectional transformers for language understanding. *NAACL*.

Jeremy Howard and Sebastian Ruder. 2018. Universal language model fine-tuning for text classification. *The 56th Annual Meeting of the Association for Computational Linguistics (ACL)*.

Kenton Lee, Luheng He, Mike Lewis, and Luke Zettlemoyer. 2017. End-to-end neural coreference resolution. In *Proceedings of the 2017 Conference on Empirical Methods in Natural Language Processing*, pages 188–197.

Nishtha Madaan, Sameep Mehta, Shravika Mittal, and Ashima Suvarna. 2018. Judging a book by its description: Analyzing gender stereotypes in the

model	weights	stage 1				stage 2			
		O	F	M	B	O	F	M	B
End2end, Uncased	0.36	0.3308	0.3439	0.3177	0.92	0.2388	0.2293	0.2484	1.08
End2end, Cased	0.54	0.3308	0.3414	0.3201	0.94	0.2243	0.2271	0.2214	0.97
Pure Bert, Uncased	0.04	0.3584	0.3649	0.3518	0.96	0.2333	0.2287	0.2381	1.04
Pure Bert, Cased	0.06	0.3544	0.3530	0.3558	1.01	0.2349	0.2357	0.2341	0.99
Ensemble (raw)		0.2961							
Ensemble (clipped)		**0.2922**	0.3021	0.2823	0.93	**0.1947**	0.1983	0.1911	0.96

Table 3: Log loss scores of single models and the ensemble for both stages, **competition version**, with Overall, Feminine, Masculine and Bias (M/F). Stage 2 results were evaluated after competition ended using the solution provided by Kaggle, except the final score 0.1947 (in bold), which placed 7th in the competition.

model	weights	stage 1				stage 2			
		O	F	M	B	O	F	M	B
End2end, Uncased	0.36	0.3244	0.3402	0.3086	0.91	0.1901	0.1820	0.1984	1.09
End2end, Cased	0.44	0.3239	0.3345	0.3133	0.94	0.1871	0.2017	0.1723	0.85
Pure Bert, Uncased	0.08	0.3486	0.3593	0.3378	0.94	0.2269	0.2322	0.2215	0.95
Pure Bert, Cased	0.12	0.3492	0.3446	0.3539	1.03	0.2158	0.2145	0.2171	1.01
Ensemble (raw)		0.2875							
Ensemble (clipped)		**0.2846**	0.2947	0.2744	0.93	**0.1799**	0.1829	0.1769	0.97
More unbiased version		0.2855	0.2929	0.2780	0.97	0.1817	0.1858	0.1776	0.96

Table 4: Log loss scores of single models and the ensemble for both stages, **post-competition version**, with Overall, Feminine, Masculine and Bias (M/F). Stage 2 results were evaluated after competition ended using the solution provided by Kaggle. The stage 2 final score 0.1799 would rank third place on the leaderboard. Last row is a more gender-unbiased version with different ensemble weights.

man bookers prize winning fiction. *arXiv preprint arXiv:1807.10615*.

Gabriel Pereyra, George Tucker, Jan Chorowski, Łukasz Kaiser, and Geoffrey Hinton. 2017. Regularizing neural networks by penalizing confident output distributions. *arXiv preprint arXiv:1701.06548*.

Matthew Peters, Mark Neumann, Mohit Iyyer, Matt Gardner, Christopher Clark, Kenton Lee, and Luke Zettlemoyer. 2018. Deep contextualized word representations. In *Proceedings of the 2018 Conference of the North American Chapter of the Association for Computational Linguistics: Human Language Technologies, Volume 1 (Long Papers)*, pages 2227–2237.

Alec Radford, Karthik Narasimhan, Tim Salimans, and Ilya Sutskever. 2018. Improving language understanding by generative pre-training.

Sravana Reddy and Kevin Knight. 2016. Obfuscating gender in social media writing. In *Proceedings of the First Workshop on NLP and Computational Social Science*, pages 17–26.

Christian Szegedy, Vincent Vanhoucke, Sergey Ioffe, Jon Shlens, and Zbigniew Wojna. 2016. Rethinking the inception architecture for computer vision. In *Proceedings of the IEEE conference on computer vision and pattern recognition*, pages 2818–2826.

Kellie Webster, Marta Recasens, Vera Axelrod, and Jason Baldridge. 2018. Mind the gap: A balanced corpus of gendered ambiguous pronouns. In *Transactions of the ACL*, page to appear.

Qizhe Xie, Zihang Dai, Eduard Hovy, Minh-Thang Luong, and Quoc V Le. 2019. Unsupervised data augmentation. *arXiv preprint arXiv:1904.12848*.

Ziang Xie, Sida I Wang, Jiwei Li, Daniel Lévy, Aiming Nie, Dan Jurafsky, and Andrew Y Ng. 2017. Data noising as smoothing in neural network language models. *Fifth International Conference on Learning Representations (ICLR)*.

Adams Wei Yu, David Dohan, Minh-Thang Luong, Rui Zhao, Kai Chen, Mohammad Norouzi, and Quoc V Le. 2018. Qanet: Combining local convolution with global self-attention for reading comprehension. *Sixth International Conference on Learning Representations (ICLR)*.

Xiang Zhang, Junbo Zhao, and Yann LeCun. 2015. Character-level convolutional networks for text classification. In *Advances in neural information processing systems*, pages 649–657.

Gendered Pronoun Resolution using BERT and an extractive question answering formulation

Rakesh Chada

Jersey City, NJ

rakesh.chada@gmail.com

Abstract

The resolution of ambiguous pronouns is a longstanding challenge in Natural Language Understanding. Recent studies have suggested gender bias among state-of-the-art coreference resolution systems. As an example, Google AI Language team recently released a gender-balanced dataset and showed that performance of these coreference resolvers is significantly limited on the dataset. In this paper, we propose an extractive question answering (QA) formulation of pronoun resolution task that overcomes this limitation and shows much lower gender bias (0.99) on their dataset. This system uses fine-tuned representations from the pre-trained BERT model and outperforms the existing baseline by a significant margin (22.2% absolute improvement in F1 score) without using any hand-engineered features. This QA framework is equally performant even without the knowledge of the candidate antecedents of the pronoun. An ensemble of QA and BERT-based multiple choice and sequence classification models further improves the F1 (23.3% absolute improvement upon the baseline). This ensemble model was submitted to the shared task for the 1st ACL workshop on Gender Bias for Natural Language Processing. It ranked 9th on the final official leaderboard.

1 Introduction

Coreference resolution is a task that aims to identify spans in a text that refer to the same entity. This is central to Natural Language Understanding. We focus on a specific aspect of the coreference resolution that caters to resolving ambiguous pronouns in English. Recent studies have shown that state-of-the-art coreference resolution systems exhibit gender bias (Webster et al., 2018) (Rudinger et al., 2018) (Zhao et al., 2018). (Webster et al., 2018) released a dataset that contained an equal number of male and female ex-

amples to encourage gender-fair modeling on the pronoun resolution task. A shared task for this dataset was then published on Kaggle[1]. The task involves classifying a specific ambiguous pronoun in a given Wikipedia passage as coreferring with one of the three classes: first candidate antecedent (hereby referred to as **A**), second candidate antecedent (hereby referred to as **B**) or neither of them (hereby referred to as **N**). The authors show that even the best of the baselines such as (Clark and Manning, 2015), (Wiseman et al., 2016), (Lee et al., 2017) achieve an F1 score of just 66.9% on this dataset. The limited number of annotated labels available in this unbiased setting makes the modeling a challenging task. To that end, we propose an extractive question answering formulation of the task that leverages BERT (Devlin et al., 2018) pre-trained representations and significantly improves (22.2% absolute improvement in F1 score) upon the best baseline (Webster et al., 2018). In this formulation, the task is similar to a SQUAD (Rajpurkar et al., 2016) style question answering (QA) problem where the question is the context window (neighboring words) surrounding the pronoun to be resolved and the answer is the antecedent of the pronoun. The answer is contained in the provided Wikipedia passage. The intuition behind using the pronoun's context window as a question is that it allows the model to rightly identify the pronoun to be resolved as there can be multiple tokens that match the given pronoun in a passage. There has been previous work that cast the coreference resolution as a Question Answering problem (Kumar et al., 2016). But the questions used in their approach take the form "Who does "she" refer to?". This would necessitate including additional information such as an indicator vector to identify the exact pronoun to be re-

---

[1]https://www.kaggle.com/c/gendered-pronoun-resolution

Proceedings of the 1st Workshop on Gender Bias in Natural Language Processing, pages 126–133

Florence, Italy, August 2, 2019. ©2019 Association for Computational Linguistics

Number of examples	Stage 1				Stage 2			
	T	**A**	**B**	**N**	**T**	**A**	**B**	**N**
5-Fold Dev (80-20 split)	2454	1105	1060	289	4454	1979	1985	490
Test	2000	874	925	201	760	340	346	74

Table 1: Stage 1 and Stage 2 Dataset statistics.

solved when there are multiple of them in a given passage. Furthermore, their approach doesn't impose that the answer should be contained within the passage or the question text. (McCann et al., 2018) model the pronoun resolution task of the Winograd schema challenge (Levesque et al., 2012) as a question answering problem by including the candidate antecedents as part of the question. An unique feature of the question answering framework (referred to as CorefQA) we propose is that it doesn't require the knowledge of the candidate antecedents in order to produce an answer for the pronoun resolution task. The model "learns", from training on the QA version of the shared task dataset, the specific task of extracting the appropriate antecedent of the pronoun given just the Wikipedia passage and the pronoun's context window. We also demonstrate other modeling variants for the shared task that use the knowledge of the candidate antecedents **A** and **B**. The first variant (CorefQAExt) is an extension of the CorefQA model that uses its predictions to produce probabilities over **A**, **B** and **N**. The second variant (CorefMulti) takes the formulation of a SWAG (Zellers et al., 2018) style multiple choice classification and the final variant (CorefSeq) takes the standard sequence classification formulation. An ensemble of CorefQAExt, CorefMulti and CorefSeq models shows further performance gains (23.3% absolute improvement in F1 score).

2 Data

The dataset used for this shared task is the GAP dataset (Webster et al., 2018) where each row contains a Wikipedia text snippet, the corresponding page's URL, the pronoun to be resolved, the two candidate antecedents (**A** and **B**) of the pronoun, the text offsets corresponding to **A**, **B**, pronoun and boolean flags indicating the pronoun's coreference with A and B. The Kaggle competition for this shared task was conducted in two stages. Table 1 shows the aggregate statistics for each stage.

The 5-Fold Dev row represents the number of examples used for 5-fold stratified cross validation done based on the gender of the pronoun. This could lead to different distributions of A and B during the training of each fold. We chose to do so because we wanted to retain the perfect balance between male and female representations during training and thereby minimize the bias from the data. The columns **T**, **A**, **B** and **N** refer to the total number of examples, the number of examples where the pronoun's antecedent is A, B and neither respectively. We should note that for the question answering model, we exclude all the neither examples from the training data as we dont have an exact answer. While this seems destructive, the model doesn't need, by design, an explicit supervision on the "neither" examples to predict an antecedent that's neither A nor B. The male and female pronoun examples are equally represented (50-50 split) in the development, validation and test datasets - with the exception of stage 2 test dataset. The stage 2 test dataset has 377 male and 383 female examples. We use lower-cased BERT word-piece tokenizer for preprocessing. This comes with a pre-built vocabulary of size 30522.

3 System Description

The final model used for submission is an ensemble of the question answering (CorefQAExt), multiple choice (CorefMulti) and sequence classification (CorefSeq) models. We describe each of these models in the following sections. We chose the pytorch-pretrained-bert[2] library to implement all models. The source code is available at `https://github.com/rakeshchada/corefqa`

---

[2]`https://github.com/huggingface/pytorch-pretrained-BERT`

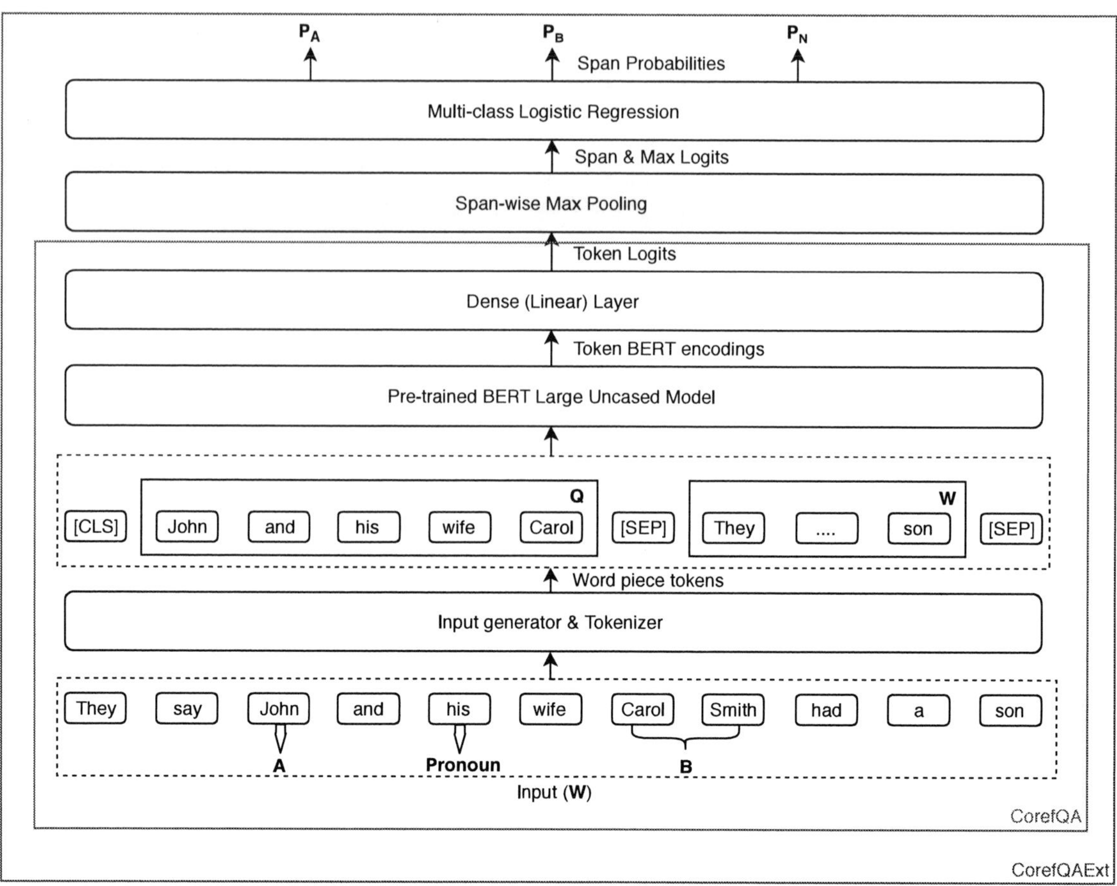

Figure 1: Architecture of CorefQA, CorefQAExt models

3.1 Question Answering System (CorefQA, CorefQAExt)

3.1.1 Inputs and Architecture

The architecture of this system is shown in Figure 1. The input **I** to the system can be represented as **I** = "[CLS] **Q** [SEP] **W** [SEP]" where **Q** represents the question text, **W** represents the Wikipedia passage text and [CLS], [SEP] are the delimiter tokens used in the BERT model. The question text **Q** is the pronoun context window of up to 5 words. The context window is the pronoun itself and its two neighboring words to the left and right. So, if **W** is *"They say John and his wife Carol had a son"*, then **Q** would be *"John and his wife Carol"* assuming *"his"* is the pronoun to be resolved. In the case where there are less than two words on a given side, we just use the words available within the window - so these cases would lead to the window with less than 5 words. The text at this point is still un-tokenized so the "words" are just space separated tokens in a given text. The an-

swer text is either **A**'s or **B**'s name ("neither" cases have been initially filtered). The rest of the architecture until the Span-wise Max Pooling layer follows the standard SQUAD formulation in (Devlin et al., 2018). It's worth noting that the architecture until this point (before the Span-wise Max Pooling layer) doesn't use candidate antecedents' **A** and **B** text or offset information. The output at this intermediate layer (Dense Layer) contains two sets of logits: start and end logits for each token. These can then be used to extract the maximum scoring span as an answer as demonstrated in (Devlin et al., 2018). We refer to the architecture until the Span-wise Max Pooling Layer as CorefQA.

3.1.2 Probability Estimation

The shared task requires the output to be probabilities over the given **A**, **B** and **N** spans. So, we implement a mechanism that combines Span-wise Max Pooling and Logistic Regression to extract probabilities from start and end logits obtained in the previous step. Since we have access to offsets of **A** and **B**, we simply extract span logits corresponding to those offsets. Span logits are calculated by taking the maximum value of each of the individual token logits in a span. This gives us four values that represent maximum logits for the start and end of A and B spans. We also calculate maximum start and end logits over the entire sequence. These six logits are then fed as input features to a multi-class logistic regression. The output of this classifier then gives us the desired probabilities $\mathbf{P}_A, \mathbf{P}_B \& \mathbf{P}_N$. We refer to this end-to-end architecture (from input layer to the Multi-class Logistic Regression layer) as CorefQAExt.

3.1.3 Training & Hyperparameters

We use Adam optimizer with learning rate of 1e-5, β_1=0.9, β_2=0.999, L2 weight decay of 0.01, learning rate warmup over the first 10% of total training steps, and linear decay of the learning rate. The maximum sequence length is set to 300 and batch size of 12 is used during training. We use BERT Large Uncased pre-trained model for initializing the weights of BERT layers. This model has 24 layers with each producing a 1024 dimensional hidden representation. The whole system is trained in an end-to-end fashion. We fine-tune the last 12 BERT Encoder layers (layer 13 to layer 24) and freeze layers 1 to 12 - meaning the parameters of those layers aren't updated during training. This leads to total trainable parameters in the order of 150 million. We didn't use any dropout. The hyperparameter C for the logistic regression is set to 0.1. This model was trained for 2 epochs on a NVIDIA K80 GPU. The training with the 5-fold cross validation finished in about 30 minutes. The average of the predictions of each fold on the test dataset is used as the final prediction. We had experimented with different choices for each of these hyperparameters - such as freezing or unfreezing more layers, choosing different learning rates, different batch sizes - but these numbers gave us the best results. Another hyperparameter the model was sensitive to was the context window size. Lower window sizes gave us better results with 5 being the ideal size.

3.2 Multiple Choice classification (CorefMulti)

Here, we formulate the task as a SWAG (Zellers et al., 2018) style multiple choice problem among **A**, **B** and **N** classes.

3.2.1 Inputs and Architecture

For each example, we construct four input sequences, which each contain the concatenation of the the two sequences **S1** and **S2**. **S1** is a concatenation of the given Wikipedia passage with an additional sentence of the form "**P** is " where **P** is the text of the pronoun in question. So, for a passage that ends with the sentence *"They say John and his wife Carol had a son"*, the sequence **S1** would be *"They say John and his wife Carol had a son. his is "* assuming *"his"* is the pronoun to be resolved. The sequence **S2** is one of **A**'s name, **B**'s name or the word *"neither"* if the pronoun in the example doesn't co-refer with **A** and **B**. Once we represent the inputs in this fashion, the rest of the architecture follows the design of BERT based SWAG task architecture discussed in (Devlin et al., 2018).

3.2.2 Training & Hyperparameters

We use a batch size of 4 for training, initialize the BERT layers with the weights from the BERT Large Uncased pre-trained model and maintain the rest of the hyperparameters the same as the ones used for CorefQAExt model. Layers 12 to 24 of the BERT Encoder are fine-tuned and the rest of the layers are frozen. We use 5-fold cross validation with test prediction averaging from each fold. This model took about 100 minutes to run on Stage 1 data on a NVIDIA K80 GPU.

3.3 Sequence classification (CorefSeq)

This involves framing the problem as a standard sequence classification task.

3.3.1 Inputs and Architecture

The input is the given Wikipedia passage without any additional augmentation. The sequence features are extracted by concatenating token embeddings corresponding to the A, B and the pronoun spans. These span embeddings are calculated by concatenating token embeddings of the start token, end token and the result of an element-wise multiplication of start and end token embeddings. The token embeddings are the output of the last encoder layer of the (fine-tuned) BERT. These features are then fed to a single hidden layer feedforward neural network with a ReLU activation. This hidden layer has 512 hidden units. A softmax layer at the output then provides the desired **A**, **B** and **N** probabilities.

Model	Stage 1					Stage 2				
	M*	F*	B*	O*	L*	M*	F*	B*	O*	L*
CorefQA	88.8	87.8	0.99	88.3	N/A[#]	93.2	91.3	**1.0**	92.2	N/A[#]
CorefQAExt	**91.1**	87.1	0.95	89.1	0.38	93.7	94.6	**1.0**	**94.2**	0.22
CorefMulti	87.9	87.4	**0.99**	87.6	0.40	92.8	92.3	0.99	92.7	0.24
CorefSeq	88.7	86.4	0.97	87.6	0.38	90.9	88.9	0.98	89.9	0.29
Full Ensemble	90.9	**89.5**	0.98	**90.2**	**0.32**	**94.1**	**94.0**	1.0	94.0	**0.20**
QAMul Ensemble[+]	91.1	88.4	0.97	89.7	0.35	93.9	**94.3**	1.0	94.1	**0.19**

* L = Log-Loss, O = Overall F1, M = Male F1, F = Female F1, B = Bias (F/M)
[#] N/A = Not Applicable
[+] Post competition Stage 2 deadline

Table 2: Stage 1 and Stage 2 Test Results. **Bold** indicates best performance.

3.3.2 Training & Hyperparameters

A dropout of 0.1 is applied before the inputs are fed from the BERT's last encoder layer to the feed forward neural network. The model is trained for 30 epochs with a batch size of 10. Layers 12 to 24 of the BERT Encoder are fine-tuned and the rest of the layers are frozen. A learning rate of 1e-5 is used with a triangular learning rate scheduler (Smith, 2017) whose steps per cycle is set to 100 times the length of training data. We use 5-fold cross validation with test prediction averaging from each fold. This model took 105 minutes to run on Stage 1 data on a NVIDIA K80 GPU.

4 Results and discussion

Table 2 shows the results of all models for Stage 1 and Stage 2. We calculate Log-Loss, Male F1, Female F1, Overall F1 score and Bias (Female F1 / Male F1) as metrics on the test data sets. As the results show, all individual models improve upon the baseline model by a significant margin with the CorefQAExt model showing the highest absolute improvement of 22.2%. It is interesting to note that the CorefQA model[3] still improved upon the baseline by 21.4% despite not using the knowledge of candidate antecedents **A** and **B**. Infact, it slightly outperforms, on the Overall Stage 1 F1 score, both CorefMulti and CorefSeq models that explicitly encode the knowledge of **A** and **B**. A few input/output samples of the CorefQA model are shown in the Supplemental Section A. It is worth noticing that this model (correctly) selects, most of the time, the spans corresponding to named entities as answers even though that

constraint wasn't explicitly encoded in its design. The CorefQA model doesn't produce probabilities over **A**, **B** and **N** classes as that information isn't available to the model. Hence, we report Log-loss as "N/A" in Table 2. The probabilities from the CorefQAExt, CorefMulti and CorefSeq are averaged to obtain the ensemble models probabilities. This ensemble model, with an Overall F1 score of 90.2, improves upon the baseline by 23.3 percentage points. This model ranked ninth on the final leaderboard of the Kaggle competition. The CorefMulti model seemed most robust to bias (0.99). The ensemble model had the best log loss in stage 2 even though the CorefQAExt model had the best Overall F1 score. This might be a reflection of the issues with probability calibration. Another explanation of this might be just the smaller stage 2 data size as compared to stage 1. Finally, although the CorefSeq model doesn't individually outperform other models, we get a better ensemble performance by including it rather than by excluding it.

4.1 Freezing BERT weights

We tried freezing all BERT layer weights for some of our initial experiments but hadn't seen much success - especially when we used the weights from the last encoder layer of the BERT. The Stage 1 Overall F1 score for the CorefQAExt model dropped down significantly to 63.6% in this setting. This improved to 72.1% if we used layer 18 weights. We also tried concatenating the last four encoder layer outputs of BERT. This resulted in an slightly better Overall F1 score of 74.4% for Stage 1. So, the performance seemed to be sensitive to the choice of the encoder layer outputs. However,

---

[3] Sample predictions shown in the Supplemental Material Section A

from the preliminary experiments, there seemed to be a big gap of about 15% on the Overall F1 when compared to the fine-tuned model. A more principled & thorough analysis of this phenomena makes an important future area of work.

4.2 Post Stage 2 deadline Results

After the competition had finished, we experimented with a few model variations on the final stage 2 test dataset that gave us interesting insights. Firstly, we tried excluding each model from the full ensemble. We noticed that we obtained a better Log Loss of 0.195 when we excluded CorefSeq. This model is listed as QAMul Ensemble in Table 2. We carried another experiment where we trained the CorefQAExt using the cased version of the BERT model. An ensembling of the uncased version with this cased version delivered further performance gains (3% absolute F1 improvement upon uncased CorefQAExt). Then, we tried ensembling the cased and uncased versions of all the three individual models - CorefQAExt, CorefMulti and CorefSeq on stage 2 test data. This resulted in an overall F1 score of 94.7% , Male F1 of 94.8%, Female F1 of 94.6%, bias of 1.0 and a log loss of 0.197.

4.3 Failed Experiments

1. We tried fine-tuning the BERT model in an unsupervised manner by training a language model on the texts extracted from the Wikipedia pages corresponding to the URLs provided in the dataset. The idea behind this one was to see if we can get better BERT layer representations by tuning them to the shared task's dataset. However, this is a computationally expensive step to run and we didn't see promising gains from initial runs. We hypothesize that this may be due to the fact that BERT representations were originally obtained by training on Wikipedia as one of the sources. So, fine-tuning on the task's dataset which is also from Wikipedia might not have added an extra signal.

2. For the CorefMulti model, we tried adding to the token embedding vector, an additional entity embedding vector that encodes the word-piece token level info of whether it belongs to one of **A**, **B** or **P**. We hypothesized this should help the model focus its attention on the relevant entities to the coreference task.

But we weren't able to make a successful use of these embeddings to improve the model performance within the competition deadline. However, this is a promising future direction.

3. For the CorefQAExt model, we appended the title extracted from the provided wikipedia page's URL into the input token sequence to evaluate if the page URL provides useful signal to the model. This made the performance slightly worse.

5 Conclusion

We proposed an extractive question answering (QA) formulation of the pronoun resolution task that uses BERT fine-tuning and shows strong performance on the gender-balanced dataset. We have shown that this system can also effectively extract the antecedent of the pronoun without using the knowledge of candidate antecedents. We demonstrated three other formulations of the task that uses this knowledge. The ensemble of all these models obtained further gains (Table 2). This work showed that the pre-trained BERT representations provide a strong signal for the coreference resolution task. Furthermore, thanks to training on the gender-balanced dataset, this modeling framework was able to generate unbiased predictions despite using pre-trained representations. An important future work would be to analyze the gains obtained from BERT representations in more detail and perhaps compare it with alternate contextual token representations and fine-tuning mechanisms (Peters et al., 2018) (Howard and Ruder, 2018). We also would like to apply our techniques to the Winograd schema challenge (Levesque et al., 2012), the Definite Pronoun Resolution dataset (Rahman and Ng, 2012), the Winogender schema dataset (Rudinger et al., 2018) and explore extensions to other languages perhaps using the CoNLL 2012 shared task dataset (Pradhan et al., 2012).

Acknowledgments

We thank the GeBNLP committee reviewers for comments on the work and thank Thomas Wolf, Prashant Jayannavar, Hema Priya Darshini, Aquila Khanam for helpful feedback on the draft. We also thank the Google AI Language team for the Kaggle competition and the team at Hugging Face Inc. for the "pytorch-pretrained-bert" library.

References

Kevin Clark and Christopher D. Manning. 2015. Entity-centric coreference resolution with model stacking. In *Proceedings of the 53rd Annual Meeting of the Association for Computational Linguistics and the 7th International Joint Conference on Natural Language Processing (Volume 1: Long Papers)*, pages 1405–1415, Beijing, China. Association for Computational Linguistics.

Jacob Devlin, Ming-Wei Chang, Kenton Lee, and Kristina Toutanova. 2018. Bert: Pre-training of deep bidirectional transformers for language understanding. *arXiv preprint arXiv:1810.04805*.

Jeremy Howard and Sebastian Ruder. 2018. Universal language model fine-tuning for text classification. In *Proceedings of the 56th Annual Meeting of the Association for Computational Linguistics (Volume 1: Long Papers)*, pages 328–339, Melbourne, Australia. Association for Computational Linguistics.

Ankit Kumar, Ozan Irsoy, Peter Ondruska, Mohit Iyyer, James Bradbury, Ishaan Gulrajani, Victor Zhong, Romain Paulus, and Richard Socher. 2016. Ask me anything: Dynamic memory networks for natural language processing. In *Proceedings of The 33rd International Conference on Machine Learning*, volume 48 of *Proceedings of Machine Learning Research*, pages 1378–1387, New York, New York, USA. PMLR.

Kenton Lee, Luheng He, Mike Lewis, and Luke Zettlemoyer. 2017. End-to-end neural coreference resolution. In *Proceedings of the 2017 Conference on Empirical Methods in Natural Language Processing*, pages 188–197, Copenhagen, Denmark. Association for Computational Linguistics.

Hector Levesque, Ernest Davis, and Leora Morgenstern. 2012. The winograd schema challenge. In *Thirteenth International Conference on the Principles of Knowledge Representation and Reasoning*.

Bryan McCann, Nitish Shirish Keskar, Caiming Xiong, and Richard Socher. 2018. The natural language decathlon: Multitask learning as question answering. *arXiv preprint arXiv:1806.08730*.

Matthew Peters, Mark Neumann, Mohit Iyyer, Matt Gardner, Christopher Clark, Kenton Lee, and Luke Zettlemoyer. 2018. Deep contextualized word representations. In *Proceedings of the 2018 Conference of the North American Chapter of the Association for Computational Linguistics: Human Language Technologies, Volume 1 (Long Papers)*, pages 2227–2237, New Orleans, Louisiana. Association for Computational Linguistics.

Sameer Pradhan, Alessandro Moschitti, Nianwen Xue, Olga Uryupina, and Yuchen Zhang. 2012. Conll-2012 shared task: Modeling multilingual unrestricted coreference in ontonotes. In *Joint Conference on EMNLP and CoNLL-Shared Task*, pages 1–40. Association for Computational Linguistics.

Altaf Rahman and Vincent Ng. 2012. Resolving complex cases of definite pronouns: the winograd schema challenge. In *Proceedings of the 2012 Joint Conference on Empirical Methods in Natural Language Processing and Computational Natural Language Learning*, pages 777–789. Association for Computational Linguistics.

Pranav Rajpurkar, Jian Zhang, Konstantin Lopyrev, and Percy Liang. 2016. Squad: 100, 000+ questions for machine comprehension of text. In *Proceedings of the 2016 Conference on Empirical Methods in Natural Language Processing, EMNLP 2016, Austin, Texas, USA, November 1-4, 2016*, pages 2383–2392.

Rachel Rudinger, Jason Naradowsky, Brian Leonard, and Benjamin Van Durme. 2018. Gender bias in coreference resolution. In *Proceedings of the 2018 Conference of the North American Chapter of the Association for Computational Linguistics: Human Language Technologies*, New Orleans, Louisiana. Association for Computational Linguistics.

Leslie N Smith. 2017. Cyclical learning rates for training neural networks. In *2017 IEEE Winter Conference on Applications of Computer Vision (WACV)*, pages 464–472. IEEE.

Kellie Webster, Marta Recasens, Vera Axelrod, and Jason Baldridge. 2018. Mind the gap: A balanced corpus of gendered ambiguou. In *Transactions of the ACL*, page to appear.

Sam Wiseman, Alexander M. Rush, and Stuart M. Shieber. 2016. Learning global features for coreference resolution. In *Proceedings of the 2016 Conference of the North American Chapter of the Association for Computational Linguistics: Human Language Technologies*, pages 994–1004, San Diego, California. Association for Computational Linguistics.

Rowan Zellers, Yonatan Bisk, Roy Schwartz, and Yejin Choi. 2018. Swag: A large-scale adversarial dataset for grounded commonsense inference. *arXiv preprint arXiv:1808.05326*.

Jieyu Zhao, Tianlu Wang, Mark Yatskar, Vicente Ordonez, and Kai-Wei Chang. 2018. Gender bias in coreference resolution: Evaluation and debiasing methods. In *Proceedings of the 2018 Conference of the North American Chapter of the Association for Computational Linguistics: Human Language Technologies, Volume 2 (Short Papers)*, pages 15–20, New Orleans, Louisiana. Association for Computational Linguistics.

A Supplemental Material

This section lists a few example input/outputs of the CorefQA model that predicts answers to the gendered pronoun resolution task using just the Context and the Question (without the knowledge of the candidate antecedents **A** and **B**).

Context: "Alice (19), Kathleen Mary (12), Gertrude (10) and Mabel (7). In the 1901 census Allen was living at Fox Lane in Leyland with his 2nd wife Margaret (Whittle), daughter of James Whittle, a coachman, & Ann Mills, whom he had married in 1900. She was some 18 years his junior."
Question: "1900. **She** was some"
Predicted Answer (Correct): "Margaret (Whittle)"

InfoBox 1: CorefQA Prediction Sample 1

Context: "He then announced that CMU will celebrate Pausch's impact on the world by building and naming after Pausch a raised pedestrian bridge to connect CMU's new Computer Science building and the Center for the Arts, symbolizing the way Pausch linked those two disciplines. Brown University professor Andries van Dam followed Pausch's last lecture with a tearful and impassioned speech praising him for his courage and leadership, calling him a role model."
Question: "speech praising **him** for his"
Predicted Answer (Correct): "Pausch"

InfoBox 2: CorefQA Prediction Sample 2

Context: "Walter S. Sheffer (August 7, 1918 - July 14, 2002) was an American photographer and teacher, born in Youngsville, Pennsylvania. He moved to Milwaukee, Wisconsin in 1945 to work at the studio of John Platz, Milwaukee's main society photographer. When Platz retired, Sheffer inherited his clientele and was able to establish his own "look" and very successful portrait studio by 1953."
Question: "Sheffer inherited **his** clientele and"
Predicted Answer (Wrong): "Sheffer'

InfoBox 3: CorefQA Prediction Sample 3

Context: "I would never write a book about the bad parts. I would mostly revel in the fantastic parts, of which there were so many." In early 2007, reports surfaced concerning Lindsay Lohan's interest in buying the rights to Nicks' life story and developing a motion picture in which she planned to play her."
Question: "in which **she** planned to"
Predicted Answer (Wrong): "Lindsay Lohan's interest in buying the rights to Nicks"

InfoBox 4: CorefQA Prediction Sample 4. The model wrongly predicts a bigger span as an answer.

Context: "The president of SAG – future United States President Ronald Reagan – also known to the FBI as Confidential Informant "T-10", testified before the committee but never publicly named names. Instead, according to an FBI memorandum in 1947: "T-10 advised Special Agent (name deleted) that he has been made a member of a committee headed by Mayer, the purpose of which is allegedly is to 'purge' the motion-picture industry of Communist party members, which committee was an outgrowth of the Thomas committee hearings in Washington and subsequent meetings ...."
Question: ") that **he** has been"
Predicted Answer (Correct): "Special Agent"

InfoBox 5: CorefQA Prediction Sample 5

Context: "Emily Thorn Vanderbilt (1852–1946) was a member of the prominent United States Vanderbilt family. The second daughter of William Henry Vanderbilt (1821–1885) and Maria Louisa Kissam (1821–1896), Emily Thorn Vanderbilt was named after her aunt, Emily Almira (Vanderbilt) Thorn, daughter of dynasty founder Cornelius Vanderbilt."
Question: 'named after **her** aunt,"
Predicted Answer (Correct): "Emily Thorn Vanderbilt"

InfoBox 6: CorefQA Prediction Sample 6

Gendered Ambiguous Pronouns Shared Task: Boosting Model Confidence by Evidence Pooling

Sandeep Attree
New York, NY
`sandeep.attree@gmail.com`

Abstract

This paper presents a strong set of results for resolving gendered ambiguous pronouns on the Gendered Ambiguous Pronouns shared task. The model presented here draws upon the strengths of state-of-the-art language and coreference resolution models, and introduces a novel evidence-based deep learning architecture. Injecting evidence from the coreference models compliments the base architecture, and analysis shows that the model is not hindered by their weaknesses, specifically gender bias. The modularity and simplicity of the architecture make it very easy to extend for further improvement and applicable to other NLP problems. Evaluation on GAP test data results in a state-of-the-art performance at 92.5% F1 (gender bias of 0.97), edging closer to the human performance of 96.6%. The end-to-end solution[1] presented here placed 1st in the Kaggle competition, winning by a significant lead.

1 Introduction

The Gendered Ambiguous Pronouns (GAP) shared task aims to mitigate bias observed in the performance of coreference resolution systems when dealing with gendered pronouns. State-of-the-art coreference models suffer from a systematic bias in resolving masculine entities more confidently compared to feminine entities. To this end, Webster et al. (2018) published a new GAP dataset[2] to encourage research into building models and systems that are robust to gender bias.

The arrival of modern language models like ELMo (Peters et al., 2018), BERT (Devlin et al., 2018), and GPT (Radford et al., 2018), have significantly advanced the state-of-the art in a wide

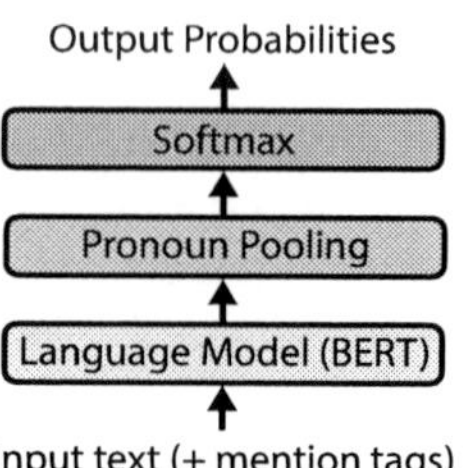

Figure 1: ProBERT: Pronoun BERT. Token embeddings corresponding to the labeled pronoun in the input text are extracted from the last layer of the language model (BERT) and used for prediction.

range of NLP problems. All of them have a common theme in that a generative language model is pretrained on a large amount of data, and is subsequently fine-tuned on the target task data. This approach of transfer learning has been very successful. The current work applies the same philosophy and uses BERT as the base model to encode low-level features, followed by a task-specific module that is trained from scratch (fine-tuning BERT in the process).

GAP shared task presents the general GAP problem in *gold-two-mention* (Webster et al., 2018) format and formulates it as a classification problem, where the model must resolve a given pronoun to either of the two given candidates or neither[3]. *Neither* instances are particularly difficult to resolve since they require understanding a wider context and perhaps a knowledge of the world. A parallel for this case can be drawn from Question-Answering systems where identifying unanswerable questions confidently remains an active research area. Recent work shows that it is possible to determine lack of evidence with

---

[1] The code is available at `https://github.com/sattree/gap`

[2] `https://github.com/google-research-datasets/gap-coreference`

[3] There is a case in the GAP problem where the pronoun in question may not be coreferent with either of the two mentioned candidates. Such instances will be referred to as *Neither*.

Proceedings of the 1st Workshop on Gender Bias in Natural Language Processing, pages 134–146
Florence, Italy, August 2, 2019. ©2019 Association for Computational Linguistics

	M	F	Total
gap-development	1000	1000	2000
gap-validation	227	227	454
gap-test	1000	1000	2000
gpr-neither (section 2.1)	129	124	253
stage 2 test (kaggle)[†]	6499	5860	12359

Table 1: Corpus statistics. Masculine (M) and Feminine (F) instances were identified based on the gender of the pronoun mention labeled in the sample. [†]Only a subset of these may have been used for final evaluation.

greater confidence by explicitly modeling for it. Works of Zhong et al. (2019) and Kundu and Ng (2018) demonstrate model designs with specialized deep learning architectures that encode evidence in the input and show significant improvement in identifying unanswerable questions. This paper first introduces a baseline that is based on a language model. Then, a novel architecture for pooling evidence from off-the-shelf coreference models is presented, that further boosts the confidence of the base classifier and specifically helps in resolving *Neither* instances. The main contributions of this paper are:

- Demonstrate the effectiveness of pretrained language models and their transferability to establish a strong baseline (ProBERT) for the *gold-two-mention* shared task.

- Introduce an Evidence Pooling based neural architecture (GREP) to draw upon the strengths of off-the-shelf coreference systems.

- Present the model results that placed 1st in the GAP shared task Kaggle competition.

2 Data and Preprocessing

Table 1 shows the data distribution. All datasets are approximately gender balanced, other than stage 2 test set. The datasets, gap-development, gap-validation, and gap-test, are part of the publicly available GAP corpus. The preprocessing and sanitization steps are described next.

2.1 Data Augmentation: *Neither* instances

In an attempt to upsample and boost the classifier's confidence in the underrepresented *Neither* category (Table 2), about 250 instances were added manually. These were created by obtaining cluster predictions from the coreference model by Lee

et al. (2018) and choosing a pronoun and the two candidate entities A and B from disjoint clusters. However, in the interest of time, this strategy was not fully pursued. Instead, the evidence pooling module was used to resolve this problem, as will become clear from the discussion in section 6.

2.2 Mention Tags

The raw text snippet is manipulated by enclosing the labeled span of mentions with their associated tags, i.e. <P> for pronoun, <A> for entity mention A, and <B> for entity mention B. The primary reason for doing this is to provide the positional information of the labeled mentions implicitly within the text as opposed to explicitly through additional features. A secondary motivation was to test the language model's sensitivity to noise in input text structure, and its ability to adapt the pronoun representation to the positional tags. Figure 2 shows an example of this annotation scheme.

> ... NHLer Gary Suter and Olympic-medalist <A> Bob Suter <A> are <B> Dehner <B>'s uncles. <P> His <P> cousin is Minnesota Wild's alternate captain Ryan ...

Figure 2: Sample text-snippet after annotating the mentions with their corresponding tags. Bob Suter and Dehner were tagged as entities A and B, and the mention 'His' following them was tagged as the pronoun.

2.3 Label Sanitization

Only samples where labels can be corrected unambiguously based on snippet-context were corrected[4]. The Wikipedia page-context and url-context were not used. A visualization tool [5] was also developed as part of this work to aid in this activity. Table 2 lists the corpus statistics before and after the sanitization process.

2.4 Coreference Signal

Transformer networks have been found to have limited capability in modeling long-range dependency (Dai et al., 2018; Khandelwal et al., 2018). It has also been noticed in the past that the coreference problem benefits significantly from global

---

[4]Corrected labels can be found at `https://github.com/sattree/gap`. This set was generated independently to avoid any unintended bias. More sets of corrections can be found at `https://www.kaggle.com/c/gendered-pronoun-resolution/discussion/81331#503094`

[5]`https://github.com/sattree/gap/visualization`

	Before sanitization			After sanitization			
	A	B	NEITHER	A	B	NEITHER	Total
gap-development	874	925	201	857(-37)(+20)	919(-32)(+26)	224(-4)(+27)	2000
gap-validation	187	205	62	184(-10)(+7)	206(-7)(+8)	64(-4)(+6)	454
gap-test	918	855	227	894(-42)(+18)	860(-27)(32)	246(-8)(27)	2000

Table 2: GAP dataset label distribution before and after sanitization. (-x) indicates the number of samples that were moved out of a given class and (+x) indicates the number of samples that were added post-sanitization.

knowledge (Lee et al., 2018). Being cognizant of these two factors, it would be useful to inject predictions from off-the-shelf coreference models as an auxiliary source of evidence (with input text context being the primary evidence source). The models chosen for this purpose are Parallelism+URL (Webster et al., 2018), AllenNLP[6], NeuralCoref[7], and e2e-coref (Lee et al., 2018).

3 Model Architecture

3.1 ProBERT: baseline model

ProBERT uses a fine-tuned BERT language model (Devlin et al., 2018; Howard and Ruder, 2018) with a classification head on top to serve as baseline. The snippet-text is augmented with mention-level tags (section 2.2) to capture the positional information of the pronoun, entity A, and entity B mentions, before feeding the text as input to the model. Position-wise token representation corresponding to the pronoun is extracted from the last layer of the language model. With GAP dataset and WordPiece tokenization (Devlin et al., 2018), all pronouns were found to be single token entities.

Let $E_p \in \mathbb{R}^H$ (where H is the dimensionality of the language model output) denote the pooled pronoun vector. A linear transformation is applied to it, followed by softmax, to obtain a probability distribution over classes A, B, and NEITHER, $P = softmax(W^T E_p)$, where $W \in \mathbb{R}^{H \times 3}$ is the linear projection weight matrix. All the parameters are jointly trained to minimize cross entropy loss. This simple architecture is depicted in Figure 1. Only $H \times 3$ new parameters are introduced in the architecture, allowing the model to use training data more efficiently.

A natural question arises as to why this model functions so well (see section 5.2) with just the pronoun representation. This is discussed in section 6.1.

[6]https://allennlp.org/models
[7]https://github.com/huggingface/neuralcoref

3.2 GREP: Gendered Resolution by Evidence Pooling

The architecture for GREP pairs the simple ProBERT architecture with a novel Evidence Pooling module. The Evidence Pooling (EP) module leverages cluster predictions from pretrained (or heuristics-based) coreference models to gather evidence for the resolution task. The internals of the coreference models are opaque to the system, allowing for any evidence source such as a knowledge base to be included as well. This design choice limits us from propagating the gradients through the coreference models, thereby losing information and leaving them noisy. The difficulty of efficiently training deeper architectures paired with the noisy cluster predictions (the best coreference model has an $F1$ performance of only 64% on gap-test) makes this a challenging design problem. The EP module uses self-attention mechanism described in Vaswani et al. (2017) to compute the compatibility of cluster mentions with respect to the pronoun and the two candidates, entity A, and entity B. The simple and easily extensible architecture of this module is described next.

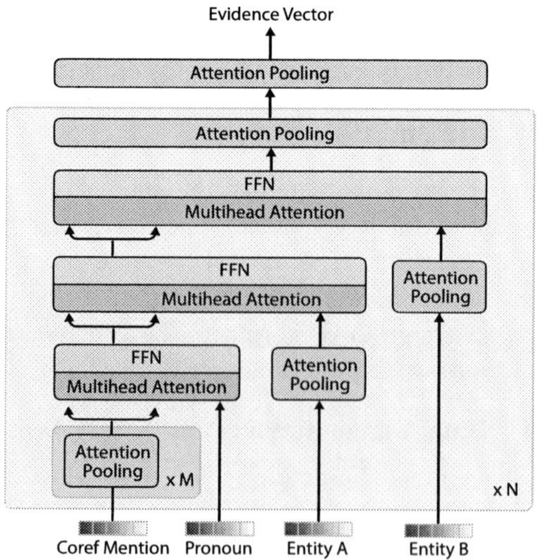

Figure 3: Evidence Pooling module architecture

Suppose we have access to N off-the-shelf coreference models and each predicts T_n mentions that are coreferent with the given pronoun. Let P, A, and B, refer to the mentioned entities labeled in the text-snippet as the pronoun and entities A and B, respectively. Without loss of generality, let us consider the *nth* coreference model and *mth* mention in the cluster predicted by it. Let $E_m \in \mathbb{R}^{T_m \times H}$, $E_p \in \mathbb{R}^{T_p \times H}$, $E_a \in \mathbb{R}^{T_a \times H}$ and $E_b \in \mathbb{R}^{T_b \times H}$, denote the position-wise token embeddings obtained from the last layer of the language model for each of the mentions, where T is the number of tokens in each mention. The first step is to aggregate the information at the mention-level. Self-attention is used to reduce the mention tokens, an operation that will be referred to as $AttnPool$ (attention pooling) hereafter. A single layer MLP is applied to compute position-wise compatibility score, which is then normalized and used to compute a weighted average over the mention tokens for a pooled representation of the mention as follows:

$$M_m = tanh(E_m W_m + b_m) \in \mathbb{R}^{T_m \times H} \quad (1)$$

$$a_m = softmax(M_m) \in \mathbb{R}^{T_m} \quad (2)$$

$$AttnPool(E_m, W_m) = A_m = \sum_{i}^{T_m} a_m E_m \in \mathbb{R}^{H} \quad (3)$$

Similarly, a pooled representation of all mentions in the cluster predicted by the nth coreference model, and of P, A, and B entity mentions is obtained. Let $A_n \in \mathbb{R}^{T_n \times H}$ denote the joint representation of cluster mentions, and A_p, A_a, and A_b, the pooled representations of entity mentions. Next, to compute the compatibility of the cluster with respect to the given entities, we systematically transform the cluster representation by passing it through a transformer layer (Vaswani et al., 2017). A sequence of such transformations is applied successively by feeding A_p, A_a, and A_b as query vectors at each stage. Each such transformer layer consists of a multi-head attention and feed-forward (FFN) projection layers. The reader is referred to Vaswani et al. (2017) for further information on $MultiHead$ operation.

$$FFN(x) = tanh(W_x x + b_x) \in \mathbb{R}^{T_p \times H} \quad (4)$$

$$C_p = FFN(MultiHead(A_p, A_m, A_m)) \in \mathbb{R}^{T_p \times H} \quad (5)$$

$$C_a = FFN(MultiHead(A_a, C_p, C_p)) \in \mathbb{R}^{T_a \times H} \quad (6)$$

$$C_b = FFN(MultiHead(A_b, C_a, C_a)) \in \mathbb{R}^{T_b \times H} \quad (7)$$

The transformed cluster representation C_b is then reduced at the cluster-level and finally at the coreference model level by attention pooling as:

$$A_c = AttnPool(C_b, W_c) \in \mathbb{R}^{N \times H} \quad (8)$$

$$A_{co} = AttnPool(A_c, W_{co}) \in \mathbb{R}^{H} \quad (9)$$

A_{co} represents the evidence vector that encodes information obtained from all the coreference models. Finally, the evidence vector is concatenated with the pronoun representation, and is once again fed through a linear layer and softmax to obtain class probabilities.

$$C = [E_p; A_{co}] \in \mathbb{R}^{2H} \quad (10)$$

$$P = softmax(W^T C + b) \in \mathbb{R}^{3} \quad (11)$$

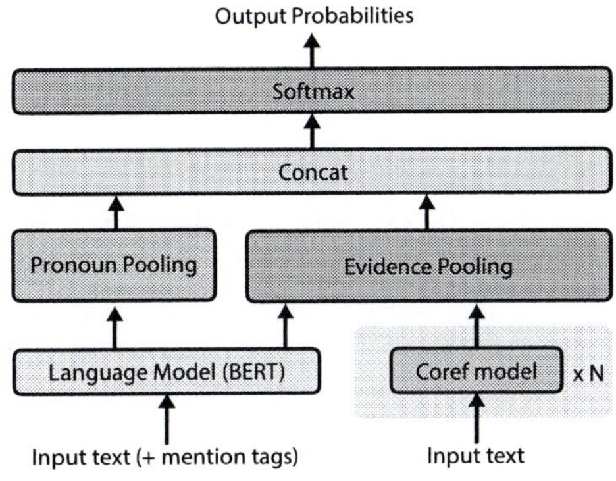

Figure 4: GREP model architecture

The end-to-end GREP model architecture is illustrated in Figure 4.

4 Training

All models were trained on 4 NVIDIA V100 GPUs (16GB memory each). The *pytorch-pretrained-bert*[8] library was used as the language model module and saved model checkpoints were used for initialization. Adam (Kingma and Ba, 2014) optimizer was used with $\beta_1 = 0.9$, $\beta_2 =$

---

[8]https://github.com/huggingface/pytorch-pretrained-BERT/. BertTokenizer from this package was used for tokenization of the text. BertAdam was used as the optimizer. This package contains resources for all variants of BERT, i.e. bert-base-uncased, bert-base-cased, bert-large-uncased and bert-large-cased.

	F1				logloss
	M	F	B	O	
Lee et al. (2017)[†]	67.7	60.0	0.89	64.0	-
Parallelism[†]	69.4	64.4	0.93	66.9	-
Parallelism+URL[†]	72.3	68.8	0.95	70.6	-
RefReader, LM & coref[‡]	72.8	71.4	**0.98**	72.1	-
ProBERT (bert-base-uncased)	88.9	86.7	**0.98**	87.8	.382
GREP (bert-base-uncased)	90.4	87.6	0.97	89.0	.350
ProBERT (bert-large-uncased)	90.8	88.6	**0.98**	89.7	.376
GREP (bert-large-uncased)	**94.0**	**91.1**	0.97	**92.5**	**.317**
Human Performance (estimated)	97.2	96.1	0.99	96.6	-

Table 3: Single model performance on gap-test set by gender. M: masculine, F: feminine, B: (bias) ratio of feminine to masculine performance, O: overall. Log loss is not available for systems that only produce labels. [†]As reported by Webster et al. (2018). [‡]As reported by Liu et al. (2019), their model does not use *gold-two-mention* labeled span information for prediction.

0.999, $\epsilon = 1e^{-6}$, and a fixed learning rate of $4e^{-6}$. For regularization, a fixed dropout (Srivastava et al., 2014) rate of 0.1 was used in all layers and a weight decay of 0.01 was applied to all parameters. Batch sizes of 16 and 8 samples were used for model variants with bert-base and bert-large respectively. Models with bert-base took about 6 mins to train while those with bert-large took up to 20 mins.

For single model performance evaluation, the models were trained on gap-train, early-stopping was based off of gap-validation, and gap-test was used for test evaluation. Kaggle competition results were obtained by training models on all datasets, i.e. gap-train, gap-validation, gap-test, and gpr-neither (a total of 4707 samples), in a 5-Fold Cross-Validation (Friedman et al., 2001) fashion. Each model gets effectively trained on 3768 samples, while 942 samples were held-out for validation. Training would terminate upon identifying an optimal early stopping point based on performance on the validation set with an evaluation frequency of 80 gradient steps. Model's access is limited to snippet-context, and the Wikipedia page-context is not used. However, page-url context may be used via coreference signal (Parallelism+URL).

5 Results

The performance of ProBERT and GREP models is benchmarked against results previously established by Webster et al. and Liu et al. (2019). It is worth noting that Liu et al. do not use *gold-two-mention* labeled spans for prediction and hence

their results may not be directly comparable. This section first introduces an estimate of human performance on this task. Then, results for single model performance are presented, followed by ensembled model results that won the Kaggle competition. $F1$ performance scores were obtained by using the GAP scorer script[9] provided by Webster et al.. Wherever applicable, log loss (the official Kaggle metric) performance is reported as well.

5.1 Human Performance

Errors found in crowd-sourced labels are considered a measure of human performance on this task, and serve as a benchmark. The corrections are only a best-effort attempt to fix some obvious mistakes found in the dataset labels, and were made with certain considerations (section 2.3). This performance measure is subject to variation based on an evaluator's opinion on ambiguous samples.

5.2 Single Model Performance

Single model performance on GAP test set is shown in Table 3. The GREP model (with bert-large-uncased as the language model) achieves a powerful state-of-the-art performance on this task. The model significantly benefits from evidence pooling, gaining 6 points in terms of log loss and 2.8 points in $F1$ accuracy. Further analysis of the source of these gains is discussed in section 6.

While it may seem that the significantly improved performance of GREP has been achieved

---

[9]`https://github.com/google-research-datasets/gap-coreference/blob/master/gap_scorer.py`

Model		Dataset	F1				logloss
			M	F	B	O	
LM=bert-large-uncased, seed=42		OOF all	94.3	93.21	0.99	93.8	.261
		OOF gap-test	94.2	93.7	0.99	93.9	.254
LM=bert-large-cased, seed=42		OOF all	94.3	93.9	0.99	94.1	.249
		OOF gap-test	94.3	93.5	0.99	93.9	.242
Ensemble:	(LM=bert-large-uncased + seeds=42,59,75,46,91)	OOF all	94.8	94.2	0.99	94.5	.195
		OOF gap-test	94.5	94.33	1.00	94.4	.193
Ensemble:	(LM=bert-large-cased + seeds=42,59,75,46,91)	OOF all	95.1	94.4	0.99	94.7	.187
		OOF gap-test	94.9	94.1	0.99	94.4	.183
Ensemble:	(LM=bert-large-uncased, bert-large-cased + seeds=42,59,75,46,91)	OOF all	95.3	94.7	0.99	95.0	.176
		OOF gap-test	95.1	94.7	1.00	94.9	.175
		Stage 2 test	-	-	-	-	**.137**[†]

Table 4: GREP model performance results in the Kaggle competition. Out-of-fold (OOF) error is reported on all data, i.e. gap-development, gap-validation, gap-test, and gpr-neither, as well as on gap-test explicitly for comparison against single model performance results. Since early stopping is based on OOF samples, OOF errors reported here cannot be considered as an estimate of test error. Nevertheless, stage 2 test performance benchmarks the model. [†]Due to a bug, the model did not fully leverage coref evidence, further gains are expected with the fixed version.

at a small cost in terms of gender bias, an attentive reader would realize that the model enjoys improved performance for both genders. Performance gains in masculine instances are much higher compared to feminine instances, and the slight degradation in bias ratio is a manifestation of this. The superior performance of GREP provides evidence that for a given sample context, the model architecture is able to successfully discriminate between the coreference signals, and identify their usefulness.

5.3 Kaggle Competition[10]

To encourage fairness in modeling, the competition was organized in two stages. This strategy eliminates any attempts at leaderboard probing and other such malpractices. Furthermore, models were frozen at the end of stage 1 and were only allowed to operate in inference mode to generate predictions for stage 2 test submission. Additionally, no feedback was provided on stage 2 submissions (in terms of performance score) until the end of the competition.

GREP model is trained as described in section 4 and out-of-fold (oof) error on the held-out samples is reported. The experiments are repeated with 5 different random seeds (42, 59, 75, 46, 91) for initialization. Finally, two sets of models are trained with bert-large-uncased and bert-large-

cased as the language models. The overall scheme leads to 50 models being trained in total, and 50 sets of predictions being generated on stage 2 test data. To generate predictions for submission, ensembling is done by simply taking the unbiased weighted mean over the 50 individual prediction sets.

Table 4 presents a granular view of the winning model performance. This performance comes very close to human performance and has almost no gender bias. As the table shows, the ensemble models achieve much larger gains in log loss as compared to $F1$ accuracy. This is expected since the committee of models makes more confident decisions on "easier" examples. Two insights can be drawn by comparing these results with the single model performance presented in section 5.2: (1) model accuracy benefits from more training data, although the gains are marginal at best (92.5 vs 93.9) given that the model was trained on approximately twice the amount of data; (2) ensembling has a similar effect as evidence pooling, i.e., models become more confident in their predictions.

6 Discussion

Results shown in section 5 establish the superior performance of GREP compared to ProBERT. This can be attributed to two sources: (1) GREP corrects some errors made by ProBERT, reflected in F1; and (2) where predictions are correct, GREP

[10]https://www.kaggle.com/c/gendered-pronoun-resolution/

139

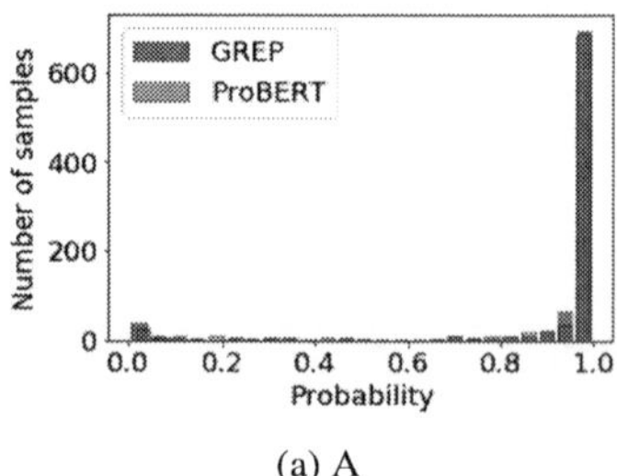
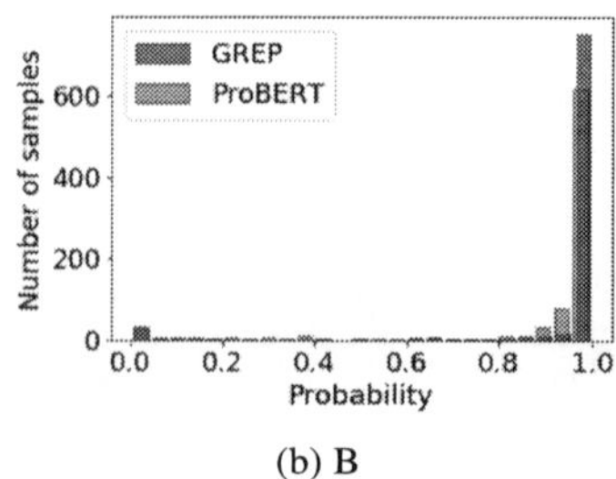
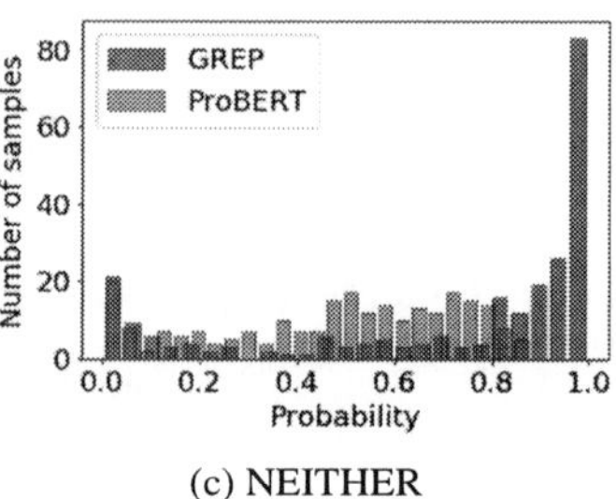

| (a) A | (b) B | (c) NEITHER |

Figure 5: Comparison of probabilities assigned by ProBERT and GREP. Figures show distribution of predicted class probabilities assigned by the models to samples from that class.

| | | GREP | |
	ProBERT	Incorrect	Correct
A	Incorrect	44	38
	Correct	28	784
B	Incorrect	37	39
	Correct	9	775
NEITHER	Incorrect	45	44
	Correct	11	146
Overall	Incorrect	126	121
	Correct	48	1705

Table 5: Class-wise comparison of model accuracy for ProBERT and GREP. Off-diagonal terms show cases where GREP fixes errors made by ProBERT and vice-versa.

is more confident in its predictions, reflected in log loss. To investigate this, error analysis is performed on gap-test.

Figure 5 shows a class-wise comparison of probabilities generated by the two models. It can be seen that GREP is more confident in its predictions (all distributions appear translated closer to 1.0), and the improvement is overwhelmingly evident for the NEITHER class. To understand the difference between the two models, confusion matrix statistics are presented in table 5. The diagonal terms show the number of instances that the two models agree on, and the off-diagonal terms show where they disagree. The numbers reveal that the evidence pooling module not only boosts the model confidence but also helps in correctly resolving *Neither* instances (44 vs 11), indicating that the model is successfully able to build evidence for or against the given candidates.

Appendix A details the behavior of GREP through some examples. The first example is particularly interesting - while it is trivial for a human to resolve this, a machine would require knowl-edge of the world to understand "death" and its implications.

6.1 Unreasonable Effectiveness of ProBERT

It would seem unreasonable that ProBERT is able to perform so well with the noisy input text (due to mention tags) and is able to make the classification decision by looking at the pronoun alone. The following two theories may explain this behavior: (1) attention heads in the (BERT) transformer architecture are able to specialize the pronoun representation in the presence of the supervision signal; (2) the special nature of dropout (present in every layer) makes the model immune to a small amount of noise, and at the same time prevents the model from ignoring the tags. The analysis of attention heads to investigate these claims should form the scope of future work.

7 Conclusion

A powerful set of results have been established for the shared task. Work presented in this paper makes it feasible to efficiently employ neural attention for pooling information from auxiliary sources of global knowledge. The evidence pooling mechanism introduced here is able to leverage upon the strengths of off-the-shelf coreference solvers without being hindered by their weaknesses (gender bias). A natural extension of the GREP model would be to solve the gendered pronoun resolution problem beyond the scope of the *gold-two-mention* task, i.e., without accessing the labeled gold spans.

Acknowledgments

I would like to thank Google AI Language and Kaggle for hosting and organizing this competition, and for providing a platform for independent research.

References

Zihang Dai, Zhilin Yang, Yiming Yang, William W Cohen, Jaime Carbonell, Quoc V Le, and Ruslan Salakhutdinov. 2018. Transformer-xl: Language modeling with longer-term dependency.

Jacob Devlin, Ming-Wei Chang, Kenton Lee, and Kristina Toutanova. 2018. Bert: Pre-training of deep bidirectional transformers for language understanding. *arXiv preprint arXiv:1810.04805*.

Jerome Friedman, Trevor Hastie, and Robert Tibshirani. 2001. *The elements of statistical learning*, volume 1. Springer series in statistics New York.

Jeremy Howard and Sebastian Ruder. 2018. Universal language model fine-tuning for text classification. *arXiv preprint arXiv:1801.06146*.

Urvashi Khandelwal, He He, Peng Qi, and Dan Jurafsky. 2018. Sharp nearby, fuzzy far away: How neural language models use context. *arXiv preprint arXiv:1805.04623*.

Diederik P Kingma and Jimmy Ba. 2014. Adam: A method for stochastic optimization. *arXiv preprint arXiv:1412.6980*.

Souvik Kundu and Hwee Tou Ng. 2018. A nil-aware answer extraction framework for question answering. In *Proceedings of the 2018 Conference on Empirical Methods in Natural Language Processing*, pages 4243–4252.

Kenton Lee, Luheng He, and Luke Zettlemoyer. 2018. Higher-order coreference resolution with coarse-to-fine inference. *arXiv preprint arXiv:1804.05392*.

Fei Liu, Luke Zettlemoyer, and Jacob Eisenstein. 2019. The referential reader: A recurrent entity network for anaphora resolution. *arXiv preprint arXiv:1902.01541*.

Matthew E Peters, Mark Neumann, Mohit Iyyer, Matt Gardner, Christopher Clark, Kenton Lee, and Luke Zettlemoyer. 2018. Deep contextualized word representations. *arXiv preprint arXiv:1802.05365*.

Alec Radford, Karthik Narasimhan, Tim Salimans, and Ilya Sutskever. 2018. Improving language understanding by generative pre-training. *URL https://s3-us-west-2. amazonaws. com/openai-assets/research-covers/languageunsupervised/language understanding paper. pdf*.

Nitish Srivastava, Geoffrey Hinton, Alex Krizhevsky, Ilya Sutskever, and Ruslan Salakhutdinov. 2014. Dropout: a simple way to prevent neural networks from overfitting. *The Journal of Machine Learning Research*, 15(1):1929–1958.

Ashish Vaswani, Noam Shazeer, Niki Parmar, Jakob Uszkoreit, Llion Jones, Aidan N Gomez, Łukasz Kaiser, and Illia Polosukhin. 2017. Attention is all you need. In *Advances in neural information processing systems*, pages 5998–6008.

Kellie Webster, Marta Recasens, Vera Axelrod, and Jason Baldridge. 2018. Mind the gap: A balanced corpus of gendered ambiguous pronouns. *Transactions of the Association for Computational Linguistics*, 6:605–617.

Victor Zhong, Caiming Xiong, Nitish Shirish Keskar, and Richard Socher. 2019. Coarse-grain fine-grain coattention network for multi-evidence question answering. *arXiv preprint arXiv:1901.00603*.

A Examples

Tables 6, 7, 8, and Figure 6 show an example of how incorporating evidence from the coreference models helps GREP to correct a prediction error made by ProBERT. While the example is trivial for a human to resolve, a machine would require knowledge of the world to understand "death" and its implications. ProBERT is unsure about the resolution and ends up assigning comparable probabilities to both entities A and B. GREP, on the other hand, is able to shift nearly all the probability mass from B to the correct resolution A, in light of strong evidence presented by the coreference solvers. Figure 6 illustrates an interesting phenomenon; while e2e-coref groups the pronoun and both entities A and B in the same cluster, the model architecture is able to harvest information from AllenNLP predictions, propagating the belief that entity A must be the better candidate. The above observations indicate that by pooling evidence from various sources, the model is able to reason over a larger space and build a rudimentary form of world knowledge.

Tables 9, 10, 11, and Figure 7 show a second example. This example is not easy even for a human to resolve without reading and understanding the full context. A model may find this situation to be adverse given the presence of too many named entities as distractor elements; and the url-context can be misleading since the pronoun referent is not the subject of the article. Nevertheless, the model is able to successfully build evidence against the given candidates, and resolve with a very high confidence of 92.5%.

Finally, a third example is shown in Tables 12 and 13. This example shows that the model doesn't simply make a majority decision, rather considers interactions between the global structure exposed by the various evidence sources.

Ground truth

Afterward, however, the company rehired him--this time as a manager, training motormen on the city's streetcars. Ching became a naturalized American citizen in 1909. In 1912, he obtained his law degree from the Evening Institute for Younger Men (now Northeastern University). The same year, he married the former [0 Anna MacIntosh.] After [0 her] death, Ching married [1 Mildred Vergosen.]

Off-the-shelf coreference model predictions

Afterward , however , the company rehired him -- this time as a manager , training motormen on the city 's streetcars . Ching became a naturalized American citizen in 1909 . In 1912 , he obtained his law degree from the Evening Institute for Younger Men (now Northeastern University) . The same year , he married the former Anna MacIntosh . After her death , Ching married Mildred Vergosen .

(a) Parallelism+URL

Afterward , however , the company rehired him -- this time as a manager , training motormen on the city 's streetcars . [0 Ching] became a naturalized American citizen in 1909 . In 1912 , [0 he] obtained [0 his] law degree from the Evening Institute for Younger Men (now Northeastern University) . The same year , [0 he] married [1 the former Anna MacIntosh] . After [1 her] death , [0 Ching] married Mildred Vergosen .

(b) AllenNLP

Afterward , however , the company rehired [0 him] -- this time as a manager , training motormen on the city 's streetcars . [0 Ching] became a naturalized American citizen in 1909 . In 1912 , [0 he] obtained [0 his] law degree from the Evening Institute for Younger Men (now Northeastern University) . The same year , [0 he] married the former Anna MacIntosh . After her death , [0 Ching] married Mildred Vergosen .

(c) NeuralCoref

Afterward , however , the company rehired [0 him] -- this time as a manager , training motormen on the city 's streetcars . [0 Ching] became a naturalized American citizen in 1909 . In 1912 , [0 he] obtained [0 his] law degree from the Evening Institute for Younger Men (now Northeastern University) . The same year , [0 he] married [1 the former Anna MacIntosh] . After [1 her] death , [0 Ching] married [1 Mildred Vergosen] .

(d) e2e-coref (Lee et al., 2018)

Table 6: Example 1 - Illustration of ground truth and coreference model predictions. Mentions belonging to a coreference cluster are color coded and indexed. Visualizations were produced using the code module at `https://github.com/sattree/gap/visualization`.

(a) Coreference model level attention weights. Indicates weightage given to evidence from each source.

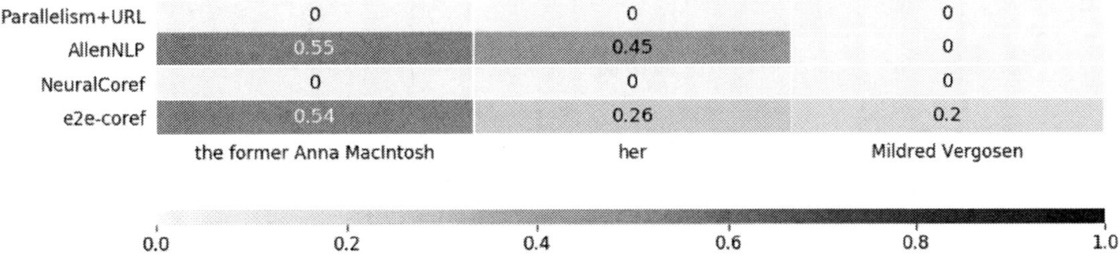

(b) Cluster mention level attention weights. Indicates weightage given to each mention within an evidence cluster.

Figure 6: Example 1 - Visualization of normalized attention scores assigned by the hierarchical attention pooling layers in the evidence pooling module

id	Pronoun	Pronoun offset	A	A offset	A coref	B	B offset	B coref	Url
test-282	her	410	Anna MacIntosh	338	True	Mildred Vergosen	475	False	http://en.wikipedia.org/wiki/Cyrus_S._Ching

Table 7: Example 1 - Sample details from GAP test set.

	P(A)	P(B)	P(NEITHER)
ProBERT	0.405	0.452	0.142
GREP	0.718	0.038	0.244

Table 8: Example 1 - A comparison of probabilities assigned by ProBERT and GREP

Ground truth

In 617, the secretary general of Wuyang Commandery (**, part of modern Handan, Hebei), Yuan Baozang (***), rebelled against Sui as well and submitted to Li Mi. He invited Wei Zheng to serve on his staff, as his secretary. Wei subsequently drafted submissions from Yuan to Li Mi, suggesting that Li Mi attack and seize nearby Wei Commandery (**, also part of modern Handan) and a large food storage that Emperor [0] Yang built, Liyang Storage (***, in modern Hebi, Henan). Li Mi was impressed, and when [2] he found out that [1] Wei wrote the submissions, he requested Yuan send Wei to him.

Off-the-shelf coreference model predictions

In 617 , the secretary general of Wuyang Commandery (** , part of modern Handan , Hebei) , Yuan Baozang (***) , rebelled against Sui as well and submitted to Li Mi . He invited Wei Zheng to serve on his staff , as his secretary . Wei subsequently drafted submissions from Yuan to Li Mi , suggesting that Li Mi attack and seize nearby Wei Commandery (** , also part of modern Handan) and a large food storage that Emperor Yang built , Liyang Storage (*** , in modern Hebi , Henan) . Li Mi was impressed , and when [0] he found out that [0] Wei wrote the submissions , he requested Yuan send Wei to him .

(a) Parallelism+URL

In 617 , the secretary general of [0] Wuyang Commandery (* * , part of modern Handan , Hebei) , [0] Yuan Baozang (* * *) , rebelled against [1] Sui as well and submitted to [3] Li Mi . [1] He invited [2] Wei Zheng to serve on [1] his staff , as [1] his secretary . [2] Wei subsequently drafted [4] submissions from [5] Yuan to [3] Li Mi , suggesting that [3] Li Mi attack and seize nearby [0] Wei Commandery (* * , also part of modern Handan) and a large food storage that Emperor Yang built , [0] Liyang Storage (* * * , in modern Hebi , Henan) . [3] Li Mi was impressed , and when [3] he found out that [2] Wei wrote [4] the submissions , [3] he requested [5] Yuan send [2] Wei to [3] him .

(b) AllenNLP

In 617 , the secretary general of Wuyang Commandery (* * , part of modern Handan , Hebei) , Yuan Baozang (* * *) , rebelled against [0] Sui as well and submitted to [1] Li Mi . [0] He invited Wei Zheng to serve on [0] his staff , as [0] his secretary . [0] Wei subsequently drafted submissions from [2] Yuan to [1] Li Mi , suggesting that [1] Li Mi attack and seize nearby Wei Commandery (* * , also part of modern Handan) and a large food storage that [3] Emperor [0] Yang built , Liyang Storage (* * * , in modern Hebi , Henan) . [1] Li Mi was impressed , and when [3] he found out that [0] Wei wrote the submissions , [3] he requested [2] Yuan send [0] Wei to [3] him .

(c) NeuralCoref

In 617 , [0] the secretary general of Wuyang Commandery (* * , part of [3] modern Handan , Hebei) , Yuan Baozang (* * *) , rebelled against Sui as well and submitted to [2] Li Mi . [0] He invited [1] Wei Zheng to serve on [1] his staff , as [0] his secretary . [1] Wei subsequently drafted [4] submissions from [5] Yuan to [2] Li Mi , suggesting that [2] Li Mi attack and seize nearby Wei Commandery (* * , also part of [3] modern Handan) and a large food storage that Emperor Yang built , Liyang Storage (* * * , in modern Hebi , Henan) . [2] Li Mi was impressed , and when [2] he found out that [1] Wei wrote [4] the submissions , [2] he requested [5] Yuan send [1] Wei to [1] him .

(d) e2e-coref (Lee et al., 2018)

Table 9: Example 2 - Illustration of ground truth and coreference model predictions. Mentions belonging to a coreference cluster are color coded and indexed.

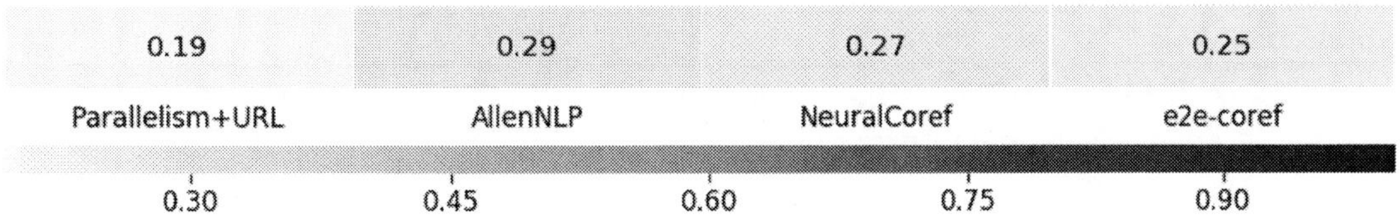

(a) Coreference model level attention weights. Indicates weightage given to evidence from each source.

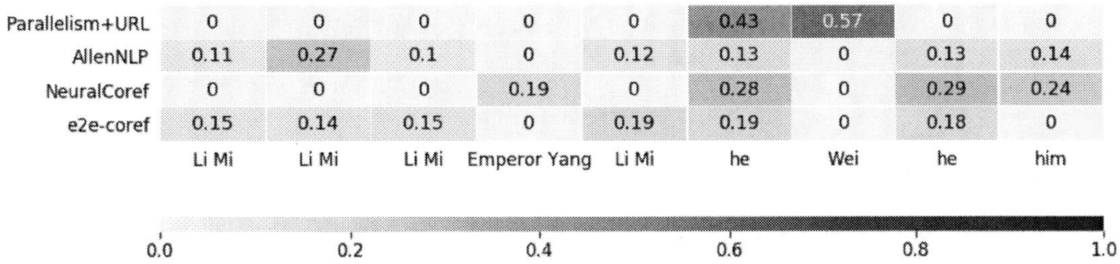

(b) Cluster mention level attention weights. Indicates weightage given to each mention within an evidence cluster.

Figure 7: Example 2 - Visualization of normalized attention scores assigned by the hierarchical attention pooling layers in the evidence pooling module

id	Pronoun	Pronoun offset	A	A offset	A coref	B	B offset	B coref	Url
test-406	he	803	Yang	636	False	Wei	916	False	http://en.wikipedia.org/wiki/Wei_Zheng

Table 10: Example 2 - Sample details from GAP test set.

	P(A)	P(B)	P(NEITHER)
ProBERT	0.790	0.038	0.172
GREP	0.055	0.020	0.925

Table 11: Example 2 - A comparison of probabilities assigned by ProBERT and GREP

Ground truth

In the following year, Richmond stirred the rivalry with the Magpies by appointing ex- Collingwood skipper Dan Minogue as playing coach. After winning the minor premiership, Richmond went on to defeat Collingwood for the flag. With [0 Dick Lee] missing for the Magpies, [1 Thorp] was able to easily blanket [0 his] replacement, Harry Curtis, and contribute significantly to the result.

Off-the-shelf coreference model predictions

In the following year , Richmond stirred the rivalry with the Magpies by appointing ex - Collingwood skipper Dan Minogue as playing coach . After winning the minor premiership , Richmond went on to defeat Collingwood for the flag . With Dick Lee missing for the Magpies , [0 Thorp] was able to easily blanket [0 his] replacement , Harry Curtis , and contribute significantly to the result .

(a) Parallelism+URL

In the following year , [1 Richmond] stirred the rivalry with [0 the Magpies] by appointing ex- Collingwood skipper Dan Minogue as playing coach . After winning [0 the minor premiership] , [1 Richmond] went on to defeat [0 Collingwood] for the flag . With Dick Lee missing for [0 the Magpies] , [0 Thorp] was able to easily blanket [1 his] replacement , Harry Curtis , and contribute significantly to the result .

(b) AllenNLP

In the following year , [0 Richmond] stirred the rivalry with [1 the Magpies] by appointing ex- [2 Collingwood] skipper Dan Minogue as playing coach . After winning the minor premiership , [0 Richmond] went on to defeat [2 Collingwood] for the flag . With [3 Dick Lee] missing for [1 the Magpies] , Thorp was able to easily blanket [3 his] replacement , Harry Curtis , and contribute significantly to the result .

(c) NeuralCoref

In the following year , [0 Richmond] stirred the rivalry with [2 the Magpies] by appointing [1 ex- Collingwood] skipper Dan Minogue as playing coach . After winning the minor premiership , [0 Richmond] went on to defeat [1 Collingwood] for the flag . With Dick Lee missing for [2 the Magpies] , [3 Thorp] was able to easily blanket [3 his] replacement , Harry Curtis , and contribute significantly to the result .

(d) e2e-coref (Lee et al., 2018)

Table 12: Example 3 - Illustration of ground truth and coreference model predictions. Mentions belonging to a coreference cluster are color coded and indexed.

	P(A)	P(B)	P(NEITHER)
ProBERT	0.028	0.968	0.003
GREP	0.724	0.263	0.012

Table 13: Example 3 - A comparison of probabilities assigned by ProBERT and GREP

Equalizing Gender Bias in Neural Machine Translation
with Word Embeddings Techniques

Joel Escudé Font and Marta R. Costa-jussà

Universitat Politècnica de Catalunya, 08034 Barcelona

`joel.escude@estudiant.upc.edu,marta.ruiz@upc.edu`

Abstract

Neural machine translation has significantly pushed forward the quality of the field. However, there are remaining big issues with the output translations and one of them is fairness. Neural models are trained on large text corpora which contain biases and stereotypes. As a consequence, models inherit these social biases. Recent methods have shown results in reducing gender bias in other natural language processing tools such as word embeddings. We take advantage of the fact that word embeddings are used in neural machine translation to propose a method to equalize gender biases in neural machine translation using these representations. We evaluate our proposed system on the WMT English-Spanish benchmark task, showing gains up to one BLEU point. As for the gender bias evaluation, we generate a test set of occupations and we show that our proposed system learns to equalize existing biases from the baseline system.

1 Introduction

Language is one of the most interesting and complex skills used in our daily life, and may even be taken for granted on our ability to communicate. However, the understanding of meanings between lines in natural languages is not straightforward for the logic rules of programming languages.

Natural language processing (NLP) is a subfield of artificial intelligence that focuses on making natural languages understandable to computers.

Similarly, the translation between different natural languages is a task for Machine Translation (MT). Neural MT has shown significant improvements on performance using deep learning techniques, which are algorithms that learn abstractions from data. In recent years, these deep learning techniques have shown promising results in narrowing the gap between human-like performance with sequence-to-sequence learning approaches in a variety of tasks (Sutskever et al., 2014), improvements in combination of approaches such as attention (Bahdanau et al., 2014) and translation systems algorithms like the Transformer (Vaswani et al., 2017).

One downside of models trained with human generated corpora is that social biases and stereotypes from the data are learned (Madaan et al., 2018). A systematic way of showing this bias is by means of word embeddings, a vector representation of words. The presence of biases, such as gender bias, is studied for these representations and evaluated on crowd-sourced tests (Bolukbasi et al., 2016). The presence of biases in the data can directly impact downstream applications (Zhao et al., 2018a) and are at risk of being amplified (Zhao et al., 2017).

The objective of this work is to study the presence of gender bias in MT and give insight on the impact of debiasing in such systems. An example of this gender bias is the word "friend" in the English sentence "She works in a hospital, my friend is a nurse" would be correctly translated to "amiga" (girl friend in Spanish) in Spanish, while "She works in a hospital, my friend is a doctor" would be incorrectly translated to "amigo" (boy friend in Spanish) in Spanish. We consider that this translation contains gender bias since it ignores the fact that, for both cases, "friend" is a female and translates by focusing on the occupational stereotypes, i.e. translating doctor as male and nurse as female.

The main contribution of this study is providing progress on the recent detected problem which is gender bias in MT (Prates et al., 2018). The progress towards reducing gender bias in MT is made in two directions: first, we define a frame-

Proceedings of the 1st Workshop on Gender Bias in Natural Language Processing, pages 147–154
Florence, Italy, August 2, 2019. ©2019 Association for Computational Linguistics

work to experiment, detect and evaluate gender bias in MT for a particular task; second, we propose to use debiased word embeddings techniques in the MT system to reduce the detected bias. This is the first study in proposing debiasing techniques for MT.

The rest the paper is organized as follows. Section 2 reports material relevant to the background of the study. Section 3 presents previous work on the bias problem. Section 4 reports the methodology used for experimentation and section 5 details the experimental framework. The results and discussion are included in section 6 and section 7 presents the main conclusions and ideas for further work.

2   Background

This section presents the models used in this paper. First, we describe the Transformer model which is the state-of-the-art model in MT. Second, we report describe word embeddings and, then, the corresponding techniques to debias them.

2.1   Transformer

The Transformer (Vaswani et al., 2017) is a deep learning architecture based on self-attention, which has shown better performance over previous systems. It is more efficient in using computational resources and has higher training speed than previous recurrent (Sutskever et al., 2014; Bahdanau et al., 2014) and convolutional models (Gehring et al., 2017).

The Transformer architecture consists of two main parts: an encoder and a decoder. The encoder reads an input sentence to generate a representation which is later used by a decoder to produce a sentence output word by word.

The input words are represented as vectors, word embeddings (more on this in section 2.2) and then, positional embeddings keep track of the sequentiality of language. The Transformer architecture computes a reduced constant number of steps using a self-attention mechanism on each one. The attention score is computed for all words in a sentence when comparing the contribution of each word to the next representation. New representations are generated in parallel for all words at each step .

Finally, the decoder uses self-attention in generated words and also uses the representations from the last words in the encoder to produce a single word each time.

2.2   Word embeddings

Word embeddings are vector representations of words. These representations are used in many NLP applications. Based on the hypothesis that words appearing in same contexts share semantic meaning, this continuous vector space representation gathers semantically similar words, thus being more expressive than other discrete representations like one-hot vectors.

Arithmetic operations can be performed with these embeddings, in order to find analogies between pairs of nouns with the pattern "A is to B what C is to D" (Mikolov et al., 2013). For nouns, such as countries and their respective capitals or for the conjugations of verbs.

While there are many techniques for extracting word embeddings, in this work we are using Global Vectors, or GloVe (Pennington et al., 2014). Glove is an unsupervised method for learning word embeddings. This count-based method, uses statistical information of word occurrences from a given corpus to train a vector space for which each vector is related to a word and their values describes their semantic relations.

2.3   Equalizing biases in word embeddings

The presence of biases in word embeddings is a topic of discussion about fairness in NLP. More specifically, Bolukbasi et al. (2016) proposes a post-process method for debiasing already trained word embeddings. (Zhao et al., 2018b) aims to restrict learning biases during the training of the embeddings to obtain a more neutral representation. The main ideas behind these methods are described next.

Hard-debiased embeddings (Bolukbasi et al., 2016) is a post-process method for debiasing word embeddings. First, the direction of the embeddings where the bias is present is identified. Second, the gender neutral words in this direction are neutralized to zero and also equalizes the sets by making the neutral word equidistant to the remaining ones in the set. The disadvantage of the first part of the process is that it can remove valuable information in the embeddings for semantic relations between words with several meanings that are not related to the bias being treated.

GN-GloVe (Zhao et al., 2018b) is an algorithm for learning gender neutral word embeddings models. It is based on the GloVe representation (Pennington et al., 2014) and modified to learn such word representations while restricting specific attributes, such as gender information, to specific dimensions. A set of seed male and female words are used to define metrics for computing the optimization and a set of gender neutral words is used for restricting neutral words in a gender direction.

3 Related work

While there are many studies on the presence of biases in many NLP applications, studies of this type in MT are quite limited.

Prates et al. (2018) performs a case study on gender bias in machine translation. They build a test set consisting of a list of jobs and gender-specific sentences. Using English as a target language and a variety of gender neutral languages as a source, i.e. languages that do not explicitly give gender information about the subject, they test these sentences on the translating service Google Translate. They find that occupations related to science, engineering and mathematics present a strong stereotype toward male subjects.

Vanmassenhove et al. (2018) compile a large multilingual dataset on the politics domain that contains the speaker information. They specifically use this information to incorporate it in a MT system. Adding this information improves the translation quality.

Our contribution is different from previous approaches in the sense that we are explicitly proposing a gender-debiased approach for NMT as well as an specific analysis based on correference and stereotypes to evaluate the effectiveness of our technique.

4 Methodology

In this section, we describe the methodology used for this study. The prior layer of both the encoder and decoder in the Transformer (Vaswani et al., 2017), where the word embeddings are trained, is adapted to use pre-trained word embeddings. We train the system with different pre-trained word embeddings (based on GloVe (Pennington et al., 2014)) to have a set of models. The scenarios are the following:

- No pre-trained word embeddings, i.e. they are learned within the training of the model.

- Pre-trained word embeddings learned from the same corpus. Specifically, GloVe, Hard-Debiased GloVe and Gender Neutral Glove (GN-GloVe) embeddings.

Also, the models with pre-trained embeddings given to the Transformer have three cases: using pre-trained embeddings only in the encoder side, see Figure 1 (left), only in the decoder side, Figure 1 (center), and both in the encoder and decoder sides, Figure 1 (right).

5 Experimental framework

In this section, we present the experimental framework. We report details on the training of the word embeddings and the translation system. We describe the data related to the training corpus and test sets and the parameters. Also, we comment on the use of computational resources.

5.1 Corpora

The language pair used for the experiments is English-Spanish. The training set consists of 16,554,790 sentences from a variety of sources including United Nations (Ziemski et al., 2016), Europarl (Koehn, 2005), CommonCrawl and News available from the Workshop on Machine Translation (WMT) [1]. The validation and test sets used are the *newstest2012* (3,003 sentences) and *newstest2013* (3,000 sentences), respectively, also from the same WMT workshop. See Table 2 for the corpus statistics.

To study gender bias, we have developed an additional test set with custom sentences to evaluate the quality of the translation in the models. We built this test set using a sentence pattern *"I've known {her, him, <proper noun>} for a long time, my friend works as {a, an} <occupation>."* for a list of occupations from different professional areas. We refer to this test as *Occupations test*, their related sizes are also listed in Table 2 and sample sentences from this set are in Table 1. We use Spanish proper names to reduce ambiguity in this particular test. These sentences are properly tokenized before using them in the test.

With these test sentences we see how "friend" is translated into its Spanish equivalent "amiga" or "amigo" which has a gender relation for each word, female and male, respectively. Note that we are formulating sentences with an ambiguous

____
[1] http://www.statmt.org/wmt13/

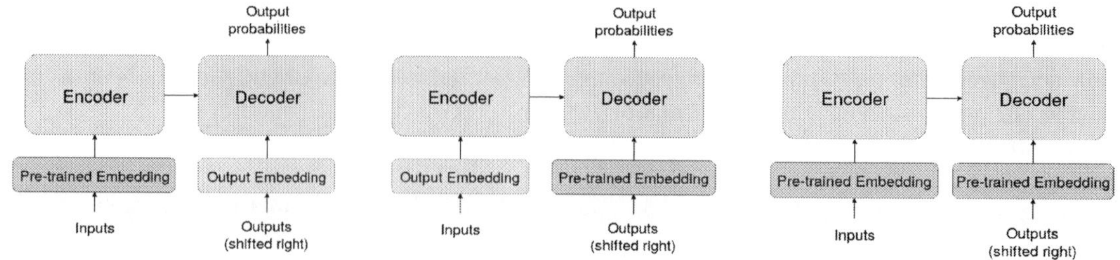

Figure 1: (Left) Pre-trained word embeddings in the encoder. (Center) Pre-trained word embeddings in the decoder. (Right) Pre-trained word embeddings in both the encoder and the decoder.

word "friend" that can be translated into any of the two words and we are adding context in the same sentence so that the system has enough information to translate them correctly. The list of occupations is from the U.S. Bureau of Labor Statistics[2], which also includes statistical data for gender and race for most professions. We use a pre-processed version of this list from (Prates et al., 2018).

5.2 Models

The architecture to train the models for the translation task is the Transformer (Vaswani et al., 2017) and we used the implementation provided by the OpenNMT toolkit[3]. The parameter values used in the Transformer are the same as proposed in the OpenNMT baseline system. Our baseline system is the Transformer witout pre-trained word embeddings.

Additionally, OpenNMT has built-in tools for training with pre-trained embeddings. In our case, these pre-trained embeddings have been implemented with the corresponding github repositories in GloVe[4], Hard-Debiasing with Debiaswe[5] and GN-GloVe[6].

The GloVe and GN-GloVe embeddings are trained from the same corpus presented in the previous section. We refer to the method from Bolukbasi et al. (2016) applied to the previously mentioned GloVe embeddings as Hard-Debiased GloVe. The dimension of the vectors is settled to 512 (as standard) and kept through all the experiments in this study. The parameter values for training the word embedding models are shown in Table 3.

Bolukbasi et al. (2016) uses a set of words to define the gender direction and to neutralize and equalize the bias from the word vectors. Three set of words are used: One set of ten pairs of words such as *woman-man, girl-boy, she-he* are used to define the gender direction. Another set of 218 gender-specific words such as *aunt, uncle, wife, husband* are used for learning a larger set of gender-specific words. Finally, a set of crowd-sourced male-female equalization pairs such as *dad-mom, boy-girl, granpa-grandma* that represent gender direction are equalized in the algorithm. In fact, for the English side, the gendered pairs used are the same as identified in the crowd-sourcing test by Bolukbasi et al. (2016). For the Spanish side, the sets are translated manually and modified when necessary to avoid non-applicable pairs or unnecessary repetitions. The sets from Zhao et al. (2018b) are similarly adapted to the Spanish language.

To evaluate the performance of the models we use the BLEU metric (Papineni et al., 2002). This metric gives a score for a predicted translation set compared to its expected output.

5.3 Hardware resources

The GPUs used for training are separate groups of four NVIDIA TITAN Xp and NVIDIA GeForce GTX TITAN. The duration time for training is approximately 3 and 5 days, respectively. In the implementation, the model is set to accumulate the gradient two times before updating the parameters, which simulates 4 more GPUs during training giving a total of 8 GPUs.

6 Results

In this section we report results on translation quality and present an analysis on gender bias.

---

[2]https://www.bls.gov/cps/tables.htm#empstat
[3]http://opennmt.net/
[4]https://github.com/stanfordnlp/GloVe
[5]https://github.com/tolga-b/debiaswe
[6]https://github.com/uclanlp/gn_glove

| (En) I've known *her* for a long time, my *friend* works as an *accounting clerk*. |
| (Es) *La* conozco desde hace mucho tiempo, mi *amiga* trabaja como *contable*. |
| (En) I've known *him* for a long time, my *friend* works as an *accounting clerk*. |
| (Es) *Lo* conozco desde hace mucho tiempo, mi *amigo* trabaja como *contable*. |
| (En) I've known *Mary* for a long time, my *friend* works as an *accounting clerk*. |
| (Es) Conozco a *Mary* desde hace mucho tiempo, mi *amiga* trabaja como *contable*. |
| (En) I've known *John* for a long time, my *friend* works as an *accounting clerk*. |
| (Es) Conozco a *John* desde hace mucho tiempo, mi *amigo* trabaja como *contable*. |

Table 1: Sample sentences from the *Occupations test* set. English (En) and Spanish (Es).

Language	Data set	Num. of sentences	Num. of words	Vocab. size
English (En)	Train	16.6M	427.6M	1.32M
	Dev	3k	73k	10k
	Test	3k	65k	9k
	Occupations test	1k	17k	0.8k
Spanish (Es)	Train	16.6M	477.3M	1.37M
	Dev	3k	79k	12k
	Test	3k	71k	11k
	Occupations test	1k	17k	0.8k

Table 2: English-Spanish data set.

Parameter	Value
Vector size	512
Memory	4.0
Vocab. min. count	5
Max. iter.	15
Window size	15
Num. threads	8
X max.	10
Binary	2
Verbose	2

Table 3: Word Embeddings Parameters.

Baseline			29.78
Pre-trained emb.	Enc.	Dec.	Enc./Dec.
GloVe	30.21	30.24	30.62
GloVe Hard-Deb.	30.16	30.09	29.95
GN-GloVe	29.12	30.13	**30.74**

Table 4: BLEU scores for the *newstest2013* test set. English-Spanish. Pre-trained embeddings are updated during training. In bold best results.

6.1 Translation

For the test set *newstest2013*, BLUE scores are given in Table 4. Pre-trained embeddings are used for training in three scenarios: in the encoder side (Enc.), in the decoder side (Dec.) and in both the encoder and decoder sides (Enc./Dec.). These pre-trained embeddings are updated during training. We are comparing several pre-trained embeddings against a baseline system ('Baseline' in Table 4) which does not include pre-trained embeddings (neither on the encoder nor the decoder).

For the studied cases, values do not differ much. Using pre-trained embeddings can improve the translation, which is coherent with previous studies (Qi et al., 2018). Furthermore, debiasing with GN-GloVe embeddings keeps this improvement and even increases it when used in both the encoder and decoder sides. We want to underline that these models do not decrease the quality of translation in terms of BLEU when tested in a standard MT task. Next, we show how each of the models performs on a gender debiasing task.

6.2 Gender Bias

A qualitative analysis is performed on the *Occupations test* set. Examples of this test set are given in Table 1. The sentences of this test set contain context information for predicting the gender of the neutral word "friend" in English, either "amigo" or "amiga" in Spanish. The lower the bias in the system, the better the system will be able to translate the gender correctly. See Table 5 for the percentages of how "friend" is predicted for each model.

"Him" is predicted at almost 100% accuracy for all models. However not all occupations are well translated. On the other hand, the accuracy drops when predicting the word "her" on all models. When using names, the accuracy is even lower for "Mary" opposite to "John".

Note that gender debiasing is shown by augmenting the percentage of "amiga" in the translation in the presence of the female pronoun while keeping the quality of translation (coherently with generic results in Table 4). Based on accuracy values from Table 5, the most neutral system is achieved with GloVe and also with Hard-Debiased GloVe pre-trained embeddings. The accuracy improves by 30 percentage points compared to the baseline system and over 10 percentage points compared to the non-debiased pre-trained word embeddings.

The quality of the translation also depends on the professions from the *Occupations test* and its predicted gender. Again, the system has no problem predicting the gender of professions in the context of "him", so we focus the analysis on the context of "her". With GN-GloVe pre-trained embeddings both in the encoder and decoder sides, the model shows a higher accuracy when predicting the gender of a profession in Spanish. Specifically, for technical professions such as "criminal investigator", "heating mechanic", "refrigeration mechanic" and others such as "mine shuttle car operator". See Table 6 for the prediction on this last profession.

7 Conclusions and further work

Biases learned from human generated corpora is a topic that has gained relevance over the years. Specifically, for MT, studies quantifying gender bias present in news corpora and proposing debiasing approaches for word embedding models have shown improvements on this matter.

We studied the impact of gender debiasing on neural MT. We trained sets of word embeddings with the standard GloVe algorithm. Then, we debiased the embeddings using a post-process method (Bolukbasi et al., 2016) and also trained a gender neutral version (Zhao et al., 2018b). We

used all these different models on the Transformer (Vaswani et al., 2017). Experiments were reported on using these embeddings on both the encoder and decoder sides, or only the encoder or the decoder sides.

The models were evaluated using the BLEU metric on the standard task of the WMT *newstest2013* test set. BLEU performance increase when using pre-trained word embeddings and it is slightly better for the debiased models.

In order to study the bias on the translations, we evaluate the systems on a custom test set composed of occupations. This set consists of sentences that include context of the gender of the ambiguous "friend" in the English-Spanish translation. This word can be translated to feminine or masculine and the proper translation has to be derived from context. We verified our hypothesis that consisted on the fact that if the translation system is gender biased, the context is disregarded, while if the system is neutral, the translation is correct (since it has the information of gender in the sentence). Results show that the male pronoun is always identified, despite not all occupations are well translated, while the female pronoun has different ratio of appearance for different models. In fact, the accuracy when predicting the gender for this test set is improved for some settings, when using the debiased and gender neutral word embeddings. Also, as mentioned, this system slightly improves the BLEU performance from the baseline translation system. Therefore, we are "equalizing" the translation, while keeping its quality. Experimental material from this paper is available online [7].

As far as we are concerned, this is one of the pioneer works on proposing gender debiased translation systems with word embedding techniques.

We did our study in the domain of news articles and professions. However, human corpora has a broad spectrum of categories, as an instance: industrial, medical, legal that may rise other biases particular to each area. Also, other language pairs with different degree in specifying gender information in their written or spoken communication could be studied for the evaluation of debiasing in MT. Furthermore, while we studied gender as a bias in MT, other social constructs and stereotypes may be present in corpora, whether individually or combined, such as race, religious beliefs

---

[7]https://github.com/joelescudefont/genbiasmt

Pre-trained embeddings	her amiga	him amigo	Mary amiga	John amigo
None	99.8	99.9	69.5	99.9
GloVe (Enc.)	2.6	100.0	0.0	100.0
GloVe (Dec.)	95.0	100.0	4.0	100.0
GloVe (Enc./Dec.)	**100.0**	100.0	90.0	100.0
GloVe Hard-Debiased (Enc.)	**100.0**	100.0	99.5	100.0
GloVe Hard-Debiased (Dec.)	12.0	100.0	0.0	100.0
GloVe Hard-Debiased (Enc./Dec.)	99.9	100.0	**100.0**	99.9
GN-GloVe (Enc.)	**100.0**	100.0	7.7	100.0
GN-GloVe (Dec.)	97.2	100.0	51.8	100.0
GN-GloVe (Enc./Dec.)	99.6	100.0	56.4	100.0

Table 5: Percentage of "friend" being translated as "amiga" or "amigo" in test sentences with female-male pronouns and proper names for the *Occupations test*. Best results in bold.

or age; this being just a small subset of possible biases which will present new challenges for fairness both in machine learning and MT.

Acknowledgments

This work is supported in part by the Spanish Ministerio de Economía y Competitividad, the European Regional Development Fund and the Agencia Estatal de Investigación, through the post-doctoral senior grant Ramón y Cajal, the contract TEC2015-69266-P (MINECO/FEDER,EU) and the contract PCIN-2017-079 (AEI/MINECO).

References

Dzmitry Bahdanau, Kyunghyun Cho, and Yoshua Bengio. 2014. Neural machine translation by jointly learning to align and translate. *CoRR*, abs/1409.0473.

Tolga Bolukbasi, Kai-Wei Chang, James Y. Zou, Venkatesh Saligrama, and Adam Kalai. 2016. Man is to computer programmer as woman is to homemaker? debiasing word embeddings. *CoRR*, abs/1607.06520.

Jonas Gehring, Michael Auli, David Grangier, Denis Yarats, and Yann N. Dauphin. 2017. Convolutional sequence to sequence learning. *CoRR*, abs/1705.03122.

Philipp Koehn. 2005. Europarl: A Parallel Corpus for Statistical Machine Translation. In *Conference Proceedings: the tenth Machine Translation Summit*, pages 79–86, Phuket, Thailand. AAMT, AAMT.

Nishtha Madaan, Sameep Mehta, Shravika Mittal, and Ashima Suvarna. 2018. Judging a book by its description : Analyzing gender stereotypes in the man bookers prize winning fiction. *CoRR*, abs/1807.10615.

Tomas Mikolov, Kai Chen, Greg Corrado, and Jeffrey Dean. 2013. Efficient estimation of word representations in vector space. *CoRR*, abs/1301.3781.

Kishore Papineni, Salim Roukos, Todd Ward, and Wei jing Zhu. 2002. Bleu: a method for automatic evaluation of machine translation. In *Proceedings of the 40th Annual Meeting of the Association for Computational Linguistics*, pages 311–318.

Jeffrey Pennington, Richard Socher, and Christopher D. Manning. 2014. Glove: Global vectors for word representation. In *Empirical Methods in Natural Language Processing (EMNLP)*, pages 1532–1543.

Marcelo O. R. Prates, Pedro H. C. Avelar, and Luís C. Lamb. 2018. Assessing gender bias in machine translation - A case study with google translate. *CoRR*, abs/1809.02208.

Ye Qi, Devendra Sachan, Matthieu Felix, Sarguna Padmanabhan, and Graham Neubig. 2018. When and why are pre-trained word embeddings useful for neural machine translation? In *Proceedings of the 2018 Conference of the North American Chapter of the Association for Computational Linguistics: Human Language Technologies, Volume 2 (Short Papers)*, pages 529–535, New Orleans, Louisiana. Association for Computational Linguistics.

Ilya Sutskever, Oriol Vinyals, and Quoc V. Le. 2014. Sequence to sequence learning with neural networks. *CoRR*, abs/1409.3215.

Eva Vanmassenhove, Christian Hardmeier, and Andy Way. 2018. Getting gender right in neural machine translation. In *Proceedings of the 2018 Conference on Empirical Methods in Natural Language Processing*, pages 3003–3008, Brussels, Belgium. Association for Computational Linguistics.

Pre-trained word embeddings	Prediction *La conozco desde hace mucho tiempo,*
None	*mi amigo trabaja como mecánico de refrigeración.*
GloVe (Enc)	*mi **amiga** trabaja como mecánico de refrigeración.*
GloVe (Dec)	*mi **amiga** trabaja como mecánico de refrigeración.*
GloVe (Enc+Dec)	*mi **amiga** trabaja como mecánico de refrigeración.*
GloVe Hard-Debiased (Enc)	*mi amigo trabaja como mecánico de refrigeración.*
GloVe Hard-Debiased (Dec)	*mi **amiga** trabaja como mecánico de refrigeración.*
GloVe Hard-Debiased (Enc+Dec)	*mi **amiga** trabaja como mecánico de refrigeración.*
GN-GloVe (Enc)	*mi **amiga** trabaja como mecánico de refrigeración.*
GN-GloVe (Dec)	*mi **amiga** trabaja como mecánico de refrigeración.*
GN-GloVe (Enc+Dec)	*mi **amiga** trabaja como **mecánica de refrigeración**.*
Reference	*mi amiga trabaja como mecánica de refrigeración.*

Pre-trained word embeddings	Prediction *La conozco desde hace mucho tiempo,*
None	*mi **amiga** trabaja como operador de un coche de enlace a las minas.*
GloVe (Enc)	*mi amigo trabaja como operador del transbordador espacial.*
GloVe (Dec)	*mi **amiga** trabaja como un operador de transporte de camiones.*
GloVe (Enc+Dec)	*mi **amiga** trabaja como un operator de coches.*
GloVe Hard-Debiased (Enc)	*mi **amiga** trabaja como mine de minas.*
GloVe Hard-Debiased (Dec)	*mi amigo trabaja como un operador de transporte de coches para las minas.*
GloVe Hard-Debiased (Enc+Dec)	*mi **amiga** trabaja como un operator de coches.*
GN-GloVe (Enc)	*mi **amiga** trabaja como operador de ómnibus de minas.*
GN-GloVe (Dec)	*mi **amiga** trabaja como un operador de transporte para las minas.*
GN-GloVe (Enc+Dec)	*mi **amiga** trabaja como **operadora de transporte de minas**.*
Reference	*mi amiga trabaja como operadora de vagones de minas.*

Table 6: Spanish predictions for the test sentences *"I've known her for a long time, my friend works as a refrigeration mechanic." "I've known her for a long time, my friend works as a mine shuttle car operator."*. Best results in bold.

Ashish Vaswani, Noam Shazeer, Niki Parmar, Jakob Uszkoreit, Llion Jones, Aidan N Gomez, Ł ukasz Kaiser, and Illia Polosukhin. 2017. Attention is all you need. In I. Guyon, U. V. Luxburg, S. Bengio, H. Wallach, R. Fergus, S. Vishwanathan, and R. Garnett, editors, *Advances in Neural Information Processing Systems 30*, pages 5998–6008. Curran Associates, Inc.

Jieyu Zhao, Tianlu Wang, Mark Yatskar, Vicente Ordonez, and Kai-Wei Chang. 2017. Men also like shopping: Reducing gender bias amplification using corpus-level constraints. In *EMNLP*, pages 2979–2989. Association for Computational Linguistics.

Jieyu Zhao, Tianlu Wang, Mark Yatskar, Vicente Ordonez, and Kai-Wei Chang. 2018a. Gender bias in coreference resolution: Evaluation and debiasing methods. In *NAACL-HLT (2)*, pages 15–20. Association for Computational Linguistics.

Jieyu Zhao, Yichao Zhou, Zeyu Li, Wei Wang, and Kai-Wei Chang. 2018b. Learning gender-neutral word embeddings. In *Proceedings of the 2018 Conference on Empirical Methods in Natural Language Processing, Brussels, Belgium, October 31 - November 4, 2018*, pages 4847–4853.

Michał Ziemski, Marcin Junczys-Dowmunt, and Bruno Pouliquen. 2016. The united nations parallel corpus v1.0. In *Proceedings of the Tenth International Conference on Language Resources and Evaluation (LREC 2016)*, Paris, France. European Language Resources Association (ELRA).

Automatic Gender Identification and Reinflection in Arabic

Nizar Habash, Houda Bouamor,[†] Christine Chung
Computational Approaches to Modeling Language Lab
New York University Abu Dhabi, UAE
[†]Carnegie Mellon University in Qatar, Qatar
{nizar.habash,cic266}@nyu.edu, hbouamor@qatar.cmu.edu

Abstract

The impressive progress in many Natural Language Processing (NLP) applications has increased the awareness of some of the biases these NLP systems have with regards to gender identities. In this paper, we propose an approach to extend biased single-output gender-blind NLP systems with gender-specific alternative reinflections. We focus on Arabic, a gender-marking morphologically rich language, in the context of machine translation (MT) from English, and for first-person-singular constructions only. Our contributions are the development of a system-independent gender-awareness wrapper, and the building of a corpus for training and evaluating first-person-singular gender identification and reinflection in Arabic. Our results successfully demonstrate the viability of this approach with 8% relative increase in BLEU score for first-person-singular feminine, and 5.3% comparable increase for first-person-singular masculine on top of a state-of-the-art gender-blind MT system on a held-out test set.

1 Introduction

The impressive progress in the last decade in many Natural Language Processing (NLP) applications, from machine translation (MT) to dialogue system, has increased awareness of some of the biases these systems have with regards to gender identities. A case in point is the *I-am-a-doctor/I-am-a-nurse* MT problem in many morphologically rich languages. While English uses gender-neutral terms that hide the ambiguity of the first-person gender reference, many morphologically rich languages need to use different grammatically gender-specific terms for these two expressions. In Arabic, as in other languages with grammatical gender, gender-blind single-output MT from En-

glish often results in أنا طبيب *ÂnA Tbyb*[1] 'I am a [male] doctor'/أنا ممرضة *ÂnA mmrDħ* 'I am a [female] nurse', which is inappropriate for female doctors and male nurses, respectively.

Part of this problem comes from human-generated data that mirrors the social biases and inequalities of the world we live in, and that results in biased models and representations. Many research efforts responded to this problem by debiasing and balancing the models created from the data through model modification or data augmentation (Font and Costa-jussà, 2019; Zmigrod et al., 2019). However, ultimately, even the most balanced and unbiased of models can be useless in gender-blind systems that are designed to generate a single text output. Such systems are doomed to unsurprisingly pass on the biases of the models they use, as demonstrated in the doctor/nurse example above. In contrast, gender-aware systems should be designed to produce outputs that are as gender-specific as the input information they have access to. The input gender information may be contextual (e.g., the input 'she is a doctor'), or extra linguistics (e.g., the gender feature provided in the user profile in social media). But, there may be contexts where the gender information is unavailable to the system (e.g., 'the student is a nurse'). In such cases, generating both gender-specific forms or a gender-neutral (gender-ambiguous) form is more appropriate.

In this paper, we propose an approach that extends the possibly biased output of gender-blind NLP systems with gender-specific reinflections. This is a monolingual postprocessing rephrasing task that wraps around a gender-blind system to make it gender-aware, through identifying if there are gender-specific phrases in its output and of-

---

[1]Arabic transliteration is in the HSB scheme (Habash et al., 2007).

155

Proceedings of the 1st Workshop on Gender Bias in Natural Language Processing, pages 155–165
Florence, Italy, August 2, 2019. ©2019 Association for Computational Linguistics

fering alternative reinflections instead. The selection of the gender-specific form is then left to the user or another automatic component has access to extra-linguistic information, such as profile gender. For example, the Arabic gender-blind MT output translating English 'I am a nurse' as أنا ممرضة *ÂnA mmrDħ* 'I am a [female] nurse' is turned into two gender-marked output options: (a) أنا ممرضة *ÂnA mmrDħ* '[First Person Singular Feminine]', and (b) أنا ممرض *ÂnA mmrD* '[First Person Singular Masculine]'. Since the output of the gender-blind NLP system is not necessarily always masculine or feminine, our approach requires two components: **gender identification** and **gender reinflection**, which can be modeled jointly or in cascade. The approach is system-independent and can be used with MT, dialogue systems, etc., as well as, to balance corpora through augmentation by adding reinflected copies of gender-specific constructions.

We focus on Arabic, a gender-marking morphologically rich language, in the context of MT from English, and for first-person-singular constructions only. We only work on first-person constructions because they tend to be gender-neutral in English. Furthermore, as sentences may involve multiple gendered references, we wanted to control for the number of combinations. We plan to extend to multiple references in future work.

Our contributions are the development of a system-independent gender-awareness wrapper, and the building of a corpus for training and evaluating first-person-singular gender identification and reinflection in Arabic. For gender identification, we compare rule-based and machine learning methods using our annotated corpus. For gender reinflection, we use a character-level neural MT (NMT) model in a single step (identify and reinflect, jointly), and as the second part of a two-step (identify then reinflect) system. Our results successfully demonstrate the viability of this approach with 8% relative increase in BLEU score for first-person-singular feminine, and 5.3% comparable increase for first-person-singular masculine on top of a state-of-the-art gender-blind MT system on a held-out test set.

Next, we discuss some related work (Section 2) and Arabic linguistic facts (Section 3). We present our Arabic parallel gender corpus in Section 4, gender identification in Section 5, and gender reinflection and MT results in Section 6.

2 Related Work

Gender bias has been detected, studied, and partially addressed for standard and contextualized word embeddings in a number of studies (Bolukbasi et al., 2016; Caliskan et al., 2017; Sutton et al., 2018; Basta et al., 2019; Garg et al., 2018; Zhao et al., 2018, 2019). These studies showed that training word embeddings on large human produced corpora such as news text leads to encoding societal biases including gender and race. Some of these studies focused on quantifying the bias, and proposed approaches for mitigating it within word embeddings.

In the context of data augmentation solutions, Lu et al. (2018) introduced *counterfactual data augmentation* (CDA), a generic methodology to mitigate bias in neural NLP tasks, where for each training instance, a copy with an intervention on its targeted words is added, replacing each with its partner, while maintaining the same ground truth. The goal here is to encourage learning algorithms to not pick up on biased distinctions. Building on CDA, (Zmigrod et al., 2019) presented a generative model that allows conversion between masculine inflected and feminine inflected sentences in four morphologically rich languages (Hebrew, Spanish, French and Italian) with a focus on animate nouns.

Specifically for MT, Rabinovich et al. (2016) presented work on the preservation of author gender. Some researchers suggested improvement through co-reference resolution (Gonzales and Tuggener, 2017; Luong and Popescu-Belis, 2016). Vanmassenhove et al. (2018) conducted a series of experiments to improve morphological agreement and improve translation quality in NMT systems for 20 language pairs (*none of which were Arabic*). They compiled large datasets from Europarl (Koehn, 2005), including speaker gender and age, and trained NMT systems with the tagged language pair. They showed that providing tags that indicate the speaker's gender to the system leads to significant improvements. Similarly, Elaraby et al. (2018) marked speaker and listener gender as meta-data input on the source sentence in an English-to-Arabic NMT system. The training data came from OpenSubtitle (Lison and Tiedemann, 2016). The authors used rules to identify the gender in the Arabic text. Prates et al. (2018) used Google Translate to translate a set consisting of a list of jobs and gender-specific sentences from a variety of gender-neutral languages into English. They showed that occupations related to science, engineering and mathematics present a strong stereotype towards the male gender. More recently, Font and Costa-jussà (2019) studied the impact of gender debiasing on NMT between English and Spanish using debiased and gender-neutral word embeddings.

Google Translate publicly announced an effort to address gender bias for a few languages in different degrees and contexts (Help, 2019). As of the time of writing this paper, the system shows both feminine and masculine translations for some single words in certain languages; and provides gender-specific pronominal translations for some gender ambiguous cases (i.e., Turkish-English MT). In our work, we also evaluate on the output of Google Translate.

This paper sits in the intersection of efforts like data augmentation for morphologically rich languages (Zmigrod et al., 2019) and gender-aware MT (Vanmassenhove et al., 2018; Elaraby et al., 2018). Similarly to Zmigrod et al. (2019), we are interested in reinflection, but we implement it as character-based NMT. While Vanmassenhove et al. (2018) and Elaraby et al. (2018) expect gender meta-information as input, we propose a gender-aware post-processing approach, that applies gender identification and reinflection.

3   Arabic Linguistic Facts

We present three specific challenges for Modern Standard Arabic (MSA) NLP with attention to gender expression and MT.

Morphological Richness   Arabic is a morphologically rich language that inflects for gender, number, person, case, state, aspect, mood and voice, in addition to allowing a number of attachable clitics (prepositions, particles, pronouns) (Habash, 2010). Wright (1955) classifies nouns according to their gender into three classes: masculine (**M**), feminine (**F**), and those that can be either masculine or feminine (**B**). Examples include طبيب *Tabiyb* 'male doctor' [M], طبيبة *Tabiybaħ* 'female doctor' [F], and words like طريق *Tariyq* 'road' [B]. Arabic adjectives have gender-specific forms (M or F). But some pronouns and some verb conjugations can be used for either masculine or feminine (B). For example, the pronoun أنا *ÂanA* 'I', and the first-person-singular perfect and imperfect verbal conjugations (e.g., كتبت *katabtu* 'I

wrote' and أكتب *Âaktub* 'I write') are all gender-ambiguous (B).

The Arabic agreement system between verbs and their subjects, and between nouns and their adjectives does not just involve gender, number, case and state, but also a lexical feature called *rationality* – a quality typically associated with human actors (Alkuhlani and Habash, 2011). For instance, while adjectives modifying rational nouns agree with them in gender and number; adjectives modifying irrational plural nouns are always feminine and singular.

Orthographic Ambiguity   Arabic is also orthographically ambiguous due to the optionality of diacritic specification in the written form. This optionality can lead to gender ambiguous orthographic forms as some gender-specific forms only differ in diacritics (short vowel specification).[2] For example, the word كتبت can be diacritized as *katabta* 'you [masc.sing] wrote' or *katabti* 'you [fem.sing] wrote', and it is ambiguous with yet two other forms: *katabtu* 'I [fem/masc] wrote' and *katabat* 'she wrote'. In this regard, orthographic ambiguity reduces gender bias. But it is still an issue for speech synthesis systems (Halabi, 2016).

In general, for first person expressions, we expect the verbal sentences to be gender-ambiguous (B), and the copular/equational sentences involving adjectives and rational nouns to be gender-specific ([M] or [F]). We will present an analysis of our data in the next section that confirms this.

Orthographic Noise   MSA *unedited* text tends to have a large percentage ($\sim$23%) of spelling errors (Zaghouani et al., 2014). Most common errors involve Alif-Hamza (Glottal Stop) spelling (ا، آ، إ، أ   *A, Ā, Ǎ, Â*), Ya spelling (ي، ى   *y, ŷ*), and the feminine suffix Ta-Marbuta spelling (ه، ة   *h, ħ*). These errors are so common, that in Arabic NLP, Alif/Ya normalization is standard preprocessing (Habash, 2010), and Alif/Ya specification is done as postprocessing (El Kholy and Habash, 2010). Since the Arabic text we use from the OpenSubtitles Corpus (Lison and Tiedemann, 2016), a collection of translated movie subtitles, has many spelling errors of the above mentioned kinds, we evaluate MT within an orthographically normalized space (more details in Section 6).

---

[2]We will use the label B to refer to inherent gender ambiguity, as well as gender ambiguity resulting from undiacritzed spelling.

157

| | Original Corpus | | | | Balanced Corpus | | | | | |
Sentences	Words	Words^{MF}	(a) Input	(b) Reinflected	(c) Input	(d) Target^{M}	(e) Target^{F}	Sentences	Words	Words^{MF}
10,242	74,702	0	B		B	B	B	10,242	74,702	0
362	2,720	422	F	M^r	F	M^r	F	362	2,720	422
636	4,710	743	M	F^r	M	M	F^r	636	4,710	743
					M^r	M^r	F	362	2720	422
					F^r	M	F^r	636	4,710	743
11,240	82,132	1,165						12,238	89,562	2,330

Table 1: Statistics of the original corpus we annotated and the balanced version we report on in the paper experiments. Words^{MF} refers to the count of gender-marking words, specifically. M^r and F^r are the reinflected versions of the F and M labelled sentences, respectively, in the same rows they appear in.

English	Original Arabic	Gender	Reinflection
I have no interest in that.	ليس لدي مصلحة في هذا	B	
He shot at me!	لقد أطلق النار علي!	B	
I'm leaving.	أنا راحلة	F	أنا راحل
I'm rich! I'm rich!	أنا غنية أنا غنية	F	أنا غني أنا غني
I am a Muslim and a Hindu and a Christian and a Jew.	أنا مسلم و هندوسي و نصراني و يهودي	M	أنا مسلمة و هندوسية و نصرانية و يهودية
I'm the new attending.	أنا الأخصائي الجديد .	M	أنا الأخصائية الجديدة .

Table 2: Examples from the Arabic Parallel Gender Corpus including original sentence, its gender and its reinflection to the opposite gender where appropriate.

4 The Arabic Parallel Gender Corpus

For the kind of experiments we conduct in this paper, we need a corpus of first-person-singular Arabic sentences that are gender-annotated and gender-translated. That is, for every sentence in such corpus, we would like the gender of the sentence's speaker to be identified as *B* (gender-ambiguous), *F* (feminine) or *M* (masculine); and for the F and M cases, we would like the equivalent opposite gender form. Such a corpus needs to also be paired with English translations to support possible MT experiments. To the best of our knowledge, no such corpus exists for Arabic, nor for any other language. We plan to make this resource publicly available.[3] We describe next the approach we followed to build this corpus.

Corpus Selection We decided to use a subset of the sentences from the OpenSubtitles 2018 corpus (Lison and Tiedemann, 2016). We selected this corpus because it has parallel English and Arabic sentences, and because it contains a lot of first-person-singular sentences. We first extracted all the English-Arabic sentence pairs that include first-person-singular pronouns in the English side: *I, me, my, myself, mine*. We used English because it is not a pro-drop language like Arabic. There

[3] http://resources.camel-lab.com

were 8.5 million sentences of this kind, 5.7 million of which do not include a second person pronoun (*you, your, yourself, yours*). In this work, we decided to focus on the first-person-singular exclusively and excluded all second person cases. Out of this rich set, we selected 12,000 sentences to be annotated. All the Arabic sentences were white-space-and-punctuation tokenized, as well as morphologically analyzed and lemmatized using the MADAMIRA toolkit for Arabic NLP (Pasha et al., 2014).

Corpus Annotation Four Arabic native speakers (three female and one male) annotated the corpus. The instructions were simple. First, they are to identify the grammatical gender of the singular speaker in each sentence and then label it as F (feminine), M (masculine), or B (ambiguous). Second, for the F and M cases, the annotators are to copy the sentence and minimally modify it so that it expresses the opposite gender and remains fully grammatical; they are only allowed to use word substitutions, i.e., no additions or deletions so that the total number of words is maintained. For most words, the gender reinflection maintained the same lemma, e.g., الطبيب *AlTbyb* 'the doctor' [M] is reinflected as الطبيبة *AlTbybħ* 'the doctor' [F]. However, gender-specific nouns that cannot reinflect in the same lemma are mapped appropriately to a related lemma expressing the opposite gender. For example, the word أم *Âm* 'mother' is mapped to أب *Âb* 'father'.[4] Proper names are all treated as gender-neutral (B), even when they have strong gender-specific associations, and as such are not reinflected. The annotators were made aware of hetreo-centrist interpretations and were instructed to suspend any preconceived assumptions, e.g., the sentence تلك زوجتي 'That's my wife' is given the label B, not M. Finally, the annotators were also instructed to flag bad translations or malformed sentences. Examples from our corpus are illustrated in Table 2. The average pairwise inter-annotator agreement on a 60-sentence set that was annotated by all annotators is quite high (97.2%), suggesting the task is reasonable. The points of disagreement were plausible different interpretations. For example, the word متأخرا *mtÂxrA* 'late' in the sentence أستيقظ متأخرا *ÂstyqĎ mtÂxrA* 'I wake up late' was interpreted as an adverb (which would not gender-inflect) or as an adjective (which would).

The Original Corpus After the annotation was completed, we excluded all sentences with malformed input, sentences with Latin characters, and sentences with Arabic-Arabic gender misalignment due to annotation errors. This resulted in a set of 11,240 sentences (82,132 words), which constitute our Original Corpus Input (Table 1, column (a)). In this corpus, about 91% of all the sentences are gender-ambiguous (B). Interestingly, the M sentences are almost twice as many as the F sentences. All of the gender-specific sentences were reinflected (M → F^r and F → M^r), resulting in an additional 989 sentences (7,430 words) (Table 1, column (b)). Among the words of the first-person-singular gender-specific sentences, 1,165 are gender-specific (15.7%). The percentage of these words in the whole corpus is 1.4%.

The Balanced Corpus Given the stark gender imbalance as well as the small ratio of gender-specific sentences, we opted to balance the corpus by introducing the reinflected sentences (M^r and F^r) as if they were original input and pair them with their original input as their reinflection. In Table 1 the added sentence statistics appear in the

two additional rows under Balanced Corpus. In Table 1 columns (c), (d) and (e), we define three versions of the balanced corpus, which we will refer to and use in the rest of the paper. The first is the balanced Arabic input corpus (henceforth, *Balanced Input*), which matches the original input plus the added reinflected sentences. The second is a masculine target corpus (Target^M) containing only B, M and M^r sentences. And the last is a feminine target corpus (Target^F) containing only B, F, and F^r sentences. All three corpora naturally have the same number of sentences, words, and gender-specific words. Given the addition of the reinflected sentences, the percentage of all gender-specific sentences in the balanced corpus is 16.3% and the number of masculine and feminine sentences is the same. The balanced corpora were all divided randomly and in parallel into training (TRAIN: 70% or 8,566 sentences), development (DEV: 10% or 1,224 sentences) and blind test (TEST: 20% or 2,448 sentences). The balanced corpus DEV and TEST English side sentences were also machine translated through Google Translate's API to create the DEV^{GT} and TEST^{GT} sets[5] (See Section 6).

The Synthetic Corpus Given the very small number of gender-specific words in the corpus, we created a synthetic corpus consisting of short gender-inflected sentences using an Arabic morphological analyzer and generator (Taji et al., 2018). We covered 6,447 adjectives and 2,172 rational nouns (8,619 total) producing 25 different expressions for each in parallel, in masculine and feminine form. The 25 expressions consisted of simple nominal sentences, including constructions with كان وأخواتها 'Kan and her sisters', and إن وأخواتها 'Inna and her sisters'. For example, for the masculine adjective سعيد *sςyd* 'happy' we include the sentences أنا سعيد *ÂnA sςyd* 'I am happy', كنت سعيدا *knt sςydA* 'I was happy', لست سعيدا *lst sςydA* 'I was not happy', etc., and their feminine versions, respectively, أنا سعيدة *ÂnA sςydħ* 'I am happy', كنت سعيدة *knt sςydħ* 'I was happy', لست سعيدة *lst sςydħ* 'I was not happy', etc. The choice of expressions was influenced by a sample manual analysis, which we discuss in Section 5.1. In total, the synthetic corpus has 226,175 sentence pairs covering 5 million words on each side. We use this corpus for training purposes only.

---

[4]We are aware that sentences with gender-specific English words, e.g., *widow and widower*, will be mismatched with the reinflected Arabic. We do not consider this to be a problem from the point of view of the spirit of the task as a whole.

[5]Google Translate's API – April 22-23, 2019.

Arabic	انا مسرورة لأني بالمدينة اليوم							
English	I'm just glad I was in town tonight							
Tokens	*AnA*	*msrwrħ*	*lÂny*			*bAlmdynħ*		*Alywm*
Gloss	I	happy	for	that	I	in	the city	today
Features	pron+1s	adj+fs	li_prep	conj_sub+	1s_pron	bi_prep	noun+fsi	noun+msi
	first person singular pronoun	*feminine singular adjective*	*preposition clitic*	*subordinating conjunction*	*first person singular pronoun*	*preposition clitic*	*feminine singular irrational noun*	*masculine singular irrational noun*

Table 3: Example of the morphological features used in automatic gender identification. In the third row, the Arabic words are presented in transliteration from left to right. The features are paired with the words they are generated from. The Gloss is the literal translation of the word. The English translation is from the OpenSubtitles corpus.

5 Automatic First-Person-Singular Gender Identification

We define the task of automatic first-person-singular gender identification as taking a sentence from our Balanced Input corpus (DEV and TEST) and predicting a label from the set {B, F, M} that indicates the gender-specificity of the first person speaker. We present four models for accomplishing this task. The first is a rule-based baseline, and the other three are machine-learning models trained on the TRAIN set of the Balanced Input corpus. Two of the machine learning models and the rule-based one make extensive use of automatically determined morphological features. All system development and parameter tuning was done using the DEV set. We report only the TEST results here. The DEV and TEST results were very similar. We discuss the morphological features next, followed by the four models, then we present our results and discussion.

5.1 The Morphological Features

We started this effort with an analysis of 100 samples from the training data: 50 from B cases, and 50 from M/F cases. For each case, we manually identified how the first person singular aspect of the task, and how the gender aspect of the task are realized linguistically. We identified three categories for the first person singular: as pro-dropped subject of a verb, as the pronoun أنا *ÂnA* 'I', and as the pronominal clitics ـني+ *+ny* and ـي+ *+y* 'me, my'. As for gender-specific forms, they were associated with adjectives and rational nouns. It was interesting to see that not a single case of the B sentences had an adjective or rational noun referring to the first person. Among the gender-specific

cases, 96% of them (all but 2 cases out of 50) appeared as simple copular sentences with some variations involving كان وأخواتها 'the so-called Kan and her sisters', or إن وأخواتها 'the pseudo verbs so-called Inna and her sisters'.

For all the collected and created corpora (manually translated, synthetic and machine translated), we generated a parallel morphologically analyzed feature corpus using the MADAMIRA Arabic analysis toolkit (Pasha et al., 2014). Since MADAMIRA uses the SAMA analyzer (Graff et al., 2009) which does not provide functional features for gender and number, and rationality, we extended MADAMIRA's analyses using the work of Taji et al. (2018). We further extracted a set of specific morphological features that we determined to be relevant from the analysis we did. An example of the features associated with a sentence from our corpus is shown in Table 3.

5.2 The Rule-based Model

Given the insights developed from our initial analysis, we created a simple regular expression that operates on the morphological features discussed above. This was intended as a baseline system. The regular expression captured any context in which a first-person-singular indicator (e.g., the pronoun أنا *ÂnA* 'I', a copular verb or pseudo verb with first person subject, or a subordinating conjunction with a first person pronominal clitic) *followed by* a singular rational noun or singular adjective. The gender of the noun or the adjective determines the label for the sentence (M or F). If there is no match, the sentence receives the label B. The rule-based model does not include any lexical features and does not require any training data.

	Rule-based			Lexicalized			Delexicalized			Joint		
	P	**R**	**F1**	**P**	**R**	**F1**	**P**	**R**	**F1**	**P**	**R**	**F1**
B	92%	99%	95%	93%	98%	96%	93%	98%	95%	94%	98%	96%
F	96%	56%	71%	84%	65%	73%	91%	65%	75%	90%	72%	80%
M	81%	53%	64%	81%	57%	67%	80%	54%	64%	84%	62%	71%
Average	**89%**	69%	77%	86%	73%	79%	88%	72%	78%	**89%**	**78%**	**83%**

Table 4: First person singular gender identification results on TEST. P, R, and F1 refer to Precision, Recall and F1-score, respectively. Average is the *Macro Average* of values in its column.

5.3 The Machine Learning Models

As part of the development of the machine-learning models, we experimented with a very large number of learning algorithms, vectorization features, and hyper parameters. This included the use of sentence2vec embeddings trained on large collections of text, and neural models, which were not competitive due to the limited training data size. We only report below on the settings and models that were determined to be optimal during development.

We trained three models, all using logistic regression with a liblinear solver, and using features derived from the input sentences or their morphological features. For the input sentence, we normalized the Alif/Ya forms. We used *character* n-gram features from length 1 to length 7, *word* n-gram features (from length 1 to length 7), and morphological n-gram features (from length 1 to length 7). We imposed a limit of 20,000 features on each of the character, word, and morphological n-grams. All these models were implemented using the scikit-learn toolkit (Pedregosa et al., 2011).

The three machine learning models are as follows. The **Lexicalized Model** only used the input sentence character and word n-gram features as presented above. The **Delexicalized Model** only used the morphological n-gram features as presented above. And the **Joint Model** used both sets of features concatenated for each sentence.

5.4 Results and Discussion

Table 4 presents the results of the four models described above, on the blind TEST set. For each model, we report the precision (P), recall (R) and F1-score (F1) for the three labels (B, F, and M), and their macro averages. While F and M are balanced, B is about 84% of all cases.

With regards to the overall performance, the Joint model outperforms all models in terms of macro-average F1. Across all models, the precision, recall and F1 scores for B are the highest, which makes sense given the higher proportion of training data. We tried several techniques for balancing the corpus, but none improved the overall scores. Interestingly, the scores for F are always higher than M. This may be attributed to the fact that feminine is the *marked* feature in Arabic, where specific endings are easy to detect, e.g., the feminine singular suffix is ة +ħ.

The Rule-based model is the least performing, although it is very competitive given that it was 'human learned' from 100 examples only (50 B, and 50 M/F). If we use a comparable training set (50 B with 50 M and F pairs), the Lexicalized, Delixicalized and Joint macro average F1 scores decrease to 56%,54%, and 60%, respectively, all below the Rule-based model. The Rule-based model also has very high precision, comparable to that of the Joint model; but it trades off with the lowest recall. This is expected and typical of rule-based models.

The Delexicalized and Lexicalized models have comparable scores and generally lower precision and higher recall than the Rule-based model. The Joint model seems to successfully increase both recall and precision (with a slight reduction of precision for F in the Delexicalized model). This suggests that the Joint model brings together complementary strengths from the Lexicalized and Delexicalized models.

6 Automatic First Person Singular Gender Reinflection

We define the task of first-person-singular gender reinflection as taking a sentence with an unspecified first-person-singular gender as input and generating two gender-appropriate versions, one masculine (B or M) and one feminine (B or F). We model the task in two ways: (a) as a single reinflection system, and (b) as a two-step identify-then-reinflect system.

6.1 Gender Reinflection as Character-based NMT

We recast the gender reinflection task as a MT task that maps the text from one source gender to a target gender. We use character-based NMT, which views the input and output sentences as sequences of characters rather than words and learn to encode and decode at the character-level. The main reason for this setup is that character-level representations are reported to be good in capturing and learning morphological aspects (Ling et al., 2015; Kim et al., 2016), which is important for a morphologically rich language like Arabic. Furthermore, character-level NMT modeling requires less vocabulary and helps reduce out-of-vocabulary by translating unseen words.

Our character-based NMT system is an encoder-decoder model that uses the general global attention architecture introduced by Luong and Manning (2015). All the NMT models we use have been trained with the OpenNMT toolkit (Klein et al., 2017) with no restriction on the input vocabulary size. Specifically, we use long short-term memory units (LSTM), with hidden units of size 500 and 2 layers in both the encoder and decoder. The model is trained for 13 epochs, using Adam with a learning rate of 0.002 and mini-batches of 40 with no pre-trained embeddings. Our char-level embeddings are learned within the training of the model.

Using different combinations of the data sets presented in Section 4, we build four reinflection models.

- **in-to-M** is a model trained to map from the Balanced Input corpus (and Synthetic F) to the Target^M corpus (and Synthetic M).

- **in-to-F** is a model trained to map from the Balanced Input corpus (and Synthetic M) to the Target^F corpus (and Synthetic F).

- **M-to-F** is a model trained to map from the Target^M corpus (and Synthetic M) to the Target^F corpus (and Synthetic F).

- **F-to-M** is a model trained to map from the Target^F corpus (and Synthetic F) to the Target^M corpus (and Synthetic M).

Single Direct Reinflection System The first two models (in-to-M and in-to-F) are used for the single system reinflection approach, where no input gender identification is needed. The in-to-M

model is used to generate the M target; and the in-to-F model is used to generate the F target.

Two-step Identify-then-Reinflect System The last two models (M-to-F and F-to-M) are used in the two-step reinflection approach. We use the output of the best sentence-level Arabic gender identification model (Joint model) described in Section 5 to identify the gender of the sentence. Then, we proceed as follows. For the M target, if the identified input sentence gender is B or M, we pass the input through as is; otherwise, we reinflect the F sentence to M using the F-to-M model. And vice versa for the F target: if the identified input sentence gender is B or F, we pass the input through as is; otherwise, we reinflect the M sentence to F using the M-to-F model.

6.2 Experimental Results and Analysis

The character-based NMT reinflection models are trained using the 8,566 TRAIN sentence pairs and the 226,175 synthetic corpus sentence pairs (as discussed above). The DEV and TEST sets comprise 1,224 and 2,448 sentences, respectively. We compare two input settings: (a) the Balanced Input DEV and TEST, and (b) the English-to-Arabic Google Translate output of the English sentences corresponding the Balanced Input DEV and TEST, DEV^{GT} and TEST^{GT} (Section 4). We evaluate sentence gender reinflection against the DEV and TEST portions of the Target^F and Target^M corpora as references (also, Section 4). In addition to the single and two-step system, we include a "do-nothing" baseline that simply passes the input to the output as is.

Reinflection Evaluation Reinflection results for each setup are reported in Table 5 in terms of the MT metric BLEU (Papineni et al., 2002). It is important to note that all the reported scores are on AYT-normalized texts.[6] This normalization helps reduce the number of cases in which Alif, Ya, and Ta Marbuta are inconsistently represented in the references. The table specifies columns for Target M, and Target F, which indicate which reference is used for evaluation.

For the Balanced Input, the best performance was achieved using the two-step system. The BLEU scores are very high because most of the

---

[6]AYT refers to the orthographic normalization of Alif-Hamza forms, Ya/Alif-Maqsura forms, and Ta-Marbuta/Ha forms (Habash, 2010)

	Balanced Input				**Google Translate Output**			
	DEV		TEST		DEV^{GT}		TEST^{GT}	
Target	M	F	M	F	M	F	M	F
Baseline	97.12	97.12	97.05	97.05	12.23	11.52	11.91	11.18
Single	95.43	95.64	96.12	95.93	**12.92**	**12.70**	**12.54**	**12.08**
Two Step	**98.00**	**97.92**	**98.22**	**98.31**	12.27	11.83	11.96	11.42

Table 5: BLEU results (all AYT normalized) for the Baseline, Single and Select systems on the DEV and TEST sets of the Balanced Corpus Input (Input^{ar}) and English-Arabic Google Translate output (Input^{GT}) for both F and M targets.

words are not changed between input and reference. The single system in fact introduced errors that made it worse than the do-nothing baseline. While in the baseline, 91.75% of DEV sentences are fully accurate; the two-step system sentence accuracy is 95.42% (M) and 94.68% (F), a ∼40% error reduction on average.

For the Google Translate results, the single system outperforms the two-step system and the baseline. On the TEST^{GT} set, the single system has an 8% relative increase in BLEU score for Target F, and 5.3% relative increase for Target M. The BLEU scores are much lower than the Balanced Input case since the actual input to the Google MT was English and many gender and non-gender related translation errors occur. Also, we only have a single MT reference to compare against. We suspect that the reason the two-step system did not do as well is that the gender identification component was not trained with the kind of input (and noise) generated by MT systems. One possible solution in the future is to train the gender identification component with MT/NLP output specifically.

Finally, an interesting side observation from this experiment is that automatic gender identification for the Google Translate Arabic output showed a 10-to-1 bias of M versus F, compared to the 50-50 distribution in the Balanced Corpus and the 2-to-1 bias in the Original Corpus. This further confirms the bias towards masculine forms in single-output MT systems.

Error Examples in MT output We conducted a limited analysis to understand the behavior of the NMT reinflection systems. While there were many cases that were handled properly, and cases of under-correction where the input is passed to the output as is; there were also cases of over-correction where words that should maintain their form are treated as gender-specific and modified.

One example is the input word للدغدغه *lldγdγh* 'for tickling', which is erroneously turned into the nonsense word للدغد *lldγd*. There were also a few cases of very long repetitions in the output; as well as reduced output – simply leading to sentence length mismatch. All of these phenomena are unsurprising side effects of using character-based NMT models. In our experiments, they happened infrequently, but we plan to address them in future work.

7 Conclusions and Future Work

We presented an approach to gender identification and reinflection that can be used together with any NLP application that generates text interfacing with users. We also presented the first parallel gender corpus for Arabic. We plan on making this data set publicly available for research purposes. We demonstrated the use of the corpus in benchmarking the quality of different systems for automatic gender identification and reinflection in the context of producing gender-specific machine translation. Our results are very promising, but there is still a lot to improve.

In the future, we plan to extend our work beyond first-person sentences, annotate additional data sets, and explore other techniques for gender identification and reinflection. Among the techniques to plan to explore is word-level gender identification as a sequence labeling task. For gender reinflection, we plan to consider the approaches introduced by Cotterell et al. (2017) and Zmigrod et al. (2019). We are also planning to explore opportunities of hybrid approaches that exploit existing Arabic analysis and generation systems together with more advanced machine learning models. Finally, we are interested in expanding this work to include Arabic dialects.

Acknowledgments

We thank the New York University Abu Dhabi students who helped with the annotation and translation of the Arabic parallel gender corpus: Fatima Alaydaroos, Aya Bouhelal, Fatema AlNuaimi, Muhannad AlRamlawi, and Ella Noll. We also thank Ryan Cotterell, for helpful discussions. Finally, we thank the reviewers for their extremely helpful remarks and feedback.

References

Sarah Alkuhlani and Nizar Habash. 2011. A corpus for modeling morpho-syntactic agreement in Arabic: Gender, number and rationality. In *Proceedings of the 49th Annual Meeting of the Association for Computational Linguistics (ACL'11)*, Portland, Oregon, USA.

Christine Basta, Marta Ruiz Costa-jussà, and Noe Casas. 2019. Evaluating the underlying gender bias in contextualized word embeddings. *CoRR*, abs/1904.08783.

Tolga Bolukbasi, Kai-Wei Chang, James Y Zou, Venkatesh Saligrama, and Adam T Kalai. 2016. Man is to computer programmer as woman is to homemaker? debiasing word embeddings. In *Advances in Neural Information Processing Systems*, pages 4349–4357.

Aylin Caliskan, Joanna J. Bryson, and Arvind Narayanan. 2017. Semantics derived automatically from language corpora contain human-like biases. *Science*, 356.6334.

Ryan Cotterell, Christo Kirov, John Sylak-Glassman, Géraldine Walther, Ekaterina Vylomova, Patrick Xia, Manaal Faruqui, Sandra Kübler, David Yarowsky, Jason Eisner, and Mans Hulden. 2017. CoNLL-SIGMORPHON 2017 shared task: Universal morphological reinflection in 52 languages. *CoRR*, abs/1706.09031.

Ahmed El Kholy and Nizar Habash. 2010. Orthographic and morphological processing for English-Arabic statistical machine translation. In *Proceedings of Traitement Automatique des Langues Naturelles (TALN)*, Montréal, Canada. Montréal, Canada.

Mostafa Elaraby, Ahmed Y Tawfik, Mahmoud Khaled, Hany Hassan, and Aly Osama. 2018. Gender aware spoken language translation applied to English-Arabic. In *Natural Language and Speech Processing (ICNLSP), 2018 2nd International Conference on*, pages 1–6. IEEE.

Joel Escudé Font and Marta R Costa-jussà. 2019. Equalizing gender biases in neural machine translation with word embeddings techniques. *arXiv preprint arXiv:1901.03116*.

Nikhil Garg, Londa Schiebinger, Dan Jurafsky, and James Zou. 2018. Word embeddings quantify 100 years of gender and ethnic stereotypes. *Proceedings of the National Academy of Sciences*, 115(16):E3635–E3644.

Annette Rios Gonzales and Don Tuggener. 2017. Co-reference resolution of elided subjects and possessive pronouns in Spanish-English statistical machine translation. In *Proceedings of the 15th Conference of the European Chapter of the Association for Computational Linguistics: Volume 2, Short Papers*, volume 2, pages 657–662.

David Graff, Mohamed Maamouri, Basma Bouziri, Sondos Krouna, Seth Kulick, and Tim Buckwalter. 2009. Standard Arabic Morphological Analyzer (SAMA) Version 3.1. Linguistic Data Consortium LDC2009E73.

Nizar Habash, Abdelhadi Soudi, and Tim Buckwalter. 2007. On Arabic Transliteration. In A. van den Bosch and A. Soudi, editors, *Arabic Computational Morphology: Knowledge-based and Empirical Methods*, pages 15–22. Springer, Netherlands.

Nizar Y Habash. 2010. *Introduction to Arabic natural language processing*, volume 3. Morgan & Claypool Publishers.

Nawar Halabi. 2016. *Modern standard Arabic phonetics for speech synthesis*. Ph.D. thesis, University of Southampton.

Google Translate Help. 2019. Get gender specific translations. https://support.google.com/translate/answer/9179237.

Yoon Kim, Yacine Jernite, David Sontag, and Alexander M Rush. 2016. Character-aware neural language models. In *Thirtieth AAAI Conference on Artificial Intelligence*.

Guillaume Klein, Yoon Kim, Yuntian Deng, Jean Senellart, and Alexander M Rush. 2017. Opennmt: Open-source toolkit for neural machine translation. *arXiv preprint arXiv:1701.02810*.

P. Koehn. 2005. Europarl: A parallel corpus for statistical machine translation. In *MT summit*, volume 5. Citeseer.

Wang Ling, Isabel Trancoso, Chris Dyer, and Alan W. Black. 2015. Character-based neural machine translation. *CoRR*, abs/1511.04586.

Pierre Lison and Jörg Tiedemann. 2016. OpenSubtitles2016: Extracting Large Parallel Corpora from Movie and TV Subtitles. In *Proceedings of the Language Resources and Evaluation Conference (LREC)*, Portorož, Slovenia.

Kaiji Lu, Piotr Mardziel, Fangjing Wu, Preetam Amancharla, and Anupam Datta. 2018. Gender bias in neural natural language processing. *CoRR*, abs/1807.11714.

Minh-Thang Luong and Christopher D Manning. 2015. Stanford neural machine translation systems for spoken language domains. In *Proceedings of the International Workshop on Spoken Language Translation*.

Ngoc Quang Luong and Andrei Popescu-Belis. 2016. Improving pronoun translation by modeling coreference uncertainty. In *Proceedings of the First Conference on Machine Translation: Volume 1, Research Papers*, volume 1, pages 12–20.

Kishore Papineni, Salim Roukos, Todd Ward, and Wei-Jing Zhu. 2002. Bleu: a method for automatic evaluation of machine translation. In *Proceedings of ACL*, Philadelphia, USA.

Arfath Pasha, Mohamed Al-Badrashiny, Mona Diab, Ahmed El Kholy, Ramy Eskander, Nizar Habash, Manoj Pooleery, Owen Rambow, and Ryan Roth. 2014. Madamira: A fast, comprehensive tool for morphological analysis and disambiguation of Arabic. In *Proceedings of the Language Resources and Evaluation Conference (LREC)*, pages 1094–1101, Reykjavik, Iceland.

F. Pedregosa, G. Varoquaux, A. Gramfort, V. Michel, B. Thirion, O. Grisel, M. Blondel, P. Prettenhofer, R. Weiss, V. Dubourg, J. Vanderplas, A. Passos, D. Cournapeau, M. Brucher, M. Perrot, and E. Duchesnay. 2011. Scikit-learn: Machine Learning in Python . *Journal of Machine Learning Research*, 12:2825–2830.

Marcelo O. R. Prates, Pedro H. C. Avelar, and Luís C. Lamb. 2018. Assessing gender bias in machine translation - A case study with google translate. *CoRR*, abs/1809.02208.

Ella Rabinovich, Shachar Mirkin, Raj Nath Patel, Lucia Specia, and Shuly Wintner. 2016. Personalized machine translation: Preserving original author traits. *arXiv preprint arXiv:1610.05461*.

Adam Sutton, Thomas Lansdall-Welfare, and Nello Cristianini. 2018. Biased embeddings from wild data: Measuring, understanding and removing. *CoRR*, abs/1806.06301.

Dima Taji, Jamila El Gizuli, and Nizar Habash. 2018. An Arabic dependency treebank in the travel domain. In *Proceedings of the Workshop on Open-Source Arabic Corpora and Processing Tools (OS-ACT)*, Miyazaki, Japan.

Eva Vanmassenhove, Christian Hardmeier, and Andy Way. 2018. Getting gender right in neural machine translation. In *Proceedings of the 2018 Conference on Empirical Methods in Natural Language Processing*, pages 3003–3008. Association for Computational Linguistics.

William Wright. 1955. *A grammar of the Arabic language*, volume I. Cambridge University Press.

Wajdi Zaghouani, Behrang Mohit, Nizar Habash, Ossama Obeid, Nadi Tomeh, Alla Rozovskaya, Noura Farra, Sarah Alkuhlani, and Kemal Oflazer. 2014. Large Scale Arabic Error Annotation: Guidelines and Framework. In *Proceedings of the Language Resources and Evaluation Conference (LREC)*, Reykjavik, Iceland.

Jieyu Zhao, Tianlu Wang, Mark Yatskar, Ryan Cotterell, Vicente Ordonez, and Kai-Wei Chang. 2019. Gender bias in contextualized word embeddings. *CoRR*, abs/1904.03310.

Jieyu Zhao, Yichao Zhou, Zeyu Li, Wei Wang, and Kai-Wei Chang. 2018. Learning gender-neutral word embeddings. *arXiv preprint arXiv:1809.01496*.

Ran Zmigrod, Sebastian J. Mielke, Hanna Wallach, and Ryan Cotterell. 2019. Counterfactual data augmentation for mitigating gender stereotypes in languages with rich morphology. In *Proceedings of the Annual Meeting of the Association for Computational Linguistics*, Florence, Italy.

Measuring Bias in Contextualized Word Representations

Keita Kurita   Nidhi Vyas   Ayush Pareek   Alan W Black   Yulia Tsvetkov

Carnegie Mellon University
{kkurita,nkvyas,apareek,awb,ytsvetko}@andrew.cmu.edu

Abstract

Contextual word embeddings such as BERT have achieved state of the art performance in numerous NLP tasks. Since they are optimized to capture the statistical properties of training data, they tend to pick up on and amplify social stereotypes present in the data as well. In this study, we (1) propose a template-based method to quantify bias in BERT; (2) show that this method obtains more consistent results in capturing social biases than the traditional cosine based method; and (3) conduct a case study, evaluating gender bias in a downstream task of Gender Pronoun Resolution. Although our case study focuses on gender bias, the proposed technique is generalizable to unveiling other biases, including in multiclass settings, such as racial and religious biases.

1   Introduction

Type-level word embedding models, including word2vec and GloVe (Mikolov et al., 2013; Pennington et al., 2014), have been shown to exhibit social biases present in human-generated training data (Bolukbasi et al., 2016; Caliskan et al., 2017; Garg et al., 2018; Manzini et al., 2019). These embeddings are then used in a plethora of downstream applications, which perpetuate and further amplify stereotypes (Zhao et al., 2017; Leino et al., 2019). To reveal and quantify corpus-level biases is word embeddings, Bolukbasi et al. (2016) used the word analogy task (Mikolov et al., 2013). For example, they showed that gendered male word embeddings like *he, man* are associated with higher-status jobs like *computer programmer* and *doctor*, whereas gendered words like *she* or *woman* are associated with *homemaker* and *nurse*.

Contextual word embedding models, such as ELMo and BERT (Peters et al., 2018; Devlin et al., 2019) have become increasingly common, replacing traditional type-level embeddings and attaining new state of the art results in the majority of

NLP tasks. In these models, every word has a different embedding, depending on the context and the language model state; in these settings, the analogy task used to reveal biases in uncontextualized embeddings is not applicable. Recently, May et al. (2019) showed that traditional cosine-based methods for exposing bias in sentence embeddings fail to produce consistent results for embeddings generated using contextual methods. We find similar inconsistent results with cosine-based methods of exposing bias; this is a motivation to the development of a novel bias test that we propose.

In this work, we propose a new method to quantify bias in BERT embeddings (§2). Since BERT embeddings use a *masked* language modelling objective, we directly query the model to measure the bias for a particular token. More specifically, we create simple template sentences containing the attribute word for which we want to measure bias (e.g. *programmer*) and the target for bias (e.g. *she* for gender). We then mask the attribute and target tokens sequentially, to get a relative measure of bias across target classes (e.g. male and female). Contextualized word embeddings for a given token change based on its context, so such an approach allows us measure the bias for similar categories divergent by the the target attribute (§2). We compare our approach with the cosine similarity-based approach (§3) and show that our measure of bias is more consistent with human biases and is sensitive to a wide range of biases in the model using various stimuli presented in Caliskan et al. (2017). Next, we investigate the effect of a specific type of bias in a specific downstream task: gender bias in BERT and its effect on the task of Gendered Pronoun Resolution (GPR) (Webster et al., 2018). We show that the bias in GPR is highly correlated with our measure of bias (§4). Finally, we highlight the potential negative impacts of using BERT in downstream real world applications (§5). The code and data used in this work are publicly

Proceedings of the 1st Workshop on Gender Bias in Natural Language Processing, pages 166–172
Florence, Italy, August 2, 2019. ©2019 Association for Computational Linguistics

available.[1]

2   Quantifying Bias in BERT

BERT is trained using a masked language modelling objective i.e. to predict masked tokens, denoted as [MASK], in a sentence given the entire context. We use the predictions for these [MASK] tokens to measure the bias encoded in the actual representations.

We directly query the underlying masked language model in BERT[2] to compute the association between certain **targets** (e.g., gendered words) and **attributes** (e.g. career-related words). For example, to compute the association between the target *male gender* and the attribute *programmer*, we feed in the masked sentence "[MASK] is a programmer" to BERT, and compute the probability assigned to the sentence '*he is a programmer*" (p_{tgt}). To measure the association, however, we need to measure how much *more* BERT prefers the male gender association with the attribute *programmer*, compared to the female gender. We thus re-weight this likelihood p_{tgt} using the prior bias of the model towards predicting the male gender. To do this, we mask out the attribute *programmer* and query BERT with the sentence "[MASK] is a [MASK]", then compute the probability BERT assigns to the sentence '*he is a [MASK]*" (p_{prior}). Intuitively, p_{prior} represents how likely the word *he* is in BERT, given the sentence structure and no other evidence. Finally, the difference between the normalized predictions for the words *he* and *she* can be used to measure the gender bias in BERT for the *programmer* attribute.

Generalizing, we use the following procedure to compute the association between a target and an attribute:

1. Prepare a template sentence
   e.g."[TARGET] is a [ATTRIBUTE]"
2. Replace [TARGET] with [MASK] and compute p_{tgt}=P([MASK]=[TARGET]| sentence)
3. Replace both [TARGET] and [ATTRIBUTE] with [MASK], and compute prior probability p_{prior}=P([MASK]=[TARGET]| sentence)
4. Compute the association as $\log \frac{p_{tgt}}{p_{prior}}$

[1] https://bit.ly/2EkJwh1
[2] For all experiments we use the uncased version of BERT$_{\text{BASE}}$ https://storage.googleapis.com/bert_models/2018_10_18/uncased_L-12_H-768_A-12.zip.

We refer to this normalized measure of association as the *increased log probability* score and the difference between the increased log probability scores for two targets (e.g. he/she) as *log probability bias score* which we use as measure of bias. Although this approach requires one to construct a template sentence, these templates are merely simple sentences containing attribute words of interest, and can be shared across multiple targets and attributes. Further, the flexibility to use such templates can potentially help measure more fine-grained notions of bias in the model.

In the next section, we show that our proposed *log probability bias score* method is more effective at exposing bias than traditional cosine-based measures.

3   Correlation with Human Biases

We investigate the correlation between our measure of bias and human biases. To do this, we apply the log probability bias score to the same set of attributes that were shown to exhibit human bias in experiments that were performed using the Implicit Association Test (Greenwald et al., 1998). Specifically, we use the stimuli used in the Word Embedding Association Test (WEAT) (Caliskan et al., 2017).

Word Embedding Association Test (WEAT): The WEAT method compares set of target concepts (e.g. male and female words) denoted as X and Y (each of equal size N), with a set of attributes to measure bias over social attributes and roles (e.g. career/family words) denoted as A and B. The degree of bias for each target concept t is calculated as follows:

$$s(t, A, B) = [\text{mean}_{a \in A}\text{sim}(t, a) - \text{mean}_{b \in B}\text{sim}(t, b)],$$

where *sim* is the cosine similarity between the embeddings. The test statistics is

$$S(X, Y, A, B) = [\text{mean}_{x \in X}s(x, A, B) - \text{mean}_{y \in Y}s(y, A, B)],$$

where the test is a permutation test over X and Y. The p-value is computed as

$$p = \Pr[S(X_i, Y_i, A, B) > S(X, Y, A, B)]$$

The effect size is measured as

$$d = \frac{S(X, Y, A, B)}{\text{std}_{t \in X \cup Y}s(t, A, B)}$$

Category	Templates
Pleasant/Unpleasant (Insects/Flowers)	T are A, T is A
Pleasant/Unpleasant (EA/AA)	T are A, T is A
Career/Family (Male/Female)	T likes A, T like A, T is interested in A
Math/Arts (Male/Female)	T likes A, T like A, T is interested in A
Science/Arts (Male/Female)	T likes A, T like A, T is interested in A

Table 1: Template sentences used for the WEAT tests (T: target, A: attribute)

Category	Targets	Templates
Pleasant/Unpleasant (Insects/Flowers)	flowers,insects,flower,insect	T are A, the T is A
Pleasant/Unpleasant (EA/AA)	black, white	T people are A, the T person is A
Career/Family (Male/Female)	he,she,boys,girls,men,women	T likes A, T like A, T is interested in A
Math/Arts (Male/Female)	he,she,boys,girls,men,women	T likes A, T like A, T is interested in A
Science/Arts (Male/Female)	he,she,boys,girls,men,women	T likes A, T like A, T is interested in A

Table 2: Template sentences used and target words for the grammatically correct sentences (T: target, A: attribute)

It is important to note that the statistical test is a permutation test, and hence a large effect size does not guarantee a higher degree of statistical significance.

3.1 Baseline: WEAT for BERT

To apply the WEAT method on BERT, we first compute the embeddings for target and attribute words present in the stimuli using multiple templates, such as "TARGET is ATTRIBUTE" (Refer Table 1 for an exhaustive list of templates used for each category). We mask the TARGET to compute the embedding[3] for the ATTRIBUTE and vice versa. Words that are absent in the BERT vocabulary are removed from the targets. We ensure that the number of words for both targets are equal, by removing random words from the smaller target set. To confirm whether the reduction in vocabulary results in a change of p-value, we also conduct the WEAT on GloVe with the reduced vocabulary.[4]

3.2 Proposed: Log Probability Bias Score

To compare our method measuring bias, and to test for human-like biases in BERT, we also compute the *log probability bias score* for the same set of attributes and targets in the stimuli. We compute the mean *log probability bias score* for each attribute, and permute the attributes to measure statistical significance with the permutation test. Since many TARGETs in the stimuli cause the template sentence to become grammatically incorrect, resulting in low predicted probabilities, we fixed the TARGET to common pronouns/indicators of category such as *flower, he, she* (Table 2 contains a full list of target words and templates). This avoids large variance in predicted probabilities, leading to more reliable results. The effect size is computed in the same way as the WEAT except the standard deviation is computed over the mean *log probability bias scores*.

We experiment over the following categories of stimuli in the WEAT experiments: Category 1 (flower/insect targets and pleasant/unpleasant attributes), Category 3 (European American/African American names and pleasant/unpleasant attributes), Category 6 (male/female names and career/family attributes), Category 7 (male/female targets and math/arts attributes) and Category 8 (male/female targets and science/arts attributes).

3.3 Comparison Results

The WEAT on GloVe returns similar findings to those of Caliskan et al. (2017) except for the European/African American names and pleasant/unpleasant association not exhibiting significant bias. This is due to only 5 of the African American names being present in the BERT vocabulary. The WEAT for BERT fails to find any statistically significant biases at $p < 0.01$. This implies that WEAT is not an effective measure for bias in BERT embeddings, or that methods for constructing embeddings require additional investigation. In contrast, our method of querying the underlying language model exposes statistically significant association across all categories, showing that BERT does indeed encode biases and that our method is more sensitive to them.

---

[3] We use the outputs from the final layer of BERT as embeddings

[4] WEAT was originally used to study the GloVe embeddings

Category	WEAT on GloVe	WEAT on BERT	Ours on BERT
			Log Probability Bias Score
Pleasant/Unpleasant (Insects/Flowers)	1.543*	0.6688	0.8744*
Pleasant/Unpleasant (EA/AA)	1.012	1.003	0.8864*
Career/Family (Male/Female)	1.814*	0.5047	1.126*
Math/Arts (Male/Female)	1.061	0.6755	0.8495*
Science/Arts (Male/Female)	1.246*	0.8815	0.9572*

Table 3: Effect sizes of bias measurements on WEAT Stimuli. (* indicates significant at $p < 0.01$)

Gender	Prior Prob.	Avg. Predicted Prob.
Male	10.3%	11.5%
Female	9.8%	13.9%

Table 4: Probability of pronoun referring to neither entity in a sentence of GPR

4 Case Study: Effects of Gender Bias on Gendered Pronoun Resolution

Dataset We examined the downstream effects of bias in BERT using the Gendered Pronoun Resolution (GPR) task (Webster et al., 2018). GPR is a sub-task in co-reference resolution, where a pronoun-containing expression is to be paired with the referring expression. Since pronoun resolving systems generally favor the male entities (Webster et al., 2018), this task is a valid test-bed for our study. We use the GAP dataset[5] by Webster et al. (2018), containing 8,908 human-labeled ambiguous pronoun-name pairs, created from Wikipedia. The task is to classify whether an ambiguous pronoun P in a text refers to entity A, entity B or neither. There are 1,000 male and female pronouns in the training set each, with 103 and 98 of them not referring to any entity in the sentence, respectively.

Model We use the model suggested on Kaggle,[6] inspired by Tenney et al. (2019). The model uses BERT embeddings for P, A and B, given the context of the input sentence. Next, it uses a multi-layer perceptron (MLP) layer to perform a naive classification to decide if the pronoun belongs to A, B or neither. The MLP layer uses a single hidden layer with 31 dimensions, a dropout of 0.6 and L2 regularization with weight 0.1.

Results Although the number of male pronouns associated with no entities in the training data is slightly larger, the model predicted the female pronoun referring to no entities with a significantly higher probability ($p = 0.007$ on a permutation test); see Table 4. As the training set is balanced, we attribute this bias to the underlying BERT representations.

We also investigate the relation between the topic of the sentence and model's ability to associate the female pronoun with no entity. We first extracted 20 major topics from the dataset using non-negative matrix factorization (Lee and Seung, 2001) (refer to Appendix for the list of topics). We then compute the bias score for each topic as the sum of the *log probability bias* score for the top 15 most prevalent words of each topic weighted by their weights within the topic. For this, we use a generic template "[TARGET] are interested in [ATTRIBUTE]" where TARGET is either men or women. Next we compute a bias score for each sample in the training data as the sum of individual bias scores of topics present in the sample, weighted by the topic weights. Finally, we measured the Spearman correlation coefficient to be 0.207 (which is statistically significant with $p = 4e - 11$) between the bias scores for male gender across all samples and the model's probability to associate a female pronoun with no entity. We conclude that models using BERT find it challenging to perform coreference resolution when the gender pronoun is female and if the topic is biased towards the male gender.

5 Real World Implications

In previous sections, we discussed that BERT has human-like biases, which are propagated to downstream tasks. In this section, we discuss another potential negative impact of using BERT in a downstream model. Given that three quarters of US employers now use social media for recruiting job candidates (Segal, 2014), many applications are filtered using job recommendation systems and other AI-powered services. Zhao et al. (2018)

---

[5] https://github.com/google-research-datasets/gap-coreference
[6] https://www.kaggle.com/mateiionita/taming-the-bert-a-baseline

discussed that resume filtering systems are biased when the model has strong association between gender and certain professions. Similarly, certain gender-stereotyped attributes have been strongly associated with occupational salary and prestige (Glick, 1991). Using our proposed method, we investigate the gender bias in BERT embeddingss for certain occupation and skill attributes.

Datasets: We use three datasets for our study of gender bias in employment attributes:

- *Employee Salary Dataset[7] for Montgomery County of Maryland-* Contains 6882 instances of "Job Title" and "Salary" records along with other attributes. We sort this dataset in decreasing order of salary and take the first 1000 instances as a proxy for high-paying and prestigious jobs.

- *Positive and Negative Traits Dataset[8]-* Contains a collection of 234 and 292 adjectives considered "positive" and "negative" traits, respectively.

- *O*NET 23.2 technology skills[9]* Contains 17649 unique skills for 27660 jobs, which are posted online

Discussion We used the following two templates to measure gender bias:

- "TARGET is ATTRIBUTE", where TARGET are male and female pronouns viz. *he* and *she*. The ATTRIBUTE are job titles from the Employee Salary dataset, or the adjectives from the Positive and Negative traits dataset.

- "TARGET can do ATTRIBUTE", where the TARGETs are the same, but the ATTRIBUTE are skills from the O*NET dataset.

Table 5 shows the percentage of attributes that were more strongly associated with the male than the female gender. The results prove that BERT expresses strong preferences for male pronouns, raising concerns with using BERT in downstream tasks like resume filtering.

---

⁷`https://catalog.data.gov/dataset/employee-salaries-2017`
⁸`http://ideonomy.mit.edu/essays/traits.html`
⁹`https://www.onetcenter.org/database.html#individual-files`

Dataset	Percentage
Salary	88.5%
Pos-Traits	80.0%
Neg-Traits	78.9%
Skills	84.0%

Table 5: Percentage of attributes associated more strongly with the male gender

6   Related Work

NLP applications ranging from core tasks such as coreference resolution (Rudinger et al., 2018) and language identification (Jurgens et al., 2017), to downstream systems such as automated essay scoring (Amorim et al., 2018), exhibit inherent social biases which are attributed to the datasets used to train the embeddings (Barocas and Selbst, 2016; Zhao et al., 2017; Yao and Huang, 2017). There have been several efforts to investigate the amount of intrinsic bias within uncontextualized word embeddings in binary (Bolukbasi et al., 2016; Garg et al., 2018; Swinger et al., 2019) and multiclass (Manzini et al., 2019) settings.

Contextualized embeddings such as BERT (Devlin et al., 2019) and ELMo (Peters et al., 2018) have been replacing the traditional type-level embeddings. It is thus important to understand the effects of biases learned by these embedding models on downstream tasks. However, it is not straightforward to use the existing bias-exposure methods for contextualized embeddings. For instance, May et al. (2019) used WEAT on sentence embeddings of ELMo and BERT, but there was no clear indication of bias. Rather, they observed counterintuitive behavior like vastly different p-values for results concerning gender.

Along similar lines, Basta et al. (2019) noted that contextual word-embeddings are less biased than traditional word-embeddings. Yet, biases like gender are propagated heavily in downstream tasks. For instance, Zhao et al. (2019) showed that ELMo exhibits gender bias for certain professions. As a result, female entities are predicted less accurately than male entities for certain occupation words, in the coreference resolution task. Field and Tsvetkov (2019) revealed biases in ELMo embeddings that limit their applicability across data domains. Motivated by these recent findings, our work proposes a new method to expose and measure bias in contextualized word embeddings, specifically BERT. As opposed to previous work, our measure of bias is more consistent with human biases. We also study the effect of this intrinsic bias on downstream tasks, and highlight the negative impacts of gender-bias in real world applications.

7 Conclusion

In this paper, we showed that querying the underlying language model can effectively measure bias in BERT and expose multiple stereotypes embedded in the model. We also showed that our measure of bias is more consistent with human-biases, and outperforms the traditional WEAT method on BERT. Finally we showed that these biases can have negative downstream effects. In the future, we would like to explore the effects on other downstream tasks such as text classification, and device an effective method of debiasing contextualized word embeddings.

Acknowledgments

This material is based upon work supported by the National Science Foundation under Grant No. IIS1812327.

References

Evelin Amorim, Marcia Cançado, and Adriano Veloso. 2018. Automated essay scoring in the presence of biased ratings. In *Proc. of NAACL*, pages 229–237.

Solon Barocas and Andrew D Selbst. 2016. Big data's disparate impact. *Calif. L. Rev.*, 104:671.

Christine Basta, Marta R Costa-jussà, and Noe Casas. 2019. Evaluating the underlying gender bias in contextualized word embeddings. *arXiv preprint arXiv:1904.08783*.

Tolga Bolukbasi, Kai-Wei Chang, James Y Zou, Venkatesh Saligrama, and Adam T Kalai. 2016. Man is to computer programmer as woman is to homemaker? debiasing word embeddings. In *Proc. of NIPS*, pages 4349–4357.

Aylin Caliskan, Joanna J Bryson, and Arvind Narayanan. 2017. Semantics derived automatically from language corpora contain human-like biases. *Science*, 356(6334):183–186.

Jacob Devlin, Ming-Wei Chang, Kenton Lee, and Kristina Toutanova. 2019. Bert: Pre-training of deep bidirectional transformers for language understanding. In *Proc. of NAACL*.

Anjalie Field and Yulia Tsvetkov. 2019. Entity-centric contextual affective analysis. In *Proc. of ACL*.

Nikhil Garg, Londa Schiebinger, Dan Jurafsky, and James Zou. 2018. Word embeddings quantify 100 years of gender and ethnic stereotypes. *Proceedings of the National Academy of Sciences*, 115(16):E3635–E3644.

Peter Glick. 1991. Trait-based and sex-based discrimination in occupational prestige, occupational salary, and hiring. *Sex Roles*, 25(5-6):351–378.

Anthony Greenwald, Debbie E. McGhee, and Jordan L. K. Schwartz. 1998. Measuring individual differences in implicit cognition: The implicit association test. *Journal of personality and social psychology*, 74:1464–80.

David Jurgens, Yulia Tsvetkov, and Dan Jurafsky. 2017. Incorporating dialectal variability for socially equitable language identification. In *Proc. of ACL*, pages 51–57.

Daniel Lee and Hyunjune Seung. 2001. Algorithms for non-negative matrix factorization. In *Proc. of NIPS*.

Klas Leino, Matt Fredrikson, Emily Black, Shayak Sen, and Anupam Datta. 2019. Feature-wise bias amplification. In *Prof. of ICLR*.

Thomas Manzini, Yao Chong, Yulia Tsvetkov, and Alan W Black. 2019. Black is to criminal as caucasian is to police: Detecting and removing multiclass bias in word embeddings. In *Proc. of NAACL*.

Chandler May, Alex Wang, Shikha Bordia, Samuel R. Bowman, and Rachel Rudinger. 2019. On measuring social biases in sentence encoders. In *Proc. of NAACL*.

Tomas Mikolov, Ilya Sutskever, Kai Chen, Greg S Corrado, and Jeff Dean. 2013. Distributed representations of words and phrases and their compositionality. In *Proc.of NIPS*, pages 3111–3119.

Jeffrey Pennington, Richard Socher, and Christopher Manning. 2014. GloVe: Global vectors for word representation. In *Proce. of EMNLP*, pages 1532–1543.

Matthew E Peters, Mark Neumann, Mohit Iyyer, Matt Gardner, Christopher Clark, Kenton Lee, and Luke Zettlemoyer. 2018. Deep contextualized word representations. In *Proc. of NAACL*.

Rachel Rudinger, Jason Naradowsky, Brian Leonard, and Benjamin Van Durme. 2018. Gender bias in coreference resolution. In *Proc. of NAACL*.

J Segal. 2014. Social media use in hiring: Assessing the risks. *HR Magazine*, 59(9).

Nathaniel Swinger, Maria De-Arteaga, Neil Heffernan IV, Mark Leiserson, and Adam Kalai. 2019. What are the biases in my word embedding? In *Proc. of the AAAI/ACM Conference on Artificial Intelligence, Ethics, and Society (AIES)*.

Ian Tenney, Patrick Xia, Berlin Chen, Alex Wang, Adam Poliak, R. Thomas McCoy, Najoung Kim, Benjamin Van Durme, Samuel R. Bowman, Dipanjan Das, and Ellie Pavlick. 2019. What do you learn from context? probing for sentence structure in contextualized word representations. In *Proc. of ICLR*.

Kellie Webster, Marta Recasens, Vera Axelrod, and Jason Baldridge. 2018. Mind the gap: A balanced corpus of gendered ambiguous pronouns. *Transactions of the Association for Computational Linguistics*.

Sirui Yao and Bert Huang. 2017. Beyond parity: Fairness objectives for collaborative filtering. In *Advances in Neural Information Processing Systems*, pages 2921–2930.

Jieyu Zhao, Tianlu Wang, Mark Yatskar, Ryan Cotterell, Vicente Ordonez, and Kai-Wei Chang. 2019. Gender bias in contextualized word embeddings. In *NAACL (short)*.

Jieyu Zhao, Tianlu Wang, Mark Yatskar, Vicente Ordonez, and Kai-Wei Chang. 2017. Men also like shopping: Reducing gender bias amplification using corpus-level constraints. In *Proc. of EMNLP*.

Jieyu Zhao, Yichao Zhou, Zeyu Li, Wei Wang, and Kai-Wei Chang. 2018. Learning gender-neutral word embeddings.

Appendix

Topic Id	Top 5 Words
1	match,round,second,team,season
2	times,city,jersey,york,new
3	married,son,died,wife,daughter
4	best,award,actress,films,film
5	friend,like,work,mother,life
6	university,music,attended,high,school
7	president,general,governor,party,state
8	songs,solo,song,band,album
9	medal,gold,final,won,world
10	best,role,character,television,series
11	kruse,moved,amy,esme,time
12	usa,trunchbull,pageant,2011,miss
13	american,august,brother,actress,born
14	sir,died,church,song,john
15	natasha,days,hospital,helene,later
16	played,debut,sang,role,opera
17	january,december,october,july,married
18	academy,member,american,university,family
19	award,best,played,mary,year
20	jersey,death,james,king,paul

Table 6: Extracted topics for the GPR dataset

On Measuring Gender Bias in Translation of Gender-neutral Pronouns

Won Ik Cho[1], Ji Won Kim[2], Seok Min Kim[1], and Nam Soo Kim[1]
Department of Electrical and Computer Engineering and INMC[1]
{wicho,smkim}@hi.snu.ac.kr, nkim@snu.ac.kr
Department of Linguistics[2]
kimjiwon08@snu.ac.kr
Seoul National University
1 Gwanak-ro, Gwanak-gu, Seoul, Korea, 08826

Abstract

Ethics regarding social bias has recently thrown striking issues in natural language processing. Especially for gender-related topics, the need for a system that reduces the model bias has grown in areas such as image captioning, content recommendation, and automated employment. However, detection and evaluation of gender bias in the machine translation systems are not yet thoroughly investigated, for the task being cross-lingual and challenging to define. In this paper, we propose a scheme for making up a test set that evaluates the gender bias in a machine translation system, with Korean, a language with gender-neutral pronouns. Three word/phrase sets are primarily constructed, each incorporating positive/negative expressions or occupations; all the terms are gender-independent or at least not biased to one side severely. Then, additional sentence lists are constructed concerning formality of the pronouns and politeness of the sentences. With the generated sentence set of size 4,236 in total, we evaluate gender bias in conventional machine translation systems utilizing the proposed measure, which is termed here as *translation gender bias index* (TGBI). The corpus and the code for evaluation is available on-line[1].

1 Introduction

Gender bias in natural language processing (NLP) has been an issue of great importance, especially among the areas including image semantic role labeling (Zhao et al., 2017), language modeling (Lu et al., 2018), and coreference resolution (Lu et al., 2018; Webster et al., 2018). Along with these, the bias in machine translation (MT) was also claimed recently regarding the issue of gender dependency in the translation incorporating occupation (Prates et al., 2018; Kuczmarski and Johnson, 2018). That

---

Figure 1: Occupation gender bias shown in some KR-EN (Korean-English) translation systems. Note that unlike this figure, Yale romanization is utilized in the rest of this paper.

is, the prejudice within people, e.g., *cops are usually men* or *nurses are usually women*, which is inherent in corpora, assigns bias to the MT models trained with them.

State-of-the-art MT systems or the ones in service are based on large-scale corpora that incorporate various topics and text styles. Usually, sentence pairs for training are fed into the seq2seq (Sutskever et al., 2014; Bahdanau et al., 2014) or Transformer (Vaswani et al., 2017)-based models, where the decoding process refers to thought vector of the source data to infer a plausible translation (Cho et al., 2014). Under some circumstances, this may incur an association of gender-specified pronouns (in the target) and gender-neutral ones (in the source) for lexicon pairs that frequently collocate in the corpora. We claim that this kind of phenomenon seriously threatens the fairness of a translation system, in the sense that it lacks generality and inserts social bias to the inference. Moreover, the output is not fully correct (considering gender-neutrality) and might offend the users who expect fairer representations.

The aforementioned problem exists in Korean as well (Figure 1). To look more into this, here we investigate the issue with the gender-neutral

---

[1]https://github.com/nolongerprejudice/tgbi

Proceedings of the 1st Workshop on Gender Bias in Natural Language Processing, pages 173–181
Florence, Italy, August 2, 2019. ©2019 Association for Computational Linguistics

pronouns in Korean, using the lexicons regarding sentiment and occupation. We provide the sentences of the template "걔는 [xx]-해 (kyay-nun [xx]-hay), *S/he is [xx]* ", as in Prates et al. (2018), to the translation system, and evaluate the bias observed from the portion of pronouns being translated into female/male/neither. Here, *[xx]* denotes either a sentiment word regarding one's judgment towards the third person (polar), or an occupation word (neutral). Since *kyay* in Korean, which refers to *s/he*, is gender-neutral thus the translation output of the sentence becomes either *"She is [xx]"*, *"He is [xx]"*, or *"The person is [xx]"*. Although the expressions as used in the last output are optimal, they are not frequently utilized in conventional translation systems. Also, such result is difficult to be mechanically achieved since transforming all the gender-related pronouns to the neutral ones may cause loss of information, in the circumstances where the context is given (e.g., *To tell you one thing about her, [she] is [xx]*).

In this study, we collect a lexicon set of the size of 1,059 for the construction of an equity evaluation corpus (EEC) (Kiritchenko and Mohammad, 2018), specifically 324 sentiment-related phrases and 735 occupation words. For each sentence of the above template containing a lexicon, along with an alternative pronoun (formal version) and a politeness suffix (on/off), we eventually obtain 4,236 utterances to make up the EEC. We claim the following as contributions of this paper:

- Construction of a corpus with template sentences that can check the preservation of gender-neutrality in KR-EN translation (along with a detailed guideline)
- A measure to evaluate and compare the performance of translation systems regarding the preservation of gender neutrality of pronouns
- Rigorous contemplation on why the preservation of gender neutrality has to be guaranteed in translation

In the following sections, after an introduction to the literature, we describe how we made up the corpus, and how it is utilized in evaluating the conventional machine translation systems in service.

2   Related Work

It is essential to clarify the legitimate ground for the necessity of mitigating gender bias in machine learning models. For example, Binns (2017) suggests that it should be considered as a problem of individuality and context, rather than of statistics and system. The paper poses a question on the fairness of *fairness* utilized in fair machine learning, and concludes that the fairness issue in algorithmic decision-making should be treated in a contextually appropriate manner, along with the points that may hinge on *the factors which are not typically present in the data available in situ*. Although little study has been undertaken in the field of ethics in translation, we have plentiful research on the call for mitigation of gender bias in NLP models.

One of them is image semantic role labeling, as suggested in Zhao et al. (2017). It is claimed that due to the bias in the image/caption pairs that associate specific verb/mood with a specific gender, e.g., *warm tone kitchen* and *cooking* with *women*; the trained model infers the wrong gender in the captioning of some images. The primary reason is assumed to be a lack of data with cooking males in warm tone kitchen. However, since data augmentation for all the imbalance is costly and not promising, the paper proposes giving a constraint in the training phase in the way of disassociating verbs and gender information.

Other areas where gender bias is observed are classification and recommendation, as represented in a recent article[2]; in Amazon AI recruiting, the system came out to recommend the applicants who had sufficient work experience in the field, in most cases male. This incident does not merely mean that the data concerning female occupies much smaller volume than male; it also conveys that so-called "good" applicants were selected in perspective of choosing experienced and industrious workers who might have been less forced to devote their time to housework or childcare. However, it is questionable that forcing the dataset to be balanced by making the portion of female employment half is a sound solution. Instead, this is about disentangling the factors that are less directly related to working ability.

Above kind of disentanglement is required as well in the area of inference; for instance, a shared task of GenderBiasNLP[3]. For such a task, researchers find how contextual factors can be disassociated with gender information. In this paper, a similar problem is discussed in cross-lingual perspective. Along with the articles that pose the

---

[2]https://www.reuters.com/article/us-amazon-com-jobs-automation-insight/amazon-scraps-secret-ai-recruiting-tool-that-showed-bias-against-women-idUSKCN1MK08G

[3]https://www.kaggle.com/c/gendered-pronoun-resolution

problem[4], some studies have been done in an empirical viewpoint (as coreference resolution in translation) including Kuczmarski and Johnson (2018). In Prates et al. (2018) which is the closest to this work, twelve languages are investigated with about 1,000 occupations and 21 adjectives, with a template sentence, demonstrating a strong male dependency within Google translator. However, albeit its syntax being similar to that of Japanese, Korean was omitted due to some technical reasons. Here, we make the first known attempt to create a concrete scheme for evaluating the gender bias of KR-EN translation systems regarding sentiment words and occupations, and propose a measure for an inter-system comparison. Also, we state that mitigated male dependency does not necessarily mean that the system bias has reduced, rather it can imply that another social bias has been involved.

3 Proposed Method

In this section, we describe how the EEC is created and how it is utilized in evaluating gender bias in the MT models.

3.1 Corpus generation

The corpus generation scheme can be compared with Burlot and Yvon (2017) in the sense that various morpho-syntactic/semantic features are taken into account. However, here we focus more on making the template sentences help discern the gender bias regarding the translation of gender-neutral pronouns.

3.1.1 Gender-neutral pronouns

The first thing to be clarified is the distinction of gender-neutral words in Korean. Unlike some languages such as German, the Korean language does not incorporate grammatical gender. However, for the third person pronouns, there exist '그녀 (kunye), *she*' and '그 (ku), *he*', which are clearly gender-specific. Therefore, in some cases, to avoid specifying a gender (e.g., in case the speaker asks the addressee about a person whose gender is not identified), the speakers use gender-neutral pronouns such as '걔 (kyay), *s/he*'[5], which is widely used to indicate somebody that does not partici-

pate in the conversation (and who the speakers altogether know).

Note that for a native speaker, *kyay* indicates someone who is younger than or the same age as the speaker, in an informal way. Thus, '그 사람 (ku salam), *the person*' was adopted in this study as well, as a variation of *kyay* to assign formality to the utterances. For both *kyay* and *ku salam*, topic marker '은/는 (un/nun), *is*' was agglutinated to disambiguate the objectivity. In other words, all the sentiment words or the occupations introduced in the following paragraphs denote the property regarding the topic (the pronoun) of the sentence.

3.1.2 Sentiment words

Sentiment words in category of positive and negative polarity lexicons were collected from the *Korean Sentiment Word Dictionary* published by Kunsan National University[6]. The corpus is reported to be constructed by majority voting of at least three people. Among the total of 14,843 items including single words and phrases, we only took roots into account, finally obtaining 124 and 200 items for positive and negative polarity words. We selected not only single words such as '상냥한 (sangnyanghan), *kind*, positive', but also phrases such as '됨됨이가 뛰어난 (toymtoymika ttwienan), *be good in manner*, positive', sometimes including verb phrases such as '함부로 말하는 (hampwulo malhanun), *bombard rough words*, negative'. Additional adverbs were not utilized in the sentence generation.

In investigating the appropriateness of the sentiment words, two factors were considered: first, does the sentiment word belong to the category of the positive or negative lexicon? And second, does it incorporate any prejudice if categorized into positive or negative? For the first question, three Korean native speakers examined the EEC and left only the lexicons with the complete consensus. For the second question, we removed the words regarding appearance (e.g., *pretty, tall*), richness (e.g., *rich, poor*), sexual orientation (e.g., *homosexual*), disability (e.g., *challenged*), academic background (e.g., *uneducated*), occupation or status (e.g., *doctor, unemployed*), etc. This was also thoroughly checked.

3.1.3 Occupations

Occupation, which was not incorporated in the previous section since assigning sentiment polar-

---

[4]https://qz.com/1141122/google-translates-gender-bias-pairs-he-with-hardworking-and-she-with-lazy-and-other-examples/

[5]An abbreviated form of '그 애 (ku ay), *the child*'.

[6]http://dilab.kunsan.ac.kr/knusl.html

ity to it may not guarantee fairness, was taken into account to form a separate corpus. We searched for the official terms of each job and put them in the template *"S/he is [xx]."*[7]. The occupation list of size 735 was collected from an official government web site for employment[8] and was checked for redundancy.

In choosing the occupations, gender-specificity had to be concealed, which is disclosed in words like "발레리노 (palleylino), *ballerino*" or "해녀 (haynye), *woman diver*". Also, the words that convey hate against specific groups of people were omitted. By this, we made sure that the occupation words are free from sentiment polarity, even though some may be listed in the sentiment word dictionary.

3.1.4 Politeness suffix

Finally, the suffix "요 (yo)" was considered in assigning politeness to the sentences. It is usually attached at the end of the sentence; if a straightforward attachment is not available, then the last part of the sentence is transformed to guarantee the utterance being polite. Overall, the criteria regarding the construction scheme of the test set comprise three factors; formality, politeness, and polarity (occupation: neutral).

3.2 Measure

For any set of sentences S where each sentence contains a pronoun of which the gender-neutrality should be preserved in translation, let p_w be the portion of the sentences translated as female, p_m as male, and p_n as gender-neutral[9]. Then we have the following constraints:

$$p_w + p_m + p_n = 1 \qquad (1)$$
$$0 \leq p_w, p_m, p_n \leq 1$$

Consequently, by defining

$$P_s = \sqrt{p_w p_m + p_n} \qquad (2)$$

we might be able to see how the translation is far from guaranteeing gender neutrality. Note that the measure is between 0 and 1, from constraint (1)[10];

---

[7]Here, we notice that the Korean template differs regarding the role of [xx]; if [xx] is noun phrase then the template becomes "걔는 [xx]야 (kay-nun [xx]-ya)", incorporating -*ya* instead of -*hay* which fits with the modifiers.

[8]https://www.work.go.kr

[9]p_w regards words such as *she, her, woman, girl*, and p_m regards *he, him, man, guy, boy*. Others including *the person* were associated with p_n.

[10]The proof is provided in the appendix A.

maximum when p_n is 1 and minimum when either p_w or p_m is 1. This condition matches with the ideal goal of assigning gender-neutrality to pronouns in context-free situations, and also with the viewpoint that random guess of female/male yields the optimum for a fixed p_n.

For all the sentence sets namely $S_1 \cdots S_n$ and the corresponding scores $P_{S_1} \cdots P_{S_n}$, we define the average value $P = AVG(P_{S_i})$ as a translation gender bias index (TGBI) of a translation system, which yields 1 if all the predictions incorporate gender-neutral terms. S_i can be associated with whatever corpus that is utilized. Here, non-weighted arithmetic average is used so that the aspects investigated in each sentence set are not overlooked for its small volume.

3.2.1 A remark on interpretation

At this point, we want to point out that two factors should be considered in analyzing the result. The first one is the bias caused by the volume of appearance in corpora (*VBias*), and the other is the bias caused by the social prejudice which is projected in the lexicons utilized (*SBias*).

We assumed that *VBias* leans toward males and that low p_w might be obtained overall, which came out to be generally correct. However, p_w being relatively high (among sentence sets) does not necessarily mean that the bias is alleviated; rather it can convey the existence of *SBias*, which assigns female-related translation for some sentiment words or occupations. In other words, we *cannot* guarantee here that *the translation system that shows higher p_w with a specific sentence set* substantiates their not being biased, considering both volume-related and social bias-related aspects.

3.2.2 Why the measure?

Despite the limitation of the proposed measure, as explained above, we claim that using the measure may be meaningful for some reasons. First, the measure adopts square root function to reduce the penalty of the result being gender-specific, taking into account that many conventional translation systems yield gender-specific pronouns as output. Secondly, we evaluate the test result with the various sentence sets that comprise the corpus, not just with a single set. This makes it possible for the whole evaluation process to assess gender bias regarding various topics. Finally, although it is unclear if the enhancement of P_{S_i} for some S_i orig-

Sentence set [size]	Google Translator (GT)	Naver Papago (NP)	Kakao Translator (KT)
(a) Informal [2,118]	0.4018 (0.2025, 0.0000)	**0.3936 (0.1916, 0.0000)**	**0.1750 (0.0316, 0.0000)**
(b) Formal[2,118]	0.0574 (0.0000, 0.0033)	0.0485 (0.0014, 0.0009)	0.0217 (0.0000, 0.0004)
(c) Impolite[2,118]	0.3115 (0.1062, 0.0023)	0.3582 (0.1506, 0.0004)	0.1257 (0.0155, 0.0004)
(d) Polite[2,118]	0.2964 (0.0963, 0.0009)	0.2724 (0.0807, 0.0000)	0.1256 (0.0160, 0.0000)
(e) Negative [800]	0.3477 (0.1362, 0.0037)	0.1870 (0.0350, 0.0012)	0.1311 (0.0175, 0.0000)
(f) Positive [496]	**0.4281 (0.2358, 0.0040)**	0.2691 (0.0786, 0.0000)	0.1259 (0.0161, 0.0000)
(g) Occupation [2,940]	0.2547 (0.0690, 0.0006)	0.2209 (0.0496, 0.0017)	0.1241 (0.0153, 0.0003)
Average	**0.2992**	**0.2499**	**0.1184**

Table 1: The overall evaluation result for three conventional KR-EN translation systems. Note that the values for the sentence sets (a-g) denote P_s (p_w, p_n) for each sentence set S. The bold lines denote the sentence set with which each translator shows the highest score.

inates in relieved *VBias* or inserted *SBias*, the averaged value P is expected to be used as a representative value for inter-system comparison, especially if the gap between the systems is noticeable.

4   Evaluation

For evaluation we investigate seven sentence sets in total, namely (a) *informal*, (b) *formal*, (c) *impolite*, (d) *polite*, (e) *negative*, (f) *positive*, and (g) *occupation*. (a-d) contains 2,118 sentences each and (e-g) contains 800, 496, and 2,940 each. The validity of investigating multiple sentence subsets is to be stated briefly in the appendix B.

In this study, we evaluate three conventional translation systems in service, namely *Google translator (GT)*[11], *Naver Papago*[12] *(NP)*, and *Kakao translator (KT)*[13]. Overall, *GT* scored the highest and *KT* the lowest. We conduct additional analysis to catch the meaning beyond the numbers.

4.1   Quantitative analysis

VBias is primarily assumed to be shown by p_m dominating the others (Table 1). However, in some cases, *VBias* is attenuated if *SBias* is projected into the translation output in the way of heightening p_w.

4.1.1   Content-related features

Considering the result with the sentence sets (e-g) which are content-related, the tendency turned out to be different by the systems; *GT* and *NP* show relatively low score with positive sentiment words and *KT* with negative sentiment words. We suspected at first that the negative sentiment words would be highly associated with translation into a

female, but the result proves otherwise. Instead, in *GT* and *NP*, (f) the positive case shows relatively more frequent inference as female compared with (e) the negative case, although the absolute value suggests that there exists *VBias* towards men.

For all the systems, intra-system analysis demonstrates that the result regarding occupation is more biased than the others. Except for *NP*, the social bias inserted in the models seems to lower the score regarding (g). This is to be investigated more rigorously in the qualitative analysis.

4.1.2   Style-related features

The sentences in the set (b), with formal and gender-neutral pronouns, turned out to be significantly biased to male compared with (a) the informal cases, which was beyond our expectations. From this, we could cautiously infer that corpora incorporating relatively formal expressions (such as news article, technical report, papers, etc.) generally associate the sentiment or occupation words with males. With respect to politeness, the systems did not show a significant difference between (c) and (d). We infer that the politeness factor does not affect the tendency of translation much since it is largely related to the colloquial expressions which might not have been employed in the training session.

The result regarding formality reminds us of the phenomenon which has been discerned in the challenge on author profiling (Martinc et al., 2017), that the formal style is known to be predictive for identifying male authors. Undoubtedly, the identity of a writer is *not* direct evidence of s/he utilizing the expressions biased to specific gender in writing. However, a tendency has been reported that the male writers frequently assume or refer to male subject and topic, either unconsciously or to

---

[11]https://translate.google.com/
[12]https://papago.naver.com/
[13]https://translate.kakao.com/

follow the convention, in the formal writing (Argamon et al., 2003). Also, it cannot be ignored that the males are more engaged in formal writing in the real world[14], accounting for a large portion of the corpora. Thus, it seems not unreasonable to claim that, although controversial, the positive correlation between the formal text style and the male-related translation might have been affected by the occupation gender ratio[15].

The result regarding sentence style-related features shows that in giving constraint to prevent the association of gender-related features and contents while training, at least in KR-EN translation, the formality of expressions should not be neglected since it is largely influenced by the context in the corpora where the expressions and contents belong to, and even real world factors. Politeness turned out not to be a severe influence, but the politeness suffix can still reflect the relationship between the speakers, affecting the type of conversation that takes place.

4.2 Qualitative analysis

In brief, translation into male dominates due to the bias in volume, and social bias is represented mainly in the way of informal pronouns being translated into a female with relative frequency, although the content-related features do not necessarily prove it to be so. However, qualitative evaluation is indispensable for a comprehensive understanding of the bias since the quantitative result only informs us of the number, not the semantics.

The most significant result was that of occupations. *GT* reflects the bias that is usually intimated by people (e.g., experts such as *engineers, technicians, professors* are usually men, and art/beauty-related positions such as *fashion designer, hairdresser* are mainly held by women), and *KT* shows the volume dominance of male in the corpus (overall score lower than *GT* and *NP* in Table 1), with rare female cases related to design or nursing. As stated in Section 4.1, we interpreted the result regarding *GT* as *permeated SBias attenuating VBias*, and *KT* as *VBias not attenuated*.

In analyzing the result for *NP*, we observed some unexpected inferences such as *researchers* and *engineers* significantly being translated into female pronoun and *cuisine*-related occupations into male, which is different from social prejudice

---

[14]E.g., journalists, engineers, researchers; considering the gender ratio statistics.

[15]As in https://www.bls.gov/cps/cpsaat11.htm

posed by *GT* or *KT*. We assume this phenomenon as a result of technical modification performed by *NP* team to reduce the gender bias in translating pronouns regarding occupations. The modification seems to mitigate both *VBias* and *SBias* in a positive way, although the final goal should be a guaranteed utilization of gender-neutral expressions rather than a half-half guess.

4.3 Comparison with other schemes

Although the scope and aim do not precisely overlap, we find it beneficial for our argument to compare the previous studies with ours. In Kuczmarski and Johnson (2018), the paper mainly aims to perform post-processing that yields gender non-biased result in pronoun translation for Turkish, but no specific description of the evaluation was accompanied. In Lu et al. (2018), a score function on evaluating bias was suggested as a portion of matched pair among masked occupations. However, the task was not on translation, and we eschew using the suggested type of linear computation so as to avoid the arithmetic average (TGBI) not revealing the different performance on various sentence sets. Most recently, Prates et al. (2018) utilized a heat map regarding occupation and adjectives in 12 languages to evaluate Google translator. They computed the p-values relative to the null hypothesis that the number of translated male pronouns is not significantly higher than that of female pronouns, with a significance level of $\alpha = .05$. They obtained the outliers in Finnish, Hungarian, and Basque notably, but the study on Korean was omitted, and the work only incorporates a single sentence style, probably for simplicity.

Note that the aforementioned approaches are not aimed to evaluate multiple translation systems quantitatively, and omit the portion of gender-neutral pronouns in translation output; which are the strong points of utilizing the proposed EEC and measure for the evaluation of translation gender bias. Also, we take into account both *VBias* and *SBias* in the analysis, of which neither side should be underestimated. For example, someone might assume that occupation gender bias is more severe in *NP* than *GT* since the absolute numerics say so (regarding (g) in Table 1). However, such a conclusion should be hesitantly claimed since it is highly probable that *GT* inherits another kind of bias (from the corpora) that attenuates the *VBias* on males as demonstrated in Section 4.2. Our approach aims to make it possible for the evaluators (of the MT systems) to comprehend how the bias is distributed and to perform an inter- or intra-system comparison, by providing the various sentence sets of which the corresponding scores represent content- and style-related aspects of translation gender bias.

4.4 Discussion

We do not claim here that the model which yields the translation of test utterances being biased to one gender is a biased translator, nor that the distribution of gender-related content in the corpora should be half-half. However, since we decided to investigate only the gender non-specific pronouns, sentiment words, and occupations, so that the generated sentences hardly incorporate any context that determines the pronouns to be one specific gender, we claim that the translation is *recommended to* contain each gender as equally as possible for the sentence sets that are constructed, or use neutral pronouns if available. This is not about making up a mechanical equality, but about avoiding a hasty guess if the inference is not involved with a circumstance that requires the resolution of coreference.

For the user's sake, Google translator recently added the service on providing the result containing both genders as answer if the gender ambiguity is detected[16] (Kuczmarski and Johnson, 2018). This is the first known approach in service that mitigates gender bias in translation. We are encouraged to face this kind of change, although it is tentative. In the long term, we hope the translators print random or gender-neutral answers for the argued type of (or possibly various other kinds of) sentences.

Another important point is that the systems also have to distinguish the circumstances that require a random guess from the ones that gender should be specified. For example, with a sentence "걔는 생리중이야 (kyay-nun sayngli-cwung-iya)[17]", *GT* yields *"He's on a period."*, which is physiologically unreasonable. Moreover, the resolution of coreferences in long-term dependency with the specified gender is required for a correct translation of the sentences with context.

In response to concern on this study being language-specific, we want to note that the proposed methodology can be applied to other languages with gender-neutral pronouns, especially with a high similarity if the source language contains both a formality and politeness-related lexicons (e.g., Japanese). The extensibility regarding the source language has recently been displayed in Prates et al. (2018), and in this paper, a further and detailed experiment was conducted with a language that had not been investigated. For the cases of the target being non-English, we assume that the tendency depends on the presence of gender-neutral pronouns in the target language; in our pilot study utilizing Japanese as a target, the gender-neutrality of the Korean pronouns were preserved mostly in the translation. However, even for the cases where the target language incorporates gender-neutral pronouns, the proposed scheme is useful since the measure reflects the preservation of the gender-neutrality. Despite the difficulty of a typological approach regarding generalization, our study is relevant for a broader audience if the source language being analyzed fits the condition above.

5 Conclusion

In this paper, we introduced a test corpus and measure for the evaluation of multiple KR-EN translation systems. A criteria set for choosing the pronouns, lexicons, and markers was stated in detail, making up a corpus of size 4,236 and seven sentence subsets regarding (in)formality, (im)politeness, sentiment polarity, and occupation. The measurement was performed by averaging P_S for each sentence subsets where P_S denotes $\sqrt{p_w p_m + p_n}$ for p_w, p_m and p_n each the portion of the sentences with pronouns translated into female/male/gender-neutral terms respectively.

Among the three candidates, *Google Translator* scored the highest overall, albeit the qualitative analysis says that an algorithmic modification seems to be implemented in *Naver Papago* considering the result regarding occupations. Although *Kakao Translator* scored the lowest, the low score here does not necessarily mean that the translator malfunctions. In some sense, a well-biased translator is a well-performing translator that reflects the inter-cultural difference. However, we believe that the bias regarding gender should be reduced as much as possible in the circumstances where

---

[16]https://blog.google/products/translate/reducing-gender-bias-google-translate/

[17]생리중 (saynglicwung) denotes *to be in one's menstrual period*, which matches only if *kyay* is translated into a female-related term.

the gender specification is not required.

Our future work includes making up a post-processing system that detects the presence of context and assigning gender specificity/neutrality to the pronouns in the translation. Though we hesitate to claim that it is the best solution, such an approach can be another step to alleviating the amplification of gender bias in cross-lingual tasks. Simultaneously, we aim to have an in-depth analysis in the architecture or model behavior regarding training datasets, with an extended test set that encompasses contextual inference, to find out how each MT system performs better than others in some aspects.

Acknowledgement

This research was supported by Projects for Research and Development of Police science and Technology under Center for Research and Development of Police science and Technology and Korean National Police Agency funded by the Ministry of Science, ICT and Future Planning (PA-J000001-2017-101). Also, this work was supported by the Technology Innovation Program (10076583, Development of free-running speech recognition technologies for embedded robot system) funded by the Ministry of Trade, Industry & Energy (MOTIE, Korea). The authors appreciate helpful comments from Ye Seul Jung and Jeonghwa Cho. After all, the authors send great thanks to Seong-hun Kim for providing a rigorous proof for the boundedness of the proposed measure.

References

Shlomo Argamon, Moshe Koppel, Jonathan Fine, and Anat Rachel Shimoni. 2003. Gender, genre, and writing style in formal written texts. *Text-The Hague Then Amsterdam Then Berlin-*, 23(3):321–346.

Dzmitry Bahdanau, Kyunghyun Cho, and Yoshua Bengio. 2014. Neural machine translation by jointly learning to align and translate. *arXiv preprint arXiv:1409.0473*.

Reuben Binns. 2017. Fairness in machine learning: Lessons from political philosophy. *arXiv preprint arXiv:1712.03586*.

Franck Burlot and François Yvon. 2017. Evaluating the morphological competence of machine translation systems. In *Proceedings of the Second Conference on Machine Translation*, pages 43–55.

Kyunghyun Cho, Bart Van Merriënboer, Caglar Gulcehre, Dzmitry Bahdanau, Fethi Bougares, Holger Schwenk, and Yoshua Bengio. 2014. Learning phrase representations using rnn encoder-decoder for statistical machine translation. *arXiv preprint arXiv:1406.1078*.

Svetlana Kiritchenko and Saif M Mohammad. 2018. Examining gender and race bias in two hundred sentiment analysis systems. *arXiv preprint arXiv:1805.04508*.

James Kuczmarski and Melvin Johnson. 2018. Gender-aware natural language translation.

Kaiji Lu, Piotr Mardziel, Fangjing Wu, Preetam Amancharla, and Anupam Datta. 2018. Gender bias in neural natural language processing. *arXiv preprint arXiv:1807.11714*.

Matej Martinc, Iza Skrjanec, Katja Zupan, and Senja Pollak. 2017. Pan 2017: Author profiling-gender and language variety prediction. In *CLEF (Working Notes)*.

Marcelo OR Prates, Pedro HC Avelar, and Luis Lamb. 2018. Assessing gender bias in machine translation—a case study with google translate. *arXiv preprint arXiv:1809.02208*.

Ilya Sutskever, Oriol Vinyals, and Quoc V Le. 2014. Sequence to sequence learning with neural networks. In *Advances in neural information processing systems*, pages 3104–3112.

Ashish Vaswani, Noam Shazeer, Niki Parmar, Jakob Uszkoreit, Llion Jones, Aidan N Gomez, Łukasz Kaiser, and Illia Polosukhin. 2017. Attention is all you need. In *Advances in Neural Information Processing Systems*, pages 5998–6008.

Kellie Webster, Marta Recasens, Vera Axelrod, and Jason Baldridge. 2018. Mind the gap: A balanced corpus of gendered ambiguous pronouns. *Transactions of the Association for Computational Linguistics*, 6:605–617.

Jieyu Zhao, Tianlu Wang, Mark Yatskar, Vicente Ordonez, and Kai-Wei Chang. 2017. Men also like shopping: Reducing gender bias amplification using corpus-level constraints. *arXiv preprint arXiv:1707.09457*.

Appendix

A Proof on the boundedness of the measure

Let W_0, x, y, z each denote P_s, p_w, p_m, p_n. Then, from eqn.s (1-2) in the paper, we have

$$x + y + z = 1$$
$$0 \leq x, y, z \leq 1 \tag{3}$$

and

$$W_0 = \sqrt{xy + z} \tag{4}$$

Here, note that we have to show the bound for the following:

$$W(x, y, z) = xy + z \tag{5}$$

Let

$$D = \{(x, y, z) | x + y + z = 1, \\ 0 \le x, y, z \le 1\} \tag{6}$$

which is a compact, convex set, and let a Lagrangian L of W be

$$L = xy + z + \lambda(x + y + z - 1) \\ -\mu_x x - \mu_y y - \mu_z z \tag{7}$$

Then, the KKT conditions for optimizing L are given by

$$\frac{\partial L}{\partial x} = y + \lambda \pm \mu_x = 0$$
$$\frac{\partial L}{\partial y} = x + \lambda \pm \mu_y = 0 \tag{8}$$
$$\frac{\partial L}{\partial z} = 1 + \lambda \pm \mu_z = 0$$

where $\mu_x, \mu_y, \mu_z \ge 0$ and $\mu_x x* = \mu_y y* = \mu_z z* = 0$ for an optimal point $(x*, y*, z*)$.

If the optimal point lies in the interior of D, then $\mu_x = \mu_y = \mu_z = 0$. Thus, in the optimal point, to make $\frac{\partial L}{\partial z} = 0$, we have $\lambda = -1$. Thereby, to make $\frac{\partial L}{\partial x} = \frac{\partial L}{\partial y} = 0$, we have $x = y = 1$ which makes $z = 1$ that contradicts eqn. (3).

Consequently, the optimal points lie on the boundary of D which can be decomposed into the following three independent segments:

$$(a)\{x + y = 1, z = 0\}$$
$$(b)\{y + z = 1, x = 0\} \tag{9}$$
$$(c)\{z + x = 1, y = 0\}$$

At most two of (9) can be satisfied.

For (a), optimizing $L_1 = xy$ subject to $x + y = 1$ and $x, y \ge 0$ yields

$$min = 0, max = \frac{1}{4} \tag{10}$$

For (b) (and possibly (c)), optimizing $L_2 = z$ subject to $y + z = 1$ and $y, z \ge 0$ yields

$$min = 0, max = 1 \tag{11}$$

From eqn.s (9,10), we have $0 \le W \le 1$ which yields the boundedness of the proposed measure W_0. Moreover, we obtain that W_0 is maximized if $p_n = 1$ and minimized if either p_w or $p_m = 1$.

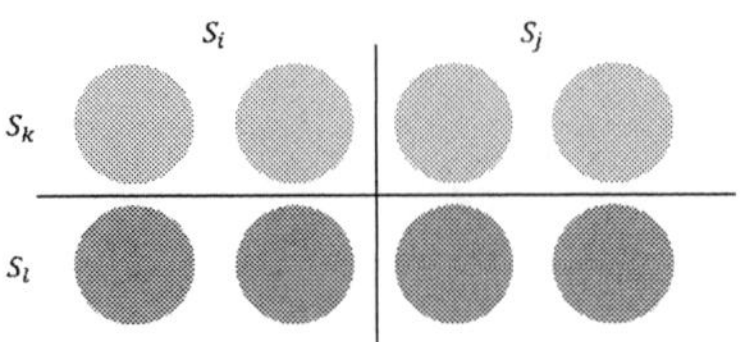

Figure 2: A brief illustration on why equal distribution is difficult to obtain for various subset pairs in deterministic system. Best viewed in color.

B A brief demonstration on the utility of adopting multiple sentence subsets

We want to recall that the conventional translation services provide a determined answer to an input sentence. This can happen to prevent the systems from achieving a high score with the proposed measure and EEC.

Let the emerald (top) and magenta (bottom) discs in Figure 2 denote the gender-neutral pronouns translated into female and male, respectively. Note that for S_i and S_j that comprise the whole corpus, P_{S_i} and P_{S_j} are both high, whereas for another sentence subset pair S_k and S_l, there is high chance of P_{S_k} and P_{S_l} being lower than the former ones. Thus, in conventional evaluating schemes as in Lu et al. (2018), arithmetic averaging may not be effective for displaying the amount of bias.

This property could have deterred adopting the proposed measure to multiple sentence subset pairs (or triplets) since a similar mean value is expected to be obtained if the number of pairs increases. However, since the utilization of p_n and square root function in the measure prevents the average from being converged into a specific value in the systems, we keep using all the sentence sets that comprise the EEC so that we can observe the tendency regarding various aspects of sociolinguistics.

Association for Computational Linguistics
209 N. Eighth Street
Stroudsburg, Pennsylvania 18360

ISBN 978-1-5108-9106-7